AF516290

Social Policy: An Introduction

Social Policy

An Introduction

Fourth Edition

Ken Blakemore and Louise Warwick-Booth

RAWAT PUBLICATIONS
Jaipur • New Delhi • Bangalore • Guwahati • Kolkata

ISBN 978-81-316-0889-0

First Indian Reprint, 2017

First Published in 2013
by Open University Press, McGraw-Hill Education, McGraw-Hill House,
Shoppenhangers Road, Maidenhead, Berkshire, England, SL6 2QL

Permission for this edition was arranged through **Open International Publishing Limited.**

Published by
Prem Rawat for **Rawat Publications**
Satyam Apts., Sector 3, Jawahar Nagar, Jaipur - 302 004 (India)
Phone: 0141 265 1748 / 7006 Fax: 0141 265 1748
E-mail : info@rawatbooks.com
Website: www.rawatbooks.com

New Delhi Office
4858/24, Ansari Road, Daryaganj, New Delhi 110 002
Phone: 011-23263290

Also at *Bangalore, Guwahati* and *Kolkata*

Printed at Nice Printing Press, New Delhi.

Praise for this book

"This textbook has always been a useful teaching resource because it combines substantial and engaging analysis with 'stand alone' extracts. The new edition adds a chapter on global social policy, updates on the Coalition Government and guides to what is in the book. The added activities are well thought out and can be adapted or expanded to suit the needs of particular students."

—Hedley Bashforth, Teaching Fellow in Social Policy, University of Bath, UK

"Social Policy: An Introduction, now in its fourth edition and eleventh year, will remain a core social policy text on reading lists across the country due to its well written and comprehensive nature. Completely revised, it has been updated and extended to reflect contemporary developments in social policy, including the policy implications of the Coalition Government, and now includes a chapter on global social policy environments reflecting the continued internationalisation of social policy debates. Updated pedagogical features, which include activities for the reader, learning outcomes at the start of each chapter and detailed case studies throughout, enhance this thought-provoking and stimulating text."

—Dr Liam Foster, University of Sheffield, UK

"It is immediately clear that a great deal of thought has been invested into designing this book. What Blakemore and Warwick-Booth have produced is a clearly laid out and well-structured analysis of impressive breadth that is a readily accessible learning instrument both for student and teacher."

—Steen Mangen, Department of Social Policy, London School of Economics and Political Science, UK

Contents

List of activities

List of tables

List of figures

List of boxes

The authors

Ken Blakemore was a senior lecturer in social policy at Swansea University. He had previously taught in Africa, in the USA (UCLA) and at universities in Coventry, Warwick and Birmingham, as well as Swansea. He has researched and written widely in several fields of social policy, including comparative education, diversity and equal opportunities, and policies on care of older people. He is now pursuing a new career in writing novels and plays for radio and the stage.

Louise Warwick-Booth is a principal lecturer at Leeds Metropolitan University, teaching health policy to a range of student audiences. She has previously taught at Sheffield University, as well as in Africa. She has researched several areas of social policy focusing upon evaluation within the public health sector.

Preface

This fourth edition of *Social Policy: An Introduction* has been revised throughout to take account of policy changes and developments since the third edition, published in 2007. I am thankful to Ken Blakemore for allowing me to have the privilege to update this book, which I have frequently used in support of my own teaching, while he has moved into different forms of writing. I am also thankful to Edwin Griggs, who was involved in updating the third edition of this text and who singly authored the criminal justice chapter. While Edwin has had no involvement in this fourth edition, I am grateful to him for passing the mantle over to me.

The framework of the book is substantially that of the earlier edition, but some new material has been incorporated, mainly in the form of a chapter on the global policy environment (Chapter 4). This has the purpose of providing a brief introduction to the growing importance of the global within contemporary policy-making. It also serves to introduce students to an area of public policy which is the subject of lively interest at the present time.

There has also been a change of UK government since the last edition, with the Coalition Government taking office in 2010. This has provided an opportunity to explore the extent to which this government has begun to make a difference to social policy. Furthermore, there has also been some evaluation of New Labour as the outgoing party and the policy legacy that they left. Therefore this edition, as well as providing an update of Coalition Government approaches, also provides a clearer picture of the achievements and failures of New Labour. To that extent the book attempts, as did its predecessors, to provide a commentary on current developments, as well as providing a foundational account of welfare institutions and policies for the beginner.

The aims of this book, like those of its predecessors, are simple: to offer a text that can be consulted briefly for single items or insights, but also to offer a piece of writing about social policy that you, the reader, might enjoy reading chapter by chapter. This fourth edition also contains activities for the reader, and learning outcomes at the start of each chapter, which should serve to stimulate thinking about social policy. Let's hope that you agree that this is a fascinating subject to explore.

Louise Warwick-Booth

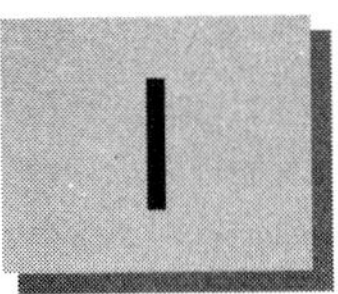

The subject of social policy

Key learning outcomes

By the end of this chapter you should:

- be able to understand what social policy is and appreciate the relationship between social policy and a range of other **disciplines**
- be able to identify and understand the key areas of social complexities associated with the policy-making process
- be able to understand how social policy influences our lives in a variety of ways

Overview of the chapter

This chapter gives an overview of what social policy is generally and then more specifically it demonstrates that many facets of policy exist within our social environment. This chapter will answer key questions such as: what is social policy and why does the subject have an identity problem? This chapter will explore the story of social policy looking at its early roots and tracing the development of the subject matter through time. The chapter also has activities woven throughout so that readers can complete these, and begin to reflect upon their own knowledge base in relation to the field. Finally, the chapter ends with an outline of what this book will cover, detailing its structure.

Social policy: an identity problem?

Social policy can be described in two ways. First, it is an academic subject to research and to study; the aim of this first chapter is to introduce you to it. Second, it is something that has an impact on the 'real' world. Government, business and voluntary organizations all have policies that are experienced by families and individuals.

What are 'policies'? In one way they can be seen as aims or goals, or statements of what ought to happen. *Social* policies aim to improve human welfare (though they often fail to do so) and to meet human needs for education, health, housing and social security.

As goals, intentions and ideas, policies can be found in the form of official government policy (legislation, or the guidelines that govern how laws should be put into operation). The ideas and proposals put forward in manifestos and glossy leaflets by the Conservative, Labour, Liberal Democrat and other political parties are examples of policies as broad ideas and stirring goals. Outside government, a company's or an organization's statement of policy on something – for instance, an equal opportunity policy – is also an example of policy expressing ideas about what ought to happen.

However, policies are living things, not just static lists of goals, rules or laws. Policy blueprints have to be implemented, often with unexpected and sometimes with disastrous results. Therefore, social policies are what happens 'on the ground' when they are implemented, as well as what happens at the preliminary decision-making or legislative stage. There is often a gulf between the concepts and goals that inspire policy and 'real' policy, the result of compromise. Social policies are often complex in how they are formulated how they are implemented, and certainly there are numerous influences affecting the policy process. Figure 1.1 shows some of the many influences which affect the policy process.

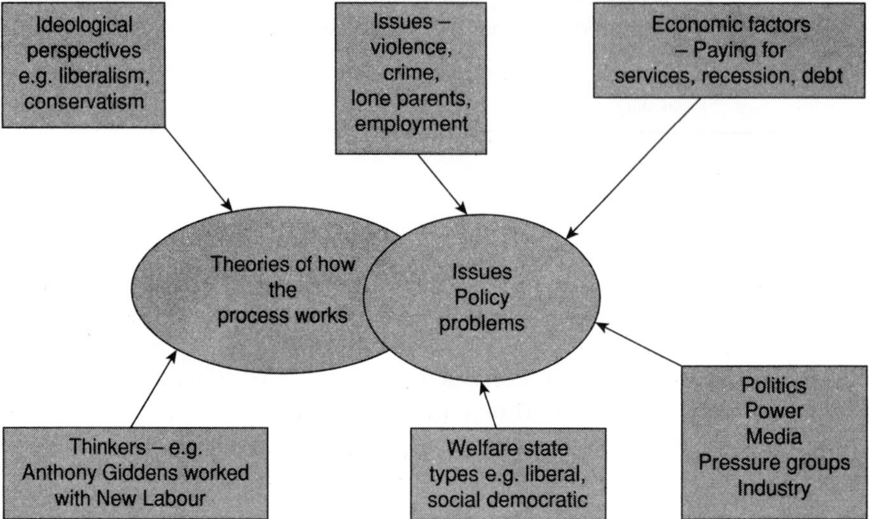

Figure 1.1 The many influences within the policy process

This probably seems complicated already but *studying* social policy is fascinating because it will involve you in thinking about:

- *what* social policies are: that is, what the content of specific government policies is, for example an Education Act or a policy about provision within the UK National Health Service (NHS) such as the availability of expensive medications for specific patient groups.
- *how* policies are developed, administered and implemented: for instance, how a new policy on tackling unemployment was conceived, what its stated and hidden aims are, how it is funded and how far it meets its objectives.
- *why* policies exist (or do not exist): why, for example, was a market approach to providing health and social services introduced in the 1980s and early 1990s? Or why, globally, are we concerned with setting targets across a range of areas such as the Millennium Development Goals?

Social policy and other subjects

So what is social policy? Social policy can be described as a field of activity decided upon and implemented by the government, and is usually a course of action and a web of decisions rather than a single decision (Hill 1997). Policy usually is a stance towards a particular topic influenced perhaps by **ideology**, media input and evidence, and involves a cluster of related decisions and actions often dealt with in a consistent fashion (Harrison and Macdonald 2008). Although this preliminary definition of social policy might be helpful, no single definition tells the whole story. The challenge facing us, therefore, is more than that of moving from simple to slightly more complicated definitions of social policy, and descriptions of various policies in areas such as education and health.

Activity 1.1 Defining social policy

Use the Internet to research a range of views from key contemporary thinkers about the field of social policy.
Pete Alcock, on YouTube, answers the question 'What is social policy?' www.youtube.com/watch?v=Ccff_50dFP4
Hartley Dean similarly addresses the question via YouTube footage: www.youtube.com/watch?v=IQ3DKpD8kao
Listen to what these two academics have to say about social policy and what it is – there are other interpretations and debates for you to watch if you find these interesting.

Watch the footage suggested in Activity 1.1 then consider if you found it interesting and useful in terms of providing a definition of the field of social policy. Hopefully you did, but definitions and descriptions are not enough. Anyone new to a subject needs something else: an image of the subject to identify with, or a glimpse of the whole thing which gives a feel for the subject, and some way of anticipating what is coming next.

To demonstrate the importance of these things, you might briefly think about a range of subjects that you are already familiar with: English literature, perhaps, or media studies, sociology, geography, history or economics. Now think of the images that each one calls up in your mind.

English and media studies bring images from drama, film and novels – some of which, incidentally, are very useful for a broader understanding of social policy and changing social conditions (see suggestions for further reading at the end of Chapter 3). Geography helps us to visualize the globe, space and particular environments such as a tropical rain forest or mountain ranges. History and sociology might prompt images of particular periods that you have been interested in – how ordinary people fared in Hitler's Germany in the 1930s, for instance. Depending on the health of your bank balance, economics might give an image of either a looming overdraft or a pile of banknotes.

Now try the same exercise with the words 'social policy' in mind. Do any images appear? If they do, you might be sufficiently well informed to consider shelving this book. If you have no clear image or impression of the subject, on the other hand, this is perfectly understandable – and you need to read on.

Social policy's identity problem – or, more precisely, its problem of *lack* of identity – has a number of causes. As with sociology, perhaps social policy's lack of a clear image is due to it being a relatively new subject compared with traditional disciplines such as history and geography. There is another reason for social policy's identity problem. It is a 'magpie' subject – a discipline that has taken bright and sparkling treasures from other disciplines such as economics, philosophy, politics and sociology. For this reason social policy is sometimes seen as an interdisciplinary subject rather than an academic discipline in its own right. As argued later, however, there is a strong case for viewing social policy as a discipline. Like the magpie's nest, social policy's base contains others' pearls of wisdom, but social policy has also developed insights, theories and **empirical research** of its own.

Like any other discipline, social policy employs a distinctive body of **theory** that individual scholars and researchers have used to test hypotheses about the impact of social policies on people's lives (see Box 1.1). Through the study of social policy as a discipline, therefore, you will gain a view of the world that is distinctly different from, but related to, the perspectives of sociology, politics and the other social sciences.

Box 1.1 Social policy research: an example

Example of a theory	*Some possible hypotheses to test the theory*
Public provision (for example of **social housing**) maintains some fairness in allocation of goods and services; market provision is bound to exclude disadvantaged groups.	1. Where social housing is sold off, poorer families tend to get left behind in sub-standard housing; they are excluded from better-quality flats or houses. **or** 2. Where social housing is sold to tenants, the purchasers are more likely to stay; there is a better mix than if people have to leave their estates to purchase a home.

An example of research that examines these hypotheses – in relation to council house sales and the African-Caribbean community – can be found in a study by Peach and Byron (1994). This may seem an outdated piece of research now, but given the issues now being reported in the media in relation to housing provision (lack of affordable homes and the 'social cleansing' of tenants), many lessons remain relevant. See Chapter 9 for further discussion of Peach and Byron's study.

Before we leave initial impressions and images, it is important to realize that experienced scholars in social policy have their personal images of the subject, just as much as do people who have only recently begun to study it. For example, Nicholas Deakin (1994: 1) gives us this personal impression:

> Towards the end of the War (which is how people of my generation still habitually refer to the Second World War) my mother took to bringing home from our visits to the children's clinic . . . small brown bottles labelled 'welfare orange juice'. My brother and I gulped down the contents willingly enough: the flavour, bland, but with a slightly bitter chemical back taste, was in every way preferable to the only

> other alternative on offer: cod liver oil. Now, forty years later, the ghost of the tang that the juice once left still appears unbidden on my palate whenever I first see the word 'welfare'; and it illustrates in a trivial but (to me) highly immediate way how the terms employed in the debate about the future of welfare have developed associations and personal references which are lodged deep in the collective unconscious of the nation.

For the millions of people of Nicholas Deakin's generation and of preceding generations, this particular impression has a lot of resonance. It expresses a deep attachment to the welfare state and might be termed a welfarist image of social policy. Does this resonate with you or did you grow up with very different experiences, and therefore hold alternative views?

More recent impressions among younger generations might be less pro-welfare or welfarist. For instance, the term welfare might be more readily associated with the frustrations of dealing with a benefits office, or with the suspicion that sometimes **poverty** is made worse by the **welfare system** rather than relieved by it (see Chapters 5 and 6).

Images of welfare and social policy (assuming these two terms are used synonymously) can therefore be negative as well as positive. The study of social policy must include a critical element. Social policies are 'nasty' as well as 'nice'. The aims and impact of social policies and the welfare system (either deliberately or unintentionally) can as often be to control people and to keep them in their place (see Chapter 6) as to liberate them or to give them a better life than they would otherwise have. The UK media often echo a range of attitudes about groups of individuals who are subject to social policy interventions, so complete Activity 1.2 to explore this further.

Activity 1.2 The media and social policy

Think about all areas of your own life that are influenced by social policies (there are many: your education thus far, the welfare system, health care and transport policy are all good starting points). Now consider how your views of each of these areas may be influenced by media coverage as well as your own experiences.

1. Use the Internet to find out more about the media reporting on a particular area of social policy that interests you, or choose some recent media coverage of a particular area. For example, at the time of writing there is media coverage about education policy in relation to how schools are tackling incidences of racism, and about the failure of health policy in providing equal care to all, focusing particularly upon diabetes patients.
2. Take time to think about the ethical debates that emerge as a result of the media reporting of the issue. How are some groups labelled in media reports? You may wish to give consideration to 'scaremongering' and its implications, the ideology underpinning the media analysis and your own **values** and beliefs. For example, terms such as '**Chavs**' and 'welfare scroungers' illustrate negative labelling. Scaremongering may also occur in relation to health fears such as hospital failings, and lack of available provision in terms of health care.
3. You also might want to think about which societal groups were more likely to be negatively affected by the reporting and how widely held some views may be.

Upon completing Activity 1.2 you should now begin to realize that social policy needs considerable analysis. Thus, a major aim of the subject of social policy is to *evaluate critically* the impact of social policies on people's lives. This is essential because social policy influences all aspects of our social world, as described here in a blog by Hartley Dean (2012),

> Social policy therefore bears on pretty much every aspect of human existence and is a subject with few boundaries. It engages with practical as much as theoretical issues. It brings rigorous analysis to bear upon major controversies to do with who gets what in society, who controls this and by what criteria the outcomes may be considered just. What's not to get excited about?

As already mentioned this involves developing theories about the role of welfare and using hypotheses to test out what is happening. As an example, we might consider the impact of quantitative easing – that is, printing more money as a mechanism to move the economy out of **recession** – and whether this has really helped those who are unemployed or indeed struggling financially. Is this policy working to move a declining economy back into growth?

To engage in an honest and objective appraisal of the social impact of this economic policy, the social policy researcher must, like any other social scientist, try to lay aside personal views and political opinions. Would an economist be the best choice of person to research the value of quantitative easing? Perhaps not, but then neither would a government spokesperson committed to this policy.

Despite the importance of **objectivity**, though, the identity of social policy as a subject *is* simultaneously bound up with values: that is, expressing what you believe in, and what you think social policies *should be* trying to achieve to make society better for everyone. You too will hold your own values which influence your perspective upon social policy. You may not at this point recognize these but we all have them, and often values are complex.

How can there be a commitment to objectivity on the one hand, and to personal and political values on the other? The tension between these two opposites will be explored by looking at the life and work of Richard Titmuss, who is perhaps the most important founder of the subject of social policy. He argued strongly that it is possible to be committed to one's values and political standpoint *and* to be objective about social conditions and the need for social reform.

We shall also explore the way in which social policy developed as a subject both before and after Titmuss made his important contribution. Before this, however, it might help to review these opening remarks about social policy by comparing the ways in which different academic subjects relate to social policy (see Box 1.2).

Box 1.2 Examples of links between social policy and other disciplines

Discipline	*Examples of social policy relevance*
Anthropology	Study of family, kinship and differences in household composition and living arrangements. Social security entitlements depend on official policy of 'what counts' as a recognized household unit.

Economics	Looking at the economic costs and 'payoffs' of particular policies and social benefits. For example child benefit has recently been reviewed and now is means tested from January 2013. This means that certain groups, based upon the amount of money that they earn, are no longer entitled to receive this benefit. Previously this was a universal benefit – everyone in the UK with children was entitled to it.
Geography	Insights into the spatial patterns of the distribution and take-up of services: for example, maps of the boundaries of general practitioners' practices, numbers of patients and visits to the doctor.
History	Study of the development of social policies through time: comparing present-day services (and attitudes to them) with examples from the past: for example, hostels for the homeless today could be compared with 'Poor Law' institutions in the past.
Philosophy	Examining the reasons or justifications for choosing one kind of policy rather than another; discussing ethical questions, such as the right of clinical commissioning groups not to provide certain kinds of services, treatment, drugs or therapy.
Politics	Investigating the social policy aims of the Labour, Conservative, Liberal Democrat, Green and Nationalist parties; or, conversely, looking at the political impact of social policies: for example, what have been the effects of the Health and Social Care Bill 2012 upon the provision of both healthcare services and **public health**?
Psychology	Studying personal perceptions of, and attitudes towards, welfare services. Psychological perspectives are important in investigating individual **need** and design of services: for example, the way prostate cancer screening is advertised and provided, and men's perceptions of this service.
Sociology	Researching the norms, values and other social pressures that affect the relationship between the welfare system and different groups: for example, reasons for racial inequalities in access to social services.

The story of social policy

In order to understand the distinctive character of social policy as a subject, we need briefly to examine its roots and the way it developed in the UK.

Early roots: social work, sociology and social administration

Concern about questions of social policy grew throughout the nineteenth century. For instance, there was mounting concern about poverty and the squalid conditions that many people had to live in at that time, concern about child labour in mills, factories and mines, and concern about lack of literacy and the threatening **power** of the uneducated masses (see Chapter 3). Such concerns remain relevant to contemporary social policy with a focus upon problems and issues always at the centre of social policy debates.

As the end of the nineteenth century neared, it became increasingly clear to a growing number of reformers that government would have to play a much larger role than before in dealing with the social problems of the day. Although some of this concern was motivated by genuine and progressive aims to improve social conditions for ordinary people, it was mixed with other more controlling and reactionary motivations. These tensions about the role of the state still exist today, with discussions of the 'nanny state' and the welfare state often framed negatively.

The work of those who led the Charity Organisation Society (COS) is a good example of this mix of motivations and aims. The COS, set up to co-ordinate charitable efforts and to eliminate problems of charities duplicating one another's work, became a highly influential advisory body in late Victorian and early twentieth-century Britain. For instance, several of its members, including Octavia Hill (see Chapter 11), served on a government commission on the reform of the Poor Law between 1905 and 1909.

In general, the COS and those who shared similar opinions were looking for a more efficient way of managing the existing system of poverty relief, rather than a radical overhaul of social policy and the introduction of universal state benefits. The COS had pioneered the development of a new kind of occupation – the social caseworker – who was often a volunteer and often a (middle- or upper-class) woman. 'Social workers', as they gradually came to be known, were responsible for investigating the needs of poor families and for finding out whether they were 'deserving' cases. There was great concern among those who ran charities at the time that no one who was 'undeserving' should receive any help, because undeserved help would compound the character faults that were then thought to cause poverty and unemployment: laziness, ignorance, immoral behaviour and dependence. These concerns about laziness, dependency and distinctions between the deserving and undeserving remain ever present in contemporary social policy debates and often may bias many people's views about the experience of inequality. Complete Activity 1.3 to reflect upon the experiences of inequality.

Activity 1.3 Beliefs about inequality

Think about your own life and experiences. What do you take for granted? How do you frame your discussions of what you need in life? The country and context in which you live influence your views about both your needs and expectations – if you lived in a non-western context, might your expectations be different? How do you think about, discuss and label those who are not in the same position as you, both richer and poorer? Do you ever consider the fairness of people's societal position? Do you agree with some media reports and political views that many poor people are lazy and could improve their lives if they wished to?

Now you have given consideration to your own views, read the following summary of Dorling's (2010) interpretation of contemporary beliefs about poverty and inequality. He argues that many widespread beliefs serve to perpetuate inequality. Despite the fact that there are enough resources for everyone, these are not distributed evenly or fairly controlled. Therefore negative views of poorer people are responsible for the persistence of inequality within contemporary society. These beliefs are:

- Elitism is efficient – those who are the best succeed, whereas those who are limited do not. This belief ignores both **equality** of opportunity and the divisive effects of privilege.
- Exclusion is necessary – those who hold elite social positions argue that exclusion is necessary as part of achievement and success.

- Prejudice is natural – if this is so then why it is generally directed at those in the lowest social orders?
- Greed is good – this view is to encourage **economic growth** via purchasing and the demand for new goods because greed is the essence of successful capitalism. Mass car ownership is one form of contemporary greed which results in congestion, pollution and further selfishness (Dorling 2010), as well as socially excluding those who are unable to afford a vehicle.
- Despair is inevitable – mental illness increases and happiness levels remain stagnant despite economic development. So is economic growth beneficial for our mental health? Debates continue and demands for economic growth persist because it is viewed as essential by established political and economic opinion.

Having completed Activity 1.3 you should be able to see how history remains important in understanding contemporary social policy. Indeed, social work in its early days was arguably more concerned with **social control** and with trying to make the poor 'respectable' than with helping them on their own terms. But the very fact that social casework was thought necessary did succeed in bringing the problems of poverty and social inequality to the attention of middle-class volunteers and opinion-formers on a scale that had never been seen before.

At the same time, journalists, radical politicians and other commentators were writing about the appalling conditions in which many British people lived. They gave first-hand accounts and vivid descriptions of slum life that were as shocking to 'respectable' society as reports of other cultures and ways of life among the 'savages' in newly conquered parts of the Empire.

As a result of both social casework investigation and journalistic reports, philanthropists began to provide funds for research on poverty and social problems as well as for schemes to help the poor directly. One famous example of this was Seebohm Rowntree's survey of poverty in York in 1901, *Poverty: A Study of Town Life* (discussed by Fraser 1984: 136–7). It showed that an alarmingly high proportion of York's population (28 per cent) was then living below subsistence level. Rowntree's survey, which was followed by other Rowntree investigations after the First World War, is a prime example of the way in which the social conscience of leading manufacturing firms (in this case, the well-known chocolate and cocoa-processing firm) was translated into social research.

Rowntree's study was more progressive and less moralistic about the poor than an earlier study by Charles Booth, *The Life and Labour of the People in London.* This was an extremely lengthy and exhaustive study of poverty carried out between 1889 and 1903. All the studies of social conditions during this period were marked by an overriding concern to discover the 'facts' of poverty. Providing statistics of poverty and simply drawing the public's attention to social problems would make a conclusive case for urgent social reform, it was thought, and would galvanize government into action. It is interesting that research into poverty continues today, as does the search for solutions via social policy.

The key to understanding earlier, problem-focused pieces of research is to realize that they were strongly motivated by a desire to be *scientific*. Rather than an appeal for social reform and action based solely upon grounds of conscience or morality, the case put forward by Booth, Rowntree and others was to be based on irrefutable evidence and an objective approach to social problems.

It is about this time – the beginning of the twentieth century – that the term 'sociology' began to gain currency as a way of summing up this scientific, statistical approach to understanding social problems. Early sociology, reflecting as it did the passion for collecting facts and statistics, came to be known as 'blue book sociology', because it was based so heavily on official reports and population censuses (published in blue covers).

All this rapidly accumulating knowledge about social conditions and social problems fostered the development of new kinds of training courses and university degrees in social work. In the relatively new municipal 'redbrick' universities of the time, such as Birmingham, and in the newly established London School of Economics and Political Science (LSE), three important strands of learning and training were fused together. These were social work, sociology and **social administration**, the last being the study of local and central government institutions, and of the framework in which services to the poor and needy were to be delivered.

The early roots of the subject of social policy (or its forerunner, social administration) were therefore entwined inextricably with practical action (social work) and research (sociology). Later, as sociology developed a more independent identity, sociologists began to deplore the idea of their subject being a problem-focused or policy-oriented discipline. Sociology became more theoretical in its concerns, though some sociologists retain an interest in 'real world' and policy issues.

The main aim of sociology, however, is to discover knowledge about society for its own sake. The main aim in social policy is to research the impact of social policies on people and society. Thus a key question for social policy is, 'what difference does a policy make?' At the same time, the subject of social policy raises other questions, focusing upon how policies develop, why certain policies are chosen over others and what the economic, political and social implications of policies are.

Box 1.3 Richard Titmuss, 1907–73

When Richard Titmuss became Professor of Social Administration at the LSE at the age of 43, he was one of the few non-graduates to have ever become a professor. Titmuss had had to leave school at the age of 14. His father, who had been thrown out of work on a small farm and became heavily indebted, died before Richard was 20. As a result, Titmuss had experienced firsthand the shock of financial insecurity.

After leaving school, Titmuss worked as a clerk, then as a more senior inspector, for an insurance company. This work deepened his knowledge of both social welfare and inequality. As Kincaid explains, 'During the 1930s Titmuss lived a double life. In working hours, the insurance office – but in the evenings and at the weekends, the actuarial skills learned in the insurance office were brought to bear on data about birth-rates, poverty and ill-health' (Kincaid 1984: 115).

By this time Richard Titmuss had married, and his wife, Kay Titmuss, further encouraged his social conscience and his drive to write on policy and welfare matters. During the Second World War, Titmuss was appointed as an official war historian, and subsequently wrote a masterpiece on the civilian experience of wartime, called *Problems of Social Policy* (1950). Of many later works, among the more important are *Essays on the Welfare State* (1958), *Commitment to Welfare* (1968) and *The Gift Relationship* (1970), the last being a study of blood donation and the significance of this as a model of altruism for the provision of welfare generally.

Richard Titmuss died of cancer in an NHS hospital and, at the time, his daughter Ann Oakley (well known for her feminist analyses of family life and housework) wrote a moving tribute to his life and work.

Coming of age: the welfare state and social administration

In 1950, Richard Titmuss was appointed as the first professor of social administration at the London School of Economics (see Box 1.3). The subject had 'come of age' and was fast becoming recognized as a university discipline in many other British universities.

Titmuss's department at the LSE became a central influence on the subject in the 1950s and 1960s. The LSE itself had been set up in the early years of the twentieth century, largely as a result of the efforts of energetic and pioneering socialist thinkers such as Sidney and Beatrice Webb. It was envisaged as a powerhouse of progressive political ideas and adult education. Its chief aims were, first, to provide a route into higher education for able students from working-class backgrounds and, second, to build a solid base of research studies on economic and social problems. Both of these functions were thought to be vital for developing the planned society led by enlightened experts that the Webbs and other socialists believed in at the time.

Under the directorship of William Beveridge (see Chapter 3, Box 3.3) in the 1920s and 1930s, the LSE became an internationally renowned centre of learning. Among the scholars who joined the LSE during Beveridge's time was Friedrich von Hayek, an exponent of right-wing ideas on economics and politics who was to have a profound effect on future leaders such as Margaret Thatcher.

Thus the early development of social administration and social policy as university subjects took place in an environment in which a variety of views and a commitment to scholarly research were highly valued.

Richard Titmuss's teaching and research activities ably met these standards. He was not only highly prolific as a writer and researcher (see suggestions for further reading at the end of this chapter). Like those who had worked in the early poverty research tradition of Booth, Rowntree and other important reformers, his aim was not simply to do factual research for its own sake. It was also to engage in research which, while still based on *empirical studies* (that is, observation of factual evidence and real-life experience), would be directed by the aims of exposing unmet need, social inequality and the ways in which policies seemed to be failing to bring social **justice**.

Why was Titmuss so committed to such values as equality and social justice, and what were the implications of this commitment for the development of social policy as a subject? See, first, the brief summary of his life and work in Box 1.3. As the thumbnail sketch of Titmuss's life indicates, the twin strands in his approach to writing about social welfare go back to his own experience.

First, there was Titmuss the dispassionate critic of social inequalities and of 'who gets what' in a society dominated by class privilege and an unfair labour market (see Chapter 6). Titmuss succeeded in elevating the subject of social administration from the tedious study of how the welfare system is administered to a more questioning analysis of why inequalities persist, even in a welfare state such as the one developed in Britain after 1945. A number of academics still continue to focus upon social inequality today, for example Professor Daniel Dorling, a geographer whose work you have already read about.

It was Titmuss who first pointed out that there are two welfare states: the obvious welfare system that provides education, health services and social security, and a less obvious system that particularly benefits the middle classes. The latter, 'hidden welfare state' includes subsidies to better-off groups in the form of tax advantages, public support for higher education (a near monopoly of students from middle-class families when Titmuss was writing) and mortgage interest tax relief (also benefitting better-off households at that time).

Second, though, there was the Titmuss who celebrated the welfare state that had been built in Britain after 1945 (see Chapter 3). He defended not only the actual services provided 'free' at the point of use, but also the values that underpinned the welfare state: the values of altruism, of community and of the collective will to improve people's lives. By contrast, the values that underpinned the market – individualism and competition – seemed to Titmuss to be destructive of human welfare. These market values are now dominant within contemporary policy-making which is neo-liberalist in ideological conception.

Not surprisingly, some have seen inconsistencies in Titmuss's ideas. How could there be a unified subject of social policy based on Titmuss's approach if it included on the one hand a strong defence of the existing welfare system, and on the other a devastating **critique** of the inequalities and injustices that it masked?

In retrospect, it is not too difficult to see how both of these views can be reconciled even though there is some tension between them. It is quite possible to point out the weaknesses and injustices of the present welfare system while at the same time drawing attention to the possibility of greater inequalities and problems if the system were to be scrapped. For instance, the NHS, despite being a largely 'free at the point of use' service, has not succeeded in eradicating inequalities in health and use of health services (see Chapter 10). But Titmuss argued that the replacement of the NHS with a completely privatized health system, as in the USA, would lead to health inequalities even greater than already existed. Again, these views have been more recently debated in relation to the recent changes to the NHS in the Health and Social Care Bill (2012) (Chapter 10).

Crisis and change: the development of social policy as a subject

In the 1970s, the Titmussian approach to the study of the welfare state was challenged from a number of directions. This was partly because, despite Titmuss's lively criticisms of the flaws in the welfare state, much of the subject of social administration seemed to have developed into a rather complacent and technical description of existing social services and how they were to be delivered.

What criticisms there were of existing social problems, unmet need and inequality seemed to be dominated by the Titmussian assumption that all would be well if a left of centre, planned and rather paternalistic approach to providing state welfare was followed. But what if there was something more fundamentally wrong with the whole approach to providing welfare through state institutions?

It was this latter question that provoked much interest in the 1970s, when 'social policy' began to replace 'social administration' as the heading or title of university courses in the subject. Students of social policy were increasingly exposed to a range of critiques of the welfare state and of the traditional welfare values that had been contained in the old subject of social administration.

These critiques (critical discussions) may be divided into *culturalist* criticisms and *materialist* criticisms of state welfare. Culturalist critiques are those that challenge the *way* that welfare services are designed and provided, and the cultural assumptions (for example about men's and women's roles in society) that underpin the manner in which services are delivered. For instance, in the 1970s a growing feminist and women's studies literature raised questions about the sexist assumptions behind many health, education and social services, and the ways in which those services could reinforce gender inequality (see Chapter 6). Interestingly, now more research is conducted upon gender inequalities with men as the focus, as men can be excluded from services, tend to die younger and face a range of health issues (White 2011). Similarly, growing awareness of racism and studies of racial discrimination pinpointed the inappropriateness of many social services to the needs of minority ethnic groups, as well as the paternalistic, 'culture blind' attitudes of those who ran them.

Materialist critiques, on the other hand, focused on material factors and the economic crisis apparently facing the welfare state. On the political left, Marxists and other kinds of socialists concentrated on the material inequalities that seemed to be inherent in the welfare state: for instance, in the provision of housing, schools and hospitals of unequal quality or standards. This kind of critique (as an example, see Gough 1979) paid less attention to the way in which welfare services are run, and was more concerned that *not enough* welfare was being provided to poorer and working-class groups in society. At the same time, though, Marxists pointed to what they saw as an uncontainable and rising demand from the working classes for more welfare services and higher social security benefits – a demand that would spiral out of control and lead to a fundamental crisis in the capitalist system.

For entirely different reasons, commentators on the political right shared with Marxists a view of the welfare state as an unmanageable economic burden upon the capitalist economy. Therefore, they too were putting forward materialist criticisms of the welfare state. However, unlike the Marxists, right-wing commentators based their criticisms on the belief that *too much* state welfare was being provided. Complete Activity 1.4, which will help you to reflect upon your own ideological viewpoints in relation to the provision of welfare.

Activity 1.4 Considering your own ideological viewpoint

Now that you have read about different views of welfare, you should be beginning to formulate an idea of where your own values sit in ideological terms. Read through the following statements, thinking about whether you agree or disagree.

Political left views about welfare

- All welfare systems should be in public control and aim to particularly support those most in need.
- Services such as health care should be free for all **consumers** at the point of consumption, irrespective of whether they have contributed to paying for the care in any way.
- The state should intervene – for example, by using legislation to influence individual behaviour – via the formulation of social policy.

Political right views about welfare

- Welfare can be provided by private contractors and made more efficient via the application of market **principles**.
- All individuals should pay for the services that they use including health care and those who can afford to pay for private health care should not have to contribute to the funding of public health care.
- The state should not 'nanny' because people are responsible for their own decisions and behaviour – we are all free to make our own choices.

Now think about what this tells you about your political values and your views of welfare – you may not necessarily agree with all the statements in a column, as individual beliefs are often complex.

Not only are individual ideological beliefs complex, as you are probably beginning to realize having completed Activity 1.4, but the interrelationship of policy sectors serves to muddy the waters of policy-making. Policy sectors overlap and all can impact upon an issue or field of social policy, as Figure 1.2 shows.

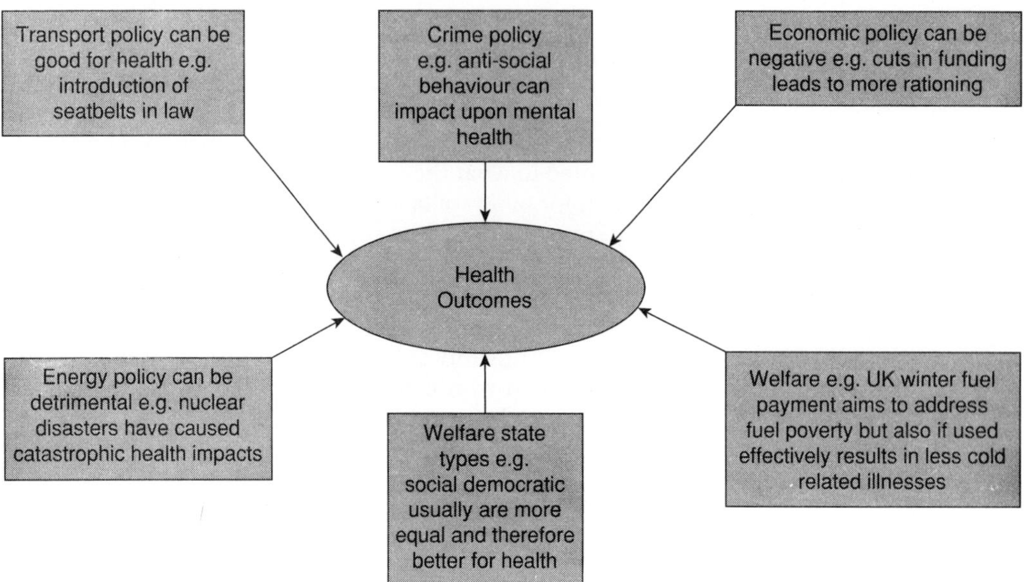

Figure 1.2 The interrelationship of policy sectors

Conclusions: the subject today

From today's vantage point many of the debates about social policy that took place in the 1970s and 1980s now seem out of date. In those days, debates were rather polarized. On the one hand, Marxist and left-wing critics of the welfare state were combining dreams of a socialist future with dire predictions of the end of capitalism. On the other, the so-called 'New Right' called for the privatization of much of the welfare system.

Neither school of thought proved to be much good at forecasting the actual development of social policy. As will be shown elsewhere in this book, Conservative government in the 1980s and 1990s did not lead to the full-scale implementation of all 'New Right' ideas, nor to the scrapping of the welfare state (though there were many significant changes). The massive rise in unemployment during the 1980s and large increases in social security spending did not result, as many Marxists had suggested, in the breakdown of the capitalist system.

The writings of Titmuss about the social policy dilemmas of the 1950s and 1960s seem in some ways to be more pertinent than the theories of the 1970s and 1980s to an understanding of today's social policy questions and the approach of government to dealing with these questions. When Titmuss was writing about the welfare state in the 1950s it was a relatively new and untried institution. Though public welfare and institutions such as the NHS enjoyed popular approval, there were strong pressures in a newly 'affluent society' to develop separate, market-based provision for the better-off and to leave the stretched public services for everyone else. There was a certain fragility about the welfare state then, and the prospect of returning to a more divided, private-insurance-based system, which has strong echoes today. For instance, in 1959, in a Fabian Society lecture, Titmuss warned of growing inequality in an 'irresponsible society' – a society in which a two-tier welfare system could develop if its middle- and upper-class members opted out of the system. This seems highly relevant to today's context. Those who can afford it are being encouraged to take out private health insurance, and there are government incentives to make personal arrangements for our pensions (instead of relying on standard state pensions), and for funding any long-term care that we might need in the future. Therefore a rereading of Titmuss's concerns about the future of the welfare state has a resonance with today's dilemmas over what direction social policy should take.

By contrast, the radical left-wing ideas of the 1970s and 1980s, preoccupied as they were with over-abstract theories about class conflict and the end of capitalism, have been argued to be less significant in analysing contemporary society. While these ideas may not have anticipated the fundamental changes in social policy since 1979 some groups do still hold the view that capitalism is the root of many contemporary inequalities and therefore needs to be addressed. The 2012 global Occupy movement raised awareness of the unjust nature of the capitalist system, and focused attention on both greed and corruption, holding media attention for a significant duration.

Despite these left-wing protests, the ideas of the New Right, which champion market-based solutions, still remain key to current social policy decisions. For example, the place of the market and competition has recently been used to change UK higher education policy, with increased tuition fees beginning to be charged from September 2012 for individuals wishing to gain an undergraduate degree, because state funding to universities is being gradually withdrawn.

However, this debate between right and left is for many less polarized than it has been in the past. The current UK New Labour party has been branded as 'Blue Labour' by some commentators due to the adoption of much more right-wing social policies. For example, it was the UK New Labour government that initially introduced tuition fees for higher education in 2003, at a capped rate of £3000 per student per annum. Moreover, **ideology** is not the only influence within the policy process. As this chapter has shown, there are numerous influencing factors (see Figure 1.1) and an interrelationship between policy sectors (see Figure 1.2) that also complicate analysis further.

Finally, any current analysis of social policy must account for the global context in which social policy is created and how national policies are now informed by key global players. **Globalization** as a process has arguably led to an increased range of global policy actors, shaping social policy, funding and provision. This is reflected in the increasing growth of global governance and the increasing importance of global organizations whose members recognize not only that poverty, social inequality and a number of other problems are interrelated but that they require action at the global level. Yeates and Holden (2009) argue that global analyses are ultimately needed to comprehend social policy formulation as well as its results (see Chapter 4).

Summary of key points

- Social policy sits within the social sciences but is influenced by a variety of disciplines.
- Social policy is itself a complex field, underpinned by complex ideological values and beliefs.
- Social policy as a discipline is crucial in helping us to understand how the welfare system impacts upon our everyday lives.

Plan of the book

In this chapter we have begun to explore how social policy has developed in recent times, both as a subject and as a programme of action 'out there' in the 'real' world. In Chapter 14 we shall return to these themes. The policies of the **Coalition Government** which was formed in 2010 will be assessed, together with broader questions about the interrelationship between social policy, economic change and social trends - for instance, the value of the concept of a 'postmodern' or 'late modern' world and its contribution to understanding current trends in social policy.

As for the filling in the sandwich - that is, all the intervening chapters - the choices that had to be made were difficult ones. For instance, there is a fundamental choice to be made between writing a book which is all 'isms and ologies' - that is, concerned primarily with theories of welfare and society - or another kind of book which provides a 'Cook's tour' of the welfare system. The drawback with the first kind is that it can easily become a semi-sociological or philosophical discussion, relatively abstract and timeless, and without much relevance to the world outside the university gates. That kind of book would not tell you much about the content of actual policies or how they were decided upon. The drawback with the second kind of book is that, after a few months, it begins to look like last summer's travel brochure. Time moves on, policies change and new Acts of Parliament are passed.

The plan of this book represents an attempt to bridge the gap between the two basic choices outlined above. The next six chapters deal with the big picture and with some important general themes in social policy, as follows:

- Chapter 2: the key ideas and principles upon which social policies are based.
- Chapter 3: the historical development of social policy.
- Chapter 4: the global social policy environment.
- Chapter 5: criminal justice policy, which also explores the boundaries of social policy and considers the usefulness of comparative approaches to the study of policy.
- Chapter 6: 'who gets what?' Questions of social and economic inequality raised by social policy, and current issues of poverty and **income** maintenance.
- Chapter 7: the connections between social policy, social control and liberation.

Although these chapters focus on general themes, they also refer to specific policy areas and examples. Chapters 6 and 7, for instance, discuss **social security benefits** policy as an illustration of both the 'who gets what?' question and the question of 'how much control do social policies exercise over us?'

The remaining chapters (before the concluding Chapter 14) also try to marry thematic approaches with specific policy areas, though the emphasis is more upon the latter than the former:

- Chapter 8 discusses education policy, using the example of the Education Reform Act 1988 and its impact on education today to reflect upon how policies are made in Britain.
- Chapter 9 traces the links between welfare and work, looking at government employment policy and its impact on the well-being of different groups, including youth, low-income workers and older workers.
- Chapter 10 defines and explores health policy, examining recent changes in the structure of the NHS and the potential impacts that these may have.
- Chapter 11 takes the example of housing to examine how rival ideologies, values and utopian dreams influence policy.
- Chapter 12 gives an account of **community care** policy, exploring at the same time 'who cares?' in today's welfare system.
- Chapter 13 discusses important changes in the way that policy is being created and implemented in the UK as a result of **devolution** of power from Westminster to the National Assembly for Wales, the Scottish Parliament and to other regional and devolved bodies. It focuses on the significance of these changes for growing differences in social policy within the UK, and it also includes a discussion of the impact of European Union (EU) social policy.

A final point, assuming that you have decided to launch into the rest of the book, is that the term 'welfare *system*' is preferred throughout the book to that of 'welfare *state*'. Interestingly, William Beveridge – a key founder of Britain's welfare system (see Chapter 3) – strongly disliked the 'welfare state' tag. As a supporter of insurance and the principle of saving for a rainy day, he disapproved of any term that seemed to encourage the idea of welfare being a bottomless pit of resources, or an institution which would unquestioningly look after people however 'undeserving' of help they were.

However, avoiding the 'welfare state' term in this book has little to do with Beveridge's preferences. Rather, it is to signal some sort of recognition that we have moved out of the twentieth-century, postwar era of 'big government' in which the state was expected to play the leading role as provider of every major welfare service.

At the same time, there is still a 'system' of welfare. Though inadequate and badly co-ordinated in parts (see Chapter 12 on community care for examples), there is a connected set of agencies making decisions about, paying for, or providing services. The structure of the welfare system is composed of:

- central and local government
- **quangos**, or quasi-autonomous non-governmental organizations (see Chapter 8 for examples in education)
- the voluntary (non-profit-making) sector
- the private (for-profit) sector and
- the informal sector of the family and community

This book is about the system; why it is run according to certain principles and not others, and – in the next chapter – what these principles mean.

Key terms and concepts

critique
disciplines
empirical research
hypothesis
ideology
implementation
models (of welfare or social policy)
objectivity
public administration
social administration
theory
values
welfare/welfare system/welfarism

Suggestions for further reading

Abel-Smith, B. and Titmuss, K. (eds) (1987) *The Philosophy of Welfare: Selected Writings of Richard M. Titmuss*. London: Allen & Unwin.

This is a convenient selection of writings about welfare, from Richard Titmuss, whose work is now seminal in the field of social policy. Much attention is paid to Titmuss in many discussions of the history of welfare analysis, and this is an excellent text giving an impression of the roots of social policy.

Baldock, J., Mitton, L., Manning, N. and Vickerstaff, S. (2011) *Social Policy*. 4th edn. Oxford: Oxford University Press

This is one of the leading UK texts on social policy and it comprehensively covers all aspects of the policy process. The fourth edition addresses key questions such as what is social policy, and why are welfare systems important? While examining the history of social policy, this book also focuses upon more recent policy issues such as migration, globalization, the UK Coalition Government as well as the recent and continuing global financial crisis.

Hudson, J., Kuhner, S. and Lowe, S. (2008) *The Short Guide to Social Policy*. Bristol: The Policy Press

This book is a short, very accessible guide to the essentials of social policy aimed at undergraduate students. As an introductory text, the book systematically and clearly provides a clear and concise overview of the major pillars of social policy. The book uses examples from around the world to give an overview of policy frameworks that different countries have developed in the fields such as education, health, employment and social security. Each chapter also usefully explains both key terms and concepts.

Walker, A., Gordon, D., Levitas, R. et al. (eds) (2010) *The Peter Townsend Reader*. Bristol: The Policy Press

This edited collection brings together the distinguished work of Peter Townsend, exploring the changes and continuities within social policy since the 1950s. Readers can also see which social issues have returned to the fore today. The book links empirical evidence, and both social theory and social policy.

2 Ideas and concepts in social policy

Key learning outcomes

By the end of this chapter you should:

- be able to understand the range of principles and concepts that underpin social policy
- be able to understand the complexity of ideology and its relationship to social policy
- be able to understand the complex relationship between social policy and inequality

Overview of the chapter

This chapter gives an overview of the key concepts that underpin social policy, focusing specifically upon equality, **equity**, justice and **need.** The chapter also explores **freedom** and rights within the policy-making context; it illustrates the complexities of these concepts in relation to differing ideological perspectives, and encourages you to think about these through the activities woven throughout. The chapter ends with a discussion about what citizenship means.

Social policy principles

The principles of social policy are the guiding ideas that underlie policies for social welfare, education, health services and the like. For instance, one policy might make the principle of *equality* a priority, while another might stress choice or freedom. This chapter is about such principles – equality, equity, need, freedom and rights – and how these words can be interpreted in different ways.

While the term 'principle' is both useful and widely used, it has a very general meaning and is potentially rather confusing. In fact it has several different but *interconnected* meanings.

First, a principle might be said to have a *moral* or ethical meaning. If someone takes a 'principled stand', they will be standing up for certain beliefs in what is right and wrong and upholding certain moral standards. A moral standard in social policy could be represented, for instance, by the principle that no individual in need, no matter how poor or for whatever reasons, should be left without access to health care. Another more contentious example might be the principle, advocated by some, that housing and social benefits should either be reduced for lone parents or be withheld unless they fulfil certain conditions, such as finding work or employment training.

As can be seen from these examples, the moralistic side of a welfare principle contains a vision of how things ought or ought not to be. Social policy reflects the *norms* and *values* of society. Many social policies have a normative element, and are drafted with the intent of influencing society or the behaviour of individuals in line with deeply held convictions and values. Table 2.1 summarizes the key ideological normative views.

Table 2.1 Ideology and approaches to social policy

Ideology	Key facets of the approach	Example policy
Conservatism	• Keen to maintain the traditional order of society. • Sees the state as having a minimal role and is keen to avoid **paternalism** and **welfare dependency.** • Values the private sector in service provision.	In the UK the current **Coalition Government** is attempting to minimize the role of the state. One way in which this is being encouraged is via 'The Big Society'. This policy is about allowing people and communities to have more power. For example, the government is keen to open up public services and allow these to be run by local communities.
Liberalism	• Views freedom of choice and the importance of the individual as central to all policy-making. • Individuals are perceived as needing to behave responsibly. • **Neo-liberalism** is a global economic approach which encourages the scaling back of state intervention and public spending while encouraging privatization.	Liberal Democrats in the UK believe in **equality of opportunity**. In the context of education this means a fair and progressive system. The party is against the use of tuition fees within higher education but now governing as part of a Coalition Government, they have not been able to achieve any reduction in fees; rather, fees have been raised.
Socialism	• Broad ideology, with differing meanings. • Left-wing normative principles include, among other things, the idea of equalizing **outcomes** for people. • Contemporary socialism involves governments attempting to reform the state, and increasing state intervention in service provision.	Cuba is a country that is often viewed as socialist because of the revolution in the 1950s, the Communist rule for many years and the heavily governed, state-planned economy. The state does provide all services but has been criticized for failing to improve general standards of living.
Nationalism	• Rather than an ideology, this is a belief system. • Nations are viewed as independent and should be self-governing: Scottish nationalism, for example. • Shared national identity is crucial in this perspective in order to promote social cohesion.	The British National Party adopts a nationalist approach and encourages the strengthening of national identity, arguing that immigration is a significant threat to this and therefore needs much tighter control. Similar arguments have been made in many other contexts such as Australia. Some countries have taken more radical steps to protect their national identity. France banned the burka in April 2011, and instituted fines for women who continue to wear them in public.

Table 2.1 Ideology and approaches to social policy (*Continued*)

Ideology	Key facets of the approach	Example policy
Feminism	• There are a range of feminist views: e.g. liberals attempt to overcome discrimination via the legal system, whereas radicals focus upon the **oppression** within domestic relationships between men and women. • Generally feminists are concerned with gender relationships and equality within these.	Feminists have influenced the policy-making process in numerous ways: for example, ensuring that equal pay is recognized in law in countries such as the UK, Australia and the Republic of Ireland.
Environmentalism; 'Green ideology'	• This encompasses a broad range of ideas. • Focus is upon the importance of the environment. • Advocates sustainability and lobbies for policies that do not damage the environment.	Many countries now have a Green Party which advocates for the environment via policy. The USA Green Party campaigns for investment in the green economy such as the renewable energy sector, arguing that this will benefit both the environment and the economy.

Table 2.1 gives an overview of differing ideological perspectives, but does not reflect the full complexity of the values that underpin policy. If you wish to explore your own values then visit Chapter 1 and complete Activity 1.4 as a starting point for reflection. Ideology remains important within the policy-making process and there remain many examples of recent policy change that seem to be based more on the government's determination to push through certain reforms based upon ideological perspective, irrespective of the evidence for or against them. The UK Coalition Government's proposals to greatly increase the number of schools that achieve academy status are just one example of this, in education policy (see Chapter 8). But even if policies are based on evidence, we could not expect to scientifically predict what the effects of social policies will be in the way that a scientist or doctor can predict what will happen if a certain medical operation or treatment is carried out (though even here we must be careful not to expect too much certainty). As well as there being issues with their implementation, policies may also have unintentional effects. For example, policies which aim to address inequalities may actually increase them. There was specific policy introduced within the UK as a direct attempt to tackle health inequalities under the New Labour Government, 1997–2010, following the commissioning of a report by Sir Donald Acheson, the Chief Medical Officer of the time. Acheson (1998) produced an independent report arguing that material disadvantage was the ultimate cause of health inequalities. This led to developments which demonstrated a political willingness to use government policy to tackle inequalities, although no additional funding was made available (Crinson 2009). However, inequalities in many areas remained the same, or had indeed worsened in some areas by the end of the New Labour term in office.

In addition to ideology, the 'principles of social policy' which refer to the *ideas* and theories that underpin social policy remain important. This definition very much overlaps with the first: principles as morals, norms or value judgements.

However, there is a valid and useful distinction between a principle as a moral statement and a principle as an idea or a theory. It is possible, as we saw in Chapter 1, to have theories about social policy that are not based *primarily* on morals or value judgements, even though such ideas might be coloured *partly* by political opinions or other biases.

For example, we may seek to define, in as objective a way as possible, what such ideas as 'freedom', 'liberty', 'justice' and 'equality' mean in social policy terms. Another example of a leading idea in social policy, which was developed in the early nineteenth century, is **utilitarianism**: a set of principles outlined by Jeremy Bentham (1748–1832) to offer what he saw as a rational alternative to governing on the basis of values or religious morals (see Box 2.1).

Box 2.1 An early principle still relevant? The example of Bentham and utilitarianism

Jeremy Bentham was born in 1748 into a prosperous middle-class family. At the age of 7 he was sent to Westminster School and, at the tender age of 12, he entered Queen's College Oxford, which 'he hated even more' than school (Warnock 1966: 7). By the age of 20 he had received 5 years of training in London as a lawyer, but his brilliant mind and wide-ranging interests led him into the world of publishing and discourse on philosophy.

Between early adulthood and middle age, Bentham established himself as a radical thinker on social, political and moral issues. Together with a circle of friends, writers and publishers, he became an influential figure, challenging government inefficiency and abuse, and recommending radical and rational solutions to social problems. His influences on policy were especially noticeable in the field of poverty and 'poor relief' (see Chapter 3), though he also put forward an ambitious scheme to reform and redesign prisons, as well as many other constitutional and administrative proposals.

In 1788, he published his *An Introduction to the Principles of Morals and Legislation* (see Bentham 1982), which contains all the main elements of what became known as 'utilitarianism' or 'Benthamism'. Though not a socialist (socialism was in its infancy), Jeremy Bentham did advocate changes that were revolutionary in their time: the vote for all adult men and women, annual parliaments, open and accountable government based on rational or scientific principles. Above all, he firmly believed that the value of any policy should be decided on its objective merits, not whether it fitted with custom and practice or with any particular religious viewpoint.

In this way, Bentham's philosophy could be summarized as 'radical and ruthless'. There is no room for sentiment or tradition, or for policies that support unearned privilege. The basic question, according to Bentham, is whether any government policy or institution serves any valuable purpose or has any *utility* (use) – hence 'utilitarianism'.

But how do we decide whether a policy has a useful function or not? Bentham's answer – and the principle he is perhaps most famous for – was to suggest that we find out what would bring 'the greatest happiness of the greatest number'. The best policy is one that minimizes the harm or discomfort to the greatest possible number of individuals, or that brings 'happiness' to the majority, even if there is a cost to the minority. Bentham's method or 'calculus' for working this out was based on the degree of pleasure or pain involved in any course of action. Not surprisingly, he was denounced by leading religious authorities of the day because he appeared to be advancing a godless doctrine that appealed to primitive or basic human instincts. In defence, Bentham's calculus of pleasures included the 'higher' things – for example, education and artistic achievement – and he suggested that policies that promote these have the greatest utility.

How does utilitarianism apply to modern dilemmas of rationing services or calculating who should benefit from welfare? The utilitarian approach to these dilemmas is to apply 'the greatest happiness of the greatest number' principle. It therefore questions whether all human life is of equal value, and whether it is immoral to weigh some people's happiness or continued life against that of others. These questions are still very much with us, as illustrated by moral dilemmas in the provision of scarce healthcare resources (see Chapter 10).

Activity 2.1 Applying utilitarian principles to healthcare rationing

When health service professionals make judgements about patients on other than medical criteria, they may stray into making utilitarian judgements: for example, whether a patient is young or old, is married or has dependants. Consciously or not, they may be asking themselves, 'What use does saving or prolonging this life have, and how far would medical help in this case add to the sum of human happiness?' Now read the following examples of individuals needing health care and think about how utilitarianism could be applied in each of these cases.

- Alice is a 90-year-old patient staying in hospital after a serious fall in which she broke her hip. She has now contracted pneumonia and is not responding well to treatment. She has no family, complex care needs and inadequate living conditions. However, she has clearly indicated that she wishes to be resuscitated if the need arises.
- James is a 35-year-old father of four young children, who has been diagnosed with a rare form of cancer. However, the cancer has spread and his illness is now terminal. Doctors are debating whether to prescribe him an expensive drug that may prolong his life and allow him to spend 'quality time' with his children. Both he and his wife have been employed since leaving school and have contributed to the welfare system by paying their taxes.
- Sarah is a 40-year-old mother of six, who has never worked or contributed to the welfare system via **taxation**. She has been in receipt of welfare benefits all of her adult life. Sarah has an unhealthy lifestyle and is now morbidly obese. She does not exercise and is not keen to implement any changes. She has visited her GP and asked for a referral for expensive bariatric surgery such as a gastric band which will help her to address her obesity.

Complete Activity 2.1, and reflect on what you think about utilitarianism now. On the one hand, utilitarianism can be seen as realistic: in this world, hard choices have to be made and it is better to be clearheaded about the relative costs and gains of a policy so that welfare can be maximized. On the other, utilitarianism can be seen as one element in an overarching Victorian philosophy of self-interest and a penny-pinching approach to public services, which may be detrimental to equality for some members of society.

Equality, equity and justice

Equality and politics

The principle of equality occupies a central place in debates about social policy, with differing views about equality evident according to ideological position.

Table 2.2 Equality and ideology

Political left views about equality	Political right views about equality
• Social policies are ideally the tools or mechanisms with which to create a fairer society by equalizing benefits from health, education and other services. • Left perspectives often defend equality by reference to people's needs. • John Rawls (1972), a liberal thinker, argues that equality should be a basic goal of every policy. As far as possible, the 'good things' of life should be shared equally: education and career opportunities, welfare services, leisure and so on. Everyone should also have the right to liberty.	• Social policies that attempt to equalize outcomes for people do so at considerable cost; they impose a burden of high taxation on people and they require a highly interventionist state and an army of bureaucrats and professionals. • The principle of freedom is threatened if social policies are too concerned with equality. • Nozick (1974) argues that any attempt to enforce patterns of justice will tend to undermine the supremely important value of liberty. For him, the only moral form of government is one that is minimal in its interventions and actions; any 'more extensive state would (will) violate the rights of individuals' (Nozick 1974: 333). • Rawls (1972) also argues that a certain amount of inequality – just enough to create rewards and incentives for the better-off people in society – will benefit not only the advantaged but also the least advantaged.

However, it is misleading to package all ideas about equality and policy neatly into either a left-wing or right-wing perspective. To begin with, and despite the popularity of the terms, there is little consensus on what being 'left wing' or 'right wing' actually means, and some writers' ideas such as those of Rawls can fit into both categories, as Table 2.2 demonstrates. The distinction between left and right in politics is thought to originate from the days of the French Revolution in the late eighteenth century, when the more liberal and radical representatives in the newly formed National Assembly were seated to the left of the presiding officer, while the more conservative members of the legislature sat on the right. As democracy developed in Europe, a similar seating arrangement became common practice in a number of parliaments. Thus a tradition grew up, associating 'left' with principles that favoured equality, radical reform and 'bigger government', and 'right' with principles that favour individual freedom and liberty over equality of outcome, a more cautious approach to change and reform, and an emphasis on reducing the role of 'big government' in people's lives.

In the contemporary **postmodern** political context, however, these earlier distinctions between left and right have become blurred. The UK is currently being governed by a coalition of Conservatives and Liberal Democrats whose ideological perspective are only partially compatible. Furthermore, there have always been considerable differences *among* fellow socialists, liberals and conservatives on the question of how much equality is desirable and how far social policies should attempt to 'correct' the inequalities and injustices of society. It has always been the case that some thinkers on the left have believed that certain inequalities are unavoidable. Some kinds of inequality might even be encouraged if they are based on rewarding merit. Conversely, it is also true that some thinkers on the right have subscribed to the idea that there should be certain basic equalities between people.

In Britain, the old left-right battle lines between the Labour and Conservative parties have been redrawn in recent times. Partly, this is a reflection of international events – in particular, the downfall of communism in the former Soviet Union (Russia) and its satellite states in eastern and central Europe. Though almost all western European socialists had already distanced themselves from repressive, corrupt and highly unequal communist regimes, the end of communism nevertheless removed an important reference point.

In short, socialism may live on as an idea, but if we define it as a set of policies to redistribute resources and to make society substantially more equal than it was, it is dead. No major political party in Britain – including the Labour Party – now supports principles of equality in the traditional socialist sense.

There is another strong reason for this. In the first half of the twentieth century, policies to redistribute wealth and to make society more equal than before held some appeal for the majority of the population. Approximately one-third of the British population enjoyed relatively high incomes and considerable wealth, while the remaining two-thirds lived either on moderate and static incomes, or in poverty. Most people could agree with the idea of **redistribution**, knowing that it would be likely to benefit them.

In more recent decades, however, the pattern of income and wealth has shifted. Although inequalities have widened, living standards for a two-thirds majority have steadily improved at the same time. A political party that stood for equality and a substantial redistribution of resources did not appeal in recent times. The Labour Party in Britain painfully discovered this in election defeat after election defeat between 1979 and 1992. Its victory in 1997 was largely attributable to its ability to distance itself from the idea that it was a high tax party with policies to help the poorer third of the population at the expense of the majority. However, the ongoing global recession may serve to move people into a different direction of voting. In May 2012 François Hollande, a moderate social democrat from the centre of the Socialist party, won the French election and became France's first left-wing president in almost 20 years. His manifesto was based upon scrapping tax-breaks for the rich and putting up taxes for high earners to finance what he argues is essential spending, including creating jobs where they are needed such as in schools.

Justifying policies for equality

Given the complexities of the current policy climate, and the general lack of support for full-blooded socialism, can equality still be defended as an important principle of social policy? As with every principle, the answer to this question depends on how the term is interpreted. Three basically different views can be identified: the goal of near-equality or **egalitarianism**; equity; and equality of opportunity. Attached to each of these definitions are somewhat different justifications for equality.

Egalitarianism

This is an ideal, an expression of equality in its 'purest' or most utopian form (Drabble 1988). It is about finding ways of ensuring that people enjoy the same results or *outcomes* in life: the same incomes, the same life span, similar levels of education and health and so on.

What would be the justification for policies to bring about a state of near-equality? Again, much would depend on the egalitarian's values or morality. The example of communism has already been mentioned. There has also been a thread of ethical or Christian socialism in British egalitarianism, and this has been a recurrent influence on thinking about social policy (see, for example, Tawney 1964). In communism or Marxism, the ultimate objective was a society in which no one unfairly exploited the labour of anyone else. Ethical socialists, however, stressed the *moral* dimension: gross inequalities are morally wrong, whereas a society of near-equals is one in which community, brotherhood and sisterhood will flourish. Note the normative ideas underlying this principle of equality.

Tawney was a Christian socialist and a leading figure in debates about equality in a welfare society. For him, equality amounted to much more than 'distributive justice' or making sure that incomes and the benefits of the welfare system were distributed equally among individuals and classes. Julian Le Grand's study *The Strategy of Equality* (1982) is an example of how the concept of distributive justice can be applied to research on 'who gets what' from the welfare system. Tawney held to a wider socialistic vision of equality. His goal and his vision of social policy was to help create a society in which people felt that they belonged to a common community – a society in which they would feel free to participate in making political decisions about their own future, and in which everyone was valued equally.

In a similar vein, Marshall – another founder of the principles of an egalitarian welfare society – argued that: 'The extension of the social services is not primarily a means of equalising incomes . . . What matters is that there is a general enrichment of the concrete substance of civilized life, a general reduction of risk and insecurity, an equalization between the more and less fortunate at all levels . . . Equality of status is more important than equality of income' (1963: 107).

However, *inequality* of income is important to egalitarians in one important respect. Large inequalities, it is argued, lead to social division and are, in themselves, morally wrong. For instance, public concern has been expressed about the enormous annual pay increases (of over 30 per cent and totalling thousands of pounds) awarded to the heads of government agencies. This has been at a time when the great majority of public sector employees, working in the same agencies, have been expected to accept much lower annual pay increases. These concerns remain ever present with media reports detailing large bonuses awarded to bankers while the general public are subjected to austerity measures in the UK.

Thus, the egalitarian's argument against inequality is relatively easy to invoke, as did Charles Dickens in his scathing attacks on the greed and selfishness of Victorian business people and corrupt public servants. However, a critique of gross inequality is not the same as making a case for *near-equality*. Here the egalitarians' arguments are harder to sustain, for a number of reasons.

First, *individuals differ*. Whether as a result of nature or nurture, every individual has a unique combination of talents, abilities, temperament and motivation. Policies trying to bring about absolute or near-equality would work against these differences, rewarding the lazy, the incompetent and the dishonest as well as the innovative, intelligent or honest.

There is a lack of justice in policies that try to ensure equal outcomes for all. Would it be just, for example, to ensure that all 16-year-olds 'achieved' the same number of GCSE passes at the same grades, even though everyone knew that a proportion of the 'successful' candidates were being rewarded for either mediocre efforts or none at all? Such a policy would immediately devalue the GCSE qualification but, more importantly, would be unjust to those who had worked hard or had the ability to achieve the better results.

The second factor is **coercion** and *lack of freedom*. In order for a state of near-equality to be maintained, very strong regulatory authorities would be needed to survey constantly individuals' incomes, redistribute wealth and monitor who was being appointed to each and every job. Not only would this cost a great deal to implement, but it would also bring about a very invasive state. Everyone's private life would have to be scrutinized regularly and closely to make sure that no one was becoming better off than anyone else. So while inequality spells lack of freedom for some because better-off individuals and groups may gain at the expense of the poor, a state of *imposed equality* would severely reduce everyone's freedom.

However, these criticisms of equality are valid only where policies are taken to extremes. It is relatively easy to put up a 'straw man' of absolute equality and then knock it down, as gurus of the New Right such as Hayek (1944), Worsthorne (1971) and Scruton (1984) have done. In arguing that the goal of equality is unattainable, they have always told cautionary tales of the horrors of repressive state socialist regimes such as the former Soviet Union. But they have never carefully considered the achievements of countries that successfully applied **social democratic** principles in the past. Countries such as Sweden and Denmark have not sought to abolish inequality completely, but have acted to reduce the extremes that arise in other capitalist economies.

So while everyone agrees that near-equality is an impossible dream, perhaps even a nightmare, this does not mean that the equality principle need be rejected altogether. In policy terms, a more acceptable and practical principle might be that of *making society more equal than it was*, rather than trying to bring about absolute equality. This is in one way a utilitarian consideration, increasing social equality not so much for the sake of it but more to maintain social order and to ensure 'the greatest happiness of the greatest number'. But, more importantly, there is also the justification of fairness – making sure that less well-off or disadvantaged groups are treated with justice.

Box 2.2 Contemporary views on justice and inequality

- Wilkinson and Pickett (2009) argue that within all societies all social problems (including crime) are strongly associated with income, being more common in the less economically well-off groups. Furthermore, the overall burden of these problems is much higher in the most unequal societies. They argue that societies that are more equal generally do better. For Wilkinson (2011) social inequality is divisive and socially corrosive, as well as unjust. Sometimes social policies contribute to these social divisions.
- Dorling (2010) highlights a range of ways in which social exclusion serves to create an unfair society. For example, in education some candidates for university entry find it more difficult to gain entry to Britain's top 'Russell Group' universities if they have been state school educated or come from a 'lower' status background, while those from public (i.e. private) schools are disproportionately represented in the 'top' universities. Again, it is clear that social policy plays a role here – for example, those with more financial capability are able to pay for higher education, and those who meet the necessary performance metrics (*specific grades*) are also more likely to secure a place.

A policy to bring about near-equality might look more justifiable if we think about it in relation to *groups* rather than individuals. For example, while accepting that individual men and women differ – the more and the less intelligent, able, rich and poor individuals – there is a strong argument that men and women as groups should be near-equals. This would mean that approximately equal proportions of women and men would occupy each occupational or income level. Sweden, for instance, has set policy targets to do just this, and aims to achieve a balance of no more than 60 per cent or less than 40 per cent of either men or women in a comprehensive list of occupations (Blakemore and Drake 1995). Other targets are arguably needed to encourage similar equality for example, there are still fewer women than men in parliament in all countries.

Similar arguments about equality and the representation of different groups at every level of society can be applied to minority groups as well as to men and women. Equal opportunity policies, for instance, aim to increase opportunities for groups who have experienced discrimination in the past because of their disability, age, sexual orientation or 'race'. As they are minority groups in the population, however, this means that equality in terms of numbers is achieved once the *proportions* of black, gay, disabled and older people in a given occupation or at a given income level match the proportions in the population as a whole. This notion of equality based on proportions – 'proportionality' – is a relatively limited definition of equality, however, because it does not include any reference to power. A business firm or a government department might employ representative proportions of women and disabled people, for instance, but this does not necessarily mean that women and disabled employees have an equal say in the shaping of policy or in sharing managerial control of the organization.

These arguments relate to notions of power within the policy process, and how policy is made, and again a range of views are discussed within the literature. Table 2.3 indicates some key theories about policy-making and views of power.

Table 2.3 Theories of power within policy-making

Theory	View of power
Decision-making	• Individuals and groups influence policy-making. • Dahl (1961) – some groups are rich in political resources and so can penetrate the policy-making process, and are able to exert more power and influence. • Power within the policy-making process is unequal.
Non-decision-making	• Power is exercised by biased agenda setting – powerful groups keep issues away from the **policy agenda**. • Decision-making is therefore limited to selected or indeed 'safe' issues.
Power as thought control	• Lukes (1974) defines power as the ability to influence others by shaping their decisions. • Power is conceptualized as thought control, with individuals sometimes voting for political parties that will not work to their advantage.

Equity

This is a useful idea that extends the concept of equality. The notion of equality tends to make us focus on sameness or similarity. Thus, if neighbours X and Y are equal, we tend to think of them having similar incomes, houses, type of car, number of children and so on. But if such an end-state were to be brought about by social and taxation policies, what would be required?

This is where the concept of equity is useful because, to reach a similar end-state or outcome, it is usually necessary to treat individuals, families and groups *equitably* rather than *equally*. An equitable approach means treating people fairly, but differently, to ensure that there is some equality between them at the end.

Dividing a cake gives a homely example to illustrate equity. Assuming that one guest feels full, two are not very hungry and a fourth is ravenous, equitable slicing would mean no cake for the first, two thin slices and one large wedge. After this, all guests should be in an equal state – full – but they have been treated unequally to achieve this. Treating them all equally, on the other hand, would have resulted in unequal or undesirable outcomes.

In social policy terms, and returning to our neighbouring families X and Y, equitable social policies would treat each household differently depending on its needs and circumstances. For example, if X's son is disabled or has special educational needs, there might be targeted grants, benefits or school facilities that would have the object of compensating the X family for additional expenditure and bringing them back to a state of near-equality with the Y family.

The problem with equitable social policies is that sometimes they do not *look* fair. Treating everyone in the same way is seen as fair, whereas treating them differently seems to smack of injustice or special favours. For example, equitable cake slicing might work with adults but try it with small children, who expect equal slices of a birthday cake. In this situation equity will almost certainly end in tears.

A more serious example is provided by public reaction to William Beveridge's wartime proposals for social security reform, which might be regarded as the cornerstone of Britain's welfare state (see Chapter 3). Above all, it was the fairness and perceived equality of the scheme that gripped the public imagination, made Beveridge into something of a hero and the 'Beveridge Report' into a best seller (Beveridge 1942). Beveridge's proposal that all contributors be treated equally, paying the same (**flat-rate**) National Insurance contributions and being able to draw the same flat-rate benefits when in need, seemed to tune in perfectly with the wartime collective spirit of equality.

Yet, in essence, Beveridge's plan owed more to liberal principles of equality than to socialist ones. Treating people 'equally' meant that the scheme did not substantially redistribute resources from the better-off social classes to the less well-off, although of course it did redistribute from the healthy to the temporarily sick and from the employed to the temporarily unemployed. A more equitable social security policy, it could be argued, would have asked the better-off to pay a little more into the scheme in return for the same benefits as everyone else – but would this have looked fair?

Applying the equity principle can also raise problems because fairness demands an accurate and accepted definition of people's *needs*. Suppose that you are again faced with a table of squabbling children at mealtime and that you have decided to distribute food in unequal, equitable portions. If you are both a parent and a student of social policy, perhaps the children will already have grudgingly learned to put up with the principle of equity. However, this does not solve the problem of deciding whose definitions of need to take into account – yours or theirs? There might be vociferous objections from the children to the *grounds* on which the size of each child's portion has been decided: 'That's not fair, he had a big slice yesterday', 'She said she's going to be sick if you give her any vegetables' and so on. You may yourself be unsure of each child's 'real' needs: is Matthew clamouring for more simply because he is showing off; is Alison hungrier than she is prepared to say, and should she be encouraged to eat more? Faced with all this, it is not surprising that parents, like welfare systems, resort to giving equal, but inequitable, benefits.

Equality of opportunity

This is another useful refinement of the meaning of equality. The equal opportunity concept might be applied first to *employment*, through policies to remove barriers of discrimination, improving access to jobs, education and training. In an age of temporary work contracts and part-time jobs, this is important. Work, despite its drawbacks, raises incomes, usually provides social contact and reduces social exclusion (see Chapter 9). Second, equal opportunity principles can be applied to improving access to, and use of, *health and social services*.

However, as with other equality principles, equal opportunity means different things to different people. Conservatives, as well as those on the left, subscribe to 'equality of opportunity'. Views from the political right stress *opportunity*, while those from the left stress the *equality* side of the equation. These differences of emphasis can result in substantial practical differences in the ways that equal opportunity policies are applied. Distinctions can be made between (a) relatively limited and modest definitions of equal opportunity (**'minimalist' principles**), and (b) more ambitious and 'tougher' approaches (**'maximalist' principles**). These distinctions are summarized in Box 2.3.

Box 2.3 Equal opportunity strategies

'Minimalist' principles	*'Maximalist' principles*
Equality policies aim to ensure that people are *treated* fairly or on an equal basis. Discrimination on grounds of gender, 'race', disability or other irrelevant criteria is unjust and illegal in most cases.	Equality policies aim to create *equal outcomes*. Policies and the law must go further than banning unfair or negative discrimination; they must also positively encourage or discriminate so that minorities and other disadvantaged groups benefit equally from employment opportunities or the welfare system.
'Fair competition' on a 'level playing field' is the hallmark of this approach. The end result or outcome (for example, being employed or receiving benefit) must be decided on *merit* or according to *need*.	There is no 'level playing field'. Historic advantages enjoyed by those in control now mean that they decide how 'merit' and 'need' are defined. Though merit is important, it may have to be redefined to avoid in-built bias against women, disabled people and others.
Individuals must be treated 'in like fashion'. The end result is unequal, but fair. *Any* discrimination, positive or negative, is wrong.	Individuals may be treated differently according to the social group or category they belong to. '**Positive action**' or 'positive discrimination' might be necessary to make sure that underrepresented groups obtain benefits or employment from which they have previously been excluded.
Quotas, or reserving certain number of jobs, educational places or services for members of minority and disadvantaged groups, are unjust.	Quotas, or at least targets, to bring the *proportions* of people in various groups (women, disabled people and others) in line with the proportions receiving employment, education and welfare are necessary because without them little will change.
'Minimalist' principles fit best with liberal or conservative principles and values.	'Maximalist' principles fit best with social democratic or egalitarian principles, though 'tough' equal opportunities policies are found in the right-of-centre dominated USA.

Under British law – for example, the anti-discrimination laws that combine legislation against discrimination on the basis of gender, race, disability, age and other categories – policy and practice are much closer to (a) than to (b). But it is better to think of equal opportunity policies on a spectrum from 'modest' to 'tough'. Particular examples do not necessarily fit neatly into either category. In the UK, for example, not all equal opportunity policies can be pigeonholed as weak. A certain amount of 'positive action' to correct gender and 'race' discrimination is allowed under British law, and in Northern Ireland a Fair Employment Act and other government action has endorsed the principle of 'proportionality' mentioned above. In the Northern Ireland case proportionality means a more equal sharing of job opportunities between the Protestant and Catholic communities than before. Although a strict policy of reserving jobs for the underrepresented Catholic minority has not been introduced, it is in Northern Ireland that the UK has moved closest to the principle of a 'tougher' approach to equal opportunities.

The summarized distinctions between minimalist policies and maximalist policies (or 'weak' and 'tough') of equal opportunity (see Box 2.3) suggest sharp differences between two types of equality policy. However, it is worth re-emphasizing that in reality these distinctions are blurred. If policies favour positive action rather than positive discrimination, for instance, we can describe them as being midway between 'weak' and 'tough'.

Positive action refers to policies that stop short of positive discrimination. Under Britain's Race Relations Act 1976, for example, it was permissible to take positive steps to encourage members of underrepresented groups to apply for work in an organization (for instance, in the way that job advertisements were worded). Other forms of positive action include additional training courses to meet the needs of underrepresented groups, career breaks for women, and improvements in facilities in the workplace that enhance disabled people's opportunities.

All these measures were designed to develop a workforce that was more representative of the population, but that did not rely on a quota system of reserving jobs for each underrepresented group. Similar principles apply to the distribution of benefits or access to social and health services. Positive action here would entail taking steps to encourage access and to enable underrepresented or disadvantaged groups to make fuller use of the services available.

However, positive action does not mean that people will automatically qualify for a service or a benefit because they are members of a minority or a disadvantaged group. Need remains the basic criterion. The object of positive action is therefore to equalize access and to ensure that everyone with needs is heard: for instance, by providing translation services to hospital patients whose first language is other than English.

Having said this, the distinction between (a) providing services strictly according to need and (b) positive discrimination in favour of a certain group is not as clear-cut as it might first appear. This point is linked to arguments about whether benefits should be **universal benefits** – that is, available to everyone in a certain category– or whether they should be targeted or **selective benefits**. This is discussed further in Chapter 6.

Need

This brings us to the important concept of need. We have already seen that 'need' is a *problematic* concept (by 'problematic', we mean a term that is not easy to define and where there is a lack of consensus about what it means). This causes difficulties when, for example, we try to decide whether one person's or one group's needs are greater than another's. To begin to consider this concept, complete Activity 2.2.

Activity 2.2 Reflecting upon need

- Before you read any further, spend five minutes writing a short list of what you think are the most important human needs. Try to list at least ten.
- Now ask yourself these questions. Is there any pattern or logic in the list you have drawn up? For example, do some needs come before others and, if so, why? Are some more basic or fundamental? (If you do not see a pattern, add some more needs and then try to prioritize the needs in some way.)
- Are your definitions of need culture-free, or do they relate only to a particular country or social group? To test this, think about whether your list would be as applicable in India or Mali, say, as in Britain or another economically developed country. Try constructing a list as if *you* were living in a village in the African Sahel, or on the streets of an Indian city.
- See www.jrf.org.uk/publications/poverty-and-social-exclusion-britain for a report that details the findings from the UK Poverty and Social Exclusion Survey in 1999, which incorporates the views and perceptions of members of the public. How do your views compare?
- Finally keep your list so that you can read on and then compare with that of Doyal and Gough (1991), presented a little further on.

Writing your own list of human needs and the questions this poses in your mind should help to identify two fundamental points about need. These points have been at the centre of social policy ever since the state began to take on certain basic responsibilities for people's welfare. The first is a central question about objectivity. Is it possible to establish a commonly accepted or objective definition of need and to distinguish clearly between those who are in need and those who are not? The second point relates to questions of responsibility and duty. How far is the state responsible for meeting certain needs? Should every citizen have rights to have their needs met, and does the community have a duty to meet them?

These questions not only are of great interest today, but also vexed the conscience of nineteenth-century Britain. In Britain, the 'new' Poor Law of 1834 showed official acceptance of a very basic responsibility of the state towards the poorest citizens. **Workhouses** and 'parish relief' were organized into a system that was designed to provide for only the absolutely destitute (see Chapter 3). In return for their freedom and loss of **civil rights**, paupers could obtain just enough from the public purse to survive. In this early example of social policy we have a definition of **basic needs**: shelter, food and perhaps some very limited medical care.

Doyal and Gough (1991: 56–9) point out that survival is too limited a definition even of basic need. As they suggest, the victim of a serious accident who is in a coma is surviving but is not able to achieve anything or to satisfy any other needs. Similarly, the example of severely malnourished victims of famine shows that people might be surviving – just – but are hardly having their basic needs met. Another problem with 'survival' as a definition of basic need is that it is rather circular: it is rather like saying that human beings 'need to live'.

For these reasons, Doyal and Gough suggest that physical health is a better definition of basic need, because 'to complete a range of practical tasks in daily life requires manual, mental and emotional abilities with which poor physical health usually interferes' (1991: 56).

The advantage of using physical health as a criterion of basic need is that it suggests certain goals. Note that Doyal and Gough talk of 'good' physical health, which takes us away from mere survival to a goal that people can aim for. However, the concept of 'physical health' also opens up problems of definition: how healthy do people have to be before we can say that their needs can be met?

Thus, it might not be possible to find completely objective definitions, even of basic needs. This is more apparent when we include Doyal and Gough's second criterion of basic needs, **autonomy**. Without autonomy, or the freedom to be able to decide and choose, human beings are arguably deprived of a need as basic as physical health. It is no use being physically healthy without the ability to realize the aspirations or objectives that make us human – secondary needs such as the need to develop oneself in various ways, to communicate and to form relationships with other human beings. As with physical health, however, autonomy is a matter of degree. There is bound to be debate about how much autonomy human beings need or, more negatively, how much they can do without. Related to this is the question of mental health. It is hard to see why only physical health should be seen as a basic need when mental illness can seriously impair quality of life and can remove people's ability to live autonomous, independent lives.

Sadly, loss or lack of autonomy is not difficult to find in the field of welfare and social policy. Older people, for example, are particularly vulnerable in this respect, because they might have been judged to be incapable of exercising autonomy. The very old are often written off as too mentally confused or frail to exercise any autonomy. Much has been made of the treatment of older people in care in the UK media recently, with documentaries demonstrating the negative attitudes of **carers**. Teodorazuk et al. (2009) argue that relationships between staff and those that they are caring for often become custodial, echoing earlier studies of confused older people in **residential care** which suggest that the staff or 'carers' sometimes exaggerate infirmities and this might actually increase them (Kitwood 1997). Such residents are not even allowed to exercise choice or autonomy in matters that they can still comprehend. Similar issues of loss of autonomy and the controlling aspects of residential care are discussed further in Chapter 7.

Box 2.4 Universal human needs?

Doyal and Gough (1991) argue that it is relatively easy to make up a list of needs – social policy research abounds with them. However, it is more difficult to decide which needs are *universal* and which definitions would permit us to compare need satisfaction in different countries or cultures.

Their list (below) has been drawn up according to one main criterion. To be included, each item must contribute towards satisfying the two most *basic* needs (physical health and autonomy). For example, they suggest that sexual relationships need not be included 'because some people manage to live healthy and autonomous lives without sex with others' (1991: 158). Do you agree with this, and in general what do you think of their list of needs?

- nutritional food and clean water
- protective housing
- a non-hazardous work environment
- a non-hazardous physical environment

- appropriate health care
- security in childhood
- significant primary relationships
- physical security
- economic security
- appropriate education
- safe birth control and childbearing

To sum up, physical health and autonomy can be seen as basic needs that, if denied, will result in people being unable to meet other, secondary needs. Putting it another way, *needs could be defined as basic if being deprived of them will lead to serious harm.*

Once basic needs have been discussed, however, there remains the question of how secondary or intermediate needs are to be identified. This is the point at which to compare your own list with that of Doyal and Gough (see Box 2.4).

Needs, wants and satisfaction

So far, our discussion of need has highlighted some of the problems encountered in trying objectively to define 'real' needs. But, while difficult, this is not an impossible task as long as we remember that there has to be some argument. In fact, debate about needs is a healthy phenomenon. For instance, it might be prompted by attempts to improve standards of welfare or to expose the hidden needs of disadvantaged groups.

Bradshaw (1972), in a pioneering discussion, suggested that there are four main ways in which people define needs.

- ***Felt need,*** according to Bradshaw, occurs when individuals are conscious of their needs. This, however, leaves open the question of whether they decide to express their felt needs or whether they are able to do so. Not all felt needs are expressed, either because those in need choose not to express them or because inequalities of power and status prevent oppressed and less powerful groups from voicing their needs. For example, some social groups views are neglected within community development settings because of their subordinate position.
- ***Expressed needs*** are publicized and known about. They become *demands,* as opposed to the hidden needs of those who are unwilling or too powerless or otherwise unable to express what they need, as just mentioned.
- ***Normative needs*** are those defined according to professional norms or standards; they are needs defined by outside observers or experts. For example, a professional counsellor might identify a need in a client that the client might accept, or on the other hand reject or fail to comprehend. Or, to give another example, social workers responsible for finding foster homes will judge whether a particular home is adequate to meet the needs of a child, as defined by their professional view and the standards laid down by their employer.
- ***Comparative need*** introduces the concept of relative judgement – that is, the needs of a group are defined relative to what other groups have or do not have. There is an element of justice here. If there are two similar groups, but only one is receiving a benefit or a service, the group not receiving welfare could be unjustly deprived and in comparative need.

The first definition – felt need – introduces a subjective element into the discussion. On the one hand, there are some needs that can be defined objectively (albeit with some disagreement among observers) and, on the other, **wants** that are apparently more to do with subjective or personal states of mind or desires. For example, a person might need a certain medical treatment that is invasive or painful, but not want it. Or a hypochondriac will be obsessed with medical treatments even though objectively these are not needed.

Remember that one way of defining a *need* is that being deprived of it causes serious harm, whereas this is not the case with things that are purely *wants*. A child might desperately want the latest computer game but arguably being deprived of it will not cause harm and might even do some good.

This distinction between wants and needs is not a clear-cut one, however. The very idea of 'felt needs' suggests that a strongly subjective element *can* enter into definitions of need. For example, pensioners on a low income might decide that keeping in touch with their grandchildren is a basic requirement (and a need to sustain important family relationships). They might decide that it is vitally important to spend a lot of their money on cards and gifts, especially on the grandchildren's birthdays or at seasonal holidays such as Christmas. But in refusing to compromise on this, they might well have to economize on heating or food costs. In this case, what appear to be unnecessary wants (cards, gifts) take the place of things that safeguard a basic need, such as physical health. For instance, they might decide that their heating must be switched off to save money, possibly risking death from hypothermia for the sake of being able to afford Christmas cards and presents.

Therefore, although being deprived of needs can be said to cause serious harm, so in some ways could being deprived of wants. The teenager who is deprived of the latest fashion item might take this want so seriously that they become depressed, feel that they are a social outcast and that their whole life has been blighted. If this happens, then we might have to take the consequences seriously: for example, shoplifting or other forms of offending.

The value of bringing the subjective element into any discussion of needs and wants is that it helps to answer the question of why *satisfaction* levels are not rising markedly in industrialized countries when, according to many objective economic criteria, needs are being met more fully than ever before.

For instance, if economic indicators of well-being are anything to go by, great progress has been made in the past few decades. British incomes rose by 230 per cent in real terms between 1950 and 1990 (Vidal 1994: 4), life expectancy has increased and ordinary people now own many more consumer goods – television sets, computers, cars, freezers and refrigerators – than could have been dreamt of in the 1950s. But whether there has been progress in meeting the full range of human needs is a much more debatable point.

This is where the subjective element is important, for as James (2007) noted in the *Guardian* newspaper,

> Selfish capitalism causes mental illness by spawning materialism, or, as I put it, the affluenza virus – placing a high value on money, possessions, appearances (social and physical) and fame. English-speaking nations are more infected with the virus than mainland western European ones. Studies in many nations prove that people who strongly subscribe to virus values are at significantly greater risk of depression, anxiety, substance abuse and personality disorder. Follow the logic? Selfish capitalism infects populations with affluenza; it fosters mental illness.

We do not have to accept the whole of this negative message. For instance, there are objective grounds for saying that health is better now than it was in the early 1960s (see Chapter 10), and economic growth has for many brought significant benefits.

Complete Activity 2.3 to reflect upon the relationship between health and growth in more depth.

Activity 2.3 Analysing economic growth and health outcomes

- Visit the website www.gapminder.org.
- Click on the second tab at the top of the page, called 'gapminder world', where you will see a graph that compares life-expectancy to levels of income. From the right-hand side of the page choose the following three countries Chad, Denmark and Georgia.
- Now go back in time to 1800 using the toolbar at the bottom of the graph and click on play. You will now have a graphical representation of changing life expectancy across the three countries.

1. Describe the different trends between income and life expectancy shown in the graph for all three countries.
2. Think about the relationship between **economics** and health as one of the possible influencing factors here.

However, despite such significant gains in both income and health, an equally important factor is whether people feel that their needs are being met and whether their quality of life is failing to improve. As societies with welfare systems become more affluent than before, perhaps they can increasingly 'afford' to be disenchanted with the costs of progress (pollution, erosion of public amenities and loss of community life) in a way that poorer, less industrialized countries cannot. Does the drive for ever-increasing growth contribute to zombie capitalism (Harman 2009) which increases our unhappiness? This has led to calls for alternative views of well-being.

Sen's theory: 'commodities', 'capabilities' and 'functionings'

The eminent Indian economist Amartya Sen has developed a view of poverty, and more generally of well-being and the standard of living, which has attracted a great deal of attention since he first put it forward. Sen's theory may be regarded as a critique and revision of economic views about well-being and at the same time his approach can be viewed as a variant of, or an application of, a 'needs' approach.

Sen criticizes what he calls the economist's and utilitarian's definitions of welfare or of value in terms of 'happiness' or utility. These, he argues, neglect a range of moral and economic issues that are important, such as exploitation (Sen 1980). He points to the urgency of basic wants and needs and the objectivity of such facts as whether a person is 'hungry, cold or oppressed' (1980: 154). Utility information (pleasure, desire-satisfaction) must be supplemented by such objective assessments. Sen therefore suggests that it is more appropriate to see demands for freedom from exploitation as a moral claim for just rewards ('equality of desert') than as 'lack of well-being' (1980: 155). Similarly, the demand for 'equal pay for equal work' is not a purely instrumental claim, which in welfarist/utilitarian terms it would be.

In developing his theory, Sen has identified, and distinguishes between, three concepts: 'commodities', 'capabilities' and 'functionings', explained in Table 2.4. The object of public policy, according to Sen, is therefore to try to ensure as fair a distribution as possible of both commodities and capabilities, which can be at the social or the individual level, involve the idea of activity, or of 'being and doing'. So, in sum, capabilities are necessary conditions to achieve functionings.

Table 2.4 Sen's theory

Concept	Explanation
Commodities	• Defined as resources, including income, health care and education. • The notion of a line or subsistence, minimum income level is based on the idea of such commodities, or the lack of them. • Sen suggests that focusing only on commodities is an inadequate basis for poverty research and for defining needs. This is because people vary in their capacities to transform commodities into 'capabilities' and 'functionings' (Sen 1980: 161).
Capabilities	• Describe the necessary conditions human beings need to enable them to function fully. • Include the ability to move about, the ability to meet our nutritional requirements, the wherewithal to be clothed and sheltered, and the ability to participate in the social life of the community.
Functionings	• Relate directly to the kinds of lives that people are able to lead – the kinds of activities they can pursue, or 'being and doing' (which, he argues, is what our concern with the standard of living and poverty is all about).

A useful feature of the capabilities concept is its connection with the idea of positive freedom – freedom as '**empowerment**' or as opportunity (see the next section for further discussion of 'positive' and 'negative' definitions of freedom). Capabilities seem to involve choice and the range of choice that individuals have: 'Capabilities . . . are notions of freedom, in the positive sense: what real opportunities you may have regarding the life you may lead' (Sen 1987: 36). So, in contrasting a capability and a functioning, the latter is an achievement and the former is 'the ability to achieve' (1987: 36).

Sen's theory is valuable for a number of reasons. It provides a systematic attempt to explore and develop a more precise characterization of well-being for social science and policy purposes than that provided by some of the standard theories on offer. It provides a corrective to some established views. Sen has drawn attention to what commodities are *for*. His theory attempts to integrate economic and sociological ideas about inequality, poverty and need – that is, economic theory based on the idea of utility or subjective preference, and social science and policy ideas based on objective notions such as need. Finally, Sen's contribution has the great merit of internationalizing the debate about issues such as poverty and need, and the political questions and moral principles these issues provoke. His discussion is as applicable to economically developed countries such as the UK as it is to developing countries such as India.

Freedom and rights

If we are coerced or told what to do throughout our lives and are deprived of rights, we cannot realize our potential to become fully human beings. However, as with equality, 'freedom' and 'rights' can easily become slogans. Difficulties begin when policy-makers or those who deliver welfare services have to decide what 'freedom' and 'rights' mean in practical terms, and on what grounds some people's freedoms might have to be removed or curtailed.

For instance, there might be a need to suspend the driving licence of a driver whose seriously failing vision and hearing pose grave dangers to other road users and pedestrians. However, difficulties arise in defining safety limits for the majority of older drivers, most of whom are safe drivers and enjoy lower insurance premiums as a result. What if a driver's vision is poor but just about adequate to drive a car along familiar routes? Or what if the driver and their partner live in a rural area, where without the use of a car it would be very difficult to visit a chemist's shop or buy groceries? Should such drivers have the freedom to take moderate risks with their own and others' safety?

Disability throws up a range of even deeper questions about freedoms and rights. The right to vote, for example, signifies an individual's full membership of society as a citizen. But should people with significant learning difficulties have the right to vote and, if not, how can their voices be heard and rights as citizens be respected? Those who champion the rights of disabled people (for instance, Oliver 1990) argue that most, if not all, of the problems they face have been created by the society around them rather than directly by their disabilities. This is a 'social' model of disability, as opposed to a 'charity' or 'victim' model. It suggests that rather than pitying disabled people as victims of their own physical or mental states, society is responsible for improving their freedoms and guaranteeing their rights. Considerable investment in redesigning housing, work environments and transport facilities is needed in order to remove the barriers to freedom experienced by disabled people.

How far and in what ways society should be expected to make such a full commitment to the rights of disabled people is an open question, and is likely to cause continuing arguments about how to balance the rights and freedoms of disabled and non-disabled people. The right to vote has also been the focus of media attention in the UK in 2011 and 2012 with debate centred upon whether those incarcerated in prison should have the right to vote. Proposed policy changes in this area follow a ruling by the European Court of Human Rights, with a decision yet to be made at the time of writing.

In following Marshall's (1950) classic distinction between **civil, political** and **social rights**, it becomes clear that individuals and groups can enjoy different types of rights and the freedoms that are associated with them. Marshall's distinctions are summarized in Table 2.5.

Table 2.5 Different types of rights

Type of rights	Definition
Civil rights	• Include basic freedoms under the law: for instance, freedom from discrimination, arbitrary arrest and detention; freedom to meet in groups and to have open discussion; freedom of the press and of expression.
Political rights	• Include the right to vote, to join and participate in political parties and to hold government accountable to democratic opinion.
Social rights	• Involve a greater commitment of resources and are represented by rights to education, social welfare and social security; in short, rights to the benefits of a welfare system.

Viewed historically, in Britain, the three categories of rights can be seen to have developed gradually, with civil rights being established first, then political rights (for men first, and for women substantially later) and finally social rights. However, Marshall stressed that there is not necessarily an inevitable process of evolution at work here, involving automatic or continued progress towards social rights.

Some countries, such as present-day Singapore, combine substantial social rights and a well-organized welfare system with rather limited political rights (see Chapter 8). Thus one kind of freedom and one set of rights does not necessarily lead to another. In fact, social welfare can bolster paternalistic governments by making them appear fair and reasonable, thus reducing basic political freedoms.

To return to particular groups in society, such as disabled people, older people or children, we may apply Marshall's distinctions to questions about the rights of each. For example, with regard to children, electoral democracies have nowhere extended them *political* rights – they cannot vote or send their own representatives to parliament. However, this does not mean that they cannot have their *civil* rights improved and, under the Children Act 1989 and many other pieces of legislation, children have legal rights to education and welfare services: *social* rights.

If we consider people with learning difficulties, it may well be that they enjoy social protection and certain social rights, but they may never be granted civil and political rights even though, in some cases, they are capable of exercising political preferences or participating in decisions made about their welfare.

Another way of looking at both rights and freedoms is to think of them either as *negative* principles ('freedom *from*' certain things that endanger liberty) or as positive principles ('freedom to' do certain things).

A negative definition of freedom would give every citizen the right to be protected from harm from others – for example, from physical assault, burglary or discrimination. Negative definitions of freedom are very much part of a classical liberal or laissez-faire philosophy. In this view, people should be allowed as many freedoms as possible. However, complete freedom, or free-for-all anarchy, would not bring genuine liberty. Laissez-faire must be coupled with strong laws to restrain those who would intentionally seek to harm or reduce the freedoms of others. Thus a liberal society such as the USA has always had relatively strong laws to limit the power of both the state and of private monopolies (which form to fix prices unfairly and exploit consumers).

A strong belief among those on the political right who subscribe to the negative view of freedom (for example, Joseph and Sumption 1979) is that *to be poor is not to be unfree*. In other words, the poor and the rich alike enjoy political rights – all can vote in parliamentary elections, for instance – and civil rights, such as freedom from arbitrary arrest. According to this view, it is not up to society or a government to bring about a state of affairs in which everyone has equal freedom of action.

To those on the political right, freedom can be fully guaranteed only in a society organized by the market, in which people are free to own as much property as they can amass and in which there is competition between individuals and businesses. Markets are seen as vital in ensuring not only freedom but also efficiency. But by their very nature, markets lead to differences and they expose inequalities. People are bound to have different amounts of talent and ability, luck and spending power. In a 'free' market, there cannot be equal freedom for everyone to be able to afford tea at the Ritz.

Why do defenders of this view, such as Hayek (1944), argue that the poor – the losers in a market-based society – are not deprived of freedom? First, civil and political freedoms are still protected. For example, a family on income support probably could not afford tea at the Ritz, but they would have as much (civil) right to enter as anyone else (in contrast to a society in which discrimination against certain groups was legal, as in the former South Africa, where a black person could legally be denied entry to a hotel). They would also have the political right to meet with others on the street outside to demonstrate about poverty, if they wished, or to write to their Members of Parliament (MPs) to complain about the inadequacy of benefit payments.

Second, this argument runs, loss of freedom involves coercion or the *intention* of someone to deprive others of freedom. In a true market, though, there is no planned intention to reduce anyone's freedom. The market operates impersonally, and its outcomes (for example, rising or falling house prices, booming demand in one industry, layoffs in another) are apparently unknowable in advance.

Does this argument ring true, especially to anyone who happens to be poor in a society dominated by the market? First, we may question the suggestion that the outcomes of living in a market-based society are unknowable. There is clear evidence that, if unchecked, inequalities tend to widen. The social gap increases between wealthy elites and a more or less permanent group of disadvantaged people, while those in the middle feel increasingly insecure about their position. Rather than an increase in freedom and the creation of a mobile society in which enterprise and individuality are rewarded, it can be argued, increasing numbers of people begin to feel unfree and the better-off tend to monopolize positions of power and influence.

Also there is an assumption that, because market forces are blind, nothing should be done to 'tinker' with them, apart from ensuring that the rules of fair competition are enforced. But it is on this point that many, including some conservatives as well as those in the political centre and on the left, agree that it is both unethical and unwise to allow the market full rein. A more positive view of freedom involves policies to make sure that it is possible for those disadvantaged by a market society to have or to do certain things: for instance, to be able to purchase adequate food or housing and to be educated.

In one sense, the whole of social policy and its history revolves around this question: *how far* should the state step in to mitigate the effects of a society based on the market and on competition? How far can it guarantee rights to both freedom and security for every citizen, which implies not only 'freedom from' discrimination or harm, but also 'freedom to' enjoy a certain standard of living and welfare?

As we have seen, there are flaws in the pro-market, 'negative' concept of freedom. On the other hand, there is also growing acceptance in social policy of the limits of 'positive' views of freedom. Partly because of the spiralling costs of welfare systems and also because of worries about the creation of welfare dependency, politicians and policy-makers in every major industrial country have introduced reforms to limit the automatic right to welfare. For example, policies to shift people on benefits into work in Britain, the USA and elsewhere emphasize the *responsibilities* of these individuals rather than their *rights*. Although for critics there is a lack of recognition of the structural determinants of unemployment – not all on benefits wish to be so, and in the current economic climate unemployment remains a serious problem, especially for young adults.

Citizenship

Having looked, in the previous sections, at ideas about equality, needs, rights and freedom, let us now turn to look at a concept which puts together all these ideas, and which is important for thinking about the meaning and purpose of the welfare state. This concept, citizenship, is one that has undergone something of a revival and reformulation in recent decades. But what is 'citizenship'?

First, citizenship implies membership – membership of a particular type of community, namely, the nation-state: 'Citizenship is a status bestowed on those who are full members of a community' (Marshall 1964: 92). How is such membership defined, and what are the markers or identifiers of citizenship? They include, for example, nationality and right of residence, the possession of a passport and the right to participate in elections. They also include the right to work and the right to a range of social benefits. Thus the general principle of citizenship poses some fundamental questions, such as 'who is a citizen?' and, perhaps more importantly, 'who are non-citizens'? What is citizenship's connection with social policy, and do the formal rights attached to being a citizen match up with substantial rights, or the experiences people have when they make use of the health service or a social service, or when they claim benefits or try to enter the job market to find work?

In social policy, the concept of citizenship was developed by T.H. Marshall in 1949, in a series of lectures exploring the nature of the recently developed welfare state. Marshall was offering an account of the remodelling of the social services by the postwar Labour government, interpreting these in the light of an expanded conception of citizenship as an expression of social rights. Marshall was the first to suggest that the concept of citizenship had mutated and developed in the modern period, so that by the mid-twentieth century it had come to include welfare entitlements. Marshall debated the nature of modern capitalism and its relation to democracy, and of the competing conceptions of equality and inequality that arise from the conflict and conjunction of these two. His contribution to the understanding of a modern conception of citizenship is, therefore, a major one and continues to be vigorously explored (Bulmer and Rees 1996).

Social and policy changes since the late 1970s arguably helped to revive interest in the concept of citizenship. One social change was the dramatic increase in income inequality in the UK, USA and other anglophone countries resulting from greater inequality in earnings from paid employment, the growth of unemployment and growing polarization between two-earner and no-earner households (see Chapter 6). There was a growth, in the 1980s, of social polarization, of a 'north–south divide' and of social exclusion.

Accompanying these developments and associated with them was the discovery, or rediscovery, of the contentious concept of an '**underclass**', a class with, allegedly, only a tenuous connection with mainstream norms and values, to the labour market and paid work, and to conventional family life. Murray's (1994) writings on the underclass associated it with the rise in criminality in this period, and defined it not simply as a group defined by its poverty or unemployment but one outside, and sometimes in opposition to, mainstream society. Although many of Murray's conclusions were subsequently challenged and shown to be unfounded, they nevertheless stimulated a debate about the degree to which some sections of the population had come to be seen – and maybe saw themselves – as 'non-citizens'. Another important social development since the early 1980s has been the advent of movements – so-called 'new social movements', associated with, among others, gender, race, disability and sexuality – for liberation and empowerment, which have explicitly questioned the extent to which citizenship rights had been equalized in postwar Britain (Lister 1998).

Marshall believed that citizenship was a dynamic and developing concept and he certainly did not believe that Britain had reached the end of the road with regard to bringing equal citizenship rights to all. For him, social class differences and inequalities still seemed to raise barriers to full and equal use of the welfare state. He also devoted some space to discussing the extent to which there could be genuine equality in the possession of civil rights, given unequal access to courts and litigation because of their costs.

The aforementioned 'new social movements', to do with gender, race, disability and sexuality, among others, have reignited the debate about the boundaries of citizenship in contemporary societies such as Britain, and have posed again the question of the extent to which citizenship's formal attributes are matched by substantial ones. In other words, is the equal status which is the promise of citizenship matched by real equality of rights? Formally, every adult British national resident in the UK is a citizen, equal in the possession of the basic package of citizenship rights described above (with some limited exceptions, including peers and criminals!), but real equality of status, it is claimed, does not exist.

Marshall neglected the dimensions of race, ethnicity and culture, understandably, perhaps, since the UK had a much smaller ethnic minority population at the time of his lectures. These are issues of great interest and importance at the present time because of their significance as sources of social division – for instance, in relation to heated public debates about the social rights of migrants, particularly those who have travelled to work in the UK from new member states of the EU in eastern Europe. Marshall's focus was on class divisions as the major determinant of social inequality and the main challenge to citizenship, and he could not have foreseen the difficulties that were to arise in deciding how far social rights should be extended to include not only EU migrants but also to people migrating to the UK from countries outside the EU, and to those seeking asylum. Interestingly the UK government has created a citizenship test; to learn more, complete Activity 2.4.

Activity 2.4 British citizenship

In 2005 the UK government, in focusing much more upon citizenship, introduced a test for individuals from other countries who wish to become British.

- Visit this website to get more information about the test: http://lifeintheuktest.ukba.homeoffice.gov.uk.
- Now visit www.ukcitizenshiptest.co.uk and click on the 'Begin test' button at the bottom right-hand corner of the page. Here you can complete a practice test and get a score at the end, telling you if you have passed or failed.

The concept of citizenship has also become more important in the **global policy** arena, linked with the growth of globalization and the increasing connectedness of many aspects of life across the globe. If you search the Internet using the term 'global citizenship' you get a huge number of hits, detailing what the concept is and how it can be applied in schools, for example. Do you consider yourself to be a global citizen? Perhaps you haven't thought about this before but, as Scholte (2000) argues, there has been a growth of global consciousness in facing problems that span the globe. Thus, many are concerned about food supply, inequality, **climate change** and the sustainability of the planet.

Conclusions

From this chapter you should have gained an insight into some basic principles of social policy: equality, need, freedom and rights. But, before we leave this discussion, there is a word of warning: any debate about concepts is bound to exaggerate their importance. It is easy to elevate them to a position of influence over social policy that in reality they do not always have. Therefore, to end the chapter, it might be worth thinking about the following points in order to keep the principles of social policy in perspective.

First, *in reality, social policies are based on conflicting principles.* There is rarely, if ever, a clear and unambiguous set of principles underlying any single policy or welfare system. Sometimes rival groups, each with its own set of principles, support the same policy. The Child Support Agency (CSA), for example, was in the beginning supported by both feminist opinion (because it seemed as though more absent fathers than before would have to recognize their responsibilities) and conservatives who subscribe to 'traditional family values' and responsibilities. Similarly, feminists and conservatives might combine to support a policy to restrict or ban pornography. When a new policy comes to be implemented, though, these temporary alliances of principles and groups easily shatter.

Second, *rarely, if ever, do the ideas and stated principles put forward by a government actually determine policy.* For instance, looking back to any government that has tried to implement reform it is clear that existing principles are not easily discarded but that policy change tends to be incremental. The Coalition Government's 2012 Health and Social Care Bill thus builds upon previous New Labour policies which emphasized the use of market provision within health service delivery; for example, by creating Independent Sector Treatment Centres and using private providers to reduce waiting lists. The British welfare system today continues to operate on a mix of conservative and social democratic principles, and the introduction of new principles and ideas by Tony Blair's 'New' Labour government 1997–2010 – summarized as the 'Third Way' – did not have a significant effect on the direction of social policy. Policy broadly continued along the lines set by previous Conservative governments. Similarly, the current UK Coalition Government is again continuing several major policies, with the Liberal Democratic influence largely invisible. In this sense the principles and ideas which are supposed to guide policy are actually more like fig leaves that vainly attempt to disguise what governments are doing.

Third, *so-called principles are often rationalizations for decisions that would have been taken anyway.* For instance, continuing the example of the impact of Conservative principles, it is likely that the slow-down in Britain's economic growth in 2008 would have led to a sharp brake on welfare expenditure, whichever political party had come to power in 2010. The Coalition Government approach is just one of several possible ways in which British politicians and policy-makers could have tried to justify to the electorate what was inevitable: tougher limits to welfare expenditure.

Despite these three points, however, principles can still be seen as important – even if they do not always play a strong, decisive role in shaping policy. For one thing, they act as signposts towards new developments in social policy and they can be invoked as goals or targets by those who wish to move policies in a new direction. David Cameron's drive to inject market and business principles into the welfare system is a case in point.

This chapter has examined principles, such as equality and need, which were once the bedrock of social policy. As mentioned in Chapter 1, students of social policy were traditionally tutored in a framework of mainly social democratic principles. The merits of the welfare state would have largely been taken for granted, just as there would have been trust in the idea of improving state-provided welfare services to meet needs.

However, as a result of profound economic and social change, including the splintering of former class divisions and allegiances, we can no longer take for granted all the old aims and principles of the welfare state. This does not mean that principles or concepts of equality and inequality are irrelevant, but it does mean that such principles have to be rethought and reconsidered to understand better the role of social policy in a more uncertain world.

Summary of key points

- There are many key concepts in social policy such as equality, need, freedom and rights. However, while these are basic principles, there are many influences at work within the policy process.
- It is often the case that the ideas and stated principles put forward by a government do not actually determine policy because of economic realities and the complexities of the political process.
- The principles that underpin social policy decisions are more often than not used as rationalizations for decisions that would have been taken anyway.

Key terms and concepts

autonomy
basic needs
civil rights
comparative need
egalitarianism
equality
equality of opportunity
equity
expressed needs
felt need
freedom
ideology
justice
minimalist and maximalist policies (of equal opportunity)
need
normative needs
normative policies
political rights
positive action
power
principles
social rights
utilitarianism
wants

Suggestions for further reading

Doyal, L. and Gough, I. (1991) *A Theory of Human Needs.* Basingstoke: Palgrave Macmillan.

This book provides a thorough exploration of concepts of need and the policy dilemmas that arise in trying to meet them. The book argues that human beings have both universal and objective needs for health and autonomy. It also explores how both developed and underdeveloped economies work in relation to meeting their citizens' needs.

Drake, R. (2001) *The Principles of Social Policy.* Basingstoke: Palgrave Macmillan.

This book wrestles with complex ideas – and wins! – and in the process provides an admirably clear and stimulating range of examples of the ways in which principles and ideas shape social policy.

Farnsworth, K. and Irving, Z. (eds) (2011) *Social Policy in Challenging Times: Economic Crisis and Welfare Systems.* Bristol: Policy Press.

This book is an edited collection of chapters in which the economic crisis is analysed in relation to the impact it is having upon welfare systems. The economic crisis is shown to be reshaping welfare in a variety of different ways across national contexts. Future welfare trajectories are also analysed.

Fraser, D. (2009), *The Evolution of the British Welfare State,* 4th edition. Basingstoke: Palgrave Macmillan.

This book contains a concise and readable introduction to the history of social policy discussing the emergence of the welfare state and utilitarianism. The book deals with all main areas of social policy.

Rowlingson, K. and McKay, S. (2012) *Wealth and The Wealthy: Exploring and Tackling Inequalities between Rich and Poor.* Bristol: Policy Press.

This book explores the concept of wealth and how policy might be used to tackle inequalities in wealth. It covers policy issues in relation to taxation, education, pension and housing, drawing upon a wide range of data offering interesting analysis and debate. It covers concepts such as equality of opportunity and fairness.

3 The development of social policy in Britain

Key learning outcomes

By the end of this chapter you should:

- be able to understand the development of **welfare** in Britain
- be able to understand the relevance of history in relation to contemporary social policies
- be able to understand how British welfare is different from that in other countries

Overview of the chapter

This chapter gives an overview of the historical development of British welfare, putting Britain's overall approach to social policy in its historical context. In detailing the historical development of the welfare state the chapter demonstrates the legacy of previous social policy outlining how this still remains important within contemporary Britain. The chapter explores welfare development, public health reform and educational changes to provide a then-and-now picture of policy. The chapter ends on a comparative note looking at types of welfare states across the globe.

The importance of history

Any country's social policy can be seen as part of what Jones (1985) calls a whole system: that is, its economy and level of development, political system and social structure; hence the need to explore historical developments. Many other countries have systems that developed in different ways and thus have differential **models** of provision today. In Chapter 2 we looked at social policy in a general way, focusing on key principles that are not specific to any particular time or place. However, in this chapter we will focus on welfare development in Britain to provide some historical background to particular social policy areas discussed elsewhere in the book: notably, education (Chapter 8) and health policy (Chapter 10). There will also be some discussion of the history of the Poor Law and nineteenth-century attempts to deal with the problem of poverty. This has relevance for social security and poverty today (Chapter 6) and for social control and social policy (Chapter 7). To understand fully a particular area of policy, there is no substitute for careful study of the history books. Further reading suggestions on the history and development of the British welfare state are given at the end of the chapter. As a starting point Box 3.1 demonstrates the connections between historical policy and current issues.

Box 3.1 Themes in present-day and historical social policy

Key issues in present-day social policy	*Historical examples and comparisons*
Welfare dependency; activation; dealing with problems of **social exclusion** and the possible formation of an underclass. Renewed interest in public health and preventive policies; cost effectiveness, efficiency savings and economic recession. **Payment by results.**	The reform of the Poor Law; the 'workhouse test' and distinctions between the '**deserving**' and '**undeserving' poor**. Public health reforms: government regulation of housing and working conditions.
Devolution of control in education; the academies programme in which state-funded schools can run their own affairs, as do private schools, and opt out of the national curriculum and national pay scales for teachers; performance monitoring, such as publishing school league tables.	Developing system of state education; deciding the appropriate roles of central government, local authorities and churches; 'payment by results'.

Box 3.1 shows that looking at the big picture of social policy development helps to put the issues of today in perspective (Jones 1985). Present-day policy changes can have earth-shattering importance attributed to them when, in the broader context of the past 50 or 100 years, they are relatively minor adjustments. This is reflective of the incremental theory of policy-making, which is one view of the policy-making process. Table 3.1 outlines different models of the policy-making process and examples of each of these theories from a range of contexts.

Given the importance of history for understanding contemporary policy, we will now explore some of the key developments in social policy that occurred before the welfare state was born. Though these are influences from much further back in time, they still remain important. This is partly because nineteenth-century policies towards poverty, for instance, left a legacy in the form of deeply entrenched ideas that still remain today. Understanding the significance of history also helps us to see that there are certain long-lasting *themes* in social policy, as already indicated in Box 3.1.

Example 1: from workhouse to workfare?

Laws governing the provision of help to the poor have long existed in Britain. Such 'poor laws' are among the earliest forms of social policy. The first comprehensive Poor Law in

Table 3.1 Theories of the policy-making process

Theory about policy development	Explanation	Policy examples
Rationalist theories	• Policy-making is a linear process. • A problem is identified and solved. • Policy-makers approach the problem rationally.	• This theory is criticized as a view because policy problems are not always clearly identifiable or agreed upon: for example, climate change has long been debated as a policy problem, as have the solutions to it.
Incrementalist theories	• Policy-makers do not start with a blank sheet or perfect knowledge. • Policy-making is about reacting and responding to past policy change. • Budget and resource decisions play a part. • Policy change is always in small steps (incremental).	• New Labour gradually extended the concept of conditionality into the **welfare system** over 1997–2010 as part of retrenching provision. • The UK Coalition Government since 2010 has continued along similar lines.
Marxist theories	• Policy is made by the powerful. • Power in policy-making is economic, driven by business interests.	• Despite increasing concerns about growing global obesity levels, the food industry continues to influence policy. • In 2004 the **World Health Organization** (WHO) warned that there is a direct connection between eating too much sugar and a whole host of diseases linked to obesity. The sugar industry fought hard to undermine research evidence and threatened to have US Congress withdraw WHO funding if dietary guidelines linked to sugar were published. The guidelines were not published and obesity continues to increase.
Network theories	• Policy is made by networks of actors who cluster together focusing upon specific interests.	• The Coalition for a Global Social Floor, consisting of a basic set of social security benefits for all citizens, is an example of a policy network. • The network aims to ensure that basic **human rights** related to welfare (access to essential services) are met across the world.
Pluralist theories	• Policy emerges from the interaction of different parties at all stages of development and **implementation**. • Different groups hold brokerage positions, bargaining for change depending upon their interests.	• Interests groups, of which there are many, campaign for change in policy via advocacy. • Greenpeace is a global interest group campaigning for change related to the environment in a context influenced by many other interests.

England and Wales was passed at the end of Elizabeth I's reign, in 1601. In 1834, however, there came a major turning point. Previous legislation about how the poor should be helped was superseded by a revised or 'New' Poor Law that departed from previous policy in a number of important ways. This change illustrates a common theme and a central debate in social policy, about *how much* welfare should be provided to the poor and *what kind* of welfare it should be.

From the earliest days, and including the original 1601 Act, poor laws had always emphasized this distinction between the 'deserving' poor and the 'undeserving' poor. However, nineteenth-century critics of the old system for helping the poor pointed out that it did not have a sufficiently *deterrent* effect. Under the 'New' Poor Law, individuals were expected to submit to degrading and shameful procedures to receive any benefit. Thus only the truly deserving, the completely destitute, would be prepared to come forward for help. It is for this reason that we link the poor laws with **stigmatization**, for to be seen as a pauper or – in the old language – to 'go on the parish', was a permanent scar or blight upon one's reputation and that of one's family. Complete Activity 3.1 to reflect upon your own attitudes to poverty.

Activity 3.1 Reflecting upon poverty and stigmatization

Read the following example of an individual experiencing poverty and then take time to reflect upon the questions listed below.

> Janet Booth is a 30-year-old single woman. She is homeless and lives in shelters. Janet has always been poor, having come from a poor family. She left school early to get a job in a fast-food restaurant to support her family. She married young but after a separation has been left without anywhere to live; her family are unable to accommodate her. She finds it difficult to gain long-term employment. She has developed an alcohol dependency while being homeless.
>
> 1. How willing would you be to employ Janet?
> 2. Would you make friends with Janet?
> 3. Do you think that Janet may be a danger to others?
> 4. Do you think that Janet is to blame for her situation?
> 5. Should Janet be entitled to support from the welfare system?
> 6. Could Janet do more to help herself?

Now that you have considered your own views, what do they tell you about how you see poverty? Are you keen to socially distance yourself from Janet: for example, by not associating with her? Do you think that she can do more to help herself despite the large disadvantage she has faced from birth? Have you ever thought about how your attitudes to the poor are shaped by history?

The last remnants of the Poor Law system were scrapped in 1948. However, it is still possible to show how the tougher attitudes towards the poor evident in the 1834 Act had a long-lasting and deeply transforming effect on British social policy and public attitudes towards poverty. It increased the shame and stigma associated with being poor and being dependent on public welfare. It also cemented the connection between work and respectability on the one hand, and between unemployment and irresponsibility on the other. This deep-rooted idea, that it is only through being in paid work that one can fully demonstrate responsibility as a citizen, is still evident in the aims and **values** that underlie the policies of **workfare** developed in the USA and adopted, to an extent, in the UK.

The concept of *eligibility* is highly important to an understanding of the historical preoccupation with how to distinguish between 'deserving' and 'undeserving' poor people. To be eligible for assistance under the nineteenth-century Poor Law, a person in poverty not only had to be willing to forgo certain liberties and to experience degrading conditions, but also had to fit into one of several tightly defined categories of 'deservingness'. There were not only the simply destitute, for example, but also those who had been abandoned or orphaned, women who had been widowed and had no family support, or disabled or chronically ill people.

Throwing greater responsibility for welfare upon individuals and their families is bound to increase the role and significance of **means tests**, or assessments of people's **incomes**, savings and ability to draw upon family help. Therefore the example of the Poor Law of 1834 also helps us to review the history of the means test and to appreciate its significance in the development of British social policy.

From the present-day standpoint, and from the point of view of the poor in the nineteenth century, the Poor Law of 1834 represented a step backwards. It removed traditional 'rights' to assistance, however limited, and challenged the idea that social policies should automatically evolve towards a more generous treatment of the disadvantaged.

The workhouse was a central element in the earliest Poor Laws, aiming to make those who received public assistance contribute to their own keep. However, there was always a moral aim too. The workhouse was to be an institution to correct laziness and to reform the character. It would also serve as an example to others, acting as a harsh reminder of what could happen to those who turned to the public authorities for help. Views of poverty as a result of laziness are still widely evident today as demonstrated in the following quotations.

> The Work and Pensions Secretary, Iain Duncan Smith said that increasing 'benefit income' simply pushes the 'family further into dependency' and makes it less likely that their children will ever escape from poverty. He warned that extra money provided to dysfunctional families may simply be spent on drugs or gambling, rather than on helping children. (Winnett 2011)

Historically, harsh treatment of the 'undeserving' had been accompanied by traditions of providing charitable support to the needy and deserving. And to supplement this there had developed a widespread informal practice of giving a **dole** of bread, the staple food, or an equivalent weekly payment in money, to low-paid labourers and their families who would otherwise starve.

The latter form of support, an early form of income support, was tagged with the name of the parish said to exemplify the practice: Speenhamland. But although the **Speenhamland system** was widespread, it was not based on law or formal rights. Nevertheless, it represented an expectation that the working poor would be helped, and that they could receive such help while continuing to work from, and live in, their own homes. Notions of deserving and undeserving poor are constantly reported within the UK media.

> The problem is, for every claimant who makes you want to scream in frustration because they're perfectly happy to be living off the State, you meet another who makes you want to weep because they are so desperate to find work. Any work. (Humphrys 2011)

So despite the Poor Law of 1834 seeking to challenge historical approaches to poverty, attitudes remain very similar in contemporary Britain. Not only did it seem to reformers that relief of poverty was leading to ever-rising and unmanageable public expenditure, but also the rising laissez-faire orthodoxy in economics suggested that it was wrong to interfere in the labour market by subsidizing poorer workers' wages. Such subsidies were encouraging employers to pay their workers a lower wage because they knew that the parish would make up each labourer's income to subsistence level. In a free market, it was held that supply and demand should determine the price of labour, as it does any other commodity.

In the Poor Law reforms of 1834, the distinction between *poverty* and ***pauperism*** or 'indigence' was redrawn and reaffirmed. The law accepted no responsibility for trying to reduce inequality and poverty in the broader sense. The poor laws were only to assist the completely destitute – the paupers. Responsibility is another key theme which is ever-present in contemporary policy debates around welfare. Tony Blair, the former Prime Minister, discussed the responsibilities held by citizens as well as their rights. Similarly David Cameron (2010) said

> At the heart of the breakdown of trust in society is a breakdown of personal responsibility…The more responsibility we give people, the more likely they are to make ethical decisions.

Thus notions of personal responsibility are central to understanding historical welfare development as well as contemporary changes. Other themes such as eligibility also emerged in the context of workhouse development, and are still central to current debates. Reformed workhouses and other institutions were run according to centrally defined principles and rules, so that no paupers would be treated better in some workhouses than in others. The rationale for this was the principle of **less eligibility**, the idea that no one receiving public assistance should be in a more 'eligible' (satisfactory) position than any wage earner. To have paupers in a better financial position than wage earners would undermine the wage economy. Less eligibility and the uniformly harsh conditions of the workhouse were introduced to prevent the poor from seeking out the more generous or liberal institutions, and to deter the 'roving beggar'. While the specific meaning of historical eligibility is no longer applicable today, the concept is still present in today's discourse about the provision of welfare. Complete Activity 3.2 to explore the idea of eligibility further.

Activity 3.2 Eligibility and media representations of welfare recipients

There are constant discussions in the UK media about individuals in receipt of welfare, with headlines such as:

> '£44k scrounger who "couldn't walk" ran two market stalls' (*The Sun*, 20 April 2012)
> 'I want more, says 12-baby scrounger' (*The Sun*, 22 June 2012)
> 'Cameron: You're never too sick or too thick to work' (*Metro*, 26 June 2012)

Use the Internet to find other reports such as these – what do the majority of reports tell you about media representations of welfare claimants? Are there any positive stories or representations? Finally think about how widely these views may be held and how these relate to the concept of eligibility.

Historically the Poor Law institutions took on more specialized functions, some becoming infirmaries or hospitals where people without any means could obtain medical treatment, many becoming mental asylums, others institutions for older people and so on. Eventually, as local government was reformed and expanded, it took over Poor Law institutions: for example, there were municipal or local-authority-run hospitals before the NHS was introduced in 1948.

The historical example of the policy of the workhouse provides a classic example of the gap between a stated policy and outcomes. In the large and rapidly growing urban centres of industrial Britain it was not uncommon to find that many thousands of workers could be thrown out of work overnight as one or more factories or companies suddenly went out of business. To expect masses of labourers to submit to the workhouse test, with possibly permanent effects on workers' family stability, earning power and respectability, was simply unrealistic. While workhouses no longer exist, the legacy of attitudes to those who face unemployment is clear. Sage (2012) shows that increasingly in the UK the general public believe that benefits are too high. Many believe that stronger sanctions should be applied, for example, to single parents in receipt of welfare (Hills 2002).

Example 2: public health reform

One of the leading policy issues today is about the balance of resources to be devoted, on the one hand, to public health and **preventive** strategies, and on the other to individual care and curative strategies in medicine. Recent restructuring of the UK public health system and the NHS reflects this (see Chapter 10 for further discussion). Health services and public health are constantly reformed.

Everyone agrees that it is much better to prevent illness in the first place than to have to deal with its consequences. However, a certain amount of illness cannot be prevented. This means that there will always be a demand for individual solutions and treatments for illnesses. Such demands are linked into technological developments, the expansion of treatment possibilities, increased knowledge among the public and changing expectations.

The history of public health in Britain illustrates both the connection between environment and health and the conflict of interests between public needs (public health, preventive strategies) and individual needs (for ***curative medicine***).

The nineteenth century was *the* age of public health and environmental improvement. This is not to say that progress in health was smoothly achieved or always centrally planned. Public health reforms were brought about after protracted struggles between progressives and reactionaries, between central government and local authorities, and between the mean-spirited and those who championed public spending on unglamorous sewer-building, better water supplies and health inspectors. However, by the end of the century, Britain had developed a comprehensive system of laws governing health standards (see Table 3.2) on page 53.

Why did the Victorians put so much effort into improving public health? First, there was an increasing threat of infectious disease in the squalid conditions of Britain's rapidly expanding towns and cities. As a result of rural–urban migration the populations of Birmingham and Manchester doubled between 1801 and 1831, while those of Glasgow tripled and of Leeds more than quadrupled in the same period (Fraser 1984: 57).

Historians are uncertain about how much the death rate went up in the first quarter of the nineteenth century, but it is certain that there was a marked increase. Overcrowding

Table 3.2 Historical health reforms compared to contemporary health reforms

Nineteenth-century health reforms	Contemporary health reforms
A Central Board of Health was set up in 1831 by government to deal with a major outbreak of cholera.	An updated UK Influenza Pandemic Preparedness Strategy was published on 10 November 2011. This is to help deal with a large-scale influenza epidemic such as the global swine flu outbreak that occurred in 2009.
Report on the Sanitary Condition of the Labouring Population of Great Britain, 1842: a pioneering and scathing report on the environmental causes of disease led by Edwin Chadwick. Resulted in the Liverpool Sanitary Act 1846, a model for the times: a local medical officer and staff were appointed to oversee water supply and sewerage improvements.	UK water supplies and sewerage collection services are now privatized. Numerous agencies regulate this provision such as The Environment Agency and the Drinking Water Inspectorate.
The Public Health Act 1848 set up a national General Health Board. Local authorities were permitted, but not obliged, to set up local boards to improve sanitation, build waterworks and so on.	The UK Health and Social Care Bill 2012 is currently changing the way in which public health responsibilities are organized. The creation of Public Health England, in April 2013, aims to create a service that can protect and improve the health and well-being of the population.
The Medical Act 1858 established a General Medical Council to control a register of qualified doctors and to regulate training.	The General Medical Council still exists today performing the same function, focusing upon the maintenance of standards in medicine.
The Sewage Utilization Act 1865 laid down national standards for safe sewage disposal.	A European Directive, the Urban Waste Water Treatment Directive was agreed in 1991. The Directive has requirements for sewerage (or collection systems) to be established and sets standards for sewage treatment.
The Public Health Acts 1872 and 1875 were two pieces of legislation that consolidated and clarified all earlier regulations. Together, they laid down the duties of local authorities with regard to environmental health (for example, duties to inspect housing and maintain sanitary standards) up to 1936.	Local authorities still hold responsibilities with regard to environmental health. Their responsibilities have also increased as they have become public health teams (see the Health and Social Care Bill, 2012). Local authorities are now also expected to lead health improvement, pulling together the work done by the NHS, social care, housing, environmental health, leisure and transport services.

and inadequate housing, poor or non-existent sanitation and infected water supplies all contributed to a high death toll and worsening health.

Urbanization on such a vast scale and at such a pace was unprecedented. Further, in a profoundly unequal society, most members of the privileged classes had little or no idea of the changing circumstances of the mass of the working population, or of the impact of death and disease upon them. Fear filled the vacuum left by lack of knowledge – fear of cholera and other deadly diseases, and fear of the contaminating mob. By preventing infectious disease in the general population, the middle and upper classes were protecting themselves. Such fears still remain present. Ollila (2005) argues that current global health priorities reflect health-related problems in developing countries that are perceived to threaten the vital interests of industrialized countries.

More than narrow self-interest was involved, however, because concern with public health was inextricably bound up with a mission to control and to 'civilize' the masses. The Victorians often mixed together images of the poor, of slums and of contamination. Welfare reform historically was linked to environmental conditions. Edwin Chadwick, a nineteenth-century champion of public health, 'embraced wholeheartedly the environmental theory of disease prevention, brushing aside the claims of curative medicine' (Klein 1984: 13).

Basing his conclusions on varying rates of disease and death in different localities, Chadwick traced the connection between poor social conditions, inadequate sanitation and illness. But he was by no means the first or the only person to conduct research on the social causes of disease. From the late eighteenth century onwards, doctors carried out a number of studies of the connections between urban living conditions and disease. Though the scientific causes of infection were not fully understood, the medical profession had therefore played a leading part in establishing the evidence for *public* health reform.

As medicine developed in the nineteenth century, this early link between medical research and public health began to wane. Gradually, doctors for a variety of reasons began to focus less on public health and more on individualized and curative care.

Historical evidence shows that the commonest illnesses of the nineteenth century were acute infectious diseases such as typhoid, influenza, tuberculosis and pneumonia, which had little or no medical remedy at the time (McKeown 1979). From the late nineteenth century and through the first half of the twentieth, the terrible toll of the acute killing diseases, which were particularly prevalent among children, was gradually reduced. But in most cases this was *not* achieved by medical discoveries or by improvements in individual medical treatment such as immunization. Social policies on public health and sanitation, housing and the working environment, and the regulation of food storage and hygiene, all reduced the opportunities for infectious diseases to spread. As McKeown has demonstrated, much if not all the improvement in death rates in the twentieth century came *before* the introduction of effective medical treatments such as immunization against tuberculosis and diptheria or the introduction of antibiotics to counter respiratory infections.

Thus modern medicine has its limitations and has not single-handedly reduced the death rate. The social causes of disease has also received contemporary attention, via the work of the World Health Organization, whose Commission on the Social Determinants of Health 2008 focused upon inequalities in health related to social factors. However, this does not devalue the contribution of medicine to the management of illness and pain (see Chapter 10). As long as individualized medical care retains the lion's share of the resources devoted to health, though, there is likely to be continuing conflict of interests between what individuals want and public health interests.

Example 3: education, the role of government and the concept of the 'contract state'

'Must welfare be provided by the state?' is a leading question in social policy. One way of answering it is to look at what happened in history when the state, or government, did *not* take on a welfare-providing role. In the times before the era of 'big government' and the twentieth-century expansion of the state, people asked whether it was right for central government to provide any services at all.

Education is a good example of this debate because, in Britain, arguments about the proper role of central government have continued uninterruptedly from the nineteenth to the twenty-first centuries. Compared with other educational systems, Britain's had been relatively decentralized (Rust and Blakemore 1990). For example, only since 1988 have we had a National Curriculum defined by central government, although adherence to this is changing under current reform. In this and in other ways, British educational policy has been rather different from the French, German and other European systems.

More contemporary questions about welfare also relate to how much welfare should be provided by the state and the decentralization of provision, with the state having less involvement in welfare provision in some areas including in education.

The development of a 'contract state' in education

Before 1870, the responsibility for providing, paying for and running schools lay largely in the hands of the voluntary sector (churches and charitable institutions) and the private sector ('public' schools, many of which were then of inferior quality but some of which were to become exclusive, elite institutions). As Best (1979: 173) explains, 'Readers... will perhaps be astonished to learn that there were few primary schools... for which the state had full responsibility in 1850, very many for which it had no responsibility at all, and that its responsibility for the rest lay with a variety of religious organisations.'

In a slow process of educational reform from about 1850, the state did come to accept growing responsibility and became a **contract state**. The *contract state* is about more than regulation. It also includes the idea of government (central or local) paying for services and entering into contracts with non-governmental organizations (NGOs) to provide services. The authorities laid down standard definitions of quality (for example, mastering the 'three Rs' of reading, writing and arithmetic) and tried to enforce these standards in contracts with providers. For instance, in the nineteenth century, churches agreed to have their schools regulated and inspected in return for religious freedom, grants from government and the right to run the schools.

Despite pressures for change, government policy in education continued to be one of delay. In the words of Best, the period up to 1870 can be seen as 'thirty and more years of dithering' in education policy (1979: 177). A review of education policy in 1861 (the Newcastle Commission) advised that the voluntary, largely church-run system should remain, but should be improved in efficiency by a system of payment by results. This policy not only delayed direct state involvement in providing education but also perpetuated rivalries in the voluntary sector of churches.

However, the efficiency drive after 1861 had a dramatic effect on the classroom. Individual schools' grants, and thus teachers' salaries, were dependent upon how many children attended the school regularly, and whether performance in standard tests of numeracy, literacy and basic factual knowledge was satisfactory. Less efficient schools would get less support. As might be expected, rote-learning and strict discipline in the classroom overshadowed interest and educational stimulation, while anything like fun or enjoyment would have been very rare indeed. Also, payment by results did nothing to reduce the huge class sizes that were prevalent in urban schools at the time. Sometimes a single teacher would be responsible for over 100 pupils, aided by monitors or pupil-teachers.

At this stage, British education policy illustrates clearly the meaning of a contract state: that is, regulation by central government, a 'purchaser' role for the government department responsible for a particular service such as education, and competition between providers.

It is valuable to compare Lowe's payment by results scheme of the nineteenth century with the education reforms of the Conservative government in 1988 (see Chapter 8). The Education Reform Act 1988 introduced a competitive market into the school system, standard ways of assessing children's school performance and the publication of school results in attainment 'league tables' in England and Wales.

As another step towards the reintroduction of a 'contract state' approach, Blair's government (1997–2010) developed a policy of removing 'failing' schools and 'failing' local education authorities from the state sector altogether. A number of schools and local education authorities have been placed under the control of private companies, signalling the return of the state's regulator role, while private or non-governmental agencies manage provision of the service. The current Coalition Government approach is an extension of this: the Academies Bill (2010) facilitates a move from a state-run to a free-market approach to schooling (see Chapter 8).

In the late nineteenth century, however, the contract state principle of funding and providing education was on the wane. It was supplemented, at first, by another way of organizing education – the direct provision of schools by public bodies known as school boards. Then, from the early 1900s on, local education authorities increasingly took over and developed a state sector of education. In the twentieth century, the state (local education authorities and a central Department for Education) became the main provider. This landscape of state provision is now shifting because contemporary state provision of services is being retrenched.

The development of a welfare state

In the first four decades of the twentieth century, a different set of principles and a different model of social policy gradually replaced the classic, laissez-faire ideas of the nineteenth century (see Chapter 7 for further discussion of the development of social policy in the twentieth century).

In health, income maintenance, housing and other important policy areas, as well as in education, government began to act according to more interventionist principles. These have been summed up as *social liberalism* (to distinguish them from classical, nineteenth-century liberalism) and, in health care and income maintenance, were based on the idea of individuals protecting themselves with insurance from the risks of illness, unemployment and other causes of loss of income.

However, to see the early decades of the twentieth century as a complete change from nineteenth-century laissez-faire would be wrong. Despite a growing willingness by governments to improve social welfare and to build up a system of social insurance, economic policies were still largely constrained by the thinking of classical liberalism. In the face of economic slumps in the 1920s and 1930s, governments could think of little else to do but reduce public expenditure, balance the books and try to alleviate the worst effects of economic depression – unemployment and poverty – by providing meagre and strictly means-tested benefits. Does this sound familiar? At the time of writing current UK policy, and indeed that of other countries, is also focused upon reducing public spending because of the recession that began in 2008. The retrenchment of welfare is part of such public spending cuts although in the UK debates abound about whether this is the result of economic recession or is linked to the ideological values of the Conservative Party within the Coalition. Complete Activity 3.3 to investigate this further.

Activity 3.3 The changing provision of welfare

To explore the many places in which welfare retrenchment is taking place, use the Internet and your university library catalogue to search for academic articles related to this issue. Begin by using search terms such as welfare retrenchment in Europe and the future of welfare (select a country to add to this term too).

Choose an academic article of interest and read it. Consider the following questions.

1. Why is welfare retrenchment taking place?
2. Are the explanations of such policy changes clear to you?
3. Do you agree with the policy changes being made?
4. What do you think the impact of these policies is likely to be?

Despite historical limitations, the landmarks of social policy in the 1920s and 1930s represent some achievement in the face of economic adversity, as the list in Box 3.2 indicates.

Box 3.2 Landmarks of social policy in the 1920s and 1930s

- *The Housing Act 1919* launched an ambitious postwar house-building programme (see Chapter 11).
- *The Unemployment Insurance Act 1920* extended insurance cover under the state insurance scheme (introduced in 1911) to almost all workers, except those in agriculture, earning up to £250 per year.
- *The Contributory Pensions Act 1925* replaced the original 1908 (non-contributory) old age pension scheme and extended benefits to widows and orphans.
- *The Hadow Report 1926* on the future of education firmly established the notion of 'primary' and 'secondary' stages and paved the way for later reform in 1944.
- *The Unemployment Insurance Act 1927* provided help for long-term unemployed people who had insufficient contributions to benefit from the scheme, but also toughened benefit rules and the 'seeking work' test of eligibility.
- *The Local Government Act 1928* transferred many of the functions of the Poor Law guardians (officials) to local authority committees (public assistance committees), including responsibility for administering means tests. It also exhorted local authorities to reorganize services according to function (for instance, a health services committee to supervise services for all in the local area) rather than a public assistance committee to deal with the health needs of 'ex-paupers'.
- *The Unemployment Act 1934* restored cuts to dole payments which had been made in 1931; it also clearly separated poverty relief from unemployment insurance.

The interwar period of social policy demonstrated that there were severe limitations to the insurance principle as a way of providing security of income and health care for everyone. Though government schemes for pensions, health and unemployment insurance were extended and improved in the 1920s and 1930s, mass unemployment and the persistence of poverty meant that millions of people could not adequately insure themselves. The poor were forced to rely on the dole and, as in the nineteenth century, had to submit to degrading and humiliating means tests to obtain any assistance.

Beveridge: the man and the plan

It is against this historical background that the contribution of one man, William Beveridge (see Box 3.3), should be judged. Perhaps more than anyone else, Beveridge can be seen as the main architect of Britain's welfare system.

Box 3.3 William Beveridge, 1879–1963

William Beveridge came from a well-off, upper-middle-class background. His father was a prominent judge who worked for the colonial service in India. After a public school education, followed by a classics degree at Oxford University and law in London, Beveridge decided not to follow his father into a career in law, but went to live in a university settlement house, Toynbee Hall.

In doing this, Beveridge demonstrated that he had both a social conscience and an interest in social questions. University settlements were charitable institutions for graduates with reforming ideas to engage in social work with the poor. Although Beveridge's work at Toynbee Hall, as a warden, was more like that of a university tutor than a community worker, and did not involve him very much in contact with local people, he began to establish himself as an influential commentator on social issues, and especially on problems of unemployment and poverty.

In 1906, Beveridge left Toynbee Hall to work as a journalist, reporting mainly on social policy issues for the *Morning Post*. Then, in 1908, he became a civil servant and an important government adviser (to Winston Churchill at the Board of Trade), helping to frame legislation on labour exchanges (job centres) and advocating the introduction of compulsory insurance of workers against loss of income from unemployment.

Thus William Beveridge's formative years were very much tied up with the social reforms of the Liberal government of 1906–14, and it was this commitment to both Liberal ideas and social insurance which shaped his later, and much greater, impact on social policy in the 1940s. Between the wars, however, Beveridge took an academic post as Director of the LSE, successfully building it up from a relatively small workers' education college to a leading university institution (see Chapter 1).

Though concentrating on academic affairs at this time, Beveridge maintained a strong interest in practical action and in devising more efficient and comprehensive approaches to social insurance than the piecemeal system that developed in the 1920s and 1930s. For instance, he was in close communication with Seebohm Rowntree, the social reformer and investigator of poverty, whose 1937 book, *The Human Needs of Labour*, was very influential in shaping Beveridge's ideas on minimum incomes and the levels of benefit necessary to maintain subsistence.

In the early years of the Second World War the government cold-shouldered Beveridge's earnest desire to help with the emergencies of wartime planning and, as has often been reported, he rather unwillingly (and with tears in his eyes) accepted what seemed to be the rather mundane task of tidying up workers' insurance schemes.

The government report that emerged from this effort in 1942, *Social Insurance and Allied Services*, was a triumph. It was a tribute not only to Beveridge's outstanding ability to bring order and simplicity to complex administrative matters, but also to his bold and imaginative use of language. His scheme promised to vanquish the five 'giants' of Want, Ignorance, Squalor, Disease and Idleness and, for the first time in British history, presented both a vision of a community in which everyone would be cared for and the practical means for attaining that vision.

The Beveridge report became a huge bestseller. People formed long queues to obtain copies and a quarter of a million were sold in the first year. It had caught the mood for welfare reform and became an important element in wartime propaganda.

As a result, Beveridge's plan became the most significant part of the blueprint for the welfare state created by the postwar Labour government of 1945–51. However, it is important to remember that although Beveridge's plan became part of a Labour programme, neither Beveridge himself nor the underlying principles of the social security system he devised were particularly socialistic. William Beveridge had always resisted the idea of joining left-wing groups such as the Fabian Society or the Labour Party and, in 1944, he became a Liberal MP (losing the seat in the 1945 election). Similarly, his blueprint for social security, though comprehensive and universal in its coverage, did not involve redistribution of money from richer to poorer sections of society. Rather, it was intended to provide a basic foundation of support for everyone, and Beveridge assumed that many would turn to the private sector of insurance to add to the coverage provided by state schemes.

His plan for a complete overhaul of Britain's social policies was written in the middle of the Second World War, in 1942. Full-scale war had dramatic effects on social policy, just as it did upon the role of government in all areas of life. The war was a particularly distinctive experience for Britain because the country successfully resisted invasion but, in the early years of the war, was brought to the brink of defeat. It was also a war that involved the whole population. In these extreme times, and as a result of the Blitz, food rationing and other common adversities, British people discovered a new sense of equality and purpose.

The significance of the so-called 'wartime spirit' can be overemphasized. There is no doubt, however, that Beveridge's proposals on welfare were hugely popular because they chimed in with wartime hopes and goals: the idea that, if the war was to be won, it had to be won for the purpose of creating a better society than that of the 1930s.

The Beveridge report was a revolutionary step forward in British social policy in the sense that it revised the social security system completely. Implementation of the social security reforms was carried out by the Labour government elected after the war, apart from legislation on family allowances that had already been passed by the preceding coalition government. Clement Attlee's Labour government introduced the following social security schemes in the National Insurance Act 1946 and the National Assistance Act 1948:

- sickness and unemployment benefits
- retirement pensions (for men at 65 and women at 60)
- maternity benefits, widows' benefits and a death grant
- a National Assistance Board to replace the Poor Law

The Beveridge report had also established the need for policies of **full employment** and a national health service. Without these two supporting planks, Beveridge argued, his proposals for children's and family allowances, pensions and unemployment insurance would not work. His plan was also revolutionary in that it suggested *universal* coverage of the whole population (wage earners, the self-employed, people not employed, dependants) and provision of a wide range of benefits *without having to submit to a means test*. Complete Activity 3.4 to explore the current range of benefit provision in the UK.

Activity 3.4 Exploring the range of UK benefit provision

Since the creation of the welfare state in the 1940s, there have been many changes in the provision of benefit. You are no doubt familiar with some benefits such as those that receive media attention, including child benefit and jobseeker's allowance. However, do you have any idea of the full extent of UK welfare provision?

1. Go to the website for the Department for Work & Pensions (www.dwp.gov.uk) and explore the range of benefits that are provided. Are you surprised in any way by the provision?
2. Many benefits also remain means tested, despite the historical stigma that has been outlined throughout this chapter. Go to www.direct.gov.uk/en/diol1/doitonline/doitonlinebycategory/dg_172666 and use the benefits advisor tool to gain insight into the experience of applying for benefits.

On the other hand, Beveridge's plan in some ways looked back to the problems of the 1930s rather than forward to a postwar world. The principle was of **flat-rate contributions and benefits**, where everyone paid in the same amounts of National Insurance and received the same benefits. This may be equal and fair (see Chapter 2) but it also means that the National Insurance scheme could gather in only relatively modest sums. National Insurance contributions alone were not enough to fund an adequate level of benefits. In addition, the idea of a ***national minimum standard of living***, though in one respect a radical breakthrough, assumed a very meagre definition of basic necessities for survival. Therefore, while Beveridge's welfare system did bring a comprehensive range of benefits to all and successfully established the notion of care 'from the cradle to the grave', it had several flaws. The legacy of Beveridge's plan posed challenges immediately after it was implemented, as well as leaving a legacy of issues for contemporary policy makers, summarized in Table 3.3.

Conclusions: Britain's welfare history in comparative context

The years 1945–51 can be seen as the period in which the main structure of Britain's welfare system was built. From 1951 to 1964, a period of Conservative administration, Beveridge's system was continued, but earnings-related contributions and benefits were introduced. As mentioned, there were difficulties in funding the system from flat-rate contributions.

In the 1960s and early 1970s, a wider range of benefits and support for families, the unemployed, the disabled and chronically ill people extended the Beveridgian welfare system. Against a background of **economic growth** and rising prosperity for the majority, coupled with the 'rediscovery' of poverty among a minority, expectations of the welfare system grew.

Table 3.3 Challenges posed by Beveridge's system

Historical challenges	Contemporary challenges
Poverty: this still persisted because benefits for older people, disabled people and the long-term unemployed were set at low levels. Beveridge had intended means-tested benefits to be a little-used safety net, but for a growing number of people on low incomes they became an indispensable and long-term support. Thus Beveridge's vision of a welfare system with little or no use of means tests was never realized.	Poverty: this still remains a significant challenge in the UK. This was recognized by the New Labour Government, which particularly focused its policies on addressing child poverty. The current Coalition Government is reducing welfare spending in ways that are likely to impact negatively upon some children and families, such as reducing child tax credits and child benefit for higher earners. The government is introducing new indicators to measure its policies in this area too, encouraging families to become financially independent.
Continued funding of the system: demands upon the benefit system grew in the postwar period, as the government found that it was impossible to find the money for benefits from National Insurance contributions alone and the social security coffers had to be topped up from tax revenues. The idea that state benefits are paid from insurance funds – a pot of gold to which people have contributed over the years – is a fiction. Britain's benefits are paid for mainly by *current* contributions to the system through tax and National Insurance contributions, not by contributions made in the past. The entire system runs with only a few months' money in hand.	This remains a challenge for all governments. In the 2012 budget, the Chancellor, George Osborne, announced that by 2017 the cost of funding the UK welfare system would take one-third of all public spending. Consequently, he also announced a cut of £10bn in welfare spending in 2016–17. The forecast bill for benefits, state pensions and tax credits in that year is £229bn.
Gender assumptions: Beveridge's plan, as adopted and revised by the Labour government in its Social Security Act 1946, contained the old-fashioned sexist assumption that married women would be treated mainly as dependants of their husbands, not as wage earners or breadwinners in their own right, thus feminists criticize this approach. The gendered nature of the welfare system is further discussed in Chapter 7.	Many contemporary policies are not obviously gender biased, but they still have differential gender effects. Policy-makers have been accused of being gender blind in relation to social security provision, as they assume household payment rather than considering the implications of provision across the life-course (Bellamy et al. 2006).

Although there were clear differences of emphasis in social policies between the two main political parties, Conservative and Labour, the period up to 1979 can be seen as one of basic consensus or agreement about welfare. In other words, as Conservative and Labour governments succeeded one another, they were unlikely to rip up the social policies of the previous government and were predisposed to expand the role of the state as a provider of welfare.

Margaret Thatcher's period of office as a Conservative prime minister from 1979 to 1990 is often presented as a radical break with the past and as the period in which Britain turned its back on the Beveridgian welfare state. In the following chapters on social security, education, employment, health and housing, you will be able to make your own judgements about how far this was actually the case. However, radical and across-the-board changes in social policy certainly did not occur in the first two governments led by Mrs Thatcher (1979–87), when economic policy and political items dominated the agenda (Deakin 1994). It was during Mrs Thatcher's third term that important social policy reforms began in earnest. There were major reforms in education, health and community care, and additional reforms in housing, where policies had already brought great change through the sale of council houses to council tenants (see Chapter 11).

However, as far as social security – the cornerstone of the Beveridgian welfare system – was concerned, the fundamental structure of the old Beveridge system was left untouched by the social security reforms of the 1980s. The Conservatives' Social Security Act 1985 introduced some important and contentious changes, such as the Social Fund, which replaced certain rights to benefits with a more discretionary relief system. Also, the names of the major benefits and welfare schemes were changed, but the underlying system of benefits designed and established in the 1940s could still be seen. However, at the time of writing, the current Coalition Government plans to merge a number of benefits into one Universal Credit scheme (by 2017) and this perhaps represents the first truly fundamental break with the remnants of Beveridge – though it remains to be seen whether the government will succeed in implementing this radical reform.

Change to the 'British model' or the basic Beveridgian welfare state has so far proved to be more evolutionary than revolutionary as governments often tinker around the edges of provision without making major reform. However, evolutionary change can be fundamental in the long run. There are already signs that within one or two decades some of the key elements in the original Beveridge scheme could disappear into the sands, particularly given the continued challenge of funding the system. The recent changes to the NHS are the most radical reform it has ever experienced, with the outcomes yet to be seen (see Chapter 10).

How then can the British experience of the development of a welfare system be summed up? What sort of welfare system has Britain developed, and how does it compare with others? Chapter 4 outlines the importance of the global context for policy-making next, and here for the purposes of comparison it is worth considering three main types or clusters of welfare state or 'welfare regimes', which have been identified by Esping-Andersen (1990). These are summarized in Table 3.4.

Table 3.4 Types of welfare states; comparative global context

Type of welfare state	Examples
Liberal welfare states • Those in which government provides only a minimum level of welfare services. • Health and welfare services are basic and state-provided services are **residual** – that is, mainly for the poor. • It is expected that the family and religious or charitable institutions will play a major part in providing health and social welfare services. • The state organizes and subsidizes social insurance schemes that protect the better-off and those in middle-class occupations.	USA Australia Portugal Spain Greece
Corporatist welfare states • Less dependent on the market and a more laissez-faire approach than liberal welfare states. • Have well-developed welfare systems with the government leading both organization and provision of health, welfare and education services. • Can be both privately or publicly funded (or mixed). • Often conservative in their approach.	Belgium France Germany Ireland
Social democratic welfare states • Emphasis is on social equality. • High levels of public money spent upon welfare and social security. • Services are comprehensive, available to all and of a very high standard. • Social democratic welfare states such as Sweden place a lot of emphasis on the work ethic and the importance of keeping people in work, which is supported by welfare provision.	Sweden

It is very important to note that the classification of different countries' welfare systems into 'liberal', 'corporatist' and 'social democratic' types is an oversimplification. Any attempt to sketch the big picture, which Esping-Andersen (1990) has done with these three models, is bound to mean that particular countries do not fit a particular model exactly, and that countries contain elements of more than one type of welfare system. Sweden, for instance, has been portrayed as a corporatist welfare state (Mishra 1990). Further, recent economic change and the integration of Sweden into the European monetary union means that the 'traditional' Swedish welfare state is under threat. On the other hand, economic growth and policy reforms in the southern European countries mean that they are adopting elements of the corporatist and social democratic models.

Interestingly, Britain does not easily fit any of these models. This could mean that Britain genuinely differs from much of Europe in its approach to social policy and is better compared with countries outside Europe, such as Canada or the USA, or that Britain is a 'one-off' and very distinctive example unlike any other welfare system. However, it could also mean that the models themselves are flawed and must be adapted in some way to incorporate the British case.

Britain's history of welfare development has shown that, along with Sweden (which interestingly did not, as a neutral country, share the direct impact of war on welfare), it led Europe in introducing a comprehensive and universal welfare system. In that sense, the early emphasis on equality and citizenship, rights to a wide range of benefits and 'free' health care all point to Britain being a prototype of the social democratic model. However, as already discussed, Britain developed a welfare system that was founded upon liberal rather than social democratic principles and a rather basic or minimal idea of how much help people should receive in times of need.

Although the welfare state of the 1940s represented a tremendous leap forward, once the system was in place the British approach has been to expand it cautiously. Britain is not easily portrayed as a 'liberal' type of welfare system but, as a medium spender on welfare, neither has it kept up with social democratic regimes to develop as comprehensive and advanced a welfare state as exists in Denmark, Norway and Sweden. Nor has the corporatist system of joint provision of welfare by the government, employers and unions – as in Germany – ever been developed in Britain.

In conclusion, Britain's welfare system today represents an interesting mix of principles and influences from the past. There is still a relatively strong foundation of welfare state principles and a commitment to provision of universal benefits. As will be shown in Chapter 6, the proportion of the nation's wealth spent on welfare services and social security has not changed much since the 1970s, despite Mrs Thatcher's pledge to cut back the welfare state. Currently there are similar pledges being made by the Coalition Government, yet it remains to be seen if these will be significant.

However, one important change in the direction of policy, especially since the late 1980s, has reintroduced into the 'British model' elements of the pre-1940s or even the nineteenth-century approach to social welfare. This trend is noticeable, for instance, in the tightening of rules governing eligibility for benefits and making some benefit conditional upon claimants' 'good behaviour' (such as seeking work or training). It also appears in the stress upon individual responsibility for welfare (as in official views of the causes of illness) and in the revival of the concept of a contract **state** through the privatization of services and the development of a market in public welfare services. For all these reasons, therefore, the British model combines elements of the liberal or residual type of welfare system with remnants of a social democratic approach.

Summary of key points

- Following the creation of Britain's welfare state, there have always been problems related to its funding, which continue to influence policy decisions today.
- British political parties often agree in general about policy related to decisions; there is a welfare consensus in many areas. Thus, changes to welfare provision are incremental and evolutionary rather than radical.
- The model of British welfare does not fit any 'classical' type, and it is an interesting mix of principles and approaches now increasingly based upon eligibility.

Key terms and concepts

contract state
corporatist welfare states
deserving and undeserving poor
dole
flat-rate
less eligibility
liberal welfare states
means tests
pauperism
payment by results (in education)
public health
residual (approach to provision of state services)
social democratic welfare states
stigmatization
welfare dependency
'whole system' comparisons
workfare
workhouse

Suggestions for further reading

Fraser, D. (2009) *The Evolution of the British Welfare State*, 4th edition. Basingstoke: Palgrave Macmillan.

This is a highly recommended text book which gives an account of the history of the British welfare state up to the present day. The book also contains useful appendices of contemporary documents and an updated bibliography of the subject.

Glennerster, H. (2007) *British Social Policy since 1945*, 3rd edition. Oxford: Wiley-Blackwell.

This is an interesting and readable text on the history of social policy in Britain. The book covers the period from the end of the Second World War to the present day and explores the Welfare State and how that relates to contemporary conceptions of social policy, and which continue to dominate current debates. Glennerster argues that social policy can only ever be understood in the context of the political and economic concerns of the time.

Harris, J. (1997) *William Beveridge: A Biography.* Oxford: Clarendon Press.

This edition of Harris's biography of William Beveridge uses extensive archive material to document both his private and public career. It outlines the origins of the Beveridge Plan and discusses how it was received. It also shows how Beveridge's personal history helped to shape his contribution to twentieth-century social reform.

Kennett, P. (2008) *Comparative Social Policy*. Cheltenham: Edward Elgar.

The current context of social policy is one that needs to examine other countries and a broad policy context beyond national boundaries. It is in this context that this book brings together the work of key commentators in the field in order to provide comparative analysis and comprehensive coverage of contemporary debates and issues in cross-national social policy research.

Timmins, N. (2001) *The Five Giants: A Biography of the Welfare State.* London: HarperCollins.

Nicholas Timmins offers an outstandingly enjoyable and informative read: it is written in a pacy and readable style that brings the subject fully alive.

4 The global social policy environment

Key learning outcomes

By the end of this chapter you should:

- be able to understand the importance of global policy-making and global governance
- be able to understand the key global policy-makers and their impact at the national level
- be able to understand how the globalization of the policy-making process is impacting in diverse ways across the world

Overview of the chapter

This chapter introduces the importance of the global context and global actors in contemporary policy-making. Traditional national boundaries still exist in relation to policy-making. However, current policy actors face many global challenges, and in recent years there has been a proliferation in the numbers of agencies and actors involved in policy-making at the global level. The chapter also examines the importance of global governance and the key global economic players that influence current policy decisions and implementation. The chapter also considers how health issues are framed by the processes associated with globalization. Globalization is a process that influences patterns of policy-making, power, inequalities and the environment – all of which are discussed in this chapter.

The current context of policy-making

Much policy-making is done at the level of the nation-state, and previous chapters have discussed policy at such a level. But the world is changing and as a consequence anyone now studying social policy needs to look beyond national boundaries to explore and capture the full range of activity within this field.

The European Union has grown in importance in terms of policy-making, influencing what happens at the national level in many areas, such as employment and social security. There are now many laws enacted at the European level which must be adhered to by member states. For example, the European Directive on Working Hours was enacted to improve employment conditions by setting a maximum 48-hour working week.

However, it does include article 18, which allows member states to opt out if they can meet a certain number of conditions. For example, workers can sign individual opt-out agreements, and employers must keep records of staff who work more than 48 hours a week. This legislation often features in the news following trade disputes or breaches of the legislation.

Many UK local authorities have connections to Brussels to keep in touch with policy developments at the European level. Furthermore, there has also been a significant development of global policy-making institutions, which have also moved into policy-making in a number of areas. Debates abound about whether these changes are positive and the impact that they have at the individual level, but, irrespective of differing views, there is no doubting the rising significance of both global policy-making and the trend towards globalization itself.

Globalization

Globalization has been defined in a number of different ways in the academic literature. It has social, cultural and economic components or elements to it, and writers disagree about the impact of each of these aspects of globalization on national policy-making. While the idea of global social change is not new, the rapid change that has occurred since the early 1980s is. This pace of change, combined with technological development, has led to the increased social, economic and political interconnectedness of the world. Giddens (2009: 126) defines globalization as 'the fact that we all increasingly live in one world, so that individuals, groups and nations become ever more dependent'. Martell (2010) offers a more detailed summary of the concept of globalization, illustrated in Box 4.1.

Box 4.1 The concept of globalization

1. It is global in distance, reaching all continents and covering economic, political and cultural relationships.
2. It is globally inclusive; it involves inputs from across continents and many countries within them.
3. It involves interdependency; it is about more than just interconnectedness. Trade declining in one country will affect the host country as well as the country receiving the goods.
4. It involves stability and regularity; structures and systems exist which are related to the processes of globalization such as global policy-making institutions.
5. It involves global consciousness – the concept is not just about people doing things globally, but also about a growing awareness of the world as one space.

Whichever definition is used, there are implications for policy-makers. The world is much more interconnected than it was. Now complete Activity 4.1 to explore the implications of globalization.

Activity 4.1 Exploring globalization and its implications for the policy-making process

Look at 'The Globalization Website' and read in more depth about globalization: http://sociology.emory.edu/faculty/globalization/issues01.html.
This will help you to complete the following task.
Debate the implications of globalization for policy-makers.

1. What does the increased social connectedness of the world mean in policy-making terms?
2. Has there been a globalization of the policy-making process itself?
3. Finally, reflect upon how globalization and global awareness affect your views of your place in the world. If you have lived in or visited any other countries (perhaps a developing country?) consider how this might have affected your perceptions of globalization.

Completing Activity 4.1 should have helped you to think about how globalization might have created new challenges for policy-makers. For example, globalization has been described as a massive threat to the environment, causing environmental damage and contributing to health problems (Feacham 2001). Globalization contributes to climate change in several ways – for example, through increased travel and pollution, the increased use of energy sources and the increased consumption of consumer products and associated waste (Wilkinson 2005). These issues are explored later in this chapter. Research on globalization shows many ways in which the process is related to policy-making (see Table 4.1).

Thus globalization in its various forms presents many challenges to policy-makers and it can pose threats to human health and welfare in several ways. This raises a key issue: is global policy-making or governance becoming a reality – and should it be?

What is global governance?

There is an increasing number and range of global policy actors which shape social policy, funding, provision and governance. Governance at the global level has recently grown following the recognition that a number of problems are obviously interrelated and require action at the global level. Yeates and Holden (2009) argue that global analyses are thus required to understand policy-making and related impacts. Similarly, Scholte (2000) describes an increasing global awareness of worldwide problems. While the term 'global governance' has become frequently used in the policy literature, its meaning remains wide-ranging. Similar to the concept of globalization, the term does not have a single definition. The Commission on Global Governance (1995: 2) defines it as the 'sum of the many ways individuals and institutions, public and private, manage their common affairs'. A key question that is now frequently discussed is, why do we need global governance?

Why do we need global governance?

George and Wilding (2009: 27) argue that 'a global approach is needed to deal with problems that are global in character' and that more and more issues are global in both their implications and impact. Their justification of the need for global governance includes a list of ten areas, including greater global interdependence, support for the idea of human rights, and global problems such as environmental pollution. Box 4.2 outlines the key global challenges for contemporary policy-makers.

Table 4.1 Researching globalization and the policy-making process

Approach	Key points	Discussions about policy	Criticisms
The global polity and society approach	The concept of a global society has only become possible in the modern age because of science, technology and industry changing the social world in which we live.	The development of collective consciousness can be used to help solve global problems, through policy-making.	Some argue that the notion of global consciousness is utopian.
The **global capitalism** approach	Globalization is driven by globalizing capitalism, and in particular the interests of the economically powerful.	Policy-making is aligned with capitalism to encourage economic growth at all costs, and many argue that such policies exacerbate inequality in numerous ways.	The evidence in this area is both confusing and contradictory.
The world-systems approach	This area of research examines changing roles and relationships within the international division of labour.	Inability to control transnational companies has been identified as an issue for policy-makers: for example, the use of using cheap labour in lower-income countries to increase profits.	This approach needs to examine the role that such companies play in providing employment and facilitating **development**.
The global culture approach	Here globalization is described as being driven by mass media. This is seen as a threat to national and local identities.	There is a lack of governance of the media and insignificant policy in this area.	The approach ignores those without access to the media and does not account for cultural resistance and individual agency in interpreting media messages.

Adapted from Sklair (2002)

Box 4.2 Contemporary challenges for global policy-makers

- the current global economic crisis
- increasing polarization of wealth and poverty both within and between countries
- increasing population
- migration of populations
- population changes such as the ageing population
- food supplies and sustainability
- increased demands for energy
- environmental challenges such as climate change, sustainable development and pollution
- technological development
- conflict and war, including terrorism
- health challenges – infectious diseases, life-style diseases, changing patterns of disease and inequalities

The list in Box 4.2 is not exhaustive and thus there may be other issues that you can think of to add to the list. Clark (2001), for example, adds ethnic conflicts, failed states and weapons of mass destruction as issues in need of global governance. Despite debate about the issues, there are clearly numerous global social problems and therefore the need for global social policies which attempt to address them. George and Wilding (2009) list a number of areas in which there is a need for global social policy:

1. To mitigate the effects of global competition – it is negatively affecting national welfare states, therefore collaboration is needed between states to resolve this problem.
2. To support human rights – this is linked to concepts of global human citizenship and global justice.
3. To support a global approach to economic problems – this is very topical at the time of writing, as effective social policy-making and planning require economic stability and growth.
4. To champion globalization as a positive mechanism for economic development; however, it has social costs and much evidence suggests that it increases inequality.
5. To address the expectations created by globalization, which can have the effect of fuelling public demand for action in tackling environmental problems, developing women's rights and fostering development.

Not everyone will agree with these reasons. However, it is clear that new patterns of governance are emerging to cope with contemporary challenges. The economic problems many countries in the world are facing today, following the dire financial crisis which began in 2008, raises questions about how effective current global policy is. There are obviously financial limits to what policy can achieve, too, and thus complex decisions need to be made about which policies should be supported. The relationship between economics and social policy-making at the global level thus needs consideration. Now complete Activity 4.2 to help you explore the relationship between policy-making and economics.

Activity 4.2 Exploring the relationship between economics and global priorities

Go to www.ted.com/talks/bjorn_lomborg_sets_global_priorities.html, and watch Bjorn Lomberg talk about what issues he would tackle first from a range of **global priorities**, if he had $50 billion to spend.

After watching take time to reflect upon the following questions:

1. Do you agree with his views and the list of priorities that he identifies?
2. If you were a policy-maker with the same amount of money, which would you attempt to solve first, AIDS or global warming?
3. Have the issues changed since this speech was made, and what does this say about the effectiveness of current policy in these areas?

Now that you have considered the key global priorities and had time to think about which should be tackled first, let us turn to exploring the key players in global policy-making and the roles that they take.

Key global policy-makers

There are many agencies and organizations acting on the world stage (Beck 1999). However, we may identify some key global institutions that everyone agrees have a major impact on social policy, as Table 4.2 indicates.

Table 4.2 Summary of key global actors

Organization	Description	Example policies
The United Nations	An international organization with a remit to maintain international peace and security, to develop friendly relations among nations and promote social progress as well as better living standards and human rights.	UNICEF (an arm of the UN) and its partners vaccinate 58 per cent of the world's children, saving 2.5 million lives a year (UN 2012). The World Food Programme provides food to 90 million people in 73 countries (UN 2012).
The **World Bank**	This organization provides low-interest loans to lower-income countries, imposing policy conditions and repayment terms. It cites one of its aims as the reduction of poverty via investing in people.	The bank provides loans for a variety of purposes including development and resettlement. The reduction of investment in public services as part of loan conditions (Stigliz 2006) has led to many criticisms that the work of the bank increases inequalities.
The World Trade Organization (WTO)	Established in 1995, its role is to regulate international trade. It aims to promote free trade and stimulate economic growth.	The WTO's policies provide a framework for negotiating and formalizing trade agreements. The WTO also resolves trade disputes and attempts to enforce participants' adherence to agreements. Its policies have been criticized for making health care and medicines unaffordable for many (Yuill et al. 2010) through the use of trade-related intellectual property rights (TRIPs), which prevent the production of generic and more affordable medicines.
International Monetary Fund (IMF)	The IMF aims to encourage economic growth and stability. Its remit also involves working with lower-income countries in order to stabilize their economies and reduce poverty.	Work includes economic surveillance to track the economic health of its 188 member countries. The IMF also provides policy advice and can lend to countries in difficulty, which often involves the provision of technical assistance to help countries improve economic management.
The World Health Organization	Established in 1948, this is the UN's specialist agency for health, aiming to attain the highest possible level of health for all people.	Policy eradication programmes such as those tackling smallpox, malaria and cholera have had varied success, but have led to observable health improvements. However, the Health for All target by 2000 was not achieved, as the goal to provide universal primary health care across the world was not reached in many areas as a result of funding and other organizational problems.
Bilateral Organizations such as DIFD (the UK's Department for International Development) and USAID, the American aid agency	These organizations often provide development aid, donated from one country to another.	DIFD provides development aid to support poverty reduction, including supporting countries in crisis.
Non-governmental organizations	These global players have a variety of remits depending upon their focus, such as disaster relief or poverty alleviation.	The Gates Foundation, by 2002, has granted $2.8 billion of health funding, starting the Global Alliance for Vaccines and Immunization (GAVI), an independently governed initiative (Yamey 2002).

Table 4.2 gives some indication of the variety of organizations operating under the rubric of global governance, though is by no means exhaustive. It also provides a flavour of the areas of work that these organizations engage in. Global policy-making organizations such as those listed in Table 4.2 demonstrate the expansion of policy-making and all associated complex relationships (Rosenau 1997).

These changes have led to some criticism of some of these organizations (Wilkinson 2005). For some theorists such as Sklair (2002) these organizations represent the transnational capitalist class at work, a view echoed in many recent public protests during high-profile meetings of the World Trade Organization, the World Bank, the G8 Summit and the European Union.

Academics have also expressed dissatisfaction about the lack of transparency of the work of these organizations and their flawed responses to international debt relief, poverty reduction and environmental issues (Wilkinson 2005). Ollilia (2005) has argued that global policy-making is aligned with industrial and trade policies to the detriment of global health. Cammack (1999) also suggests that current global policy-makers are part of undemocratic forces shaping the world order. There is also the issue of power differentials between countries across the world. Many global policy-making organizations are multilateral, meaning that they are run on behalf of a number of governments and their representatives. Clearly, some countries have more resources and military power than others and some actors have been left out of the processes of governance at the global level.

Many non-governmental organizations (NGOs) have also received criticism for the way in which they operate. The large growth of NGOs since the 1990s has led to them being seen as a 'magic bullet' for resource-poor countries in terms of both development and governance problems (Vivian 1994). Within the African context, NGOs came to rival governments in terms of service provision, with some suggesting that they were more capable of delivering development (Fowler 1998) than governments themselves. Non-governmental organizations were also seen favourably as offering better alternatives to the tough 'structural adjustment' solutions imposed by the IMF and World Bank, which often demand severe reductions in social spending on health, education and infrastructure (Brautigam 2000). Ultimately the growth in NGOs led commentators to suggest that now they also hold too much influence in terms of policy-making, especially when they are based in the global north and working in the global south (Manji 2000).

However, there are alternative positive views of global governance: it need not be a negative influence on welfare. The Millennium Development Goals created by UN member states can be described as an example of the positive role of global governance in that they are a set of targets aiming to tackle poverty and inequality, health and environmental issues, and to promote a fairer world (Davies 2010). Table 4.3 outlines these goals in detail.

However, despite the broad scope of these goals, critics have questioned levels of political commitment to their achievement, and some remain cynical about the commitment of global actors to the targets. Oxfam (2010) argues that donors need to provide more economic support in order to ensure that the goals are met. Furthermore, the goals themselves remain open to interpretation: for example, defining extreme poverty is difficult, and measuring 'promotion' and making reductions to sometimes unspecified levels are both vague targets. Analysis of progress has also highlighted delays in implementation and the resistance of higher-income countries. Furthermore, there are many local contingent factors that compromise progress: wars, corruption and transnational corporations serving their own interests (Macdonald 2007).

Table 4.3 The Millennium Development Goals; an example of positive global policy-making?

Goal	Description
1	To eradicate extreme poverty and hunger, with targets • to reduce by half the proportion of the world's poor living on less than $1 a day, and • to halve the number of people suffering from hunger.
2	To achieve universal primary education for both boys and girls.
3	To promote gender equality via strengthening the rights of women, especially educationally.
4	To reduce child mortality by two-thirds and to increase immunization of young children against measles.
5	To reduce maternal mortality by three-quarters through improved medical provision during both pregnancy and childbirth.
6	To halt, as well as possibly begin to reverse, the spread of AIDs, malaria and tuberculosis.
7	To halve the number of people without access to safe drinking water and basic sanitation as well as improving the living conditions of 'slum' dwellers.
8	To develop global partnerships to improve debt-relief initiatives and access to technology.

Source: UNDP (2010)

However, there is also a range of other positive social policy which has emerged at a global level. Examples include:

1. The Framework Convention on Tobacco Control. This WHO framework is an evidence-based treaty supporting regulatory strategies to reduce tobacco consumption. It was developed as a response to the worldwide 'epidemic' or increase in tobacco use. The framework covers price and tax measures to reduce demand, encouraging protection from exposure to tobacco smoke and regulation in other areas. The framework was signed by 168 signatories, including the European Community.
2. The WHO's 2008 report, 'Closing the Gap in a Generation: Health Equity through Action on the Social Determinants of Health' (WHO 2008). This report outlined the need to tackle social inequality as the major underlying cause of health inequalities. The report made three cross-cutting recommendations:
   a. to improve daily living conditions,
   b. to tackle the unequal distribution of power, money and resources, and
   c. to measure and understand the problem and assess the impact of any action taken.

Thus, global governance has developed some positive recommendations and related policies. However, there are often gaps between recommendations for policy-makers and implementation of policy. Questions remain about the effectiveness of how goals can be translated into meaningful action and how influential the organizations that set them are in driving forward policy.

Wilkinson (2005) argues that the literature has yet to capture the full extent of what is happening in relation to global policy-making and more problematically that there is an absence of discussion which explores alternatives to global governance in its current form. The accountability of many transnational organizations is increasingly receiving attention. Bexell et al. (2010) pinpoint lack of accountability as a key democratic deficit in many global policy-making arenas. Furthermore, Seckinelgin (2009: 206) argues that international policy-making organizations remain detached from the very groups that they target and that 'considerations of inequality of access to political decision-making remain absent at the international level'.

At the time of writing, the global financial crisis presents perhaps the most glaring set of examples of economic problems that have had serious social implication in many countries. The causes of the financial crisis remain in debate; however, many argue that the current governance of global finance based upon the Bretton Woods institutions (the World Bank and the IMF) in conjunction with the WTO is simply failing. And despite the seriousness of the crisis, Harman (2009) and others suggest that the global governance of finance is not being reformed effectively or fundamentally. So what questions does this raise?

The global economy

Shaxon (2011: 73) is heavily critical of institutions such as the IMF and the World Bank (described in Table 4.2), describing them as 'the handmaidens of globalization, unfettered trade and capital flows, and the instrument of Wall Street Bankers'.

> Shaxon's pessimistic description of the global economy shows capital flowing across borders into secret off-shore systems which are outside the restriction of usual banking regulations and taxation channels. For Shaxon, such amounts of money illicitly and illegally leaving countries results in large-scale inequalities. Furthermore, these off-shore banking practices played a fundamental role in the banking crisis.
>
> (Henry 2003)

Arguably, then, policy-making in this area is not working to benefit all. Rather, it is aligned with the interests of the capitalists, as suggested by Sklair (2002).

According to this view, management of the global economy is dominated by a neo-liberal approach which favours privatization, profit-making and competitive markets. In these ways, economic globalization has resulted in the development of large private corporations and banks increasing their influence on domestic policy-making. Lechner and Boli (2012) argue that current economic policy at the level of the global has resulted in

- corporate **deregulation**, and unrestricted capital flows across the world
- increased privatization
- socially harmful production
- unbalanced, environmentally damaging and unsustainable patterns of growth
- intense promotion of **consumerism.**

Thus, there is strong argument that many global economic policies do not enhance the life of the planet or improve human welfare, but are more likely to secure the wealth of those who encourage consumerism. Complete Activity 4.3 to reflect upon some of these issues.

Activity 4.3 The limits of markets

Go to www.bbc.co.uk/programmes/p00s473l and listen to the radio programme, which discusses some of the problems of contemporary market approaches in relation to a variety of areas of social policy across the world. The forum is called 'The Limits of Markets'. Commentators discuss their ideas about the role of the market in development.

After listening to the programme list the positive and negative aspects of market approaches. Which sides of your list is the longest? What is your overall opinion about market approaches in relation to social policy?

Now let us turn to analysing the relationship between markets and the encouragement of consumerism, a worldwide social trend which has a huge impact on social policy and welfare.

Global consumerism

Global consumerism is described by many commentators as perhaps the most important facet of globalization. In the 1950s and 1960s, European consumption habits began to change, with people purchasing new consumer goods for domestic use and cars. These changing habits have long continued and now feed into cycles of demand within contemporary society (Vandenbroucke 1998). Rostow (1978) uses the growth in sales of both cars and television sets across the USA, Western Europe and Japan to demonstrate mass consumption, which now dominates particularly within high-income countries where individuals generally have more disposable income and where purchasing power and possessions are an indication of status.

The ideology of consumerism is now, in turn, worldwide, and it drives economic markets, politics and thus social policies. For instance, many questions have been raised in relation to the way in which trade operates negatively upon health, with ineffective policy implementation being a key issue in this area. For example, a large amount of evidence demonstrates the importance of breastfeeding for the health of both mothers and infants. It is obviously economically advantageous too. Breastfeeding appears to be supported via current policy in the existence of the code for marketing of breast-milk substitutes, created by the WHO during the 1980s. However, evidence suggests frequent violations of this code, with free samples often provided in hospitals in poorer countries such as Thailand, South Africa and Bangladesh (Macdonald 2006), with consequences including higher death rates, malnutrition and higher morbidity (Labbock and Nazro 1995). Companies need to make profit and growth is considered necessary at the economic level, so policy at the global level can be contradictory, as this health example demonstrates. The push to consume also impacts in relation to inequalities and environmental sustainability, the negative results of some areas of globalization and global policy-making.

Ecological unsustainability

Further questions about the impact of global economic growth and policy on human welfare are raised in debates about the environment and about climate change. Global policy-makers such as the World Bank and the World Resources Institute acknowledge that the present global system is not sustainable, and have been reporting this for some time (World Resources Institute 2000). The way in which high-income countries consume and live is impacting negatively upon the environment, and thus policy-makers have begun to afford attention to these issues. Globalization itself is seen to be a significant part of the problem (see Box 4.3).

Environmental concerns are a significant issue for contemporary policy-makers. While the effects of climate change remain debatable many writers argue that the impact will affect the most vulnerable disproportionately, with climate change effects further increasing inequalities. Sernau (2011: 315) states that 'for a time... the rich can avoid the heat brought on by global warming by buying bigger air conditioners; they can avoid breathing polluted urban air and drinking contaminated water by driving cars with cabin air filters and buying prestigious brands of bottled water. They can hope to import dwindling natural resources... and to export their waste products to locations far away'.

Box 4.3 Globalization and the environment

- The push to consume leads to environmental degradation and contributes to climate change.
- Globalization has increased international travel and therefore the associated pollution.
- Increased demands for, and use of, energy impacts negatively upon the environment.
- Consumption of consumer products leads to waste. For example, Girling (2005) argues that, in an age of gadgets, our consumption of batteries and electricity causes serious environmental damage.
- Environmental impacts are unequal: Bullard (1990: 1993) describes how, in the USA, ugly and toxic waste is often found in areas where inhabitants are black and poor. India is a clear example of a poorer country that 'recycles' much of the richer world's waste (Gould 2008).

More positive views suggest that increased global awareness of ecological problems is a positive development (Vandenbroucke 1998). However, if this awareness does not translate into action, policies to tackle the issues will have a minimal impact.

The Kyoto Protocol, for instance, is one area of global policy-making related to climate change. The Protocol's major feature is that it has mandatory targets for the reduction of greenhouse-gas emissions. There are differential targets, but the overall aim is to reduce overall emissions of such gases by at least 5 per cent below existing 1990 levels. However, debates about its effectiveness abound because not all of the leading economies have signed up to the Protocol, and some countries are not attempting to reduce their greenhouse-gas emissions. Furthermore, the first commitment period ended in 2012, when policy concerns remain focused upon economics rather than environment.

Global inequalities, consumption and policy-making

Clearly not everyone in the world is able to consume goods and services at the level of the rich, industrialized countries; great inequalities still exist. Table 4.4 shows some of these inequalities, and details some possible policy solutions.

The relationship between the global and the national

For many commentators there are questions about how influential global policy-making and global influences are at the level of the national. However, establishing the effects of policy within one society is difficult. Any impact may well vary in relation to which social groups are being discussed. As mentioned above, some effects of globalization have a bigger impact on the less well-off and the unskilled. Writers who describe globalization as strong see global forces as dominating national issues and view the contemporary national state as less powerful than it has been seen in the past. Here economics is seen as all powerful, yet local forces can include different ideologies, different traditions and opposition to global policies (Yeates 2008). Many national governments remain concerned with being perceived as a 'nanny state' that interferes in people's lives through the policy process (Joffe and Mindell 2004). Indeed, there are also many

Table 4.4 Global inequalities and policy-making challenges

Area	Impact	What is needed
Food There are a number of causal factors which lead to malnutrition and hunger including conflicts, disasters, the breakdown of local institutions and crop failures. However, weak governance and lack of effective global policy-making are also a contributory factor here.	166 million people identified as being undernourished across 22 countries experiencing crises (FAO 2010), yet the UK population spends more than £10 billion each year on convenience food such as sandwiches, chips, burgers and curries (Sharpe 2010).	Policy that supports more sustainable food consumption: for example, Vaughan (2009) argues that eliminating the millions of tonnes of food thrown away annually in countries such as the USA and the UK could lift more than a billion people out of hunger worldwide.
Health There are sharp inequalities in the funding available to support access to health care; in poorer countries, access to even basic health care may be very restricted.	The 30 most developed nations, who are all members of the Organisation for Economic Cooperation (OCED), making up 20 per cent of the world's population, account for 90 per cent of the world's total health expenditure (WHO 2007).	Policies to increase funding may not always be the most effective – the USA has the largest investments in the world (based upon **GDP**) but significant portions of the population still have limited access to care. Lower-income countries also need policy to develop an infrastructure of caring systems – 35 of the 50 worst healthcare systems are found in sub-Saharan Africa (Macdonald 2007). In lower-income countries policy should fund primary health care as well as access to education and improvements in sanitation. Labonte (2010) argues that simple solutions that can improve health have been compromised by globalization. The economic dynamics of the changing international environment ('globalization') can undermine health because it affects the ways in which governments make policy and allocate funding.
Welfare There are inequalities in the availability of social provision across the world, with some countries providing more comprehensive support than others, and many lower-income countries having little or no welfare provision at all. Welfare provision is also changing in some contexts, shaped by the influences of globalization.	Globalization is linked to the reform of welfare in many countries (Yeates and Holden 2009). Though countries vary in their approach to welfare reform, a common theme seems to be a move towards competition between providers and marketized systems of delivery.	Universal welfare policy for all. Welfare policy that supports adequate standards of living. Welfare policy that moves beyond economic investment to develop labour power and considers its contribution to the well-being of citizens.

areas of life which citizens regard as 'private' and not suitable for policy interventions across the world. However, an area that affects most of us is that of welfare policy and provision. A large area of literature explores the relationship between the global and the national state in relation to welfare policy, with many suggesting that global neo-liberalism is shifting the provision of welfare in many countries as provision is being cut back and conditionality is increasingly the norm (see Chapter 6 for a fuller discussion of these issues). What does all of this mean at the level of the individual? While it may not be possible to identify the ways in which global social policy is directly affecting our lives, it is clear that globalization has resulted in significant social change for many of us. Giddens (1994: 5) relates globalization to 'the transformation of local, and even personal contexts of social experience', because of the different levels at which globalization filters through the social structure. Martell (2010: 2) similarly argues that large-scale global processes including international political power and economics impact our individual lives, as 'the global economy and distribution of wealth affect, for example, our chances of employment alongside our material circumstances generally'. Martell also discusses how globalization can have an impact culturally and through the media. In both these analyses, globalization and global politics significantly influence our lives.

However, this impact has not been equal across the world, and it is this inequality that has resulted in large scale criticisms of current policy-making at the global level. Giddens (2009) describes how economic globalization has led to negative experiences for some. Dahlburg (1995) details the example of a garment worker located in Bangkok, working 15 hours per day, for 6 days each week and earning what would in 2013 be the equivalent of £2 per hour. Billions of workers across the world face similar conditions. Importantly, the effects of globalization are different depending upon our location and societal position. Activity 4.4 will help you to consider your own experiences.

Activity 4.4 Thinking about your relationship with globalization

How has globalization affected your life? Write down your ideas as you reflect upon your own experiences. The questions below will help you to think about this.

1. Think about the ways in which the media might have made you part of the 'global society', listing examples of your global knowledge. Do you watch the news and see reports about what is happening in other countries? Are you aware of political problems and wars in a variety of places? How does this link to ideas about global consciousness?
2. Think about how you use technology to communicate. Do you have friends on Facebook who are from other countries? Are there similar applications on your mobile phone that allow you to send messages free of charge? In what ways do you communicate across geographical divides: for example, we imagine that you usually email or Skype, rather than writing letters!
3. Give consideration to the clothes that you wear and the goods that you purchase. Look at the labels inside your clothing: where was it made? Do you shop for cheaper goods and feel pleased that you have a bargain? If so have you ever thought about the working conditions and pay of those making your clothing?

Globalization influences our lives in many diverse ways, and for most of us living in high-income countries we have experienced many benefits of the changing world. Now finally think about how your views on globalization might differ if you were living in a different country. There are communities who have to get by on very low incomes in developing countries, for instance. List what you think might be the negative and positive effects of globalization on people in this context.

Conclusions: global social policy futures

This chapter has given you an overview of the importance of globalization and global policy-making in the world today. There has been a growing recognition that many problems are global and that there is thus a need for a more coherent policy approach at the global level. The increased pace of globalization has also facilitated the need for the expansion of policy too. Consequently, there has been a growth in the number of agencies and actors working at the global level of policy-making in recent years.

There is much debate about whether such policy is positive or negative, as several examples have illustrated. Yeates and Holden (2009) argue that global economic policy is now at a crossroads. The current system is seen as failing, especially in the wake of the collapse of the US financial sector, by the European sector too. Protests have abounded in relation to the role played by many global actors such as the World Bank and the IMF, as well as the perceived dominance of the USA in world economic matters. Recent anti-capitalist protests made interesting media headlines across Europe, with the Occupy Movement aiming to initiate global change against both capitalism and austerity measures (Gabbatt 2011).

These protests have raised interesting questions about the current global economic system, yet there is no clear consensus about the way forward. The Occupy movement is by no means isolated, as there is a plethora of social movements drawing attention to various issues and campaigns for change, but the solutions being offered are diverse. There is some common agreement, however, that 'a global vision of social justice, an effective system of global governance and coherent national and transnational (global) social policies to realize and maintain it are the most desirable and viable options for the future' (Yeates and Holden 2009: 385). Labonte (2010: 240) suggests a number of achievable policies for the future, including:

- changes to global taxation to facilitate the redistribute of wealth because more equal societies have far better health outcomes across the globe (Wilkinson and Pickett 2009);
- the radical reform of current global policy-making organizations such as the World Bank and the World Trade Organization to increase public spending on education, health care, water/sanitation and other interventions which promote equality, across the world; and
- cancellation of poor countries' debts, and fairer trade systems to allow the economies of poor countries to develop.

The key underpinning argument suggested by Labonte (2010) is that a new global governance system is required which is more ethical and rights-based, and this is the real challenge. Indeed, policy-makers working at the global level also need to remain realistic about the remit of their organizations and what can feasibly be achieved through policy implementation. As a starting point Lechner and Boli (2012) argue that ten principles for democratic and sustainable societies need to be supported by collective global social policy as follows:

1. New democracy – companies now have more power than governments, so power needs to be shifted back into the hands of people and communities.
2. **Subsidiarity** – economic globalization has resulted in power shifts that reduce the importance of the local, and this needs reversing.

3. **Ecological sustainability** – economics needs to operate in a manner that does not compromise future populations.
4. Common heritage – natural resources and public services should be shared equitably among the world's population.
5. Human rights – these need to be met in relation to all.
6. Employment – the right to employment is a basic human right, thus workers need protecting, and supporting so that they can work in dignified conditions.
7. Food security and safety – achieving this will ensure more national stability.
8. Equity – currently inequalities are increasing, thus the gap between the rich and the poor needs to be reduced.
9. Diversity – this should be supported, rather than eroded via corporate-led globalization.
10. Precaution – all policy should be precautionary – if there are threats to health and humans from activity then regulation should be introduced.

Summary of key points

- Increasingly, the global nature of many issues means that policy-making is now taking place at a level above the national, with global governance evident in many areas.
- There is a range of key global actors who are involved in policy-making, with diverse interests and focus upon different priorities.
- Debates abound about whether global policy-making is positive and how it is impacting upon key issues such as social inequalities. Thus, a need for more democratic approaches has been identified.

Key terms and concepts

climate change
consumerism
development
ecological sustainability
economics
globalization
global capitalism
global policy-making
global priorities
International Monetary Fund
Millennium Development Goals
neo-liberalism
World Bank
World Health Organization

Suggestions for further reading

Deacon, B. (2007) *Global Social Policy and Governance.* London: Sage.

This book covers all key aspects of global governance, with chapters on the World Bank, the role of the United Nations and the International Monetary Fund. The book also looks at non-state actors, giving a comprehensive overview of the key global players and the areas in which they create social policies.

Lemert, C., Elliott, A., Chaffee, D. and Hus, E. (2010) *Globalization. A Reader.* London and New York: Routledge.

This book contains a full historical outline of how globalization has developed as well as acting as a comprehensive guide to all aspects of the concept. The book discusses key debates about governance, global culture, global economic issues and future challenges. This is a comprehensive collection of edited chapters that are lengthy and detailed.

Martell, L. (2010) *The Sociology of Globalization.* Cambridge: Polity.

This book gives a good overview of sociological analyses of globalization examining all aspects of the concept including cultural, political and economic. The book also explores power, inequality and conflict throughout and so is an excellent introduction to the ongoing debates and problems associated with globalization within the field of sociology.

Yeates, N. (2008) *Understanding Global Social Policy. Understanding Welfare: Social Issues, Policy and Practice.* Bristol: Policy Press.

This book is an edited collection written by leading social policy analysts. It explores and examines the impact of the global on the ways in which social policy as a field of study is constructed. The book also looks at globalizing strategies of state and non-state actors in relationship with social policy and particularly welfare. This is a student-friendly publication containing chapter summaries, boxes and diagrams, and pointers to relevant websites.

Yeates, N. and Holden, C. (eds) (2009) *The Global Social Policy Reader.* Bristol: Policy Press.

This edited collection of chapters covers a wide range of material related to global social policy, exploring the need for global policy, global issues such as poverty and inequality and the global actors and their associated policy-making. The book is usefully organized into five sections, covering all key areas and ending with discussions about the future of social policy within a global context.

5 The contested boundaries of social policy: the case of criminal justice

Key learning outcomes

By the end of this chapter you should:

- be able to understand the field of criminal justice policy
- be able to understand the connections between criminal justice policy and social policy
- be able to comparatively discuss UK criminal justice policy

Overview of the chapter

This chapter gives an overview of the field of criminal justice considering some aspects of the English and Welsh criminal justice system and its workings (the Scottish system is different), although space permits only the briefest account of its structure. This chapter also examines the connection between criminal justice policy and social policy, highlighting close links between the two despite somewhat vague boundaries. In this sense we might say that the subject matter of social policy is wider in scope than it is conventional to suppose. A final purpose is to provide a brief introduction to the topic of **comparative analysis** in social policy and suggest that it can provide a valuable perspective on UK policies. Comparative study, in our context, means the examination of the policies, programmes and services of more than one country, which is increasingly important given the developments in global policy (see Chapter 4). This chapter also includes discussions of migration, asylum-seeking, refugees, citizenship, the secret services and national security, and the emergency services (Toynbee and Walker 2005: 6), which are all related to safety.

Introduction: what is criminal justice policy?

We should begin by noting that 'criminal justice', like most other concepts in social life and the social sciences, is fuzzy, inexact and contestable in character. (The term 'penal policy' is also sometimes used to refer to the subject, but perhaps implying a more specialized focus on punishment and the treatment of offenders.) 'Law and order' is also a rough and ready term with approximately the same meaning with which you may be more familiar. So under this heading we would expect to find descriptions and discussions of such topics as the roles of police forces, courts, sentencing, punishment, prisons, probation and of what is sometimes referred to as the criminal justice 'process' generally, as well as debates on the merits of particular approaches to the problem of crime. Much criminal justice research is concerned with evaluation of the effectiveness and fairness (or lack of it) of these institutions and their workings, and this is where comparisons with other countries' policies are often made. Definitions of criminal justice differ, with broader views also examining public safety. Thus the United Nations (UN) affiliated research agency concerned with crime and criminal justice, HEUNI, employs a broad concept, 'public safety', to refer to the subject matter of criminal justice (Kangaspunta et al. 1998: 2).

There are various analytical perspectives on crime and criminal justice. On one level, a traditional focus of much criminological research has been on the workings of the criminal justice system – on how such agencies as the police, courts and prisons *actually* work, as opposed to how they are *supposed* to work (Maguire et al. 2002). On another level, there are political science or 'public policy' perspectives which analyse the politics of criminal justice in terms of the outcome of interactions between institutions and groups, such as government, Parliament, the Home Office, political parties, pressure groups, voters and public opinion (Morris 1989; Downes and Morgan 2002). In some recent criminological writing we find, at yet another level, attempts to locate and analyse the criminal justice system within a larger societal framework. This research calls attention to the impact of broad social and economic trends on crime: for example, changes in the family, an ageing population, globalization and capitalist 'restructuring' (Loader and Sparks 2002). Current debates about economic recession are also important here, with some suggesting that recession leads to increased crime rates. Crime rates did increase in the 1980s recession, hence contemporary concern. However, relationships between crime and employment are complex (Box 1987), and recent UK crime figures do not indicate the same pattern in that overall crime figures have continued to fall (ONS 2012e).

This issue of both definitions and subject boundaries is significant when we come to consider the issue of the relationship of criminal justice to social policy, because it will be seen that there are areas of overlap – drug policy and mental health, for example, are matters of concern within both the health and criminal justice systems. Figure 5.1 demonstrates overlapping areas between criminal justice policy and social policy more generally.

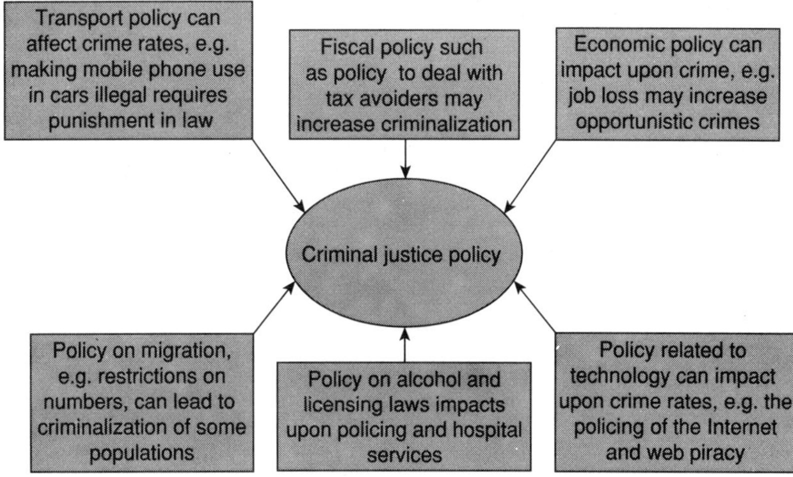

Figure 5.1 Relationship of criminal justice policy to social policy

Criminal justice, social control and social policy: a 'penal–welfare state'?

An immediate context for thinking about the connection between criminal justice and social policy has been the way that the UK Coalition Government has deliberately made the link. Following the extensive rioting in the UK in 2011, David Cameron spoke about 'Broken Britain' and the need to target troubled workless families to tackle crime rates (Travis and Stratton 2011). This is a continuation of policy in this area from the previous New Labour government, in which Tony Blair remarked in 1993, prior to coming to **power**, that a Labour government would be 'tough on crime and tough on the causes of crime'. This explicitly makes a connection between crime and social conditions which can be altered by forms of social intervention – that is, social policy. This approach will be fully explored in the later section on the Coalition Government's policies.

One way of thinking about the connection between criminal justice and social policy is in terms of the concept of social control. In Chapter 7 we examine the relationship between social policy and social control. Social policy can be regarded as something positive or negative, as welfare-enhancing or welfare-negating. Social control can be more or less overt, more or less concealed. In looking at criminal justice policy, we are concerned with another aspect of the state's relationship with society. In this case, it is

Table 5.1 Competing views of the criminal justice system

Theories about crime	View of law, order and policy
Classicism Human beings are self-interested and exercise free will. They are fully responsible for their actions.	• Individuals need both punishment and **deterrence**. • Punishments should fit the crime and be proportional – criminals should get their just deserts.
Positivism Crime is not rational and is caused by forces beyond the control of the criminal. Early analyses focused upon the biological and psychological characteristics of criminals.	• As the problem is a sickness, treatment is needed rather than punishment. • Sentences need to be individually tailored in order to effect rehabilitation.
Social positivism Individuals have some freedoms but these exist within a predetermined social framework. Different strands of the theory explain crime in a range of ways. • Social disorganization theory suggests that crime is more likely in areas where social norms have been broken. • Strain theory instead suggests that people at the lower end of the social scale are likely to use crime to achieve socially desired norms. • Subcultural theory suggests that groups of people form deviant subcultures. • Labelling theory suggests that those in less powerful positions are more likely to be labelled and then perform expected roles.	• All of these approaches hold in common the view that crime can be addressed through social programmes which alleviate underlying social conditions such as unemployment and deprivation.
Feminist perspectives Focus upon power and inequality between men and women. The position of women in society is the key to understanding men's and women's criminality.	• Solutions here need to focus upon empowering women economically, socially and politically.

that of public safety or the maintenance of law and order. Maintenance of law, order and public safety is viewed differently according to the value base that people adopt. Theories about crime are important because they serve as a stimulus for policy development as well as a rationalization of any policy approaches adopted. Table 5.1 summarizes a range of different theories about the nature of crime.

Table 5.1 shows that some understandings of crime are concerned with structural inequalities and power within society. Now complete Activity 5.1 to think further about **theories of crime**, and appropriate policy responses to the problem.

Activity 5.1 The social context of crime

Sociologists argues that crime is relatively 'normal' – we are all at some point likely to commit at least a minor crime; if this is the case then the idea that there is some biological or psychological difference between criminals and non-criminals is undermined.

1. Write down the ways in which you or people that you know have broken the criminal law. Think about driving offences as a starting point.
2. Now think about the punishments that exist in relation to the ways in which you have broken the law and the way in which the state coerces individuals into behaving in specific ways. Crime and punishment vary according to the society in which they occur, and some crimes are much more highly stigmatized than others. How do you categorize the crimes that you committed and what are your thoughts about appropriate punishments?

Criminal justice is concerned with coercion, or at least the possibility of coercion, and the state's power to coerce individuals to do things they would not otherwise do, as both Table 5.1 and Activity 5.1 have indicated. It is concerned with one of the most basic aspects of the state – its use, or potential use, of force. Historically this has been a fraught and contested issue in the justification and legitimation of political authority. The tradition of liberal political thought has, for example, been uneasy about the coercive powers of the state, and liberals have, historically, been those who sought to limit and circumscribe that authority, and have been associated with such legal–constitutional principles as 'the **rule of law**' and '**due process**' (Gray 1986). Other traditions, such as anarchism, have rejected the claim of the state to coerce and regulate its members.

This brings us to the concept of the '**penal–welfare state**' (Garland 2001: 5; Loader and Sparks 2002: 84), a concept which owes something to the work of social theorists such as Foucault (Foucault 1977; Hudson 2002: 238–40). Foucault proposed a connection between welfare and criminal justice. The welfare state is also a 'penal state' – a state based on regulation, control and punishment. 'Penality' – crime control and punishment – and welfare are two sides of the same coin, Foucault argued, and historically both developed together as aspects of the modern state, or the 'policeman state' (Gatrell 1990). This perspective highlights the ambiguity of the modern state and its functions. The modern UK state has been labelled as a 'policeman state' in recent media reports of the strategies used to control public protests about policy changes. For example, many students publicly protested about the Coalition Government's changes to tuition fees for higher education (see Chapter 8). During the protest they were 'kettled' by police, a process which involves holding protesters in a restricted area for lengthy periods of time. Some protestors argued that this approach breached their human rights (Taylor 2010), and some students used the media to complain about police intimidation and unnecessary force (BBC News 2011b). However, David Cameron condemned the protests and the violence used by a small number of protestors, and commended the police's approach (BBC News 2010b).

There have been various approaches to justification and legitimation of the state's coercive authority from within the liberal–individualist tradition, from a position broadly sympathetic to the modern state. The criminal law – that area of public law with which the criminal justice system and policy are concerned – may be justified in terms of protecting human rights; in terms of the utilitarian moral principle of maximizing overall happiness, 'utility' or well-being (see Chapter 2); or in terms of so-called 'contractarian' approaches, such as that of the celebrated theory of justice of John Rawls (see Chapter 2) (Rawls 1972). In the first case, the criminal law may be understood as protecting people's human rights to personal freedom from harm and to the ownership of property – and as imposing duties on people to respect these rights. Such rights – often referred to as 'civil rights' – may be incorporated in charters of human rights, such as those in the *European Charter of Human Rights* and its English legal manifestation in the Human Rights Act 1998. From this point of view, criminal justice is concerned with preventing and punishing rights violations or compensating victims of such violations. From this perspective, also, the state's claim to legitimacy lies in its protection of citizens' rights. There is a connection here with social policy, because one way of viewing welfare state programmes is in terms of protecting or promoting people's rights, in this case, 'social' rather than 'civil' rights (see Chapter 2).

On the other hand, the criminal law may be seen as enhancing the security and well-being of citizens, in so far as property and person are safer than they would otherwise be. People's well-being, 'utility' or happiness is enhanced. (There is a kind of cost–benefit calculation involved in this kind of reasoning. The benefits of criminal justice must be set against the costs of it, in terms of, for example, the costs of law enforcement and possible negative effects, such as punishment of the innocent, corruption, discrimination, unfair treatment, etc.)

There are contradictions, however, between protecting rights, powerful interests and democratic principles on the one hand, and powerful interests on the other. Complete Activity 5.2 to explore this area further.

Activity 5.2 The right to protest and state intervention

Use an Internet search engine such as Google to find a range of media reports about some recent UK protests. The example of the 2010–11 student protests is one area to examine. Alternatively you may be interested in exploring the 2011 Occupy movement and how this was dealt with by the state. After reading the media reports, take time to address the following questions:

1. Democracy should allow us to protest and voice opinion about policy changes; how far should the right to protest be extended?
2. Think about the role of the police in these protests. Marxist theorists describe police services as part of a state apparatus, which tends to support state interests and control the masses. What is your view of the role of the police in relation to the protests that you examined?
3. How did the media reports that you examined portray the protestors and the way in which they protested? Whose interests were best served by the reports?
4. What about the welfare of the protestors? Was this considered within the reports that you found?

The activity that you have just completed should have helped you to explore your ideas about the state and its role in criminal justice. As this chapter has already indicated, social policy and criminal justice exhibit a concern with similar topics and issues. For example, the agencies and functions of welfare overlap with those of the criminal justice system, and the objects of the two systems are to some extent the same. The criminal justice system is in practice mostly concerned with a substratum of society - the poor, the marginalized and the excluded, who make up a disproportionate share of the system's 'clients' - which is also to some extent the focus of at least some parts of the welfare system. If one's view of welfare is to see it as especially concerned with 'social problems', one would certainly be inclined to make a clear link. The probation service, for example, in terms of its methods and in terms of its client base, overlaps considerably with voluntary and statutory social work. Penal policy is much concerned with appropriate models of treatment for convicted offenders. **Rehabilitation** is a 'needs-focused' approach to the treatment of offenders, which might include a variety of strategies - medical, psychiatric, social work, educational - indistinguishable from welfare interventions in other contexts. The issues of 'safety' and 'community safety' as a focus of the criminal justice system can be seen in terms of a social welfare approach, as can the concern in recent criminal justice policy for the needs and welfare of victims. There are also connections between social work and youth justice, and the boundary between social work with young offenders and youth justice is a blurred one.

There is also an historical connection. The origins of the welfare state in the period of Liberal governments 1906–14 also saw the beginnings of significant developments in criminal justice: the introduction of borstals for young offenders, the introduction of juvenile courts and the beginnings of the probation service (Morris 1983: 167).

Finally, criminal justice policy can function as an alternative to welfare policy, and vice versa (Morris 2001: 363). Expenditure on social programmes and services may be regarded as an alternative to expenditure on law enforcement and criminal justice, given a particular interpretation of the roots of crime and criminality. The sociological interpretation of criminality sees it as arising out of poverty, deprivation, **marginalization** and exclusion (as indicated in Table 5.1). This implicitly points towards welfare solutions to the problem. International comparisons are illuminating here. Table 5.2 shows the USA's approach to law and order.

Table 5.2 suggests the USA has a punitive approach to law and order. What can we infer from this? One might infer that Americans simply prefer to spend their tax money

Table 5.2 The USA approach to law and order

Views on law and order	Policy on law and order
The USA is a relatively punitive society in relation to law and order issues. It chooses to prioritize law enforcement over social welfare as a solution to crime, disorder and social breakdown.	• Prison is used as an alternative to social security. • Some states use determinant sentencing laws – clear guidelines for certain crimes and repeat offenders. • The nation incarcerates a much higher proportion of its population than any other country. • Many states retain the death penalty. • Its law and order budget is much higher as a proportion of national income than that of the UK, European countries or Japan. The USA is also a comparatively low spender on social welfare by comparison with Western Europe.

on law and order rather than on social security, housing and health – an expression of 'American values' perhaps. Such an inference would be too hasty, but we have here an invitation to compare the criminal justice policies of different countries, and to try to arrive at explanations for the differences that we observe. This is the subject of our next section.

Comparing crime and criminal justice

> [U]nderstanding the international dimensions of punishment is both increasingly vital for the student of penology and inherently problematic.
>
> (Cavadino and Dignan 2000: 2)

In the previous section we noted some interesting differences between US and British criminal justice systems and policies. In this section we turn to consider a more systematic examination of inter-country differences. This will provide us with an opportunity for introducing the general topic of comparison and comparative study in social policy.

The question posed at the end of the previous section – why does a country such as the USA differ in its approach to criminal justice? – gives us a way into the subject, but it is worth spending a little time to consider why comparison and comparative study have come to be regarded as indispensable in any credible analysis of social and public policy. Some researchers have gone so far as to suggest that 'all research is comparative' (Pickvance 1986, cited in Kennett 2001: 42; Nelken 2002: 184) or that comparative research is 'about everything' (Mabbett and Bolderson 1999: 34). There are a number of reasons for comparative study in any area of public policy.

One has to do with overcoming the parochialism and ethno- or Anglocentrism to which we in the UK are prone. Comparative study offers the student of criminal justice as well as other policy areas the opportunity of becoming more 'reflexive', learning to avoid the error of assuming that the Anglo-American approach to law is the norm. As Chapter 4 has highlighted, there are now concerns about the global scale of crime (e.g. drug trafficking, money laundering, illegal offshore investments) and a limited country-by-country approach will not be adequate in tackling these crimes.

A second reason for increasing interest in the comparative study of criminal justice, as well as other areas of public policy, has to do with what is called **'policy learning'**. Policy-makers have become more interested, in recent years, in examining the experiences, problems and policy ideas and solutions of other countries for the light that might be shed on their own policy concerns: for what can be learned about 'what works' and what does not. There have been many examples of such 'policy learning'. The development of a rehabilitative approach to the treatment of offenders in the UK from the 1950s to the 1970s owes something to American influence, as does the decline of the rehabilitative ideal thereafter and its replacement by approaches based on 'justice' or 'deterrence'. UK rehabilitation is, however, being revisited by the Coalition Government. The growth of more punitive attitudes and treatment of offenders from the 1980s onwards, and the willingness of political parties to exploit law and order issues for electoral purposes, might be seen as evidence of American cultural influence. The idea of 'zero tolerance' policing came from the USA at the end of the 1990s, a product of its alleged success in New York. It is interesting that most of the influence seems to be from the USA to the UK, which ties into some views already described in Chapter 4 that the globalization of the policy process can be seen simply as Americanization.

However, in this context, other countries may be viewed as providing experimental situations in which policy ideas and solutions can be tested and evaluated and from which lessons may be learned. Of course, some of the use made of foreign examples has less to do with a dispassionate and scientific evaluation of alternatives than with finding opportunities to boost and promote favoured ideas: 'It is ... one of the commonest tricks in the book when advocating or criticising any social policy to declare (whether accurately or otherwise but usually in the hope that one's opponents are insufficiently knowledgeable to contradict you) that they do things so much better/worse in Ruritania' (Cavadino and Dignan 2000: 2).

A third important rationale for comparative study is that it can be employed to test theories of social and institutional change – in other words, changes in policies and governing institutions. Here, the purpose is to identify and isolate causal factors in institutional change. Why do policies change, and change in particular directions? What explains the size of the USA's prison population, by comparison with Britain's – is it a difference of ideologies and values? Or is it socioeconomic 'modernization', bound to affect all countries as they develop and 'converge' on a single uniform approach to public policy?

The second strand of comparative analysis described above, policy learning, also invites questions: for example, how effective the US approach to imprisonment is in terms of the objectives of criminal justice policy. Is it something from which we can learn or, on the other hand, is it a model to avoid? Could, or should, Americans learn from Britain or from European countries about penal policy? This is particularly interesting in the light of the growth of a global human rights culture, explicitly committed to the idea of universality and, less explicitly, to policy **convergence**. The USA's policies on incarceration and the death penalty have in fact been criticized by international bodies such as the UN on human rights grounds (Ignatieff 2005; Peel 2005).

Another between the USA and both the UK and European countries is, of course, the use of the death penalty. This was abolished in Britain in 1965, at roughly the same time that the USA imposed a moratorium on its use. This looked like a case of convergent evolution, but American policy was strikingly reversed in 1976 with a Supreme Court judgment which declared that the death penalty was, after all, legitimate. All other European countries have abolished the death penalty since the early 1980s, although several other countries still use the death penalty such as Singapore, Sudan, Iran, Iraq and China (some publicly). There are global campaigns for the abolition of the death penalty, such as the work of Amnesty International. In 2012 the World Coalition Against the Death Penalty celebrated its ten-year anniversary. However, the death penalty remains in place in many countries.

Comparison can of course be extended to cover all aspects of crime, criminal justice and law enforcement. Policy-makers in the UK have, for example, been interested in borrowing US ideas about policing. The concept of 'zero tolerance' policing is an example used in the late 1990s in Teeside and recently endorsed by David Cameron after the UK 2011 riots. Other penal concepts and ideas – parole and electronic tagging, for example – have been borrowed from foreign models.

The fact that 'penal ideas and practices are flitting around the globe like epidemics of Asian (or more often American) influenza' (Cavadino and Dignan 2000: 2) can be identified as an aspect of globalization, in terms of the flows of information and people, and the impact of multinational agencies such as intergovernmental bodies (Nelken 2002: 185). There is perhaps a tendency among criminologists to notice and highlight American influence on UK policy, while downplaying other sources of influence; there has been a comparable tendency among social policy analysts (Annesley 2003). Attention has been drawn to the 'homogenising and converging influences of the European Union on penal policy' (Nelken 2002: 175). Activity 5.3 will help you to focus on the connections between criminal justice policy and globalization.

Activity 5.3 The need for policy beyond the nation state

Chapter 4 drew attention to the importance of a global perspective. Now consider how globalization is presenting challenges to policy-makers concerned with law, order and safety.

1. Think about how the increasing interconnectedness of the world presents new areas for criminal activity, and list as many areas as you can think of. Look at news reports as a starting point if you are finding this task difficult.
2. In the absence of a global police force, what areas do you think need policy development; if you were a policy-maker what challenges would you try to tackle first?
3. Now think about some of the difficulties that may exist in using policy in tackling global criminal activity – what barriers exist to effective co-ordination of policy on crime?

The discussion so far in this chapter has focused on the desirability and importance of comparative study of criminal justice systems and policies, and Activity 5.3 should have underlined the need for an international approach to crime. However, there are difficulties in this area. There are problems of data availability and comparability, if one relies, as many researchers in the field do, on quantitative methodological approaches and the use of official statistics. These problems recur across the whole field of public policy comparison and are not unique to criminal justice (Mabbett and Bolderson 1999: 34).

Countries differ in their legal systems, their criminal law and their legal and criminal justice concepts. Apart from the data generated by large-scale social surveys of criminal justice of the kind undertaken by UN agencies (see UNODC n.d.), researchers must rely on data collected by the statistical services of each country. These are collected in the countries concerned for administrative reasons, not for the convenience of comparative researchers.

Comparison 'does have to face special difficulties. These range from the technical, conceptual, and linguistic problems posed by the unreliability of statistics, lack of appropriate data, meaning of foreign terms, etc., to the complications of understanding the differences in other languages, practices and world views which make it difficult to know whether we are comparing like with like' (Nelken 2002: 184). Legal definitions of offences differ from country to country. 'Assault', for example, may be an independent category in some countries, while others may not consider an incident to be an assault unless it results in bodily injury (Kangaspunta et al. 1998: 3). There are also procedural differences between countries in the handling of offences. In some countries, for example, traffic offences are not considered to be offences, and are handled by a special police unit or some special procedure, and may not be recorded in statistics (Kangaspunta et al. 1998: 4). The statistical classification of crime differs from country to country. 'Theft', for example, may or may not include burglary, car theft or shoplifting.

Criminal justice policy in the Netherlands

In this section we turn to an examination of criminal justice policy in another member country of the EU, the Netherlands. This is of interest for a number of reasons. First, the Netherlands is a developed, capitalist country with a high standard of living, high-quality welfare services, a long tradition of liberal democratic government, and a relatively open and tolerant culture. It is also characterized by a degree of pluralism and diversity in its social and demographic make-up, based on both religious (Protestant and Catholic, and more recently Muslim) and ethnic differences, although its population size is smaller than the UK. The criminal justice system and policy exhibit interesting differences from UK models, being based on different legal principles (Roman or civil law, rather than common law), and being rather more humane and 'progressive' in some respects. Finally, Dutch society has been subject to some of the same influences as has the UK – globalization, for example – and criminal justice policy has shifted in ways which suggest a degree of convergence.

Cavadino and Dignan (2000), drawing heavily on work by Downes (1988), provide an illuminating discussion of Dutch criminal justice policy, in terms of a concept of 'penal crisis'. From being a 'beacon of tolerance' in the 1960s, Dutch policy became increasingly harsh and the incarceration rate climbed. The severity of sentences increased and prison conditions deteriorated. These changes are documented in a more recent analysis by Tak (2008). This is further reflected in recent policy developments related to juvenile justice, such as the programme 'justice to young people' (in Dutch: *Jeugd Terecht*). The objective of this programme is to prevent first-time offending and to reduce recidivism. The Halt Programme is also a new area, in which children in the age range 12 to 18 years who commit a minor crime can get an alternative sentence. Criminal law for young adults has also been further extended. Young offenders can now be convicted according to either juvenile criminal law or adult criminal law, depending on the circumstances. The law provides the opportunity to tackle social and psychiatric problems that lead to criminal behaviour, but can also lead to more severe sentences if young people do not take the opportunities offered or fail to carry out their community service (Ministry of Security and Justice 2012). Dutch penal mildness in the earlier period is ascribed to ideological factors, such as the corporatist and Christian Democratic nature of Dutch society – socially liberal, with generous welfare state provision. Dutch penal culture had 'Enlightenment' roots. Policy was 'inclusionary' and characterized by an emphasis on 'resocialization'. Prosecutions are frequently waived (35 per cent in 1996) and prison sentences tend to be shorter (Cavadino and Dignan 2000: 12–24).

In explaining the growth of a harsher penal regime in the 1980s and 1990s, Cavadino and Dignan draw attention to general ideological and cultural changes associated with late modernity, such as the move towards a more individualized, less communitarian society. Church allegiance declined and there has been a growth of 'individualized anomie'. The Netherlands has been described by those deploring these trends as a 'victim of globalization'. Reference is made to the growth of 'American-style consumerist culture' (it is noted that the Dutch, in their multilingual nation, are open to penetration and persuasion by English-language media). There has been a growth of neo-liberal influence in public policy (although the welfare state remains relatively unscathed, despite some restructuring) (Cavadino and Dignan 2000: 17–18). The result of all this has been a decline in Dutch tolerance of criminals and criminality. There has been a 'redrawing of the boundaries of community' and the development of a policy of 'bifurcation'.

It was suggested that recent developments in Dutch penal policy exhibit a good deal of British influence (more so than American), with the Dutch Labour Party consciously imitating Britain's previous 'New Labour' government. Party politics has, however, played little part in the shift in Dutch attitudes. There has been a growth of top-down managerialism and increasing regulation and bureaucratization of the criminal justice system: 'In a country where a relatively small elite dictates penal policies, it may be that relatively rapid change is possible and even facilitated when that elite changes its mind and/or its personnel' (Cavadino and Dignan 2006: 123). The Netherlands is a small country lacking the regional **autonomy** to be found in federal states such as the USA, Germany or Australia. In the Netherlands 'the mindset of this penal elite altered significantly over a relatively short time' (Cavadino and Dignan 2000: 21). The claim that there is or was in the 1980s a 'penal crisis' in the Netherlands is rejected. There was no crisis of resources; the Dutch system is a relatively cheap one, because of its sparing use of prosecution and imprisonment (the 'waiting list' system, in which sentenced offenders were only imprisoned when a place in prison became available, helped here). Rather, it is or was a 'crisis of legitimacy', arising from popular perceptions of excessive lenience. To some extent the issue was related to the notably tolerant attitude of the Dutch towards drugs and the growing pressure from other countries such as the USA for a less relaxed attitude – an interesting example of global or international influence on domestic policy development (Cavadino and Dignan 2000: 22). Also influential was the growth of penal ideologies. Globalization in another sense has also played a part – that of transnational migration. There has been a decline in Dutch tolerance towards foreign migrants and a mental conflation of migrants with criminals (see Box 5.1). This has also been seen in many other countries, notably the UK.

Box 5.1 The criminalization of migration

- The Council of Europe (2010) has highlighted the increased criminalization of migrants across Europe in recent years with sanctions such as detainment increasingly used in a number of countries.
- Criminal law is also being used to punish individuals and businesses who engage with migrants whose immigration status is either uncertain or unauthorized.
- Illegal entry into many countries such as the UK, Greece and Italy is a criminal offence, subject to a variety of penalties.
- There has also been the criminalization of individuals seeking asylum. Many European governments have invested too much political capital in 'being tough' on asylum seekers, leading to the development and application of criminal law in this area.
- The UK Coalition Government has promised tougher new measures on migration, with the government capping numbers of migrants from outside Europe allowed entry.

Thus, the discussion of Dutch policy around migration and other areas is useful for a number of reasons, because it highlights a number of aspects of comparative analysis and its value. The authors are, to some extent, implicitly comparing Dutch policy with that of other countries, such as the UK, noting points of similarity and difference and convergence in policy, such as 'waiting lists' for imprisonment and diversion from prosecution and imprisonment. They are also attempting to explain these differences, similarities and convergences, drawing attention to penal ideologies; general social and political values in Dutch society and the character of party politics; the character of the Netherlands as a relatively small state, nonfederal in nature and regionally undifferentiated, facilitating rapid shifts in elite thinking in public policy, such as criminal justice policy. They call attention to a degree of what looks like convergence in Dutch penal policy. This is a significant concept in comparative study, which points up, in particular, political and cultural factors from outside the country which have tended to move policy in particular directions. The objectives of this particular case study, and of comparative study in general therefore, include, among others, the identification of similarities and differences; the explanation of these, especially, perhaps, the latter; and describing and examining policy and institutional change and attempting to explain these. In addition, they involve, implicitly or explicitly, a degree of policy learning. The case study seems to imply that Dutch policies – the earlier ones – are recommendable and provide a positive model that other countries might emulate.

Measuring crime

The sociological or criminological mainstream view of crime and deviance is the so-called 'social constructionist' view. Crime is the product of processes which 'construct' particular behaviour as criminal, in line with, among other things, changes in social values (Pease 2002: 947). These processes take place via the medium of the criminal law on the one hand, which labels particular behaviour as deviant, and the criminal justice system on the other. Particular societies will view particular kinds of behaviour differently. For example, in the Netherlands the age of consent is lower than the UK and attitudes towards the use of cannabis are much more relaxed than in the UK. Some crimes are much more highly stigmatized than others depending upon dominant societal views and are thus perceived as more deviant. For example, in the UK, rapists scorn paedophiles in prison due to the stigma and labelling associated with paedophilia. A good comparative example of this is the labelling as criminal in the former Soviet Union and present-day Cuba of a variety of economic activities, such commercial buying and selling, or private ownership of property, which are perfectly legal in capitalist countries. A historical example of this, already cited, is domestic violence against women, which was arguably, to some extent, legitimate and permitted in earlier times, and is now regarded as criminal. Drink-driving is punished increasingly severely in the UK, and the criminalization of other driving-related activities has also changed in recent years. For example, seatbelts now must be worn, and since 2003 it has been a criminal offence to use a mobile phone while driving.

Issues of definition and measurement loom large. A much-discussed issue is that of the 'real' incidence of crime, compared with the official recording of it. Crime statistics until the 1980s were generated first of all by what members of the public chose to report to the police, and by police practices in identifying and recording offences. The official recording of crime, therefore, is misleading as a guide to the social reality of crime, its volume, incidence and type. Since the early 1980s an alternative source of data on crime has been developed – the British Crime Survey (BCS). This is a large-scale, questionnaire-based survey of the population, conducted every two years, which seeks to measure the public's experience of crime. The BCS must be one of the largest of all such social surveys. Its data are potentially much more accurate than police figures, although not perfect. The BCS suggests that the real incidence of crime is about four times higher than that officially recorded. The number of respondents and the geographical coverage permit disaggregation of data on a local area basis. It is particularly useful in permitting us to view trends over time, a controversial and politically sensitive issue. Since the mid-1990s crime rates, as measured by the BCS, have fallen (Morris 2001: 361; Toynbee and Walker 2005: 215). The results of the 2010 British Crime Survey also demonstrate the continuing fall in crime (Travis 2010) (see Figure 5.2).

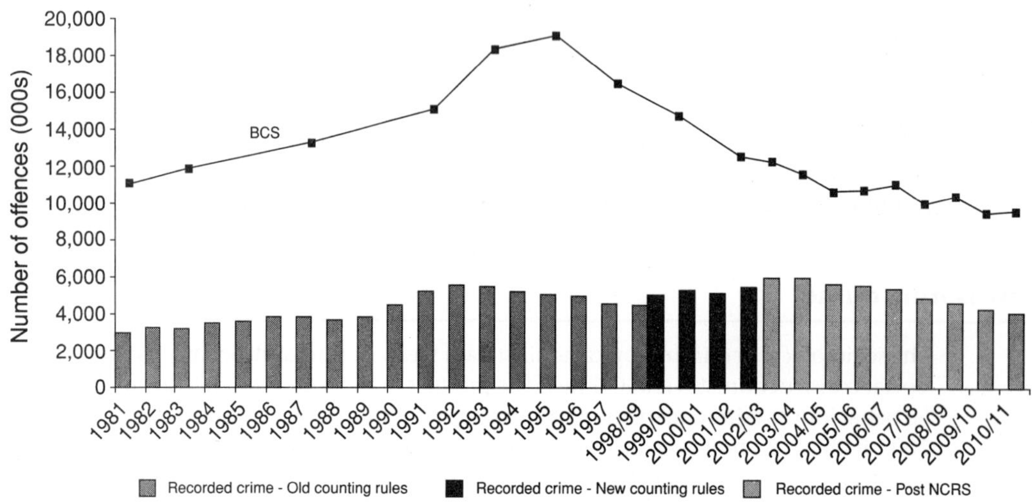

Figure 5.2 Trends in recorded crime and British Crime Survey 1981–2010/11
NCRS: National Crime Recording Standard
Source: Chaplin et al. (2011). Contains public sector information licensed under the Open Government Licence v1.0: www.nationalarchives.gov.uk/doc/open-government-licence.

Have you ever considered crime in the area in which you live? Complete Activity 5.4, which will help you to explore your local crime rates.

Activity 5.4 Local crime in your own area

Public perceptions of crime are now seen as important by policy-makers and those responsible for the delivery of services. This has resulted in new developments in the way in which the public can access crime figures in recent years. One of these new developments is the availability of online crime maps. Police services were first required to publish online crime maps on their websites in January 2009. Since January 2011 similar maps have been available providing even more local 'street-level' data via a single portal.

1. Use the Internet to visit the portal – http://police.uk.
2. Explore the portal to learn more about crime rates in the area where you live.
3. What do your local figures tell you about crime in your area?
4. How does viewing the figures make you feel in relation to both your risks and your safety?

The BCS figures must be regarded as a more accurate guide to the reality of crime by comparison with official figures. On the one hand, it appears to paint a bleaker picture of the incidence of crime – the figure is much higher than the official one – but on the other, recent figures mirror the trend of official figures; in other words, overall declining crime rates. Officially recorded crime is subject to influences – people's changing willingness to report offences; an increase in numbers of police; changing police priorities and practices (for example, greater willingness to deal with domestic violence, rape and racial attacks, which may encourage people to report these things).

Something should be said at this point about the political salience of crime and crime figures. Crime, and law and order, and what is supposed to be happening to them, have become one of the most popular topics for mass media reporting. There is a parallel here with health, and the state of the health services in Britain. It is worth observing that both these highly salient areas are also subject to extensive fictional and dramatic treatment by the broadcast media. Police dramas have always been staple television fare. Pseudo-documentary series such as *Crimewatch* also testify to the public fascination with crime, deviance and law and order. Media scares about the incidence of crime – particularly the claim that crime is 'out of control' – tend to depend on the careless use of official figures rather than crime survey figures.

Governments tend to be on the defensive in relation to issues of law and order, and highly sensitive to them. The issue of the relationship between crime, criminal justice, the media and politics will be explored in more detail in a later section.

The criminal justice process

It is useful to consider the working of the criminal justice system in terms of a *process* through which individuals move from one end to the other, or, more accurately, are lost to the system at various stages. One can examine the various stages – arrest, trial, sentencing, imprisonment or other penalties. Figure 5.3 gives a schematic account of what happens to offenders as the system handles and processes them, taking them in at one end and disposing of them at various possible 'exit points'.

It is important to realize that offenders can exit the system at various points in the process, beginning with the actions of the police. Police *discretion* is in fact one of the most interesting and significant, as well as controversial, aspects of the system.

Discretion, or choice, on the part of front-line officials or 'service providers' is an inherent and unavoidable, and in some respects desirable, aspect of many areas of public policy and social services, including health care, social care, education and, to some extent, means-tested social security. It is intimately bound up with the exercise of professional judgement (in the present context, that of police officers), and with the 'rationing' of scarce resources (in this context 'rationing' simply means the allocation or distribution of some service, good or benefit by a professional or bureaucratic authority rather than by the market).

The so-called 'attrition rate' – the rate of loss of offenders to the system as they proceed through it – is a significant and revealing statistic. It is very high; only a tiny proportion of arrested offenders make it through all the stages – arrest, prosecution, trial, sentencing – to arrive in prison, or some alternative to prison. Once an individual is arrested, the police may choose to *take no further action*, to *caution* or warn a suspect, to *impose a fixed penalty* (in the case of motoring offences) or to bring a *charge* or *summons*. It is only the last of these which sets the offender on a path through the rest of the system. Charges

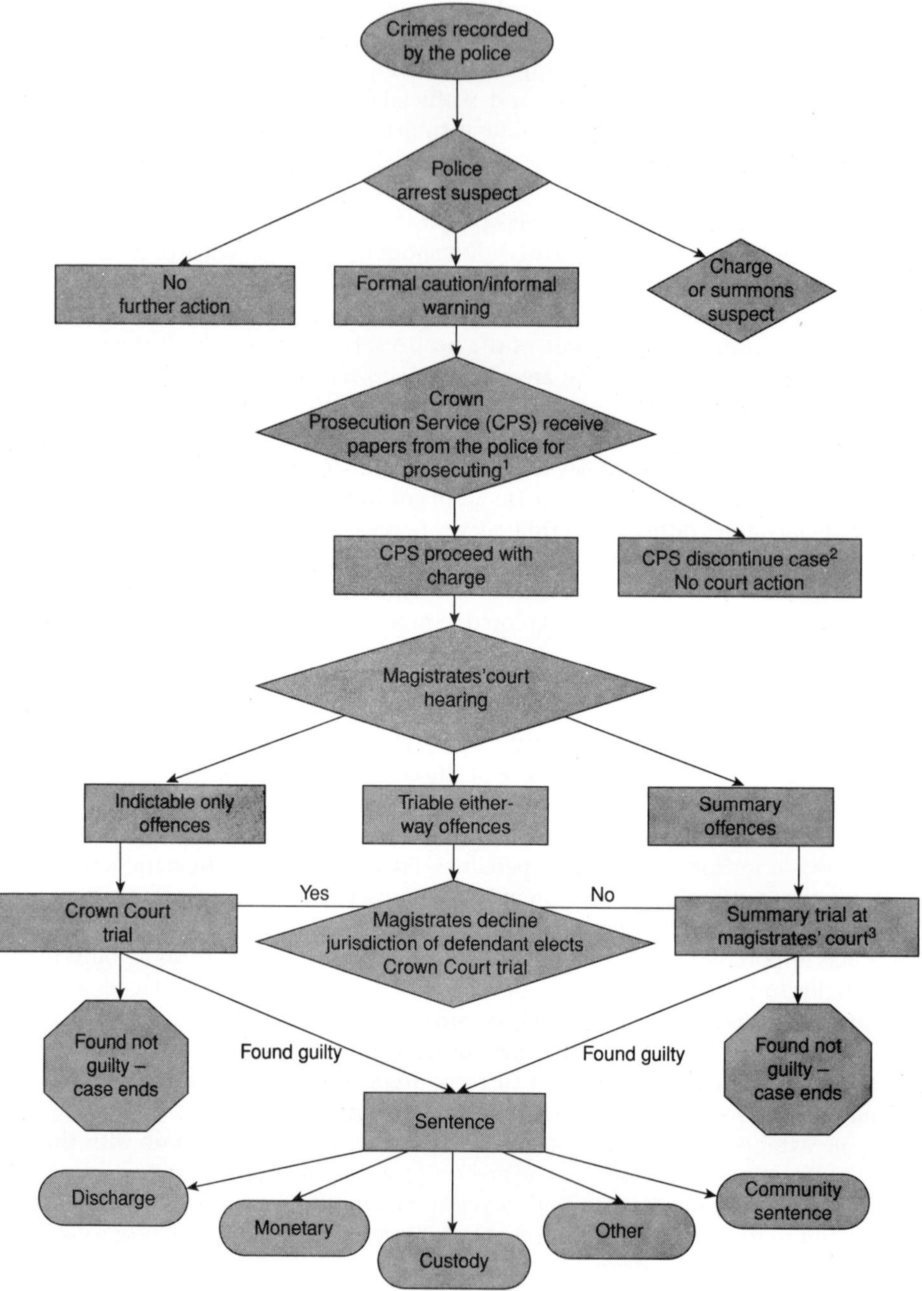

Figure 5.3 The prosecution process

1. Although the majority of prosecutions are handled by the CPS, other organizations can also bring prosecutions.

2. A case will be under continued review, and may be discontinued at any stage before the hearing at the magistrates' court, or the prosecution may offer no evidence. In addition the charge may be altered up to the final decision of the court.

3. Magistrates may commit to the Crown Court for sentence.

Source: Home Office (2000: 4). Contains public sector information licensed under the Open Government Licence v1.0.

are reviewed by the Crown Prosecution Service (CPS), which may decide that there is insufficient evidence for a successful prosecution and discontinue the case (Home Office 2000: 29). The majority of offenders – over 90 per cent – are dealt with in magistrates' courts (Home Office 2000: 18).

Equality and discrimination

These processes are of particular interest in relation to issues of equality and discrimination. There has been much concern, for example, about the numbers of African-Caribbean offenders, and about police stop and search powers which appear to be biased against young African-Caribbean males. Black people are 26 times more likely than white people to be stopped and searched by police in England and Wales (Townsend 2010). It appears, therefore, that non-whites are more likely to be stopped and searched than whites. This may be too hasty, however, and it is necessary to compare age-specific rates of stop and search for different ethnic groups to gain a more accurate picture. Such comparison reveals less of a bias.

Bias, it has been suggested, exists at other levels in the criminal justice system. Thus black people are more likely to be subject to imprisonment than white people, or those from other ethnic minorities. The findings of the Macpherson inquiry, which reported in 1999 on the murder of the black teenager Stephen Lawrence, suggested, controversially, that the police were less responsive to the policing needs of ethnic minorities than they should be (Lea 2003).

A further issue concerns the treatment of 'white-collar' crime in comparison with that of working-class crime. It has been suggested that white-collar crime is taken less seriously than blue-collar offences such as theft, burglary and robbery. White-collar crime includes, for example, fraud, embezzlement and tax evasion. The issue of tax evasion has recently received media attention in the UK, with David Cameron describing it as morally wrong (Palmer 2012). In their first month in office the Coalition Government announced their plans for the development of a new economic crime agency. The National Crime Agency came into force in 2013 led by a Chief Constable and responsible to the Home Secretary. There are also business or corporate crimes: for example, non-compliance with health and safety regulations which may endanger the life and health of workforces or consumers, the evasion of environmental and pollution controls, bribery and corruption. It has been suggested by criminologists of a Marxist persuasion that the criminal justice system is simply a tool for the social control of the working class, the weak and powerless. The 'crimes of the powerful' are overlooked, ignored or generally treated more leniently than are working-class crimes. Wacquant (2009) argues that the poor in Europe and the USA are increasingly subject to regulation by the criminal justice system.

Another issue which has been highlighted in recent accounts of law and order is that of gender, the treatment of men and women offenders, and the particular situation of women as crime victims. Feminists have drawn attention to such issues as rape and domestic violence (Heidensohn 2002: 499–500). It has been argued that the criminal justice system has been reluctant to take these issues as seriously as they deserve, and particular criticism has focused on police behaviour and the treatment of victims of rape and domestic violence. Recent comments made by Ken Clarke, the UK Justice Secretary, caused controversy when he refused to agree with the statement 'rape is rape', which led to calls for his resignation (Bingham 2011), angering both victims and feminists. A related issue is that of children as victims. Paedophilia and physical abuse of children tend to be identified as especially male offences. Crime generally is perceived as a male activity. Women's participation rate is much lower, although it is increasing (Heidensohn 2002: 493–7).

What this suggests is that issues of fairness, justice, equal treatment and nondiscrimination are live and important in the criminal justice system as elsewhere in public policy. The system is of course formally committed to justice in a more explicit way than most areas of public policy. Research seems to suggest that it falls short in various respects.

At this point we should note that a normative framework for the explicit consideration of these issues has been provided by the concept of human rights and the Human Rights Act 1998 (implemented in October 2000). The underlying principles of this legislation are not new. Britain has been a signatory of the European Convention on Human Rights, on which the law is based and whose provisions it incorporates, since 1951. Under its provisions Britons have a right of appeal to the European Court of Human Rights (ECHR) in Strasbourg. (The ECHR is an agency of the Council of Europe, and has nothing to do with the EU. The European Court of Justice, on the other hand, is an EU institution, charged with adjudicating on matters covered by EU law, and quite separate from the ECHR.) For example, the ECHR recently ruled that UK prisoners must be given the right to vote despite historical UK policy in this area which denies them this right (Bowcott 2012). With the advent of the Human Rights Act, appellants may now appear before English courts, rather than having to mount a case at the ECHR and travel to Strasbourg to seek remedy, with a considerable saving in financial and time costs. All UK public agencies, and their actions, must conform to its provisions.

The contemporary politics of law and order

Analysts have argued that the 'landscape' of law and order policy has been transformed since the early 1980s; a prevailing consensus, which was both social-scientific and political, about the nature of crime and crime control has dissipated, to be replaced by a new consensus.

The old consensus, it is suggested, was characterized by a view of crime as conceptually unproblematic, by a causal theory that understood crime as a 'presenting system of deep-seated social problems', and by the idea of crime-control policy as the province of experts and expert knowledge (Loader and Sparks 2002: 84–5). This set of understandings has been undermined and transformed since the 1970s as the result of a number of factors.

First, postwar recorded crime rates have escalated, so that crime has moved from the margins of social life 'to become a routine part of modern consciousness'. This has also involved the discovery of hitherto hidden forms of criminality – domestic violence, sexual and physical abuse of children, racial violence, and environmental pollution (Loader and Sparks 2002: 85).

Second, there have been shifts in social and cultural relations attendant upon the advent of 'late' or 'post-'modernity, involving changes in production and consumption, the family, urban ecology, the media and a 'democratization' of everyday life. These changes have contributed to an increase in opportunities and motivations for crime, as well as a greater concern about the performance and effectiveness of criminal justice agencies (Loader and Sparks 2002: 85).

Third, there have been changes in political ideology with the rise and governmental triumph of the so-called 'New Right' in the Anglophone countries. This, it is argued, has helped both to politicize issues of criminal justice and to undermine the sovereign state's claim to provide security to its citizens.

All these changes, it is argued, have heightened the profile of crime and criminal justice as issues and increased both public anxieties about them and public demands for order (Loader and Sparks 2002: 86). Another way of putting this is to say that there has been an apparent growth of *risk* (in this context, that of being a crime victim) accompanying the advent of a '**risk society**' (Loader and Sparks 2002: 92–5). So the contemporary state is expected to do *more* in the way of guaranteeing security, but paradoxically is trusted *less* in terms of being able to deliver. This is the context in which governments of the right and left have operated since the 1980s.

UK criminal justice: the Coalition Government

In this section we shall explore some aspects of the current politics of criminal justice policy, focusing on the most recent phase of policy under the UK Coalition Government which came into power in 2010.

Criminal justice as an issue had been rising in the political agenda since the 1970s, becoming more salient for voters and political parties. It is striking how little law and order mattered as an election issue before the 1970s (Morris 1989): 'Compared with the contested party politics of the economy, foreign affairs, defence, health, housing and education, those of "law and order" are of remarkably recent origin: they emerged in the mid-1960s and came decisively to the fore in the 1979 election' (Downes and Morgan 2002: 286). Prior to the General Election of 2010, law and order featured highly within all three political parties' manifestos. It was in the 1970s that the Conservative Party recognized that law and order could be an election-winning issue for them. The Conservatives presented themselves as a party that was 'tough on crime' and more successful in the fight against it than the Labour Party. Politicians in general since the 1970s have come to believe, or assert, that crime can be affected by legislative measures or, as one observer put it, that governments can attempt to 'govern through crime' (Loader and Sparks 2002: 86, citing Simon 1997). The Conservatives were seen as the party which could, and did, spend more on the police, prisons and on administering 'short, sharp shocks' to young offenders.

In fact Conservative criminal justice policy between 1979 and the 1990s was rather less punitive than the received image might suggest or lead one to expect. New Labour prior to being elected in 1997 espoused a tough on crime stance too and enacted major early legislation including the Crime and Disorder Act 1998 and the Youth Justice and Criminal Justice Act 1999. They elaborated a comprehensive strategy for crime reduction and prevention based on statutory (i.e. compulsory) partnerships between police and local authorities (Home Office 2000; Faulkner 2001). They included such measures as Anti-Social Behaviour Orders (ASBOs), 'neighbours from hell' provisions, minimum mandatory sentencing for repeat offences and electronic tagging of convicted offenders (Downes and Morgan 2002: 297). Thus, it was suggested by some critics that Labour policy differs little from that of the Conservatives – 'New Labour/Blue Labour' has been the dismissive comment of some observers. Another way of construing this phase of policy, on the other hand, is to see it as a return to a bipartisan consensus on law and order after its abandonment in the 1970s and 1980s. It is just that the grounds of the consensus have shifted 'rightwards'.

The Coalition Government elected in 2010 promised to break away from the 'old politics' and not to focus upon the numbers of those incarcerated, or the use of targets within criminal justice policy (Herbert 2010). Policy from the Coalition Government began with a focus upon the monetary cost of criminal justice provision. The 2010 Spending Review signalled large reductions in public spending including for the Ministry of Justice, which is now faced with cuts of one-quarter from 2014 to 2015 (HM Treasury 2010). This is a marked contrast to the increased spending experienced under the New Labour government, under which police expenditure had increased by 48 per cent in real terms between 1998 and 2009 (Mills et al. 2010). The Coalition Government commissioned an independent review of both remuneration and conditions of service for police officers, which recommended that more than £1bn of savings should be made. Cuts have also been made to the Crown Prosecution Service's budget, and numerous courts have been closed.

There have also been some policy changes to emerge from the *Breaking the Cycle* consultation paper (Ministry of Justice 2010), in which the rehabilitation revolution was outlined. These are summarized in Box 5.2.

Box 5.2 Breaking the Cycle (2010)

- Allows private and voluntary sector providers to deliver criminal justice services, and they are paid via 'payment by results'. This was tested in a range of pilot studies including via the Social Impact Bond at HMP Peterborough.
- Requires that prisoners work full time (this was also in New Labour's manifesto for the 2010 election).
- Establishes that rehabilitation now encompasses diversion services for those who are mentally ill and dealing with drug addiction. Diversion services aim to intervene early to ensure that those in trouble with the law are afforded the most appropriate support and help: for example that those with mental health needs have support and diversion away from the criminal justice system.
- Encourages the use of restorative justice and tougher community penalties.

Thus, the Coalition Government has introduced some new policies, as well as scrapping some existing policies such as ID cards. Payment by results is a mechanism to 'performance manage' organizations delivering criminal justice services. However, despite discussions of a clean break from the New Labour approach, there are still several areas of incremental policy change and re-labelling of existing policy, as shown in Table 5.3.

Table 5.3 Coalition Government criminal justice; new policy or new names?

Area of New Labour policy	Area of Coalition Government policy
Control orders	Control orders have now become terrorist, prevention and investigation measures.
Anti-social Behaviour Orders (ASBOs)	Now replaced with Criminal Behaviour Orders, which are similar to ASBOs: a breach can lead to imprisonment.
Gang Injunctions were introduced by New Labour.	Gang Injunctions came into force in January 2011. They can be used to restrict the movements of individuals who are identified as gang members.

For some the Coalition Government has returned to tough law and order. This can be seen by the harsh approaches taken towards public dissent, though the authorities were much criticized in the aftermath of the 2011 riots for not providing adequate policing and failing to prevent disorder. Prior to the 2011 riots, Home Secretary Theresa May was willing to grant the police more powers and discussed banning hooligans from demonstrations. Pre-emptive measures were also used to stop people protesting prior to the royal wedding in April 2011. Police powers have also been extended, and, as part of the efficiency drive to reduce paperwork, some requirements of the Police and Criminal Evidence Act 1994 have been abolished. While there has been a continuation of policy, the changes that have been made are difficult to evaluate at the time of writing as they have only recently been introduced, or are yet to be implemented.

An assessment

Success or failure in criminal justice policy is hard to establish. Since the causes of criminality 'lie deep in society', as even the Conservatives were prepared to acknowledge in their 1987 election manifesto, dramatic short-term improvements in relevant variables are unlikely and difficult to bring about through legislation and overt policy change, even if it is in politicians' interests to claim otherwise. As we have already noted, crime rates, according to the BCS, have improved since 1995. Chaplin et al. (2011) show that there has been no statistically significant change in the numbers of crime estimated from the 2010/11 British Crime Survey (9.6 million offences) compared to the previous year (9.5 million offences), showing a flattening trend in crime. Overall, the survey showed that crime remained at its lowest levels since the survey was introduced in 1981. Police recorded crime also showed a 4 per cent reduction between 2010/11 (4.2 million offences) and 2009/10 (4.3 million offences), placing it at its lowest level since the National Crime Recording Standard (NCRS) was introduced in April 2002 and mirroring the British Crime Survey.

Explaining these trends has caused debate, with competing hypotheses to explain the drop in crime since the mid-1990s. Theorists have focused upon improved property security, economic influences, social change, use of CCTV and other local crime reduction initiatives and changes in policing and the wider criminal justice system.

This pattern of falling crime in the UK is generally shared across other high-income countries as well. While there is support for the impact of improved vehicle and household security as explanations, there is little consensus on the impact of other factors. For example, in the USA prison incarceration was seen as a driver of downward crime trends, while in Canada this influence has been largely discounted (Chaplin et al. 2011).

There remains a strong link between drug and alcohol consumption and crime rates; recent crime statistics show that in 45 per cent of all violent crimes the victims believed their attackers had been drinking, and 37 per cent of domestic violence cases involve alcohol. In 2007–08, more than a million crimes involved alcohol use in some way (Directgov 2012). The issue of weekend 'binge drinking' by the young in town and city centres, to some extent a classic 'moral panic', has long gripped media and public imagination. New Labour policy in this area was inconsistent because the government, consistent with a policy of prosperity-enhancing economic deregulation, legislated to liberalize regulations on drinking hours, thus apparently increasing access to alcohol. The Coalition Government, following policy change in Scotland, has proposed a minimum price of 40p per unit for alcohol within Britain, as part of its approach to tackling binge drinking and associated issues such as crime. The Government published an alcohol strategy on 23 March 2012, stating that legislation for a minimum unit price would be introduced as soon as possible, but this was abandoned in the subsequent budget in 2013.

The Coalition Government's approach to criminal justice policy, much like New Labour's, still holds to the 'prison works' philosophy. Originally planning to offer jail sentence discounts for early guilty pleas, the Coalition Government has now instead outlined plans to hand out a greater number of life sentences and increase the amount of time serious offenders spend in prison, in what some have described as a major policy U-turn. The plan to offer 50 per cent sentence discounts to offenders submitting early guilty pleas has now been abandoned, with the media accusing the government of engaging in 'soft justice' (Mulholland 2011).

Conclusion

Much of the improvement as has been noted since 1997 in crime statistics cannot be attributed to the government's criminal justice policy. Causes may include, for example, changes in demography (shrinkage in the 'at risk' age group – essentially young males – with the passing of the 'baby boom' generational cohort and subsequent decline in birth rates since the 1980s), and greater economic prosperity and growth in individual incomes as a result of the striking decline in UK unemployment since 1993, a period of uninterrupted economic growth. In the latter case, the achievement of macro-economic stability through inflation **targeting**, and improvements in labour market efficiency and flexibility are the result of the last two UK governments, both Conservative and New Labour. As yet the economic recession does not appear to be significantly shifting crime rates. The Coalition Government policy is also not radically shifting from the New Labour project on crime which began in 1997, although there are some areas of difference such as the payment by results system for rehabilitation. However, given the large-scale changes in government policy, particularly the reduction of public spending in several areas, the long-lasting effects of the Coalition Government's policy on crime rates has yet to be seen.

Summary of key points

- Criminal justice policy is a difficult area, with many overlapping areas related to crime. Measuring crime is complex and problematic.
- Social control and power are central to criminal justice policy. However in the nation state global issues are increasingly relevant for those making criminal justice policy.
- Law and order policy is largely an area of policy continuation, with some extension of market principles and 'payment by results' by the Coalition Government.

Key terms and concepts

Coalition Government, UK
comparative analysis
convergence
deterrence
due process
globalization
human rights
penal–welfare state
policy learning
rehabilitation
risk society
rule of law
theories of crime

Suggestions for further reading

Franko, K. (2008) *Globalization and Crime.* London: Sage.

This book explores crime in the context of an increasingly connected world. It links theories of globalization with crime in exploring a range of topical issues such as terrorism, trafficking and global surveillance. The book also examines a range of responses to these issues.

Knepper, P. (2007) *Criminology and Social Policy.* London: Sage.

In this lively and engaging text, the author discusses the difference social policy makes, or can make, in any response to crime. He also considers the contribution of criminology to the debates on major social policy areas, such as housing, education, employment, health and family. The book provides criminology students with an understanding of key social policy issues, and introduces criminological theory to social policy students.

Maguire, M., Morgan, R. and Reiner, R. (2007) *The Oxford Handbook of Criminology.* 4th edition. Oxford: Oxford University Press.

This is the most comprehensive single text on the subject. It provides a history of the discipline, outlines different theoretical perspectives and covers all key areas related to crime; the criminal justice process, race and gender, crime statistics, and the media and crime. The book also has an associated Online Resource Centre, allowing students to further research the subject.

Pakes, F. (2010) *Comparative Criminal Justice.* 2nd edition. Devon: Willan Publishing.

This book examines the ways different countries and jurisdictions deal with the criminal justice process, from policing through to sentencing. Examples are taken from all over the world, with a particular focus on Europe, the UK, the USA and Australasia. The book also discusses global trends such as the rise of imprisonment, penal populism, diversion, international policing and international tribunals. Throughout the book, the role of globalization is considered.

Useful websites

EU: http://ec.europa.eu/dgs/home-affairs/what-we-do/policies/organized-crime-and-human-trafficking/crime-prevention/index_en.htm.

Visit the EU website for more information on member states' activities in relation to crime prevention, and associated social policies.

United Nations Office on Drugs and Crime: www.unodc.org.

UNODC has a role in assisting member states in tackling illicit drugs, crime and terrorism. The agency has a particular commitment to counter the world drug problem and to take concerted action against international terrorism. The website details the work the agency does and its publications.

6 Who gets what? Slicing the welfare cake

Key learning outcomes

By the end of this chapter you should:

- be able to understand the field of welfare policy
- be able understand the way in which decisions about resource allocation associated with welfare are made
- be able to comparatively discuss UK welfare policy

Overview of the chapter

This chapter gives an overview of welfare policy within the UK, discussing the key question of how the resources and services of the welfare system are shared out: in short, who gets what. As we saw in Chapter 2, important decisions about equality and need have to be taken by policy-makers, especially if social policies are aiming to reduce problems of poverty and social exclusion. Also, as Chapter 3 showed, these questions are not new. They have preoccupied governments and people since the early days of the Poor Law and the beginnings of organized social policy. This chapter will explore how dilemmas such as 'who gets what' are resolved. This chapter examines these choices within the UK context, and compares these to policy approaches used in other contexts.

What are the benefits of the welfare system?

The policy dilemmas or choices that face governments in deciding 'who gets what' can be summarized in two ways. First, there are choices to be made about *distribution* and possibly about *redistribution* of services, resources and money. And second, there are choices to be made about *funding* the welfare system and deciding who will contribute and how much they will pay. These choices are now currently being made in a context of recession or at best sluggish economic growth. The Coalition Government has stressed the need to make savings in public spending related to welfare. The Coalition has also made its ideological stance clear in arguing that the current system needs reform because it has two key problems; work incentives are poor, and the system is too complex (DWP 2013).

Choices around welfare provision are indeed complex as they focus upon a range of different areas including 'regulatory', 'distributive' and 'redistributive' public policies

(Lowi 1966; see also Blank and Burau 2004: 16). Lowi defined 'regulation' as the government's way of controlling, constraining or modifying the actions and behaviour of individuals and groups. 'Distribution' means providing some good or benefit to individuals collectively, through government action. 'Redistribution' means changing, by means of collective government action, the distribution of some good or benefit among individuals. These areas of welfare policy are illustrated in more detail in Table 6.1.

Table 6.1 An overview of welfare policy types

Policy area	Key features	Examples
Distributive and redistributive policies	Major social programmes providing benefits in cash or kind, and the revenue-raising system which pays for them.	• NHS • The education, social security and tax systems
Regulation and control	Policies and law through which the government promotes social control.	• Criminal justice is one clear policy area • Main aim of policies is to regulate the agencies providing social welfare, and to regulate individual behaviour (e.g. anti-smoking policies and health)

There are also further policy dilemmas associated with the provision of welfare, as illustrated in Box 6.1 – those of deciding how to *fund* the welfare system are key to an understanding of social policy. Directly or indirectly, therefore, the costs and benefits of the welfare system affect everyone. How far, and in what ways, people are affected will of course vary according to individual circumstances. Some people are totally dependent on welfare benefits for their incomes, while others receive no social security benefits and may make little or no use of public services.

Box 6.1 Important debates in policy related to welfare funding

- What is a basic human need? This is often open to interpretation (see Chapter 2).
- How can welfare policy ensure that all members of society have access to basic human needs and entitlements?
- Who benefits from the welfare system?
- It is just as important to ask, 'who pays for it?' It is important to reflect upon how much is paid by individuals and groups, and how much of the nation's wealth is spent on welfare. These issues have implications for people's attitudes towards the welfare system.
- How should welfare be funded? Should welfare funding be derived from taxation? Should the private sector provide funding? Should there be a mixture of provision, known commonly as a 'mixed economy' approach?
- How should welfare services be delivered and by whom? Should there be state provision? What is the role of the family? What about the role of the market?
- Should welfare policy attempt to tackle inequalities? Can welfare services address inequalities?

The notion of dependency associated with welfare provision has been well documented in the media and policy circles, and there is much debate about fairness and equity in welfare provision. While the media and politicians oversimplify these issues, portraying the beneficiaries of the welfare state as those who are not able to find employment the reality is much more complex. A career-minded childless couple, for instance, may have little or no interest in a public service such as primary education. If they plan never to have children they may resent having to pay taxes to support services they never intend to use. However, when they go shopping, visit their doctor or work with colleagues, they are indirectly experiencing the results or benefits of the education system. They are relying on the schools to have taught certain skills (reading, writing, numeracy and perhaps some technical skills) to each of the people they come into contact with. The education system may do this well or badly, and its efficiency should be of as much concern to the childless couple as to anyone else. Even though they cannot be said to be benefitting directly from the education system as parents with school-age children, they are nevertheless receiving various indirect benefits.

The very rich could also be seen as a group that might question the value of publicly provided welfare. Their children attend elite private schools, when in need of medical care they use private hospitals and they are sheltered by company welfare schemes that subsidize pensions and housing costs. Again, such people do not directly use the state system of welfare, and may therefore gain little or nothing of direct benefit from it. They pay taxes that contribute to the running of state schools and hospitals, but if they do not use the public services they do not personally regain any of the money they have contributed towards them.

However, the issue of the better off benefitting from welfare systems remains hidden because this is a complex area (Orton 2008). There are some clear examples in which the better-off are benefitting from welfare provision in the relation to health care, for instance, in what is termed 'the inverse care law'. Those on lower incomes use health services less, relative to their needs, and often have less voice in relation to influencing services once they have been accessed (Dixon et al. 2003). Differential gains have also been recorded in secondary education, with those on higher incomes being able to afford to buy homes in the catchment areas of better-performing schools. Indeed, the very rich also gain substantial indirect benefits from a public system of welfare. The doctor who treats a rich patient in a (private) hospital will probably have been trained at public expense. The roads upon which affluent people travel are publicly funded (except for a few private tolls on roads and crossing points). Those who own and control businesses depend on the welfare state being able to pick up the bill for health care for their employees. The public welfare system also helps to maintain the 'social fabric' and to prevent or minimize breakdowns of law and order. This is a function that benefits everyone, but particularly those who have most to lose. These benefits, termed **'external benefits'** by economists, go beyond individual gains or payoffs.

Nor are the benefits of a fully developed welfare system necessarily restricted to externalities, as far as the rich are concerned. The well-off also derive *direct* benefits from the welfare system. Where social security pays out universal benefits (paid to everyone automatically, irrespective of means), the better-off do regain some of the money they have paid into the system: for instance, in the form of the state retirement pension. The amounts involved may be peanuts to the rich, but they symbolize principles of being included, and of citizenship, that were established when the welfare state was launched in the 1940s. However, media images tend to not focus upon these aspects of the benefits system. Complete Activity 6.1 to explore media constructions.

Activity 6.1 The media and constructions of welfare

View the following media reports:

'Iain Duncan Smith: poverty is not solved by just more money', *The Telegraph*, 2012 www.telegraph.co.uk/news/politics/9331036/Iain-Duncan-Smith-poverty-is-not-solved-by-just-more-money.html

'Curing the cancer of welfare dependency', *The Daily Mail*, 2012 www.dailymail.co.uk/debate/article-2174074/Curing-cancer-welfare-dependency.html

1. What are these reports saying about welfare provision, and what can this tell us about how is it being represented in the media?
2. Do you think that the media reports related to welfare are fair and unbiased?
3. Consider your own personal views related to welfare provision and think about the ways in which you have personally benefited.
4. Now read the following media report: 'Sociologist urges a wider view of the welfare state', *The Guardian*, 2012, www.guardian.co.uk/society/2012/mar/20/wider-view-welfare-state. Do you agree with the points being made?

Should benefits and services be selective or universal?

Having completed Activity 6.1, you will now be aware that universal benefits, and the principle of citizenship that underpins them, are now increasingly questioned within the UK context. There have been arguments that benefits for all should be phased out in favour of targeting welfare benefits on the poor and those in greatest need. These benefits are termed *selective benefits* because they are provided selectively – that is, only to those people whose incomes have been assessed (means tested) and have been found to be below a certain level. However, as long as universal benefits and 'free' services remain (such as those provided by the NHS), middle-class and affluent people will be able to receive and use them even though they could afford to do without them or could pay for services out of their own pockets.

To those who support universal benefits, the drawback of providing 'free' services or cash benefits to everyone, including the better-off, is outweighed by the drawbacks of changing to a more selective, means-tested system. If higher-income taxpayers feel excluded from the welfare state they have a strong incentive to avoid paying taxes, and some will go to great lengths to do so. Thus there is a danger that abandoning universal benefits and a common approach to paying for welfare and health services will quickly take us towards a more divided society. Tax avoidance by those who are rich is an area that has recently begun to receive policy attention. The issue of tax avoidance is, however, a global concern and arguably means that countries lose revenue that could be used for service provision, including welfare (see Shaxon 2011). Attachment to the old ideal of universal welfare has traditionally been accompanied by fears of a return to widespread means testing. This is particularly the case in what used to be called the Labour Party's 'heartlands' – industrial areas of Britain, many of which are now in economic decline and have above-average rates of poverty. Despite these concerns, many commentators have found flaws with the universal principle, including the previous New Labour government, which attempted to reform the system. As Frank Field, who was given the task of rethinking social security, said:

> Welfare is therefore having the opposite effect from that for which it was devised [...] Welfare fraud now acts as an expelling agent, encouraging people into criminal activity. (Field 1995: 27)

Thus, while means testing is not without its flaws, the provision of universal benefits is also problematic. Toynbee refers to state pensions as an example of social security where targeted, means-tested benefits are preferable to an extension of universal benefits. She argues that across-the-board increases in state pensions would represent a 'regressive, non-redistributive and unsocialist policy' based on 'a dead old idea of a national insurance principle that never actually delivered' (Toynbee 2000: 19). The problem with selectivity, or targeting, is that such an approach involves means testing and the evidence is that many pensioners will not undergo means tests to claim extra benefits due to them. Debates have more recently been seen in relation to the universal provision of child benefit payments, which have now been amended by the Coalition Government on the basis of a more selective delivery of the payments. Thus from April 2013, families with one parent earning more than £50,000 will no longer be eligible to claim the total amount of child benefit and those earning £60,000 or more will lose all of their child benefit. This creates the anomaly that a family with two parents earning £40,000 each will keep all of their child benefit with a total household income of £80,000, while neighbours where one parent stays at home and the other earns £50,000 or more will lose out (Woodcock 2012). These examples show how opinion on the respective merits of universal and selective benefits continues to be sharply divided. The main arguments both for and against universalism and selectivism are summarized in Box 6.2.

Box 6.2 Arguments for and against selectivism and universalism

Selective benefits	*Universal benefits*
Arguments for	
Income support and benefits only given to those who need them	Inclusive: high take-up among people in eligible groups (for example, parents)
Efficient: they allow more money to be targeted on low-income families	Efficient: minimum of bureaucracy and administration costs
Reduce demand for welfare and allow public spending to be reduced or contained	Promote citizenship and sense of social unity
Arguments against	
Means testing involves complex procedures and claim forms: low take-up likely; high administration costs	Lack fairness: benefits 'wasted' on the better-off where taxes on earned incomes are low
Means testing may involve social disgrace and stigma; low take-up likely	Encourage welfare dependency and over-reliance on the state
If all benefits are related to income (means tested), a rise in income disqualifies people from benefit, acting as a disincentive to work (the poverty trap)	Wasteful: even if people improve their income, they continue to receive universal benefits

It is difficult – and perhaps rather pointless – to try to conclude that either means-tested or universal benefits would be preferable throughout the social security system. The previous New Labour government moved away from universal benefits towards more selective, or targeted, benefits. This trend has also continued under the current Coalition Government.

Gainers and losers: individuals and groups

To suggest that 'everyone benefits' from an extensive and expensive welfare system is to miss the point that some benefit much more than others do. In this chapter, we examine how there are 'gaining' and 'losing' groups in terms of how much people gain from, or lose out in paying for, the services and cash benefits of the welfare system.

The groups that stand out as either gaining or losing out in the welfare system are, first of all, income groups or – more broadly – social class groups. For instance, one way of picturing 'gainers' and 'losers' would be to think of three broad social class groups such as the rich, those on middling or average incomes, and the poor. More complicated (and accurate) divisions of social class can be constructed in order to understand inequalities between people, and the relative amounts they gain from the welfare system. Another way of looking at 'gaining' and 'losing' groups is to examine the effect of gender divisions. Do women get more out of the welfare system than men, or vice versa?

There are yet other social divisions and inequalities in the welfare system and in the wider society of which it is a part. For instance, there are divisions of age, race and ethnicity, sexual orientation, and inequalities between disabled and non-disabled people. A central question to be applied to all these social divisions is whether, or how far, the welfare system *redistributes* resources between groups. There are several possibilities.

1. The welfare system has a neutral role. It does not redistribute resources between groups to any significant degree, and its overall effect is to leave existing inequalities largely untouched.
2. The welfare system has a 'Robin Hood' role, affecting the whole spectrum of society, redistributing from the rich or better-off groups to those on average incomes and to the poor.
3. The welfare system acts like the Sheriff of Nottingham, redistributing from the poorer to the better-off sections of society. For instance, poorer and average-income groups may have to pay higher proportions of their incomes in tax and at the same time might fail to claim all the benefits they are entitled to, or underuse 'free' services.
4. There is also a possibility that the welfare system *partially* redistributes. Redistribution takes place, but within a limited range of groups. For instance, the poorest groups may take more out of the system than they are able to put into it, but the majority of people on middle incomes might be paying more than their fair share, while the rich escape with a relatively light tax burden. If this were the case, redistribution would be from the middle to the bottom, not from the top to the middle and bottom groups.
5. It is also likely that different parts of the welfare system will play different roles. For instance, the education system may play a 'Sheriff of Nottingham' role (if more is spent per head on middle-class children than those from lower- or working-class backgrounds), while social security may be a 'Robin Hood'. Or, *within* a service such as education, there may be different effects. Primary education, for instance, may have the effect of transferring resources from the better-off to the less well-off (if more is spent on inner-city schools than schools in affluent suburbs), while higher education – which people from the poorest backgrounds hardly use – may achieve the opposite.

Indeed, welfare provision across the world is disparate in terms of provision of services and the role that it plays in relation to redistribution, as Table 6.2 demonstrates.

Table 6.2 Comparative global welfare provision

Country	Welfare provision	Redistribution role of welfare
Cuba	Full responsibility rests on government to fund and deliver social entitlements. Cuba has a universal and free health, education and welfare system.	Socialist approach to welfare policy in which equity across society has been emphasized as well as universal access. Cuba has historically been committed to redistribution.
USA	Adopts a neo-liberal approach to policy and welfare provision, with welfare provided mostly by private providers. Some welfare retrenchment under the previous Bush administration; removal of the aid to families with dependent children programme.	Improved redistribution by President Obama's administration in relation to health care; Affordable Health Care Act became law in 2010, in an attempt to reduce health inequalities. Some partial redistribution.
Scandinavian countries	The Nordic model is another model of welfare implemented in countries such as Norway, Sweden, Denmark, Iceland and Finland. This approach is underpinned by social democratic principles and provides a comprehensive government-funded welfare system. Generally there are good unemployment benefits and equality of provision is key.	Provision is funded by progressive taxation, which is higher taxation of the greatest earners. Model of a redistributive approach.
Sub-Saharan African countries (except South Africa)	A range of welfare programmes exist across the continent but, given the disparity of state provision, welfare is often provided by local communities and family members in the absence of adequate state support.	Many excluded from what little welfare provision exists; thus there is an unequal system of provision that does not redistribute.

Three further points about the economics of welfare need to be borne in mind. The first two concern the nature of our contributions to the welfare system, *taxation* and *care*. The third relates to the importance of keeping a *perspective on the individual* as well as on groups in society, as far as 'gaining' and 'losing' from the welfare system are concerned.

Contributions: taxation

As mentioned earlier in this chapter, it is as important to consider how much people have to pay for welfare through the taxation system as it is to consider how much benefit they receive from the services they use. Table 6.2 highlights how some countries have a more progressive approach to taxation, which is used to fund welfare provision.

First, *tax relief* may be as important as a social security benefit in protecting the interests of better-off people. For instance, tax relief on occupational and private pension contributions makes a substantial difference to the incomes and spending power of many in the middle classes. It represents a hidden form of welfare benefit and an example of 'fiscal welfare', as discussed by Titmuss (see Chapter 1).

Income tax and national insurance (NI) contributions are *direct* taxes that by and large are argued to be *progressive*. Only those in work pay NI contributions, so that older people in retirement, among a number of other groups, are a significant section of the community who do not have to make this additional contribution. The more someone earns, the more they will be paying for commonly used services and benefits. In effect, a person who pays the top rate of tax and uses a 'free' NHS hospital service, for instance, has paid substantially more for that service than someone who has been paying a lower rate of tax. The net effect is to subsidize the hospital care of the lower earner and to transfer resources to that patient. However, the degree to which direct taxes are progressive varies. Some commentators argue that in the UK since the 1980s, the taxation system was shifted from progressive to regressive; current tax burdens fall more heavily on lower-income groups. Due to the existence of loopholes in the law allowing those who earn more to pay proportionally less tax as well as their use of tax havens (Lansley 2011), the richest in the UK are able to avoid paying as much tax, proportionally, as those in lower-income groups. High rates of direct tax upon low-income wage earners are thus unfair, as a relatively large proportion of their income will disappear in this way.

Furthermore, there is a range of *indirect* taxes in the UK, which are nearly always *regressive*, though again there are exceptions, depending on the items that are taxed. Indirect taxes such as those on cigarettes and alcohol, and value added tax (VAT) are placed on goods and services. They tend to be regressive because everyone, whether a high or low earner, must pay the same rate of tax. As a result, the better-off person loses a much lower proportion of their income through indirect taxes than the average or lower-income person. In Britain, the bottom fifth of households in income terms paid 20 per cent of their expenditure in indirect taxation, while the top fifth paid 15 per cent; therefore indirect taxes take a higher proportion of income from those with lower incomes (ONS 2011a). Given the financial challenges facing many countries, there have been a number of proposals to increase indirect taxation as a mechanism through which to increase income. For example, the Japanese government has tried to pass a bill to increase sales-related tax, and governments in China and India are also considering such moves (BBC News 2012e). This has implications for poverty and inequality across the world, because if better-off people make extensive use of certain public services, such as NHS hospitals in Britain, and those services are increasingly paid for by indirect taxation, we may well find that poorer taxpayers are subsidizing the better-off. This pattern will become more pronounced the more taxation is shifted from the direct to the indirect type. One exception to this regressive effect occurs if heavy indirect taxes are levied on purchases of luxury items or very expensive goods such as large motor cars, yachts or diamonds. In this case, better-off people will pay more tax than the average and low-income groups, for whom the luxury items are unaffordable. The effects of tax on people's incomes should not be considered in isolation. It is important to think about the way in which taxes *and* benefits (both cash benefits and 'benefits in kind', such as education and health services) together affect the final income of a household (see Figure 6.1 and Table 6.3).

Table 6.3 Direct and indirect taxes as percentages of gross income, 2009/10, in Great Britain (non-retired households grouped into five income bands)

	Bottom fifth	Second	Third	Fourth	Top fifth
All direct taxes	10.2	11.5	16.6	20.1	24.4
All indirect taxes	25.3	18.1	15.3	12.9	9.3
All taxes	35.5	29.6	31.9	32.9	33.7

Source: Adapted from ONS (2011a).

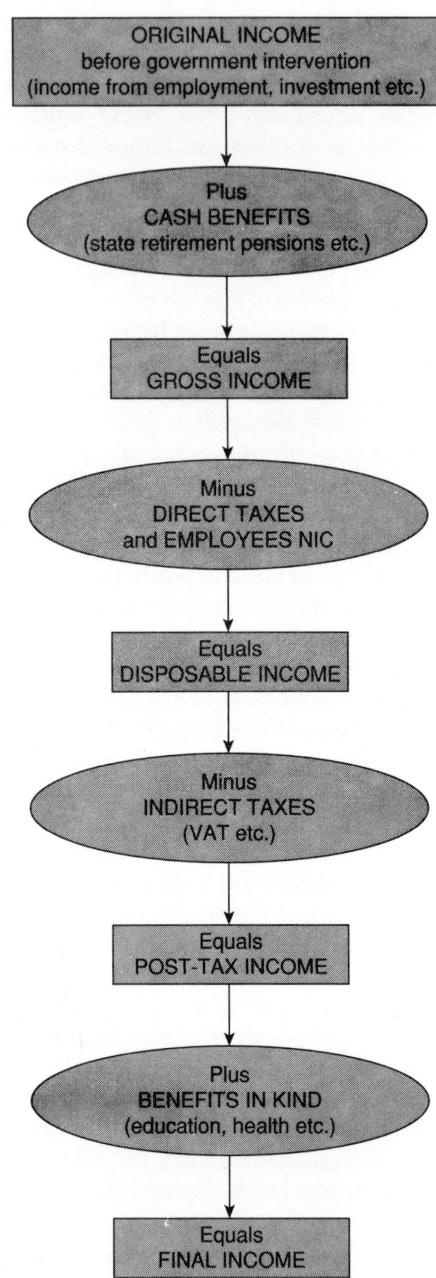

Figure 6.1 The effects of taxes and benefits on household income (reproduced by kind permission of the Office for National Statistics)
Source: Economic Trends No. 494, December 1994: 9, Crown Copyright ©

Contributions: care

A second point to bear in mind is that contributions to the welfare system are not just made in the form of money, through taxation. Economics focuses on the more easily measurable or 'objective' data – flows of money, goods and services to and from people, and to and from the various parts of the welfare system such as the health service and social services. But contributions in kind, or in unpaid domestic work, can often be missed in these measures. Taking into account only how much money people either gain or contribute to the welfare system will give an incomplete picture. By caring for relatives or a partner, people are contributing time, physical effort and emotional commitment to meeting welfare needs that otherwise the public welfare system might have to meet.

If the time and effort devoted to informal care are taken into account, the picture of who gains and loses from the welfare system changes considerably. As Ungerson (1987) and other researchers on family and **community care** have noted, women are more frequently expected to care for relatives (other than spouses) than men, and they often do so from a sense of duty. The enormous contribution to the welfare system made by family carers and volunteers raises many moral and practical questions about whether, or how much, carers should be paid for their contributions, a point that is mentioned again in relation to community care in Chapter 12.

Keeping a perspective on the individual

Although we have begun by focusing on groups (social classes, men and women, and so on) as 'gainers' or 'losers' in the great welfare distribution game, it is important not to lose sight of the individual.

Thinking about an individual's life course sheds a different light on the distribution of welfare. An individual will switch from one category or group to another during their life. Individuals might become seriously ill or be made redundant, for instance, and thus find that they become net recipients of, rather than net contributors to, the welfare system. This perspective is important, because it shows that although the welfare system might fail to distribute resources or services fairly between various groups, it might nevertheless succeed in redistributing resources from the well to the sick, from those who are employed to the unemployed, and from younger to older people.

This type of thinking lay behind another of the fundamental principles of the 1940s welfare state – the insurance principle. From an individual's point of view, the welfare system was to be thought of as a huge savings bank. For most of a person's working career, the equivalent of perhaps only £60 in services and cash benefits would be regained for every £100 'lost' in taxation and NI contributions. However, in times of need, the balance changes. Resources contributed during the 'productive' part of life are drawn upon to meet needs in a dependent phase of life.

In practice, the funding of the social security system and of welfare services does not work on the strict principles of insurance envisaged by Beveridge, the chief architect of the 1940s welfare system (see Chapter 3). Although the notion of a self-funded insurance scheme is a myth, however, the idea of an individual 'losing' or contributing and 'gaining' or receiving at different points of the life cycle is a valuable one. Historically this has led to public support for the welfare state and a willingness to tolerate taxation even when a majority are not net gainers from the system at any one point in time. However, recent research suggests that attitudes are now changing. Complete Activity 6.2 to explore changing contemporary attitudes to welfare.

Activity 6.2 Changing public attitudes to UK welfare provision

Use the Internet to visit the British Social Attitudes Survey and to look at the 29th report, published in 2012: http://bsa-29.natcen.ac.uk/read-the-report/welfare/introduction.aspx. Read the chapter summary associated with welfare as a starting point. You can also download the full chapter for a more detailed overview. View the brief slide-show detailing how attitudes have been changing.

- What does the British Social Attitudes Survey tell you about perceptions associated with UK welfare provision?
- Do you think that the recession has affected trends in attitudes? What other influences may there be? For example, think about the media's shaping of public views (and Activity 6.1), as well as political ideology and discourse.

Attitudes to welfare are also related to views on the economy and ideas about how much should be spent on welfare.

How large is the welfare cake?

Before we look at the way in which the welfare cake is sliced and at 'who gets what', we need to look briefly at the size of the cake itself and understand how welfare spending is connected to economic growth.

When an economy grows (that is, when the gross domestic product or GDP – all the goods and services produced in the country – is increasing), it is possible for government to spend larger amounts of money each year without raising the burden of taxation. If the economy stops growing or even shrinks, as is happening at the time of writing, fewer goods and services are produced, less taxation can be gathered and the government must do one or more of the following things:

- borrow money to fund the shortfall in its tax revenues,
- increase taxes, or
- reduce public spending.

In the long term, even a relatively slow-growing economy will create a significant increase in the resources available to government. For instance, a growth of 2 per cent per annum will increase the nation's wealth by a quarter over 12 years (that is, a real increase of between 24 and 26 per cent). Some industrial economies grow at a much faster rate than this. At 4 per cent growth per annum a country's wealth and income would grow by a half over the same period of 12 years.

If the population grows as quickly as the economy, however, the per capita (per head) wealth of the country will not increase and, if population growth outstrips economic growth, wealth per head will actually decline. In some parts of Africa, for instance, economic growth has been sluggish or non-existent and population growth rapid, so that standards of living in those countries have declined to the level of the 1950s.

While steady economic growth has meant some financial stability in terms of welfare provision across Europe in recent years, demographic changes have resulted in more demands upon existing welfare systems. For example, in the UK there are increasing numbers of people outside the labour force: older people, rising numbers of unemployed people and younger people who remain in the education system for longer periods than before. Indeed, the recession has added to job insecurity and instability for many individuals, with clear financial consequences evident at the individual level, and in terms of welfare provision. Stratton and Kowelle (2012) argue that rising unemployment will cost the government at least £1.5bn more than expected in welfare benefits. Indeed, rising government spending in the UK has led to austerity measures being introduced by the Coalition Government, who have argued that public spending needs to be slashed in order to reduce national debt.

Table 6.4 shows how general public expenditure has risen over previous years, and this is the case whether we look at this as increases in the actual sums of money spent (billions of pounds) or as **real increases**. A real increase translates expenditure years ago into the value of money now, or recently, by allowing for inflation and devaluation.

Table 6.4 Total managed expenditure in the UK in billions of pounds

Year	Amount (billion £)
1996/7	311.4
1998/9	315.9
1999/2000	322.0
2000/1	330.9
2001/2	343.0
2002/3	364.0
2003/4	389.2
2004/5	421.1
2005/6	455.6
2006/7	492.5
2007/8	524.2
2008/9	550.1
2009/10	582.7
2010/11	620.7

Adapted from HM Treasury (2011)

Thus we are now spending far more actual money on roads, law and order, education, social security, health services and other things than in previous years. The table conceals as much as it reveals, however, because only a few years are selected. Historically, there have been considerable fluctuations in spending as a share of GDP or national income. During the 1980s and 1990s, for instance, there were periods of low growth and high unemployment. In these circumstances the public spending share will naturally rise.

The Coalition Government's austerity plans, however, did not succeed in cutting public expenditure overall, in the first two years that they were in power (Glover 2012). The issue is the planned increases for the future of public spending, because public expenditure is predicted to rise in cash terms (taking inflation into account) over the life of the parliament. In 2010–11, it stood at £696 billion; it is projected to be £744 billion in 2015–16 (Glover 2012).

Historically, largely as a result of economic growth (but also including some gains from the sell-off or privatization of state-run services and assets), British governments have managed to fund much of the real increase in public spending without devoting a greater share of the nation's wealth to public spending. The economic cake had been growing. However, now it is not, there are concerns about the growing debt that the UK has acquired.

General government expenditure covers a wide variety of items and services. Some substantial government priorities lie outside the field of welfare or social policy, as traditionally defined: for instance, defence, trade and industry, agriculture, forestry, fisheries and food.

Table 6.5 gives an idea of the government's spending priorities and how the money is divided between 'social' expenditure (social security, health, education and so on) and other services. These priorities are not set in stone, and it is important to remember that the *proportions* of public money devoted to some areas have been declining in recent years (for instance, defence, housing), while they have been rising in others (for example, social protection).

Table 6.5 Total expenditure on services in billions of pounds, 2008–9 to 2011–12

	2008–9 outturn	2009–10 outturn	2010–11 outturn	2011–12 outturn
Defence	37	38	39	39
Public order and safety	34	34	33	32
Housing and community amenities	15	16	13	10
Health	110	118	121	121
Education	83	88	92	92
Social protection	205	225	232	242
General public services	52	52	67	69

Adapted from ONS (2012d)

Table 6.5 shows how government spending is static or declining in some areas such as defence, law and order, housing and education, but steadily increasing in health and social protection (welfare benefit provision). The current Coalition Government has announced significant spending cuts in public services and benefits with the passing of the Welfare Reform Act in 2012. This has led to concerns about impacts upon the poorest families in the UK and other at-risk groups such as the disabled (Ross 2012).

Social security: who benefits?

There are basically two kinds of social security benefit: **non-contributory benefits** and grants (which people qualify for on grounds of need or because they fall into a particular category, such as parents or children) and **contributory benefits**, which are based on the principle of insurance. People are eligible for these if they have paid into – contributed towards – the benefits system through NI (or have had credits paid on their behalf by the government or employer).

Non-contributory benefits

Non-contributory benefits are either income-related (conditional on a means test of some kind) or non-income-related – that is, paid irrespective of the level of income a person has. Historically these have included benefits such as attendance allowance and disability living allowance, although other non-income-related benefits include war pension, severe disablement allowance, industrial injuries disablement benefit and disability working allowance. None of these benefits has been taxable. Historically the UK child benefit payment was universal but, after recent policy changes, this is no longer the case.

By far the biggest item of expenditure of all non-contributory benefits is the income-related (that is, means tested) income support, which is taxable. This is the benefit upon which many poorer families and individuals rely. It is the descendant of a long line of means-tested assistance to the poor, beginning with 'outdoor relief' under the Poor Law (see Chapter 3). When the Poor Law system was abolished, national assistance was introduced in 1946 as a safety net for people in poverty not adequately covered by the contributory benefits scheme. National assistance was in turn replaced by supplementary benefit, which established a set of rights to a wide range of benefits until income support was introduced in 1986. In 1996, those out of work and on low income were switched to the jobseeker's allowance. This benefit required claimants to be available for full-time work (at least 40 hours per week) and to be actively seeking work. The Coalition Government has begun to make significant changes to the structure of the UK benefits system after passing the 2011 Welfare Reform Bill. This Act was based upon the 21st Century Welfare Consultation Paper and the 2010 White Paper *Universal Credit: Welfare that Works*. The results of this Act in relation to benefit provision are as follows.

Universal credit is a new benefit delivered as a single payment for people who are looking for work or on a low income. The idea of this single payment is that it will simplify current benefits provision by bringing together a range of working-age benefits into a single streamlined payment. It is also tied to conditionality in the sense that it aims to improve work incentives and reduce in-work poverty. It was launched in 2013 and the government aims to fully introduce it by 2017. It will replace:

- income-based jobseeker's allowance,
- income-related employment and support allowance,
- income support,
- child tax credits,
- working tax credits, and
- housing benefit.

The DWP (2013) describe the new system as follows:

1. Universal credit will be available to people who are in work and on a low income, as well as to those who are out of work.
2. There will be an online application system with the expectation that all claimants will apply online and manage their account online.
3. The benefit aims to be more flexible than the previous system, tracking claimants' changing circumstances as they move in and out of work. It aims to give an incentive to work for any period of time that is available.
4. Those on low incomes will remain eligible for universal credit even when they first start a new job or increase their part-time hours.
5. The benefit will be paid on a monthly basis into a bank account.
6. Support with housing costs are included within this one monthly payment.

These are not the only changes to ongoing benefit provision: other changes (DWP 2012c) include:

- Disability living allowance is to be replaced by the 'personal independence payment' from 2013.
- Council tax benefit will be abolished from April 2013 and replaced by a system of localized support (by which local government/councils will be given a fixed amount of money each year to provide support).
- Pension credit will be changed from October 2014, broadened in scope to include help with eligible rent and dependent children.
- The social fund is also being reformed to introduce new local assistance.
- Educational support allowance is limited to a 12-month period, with this change taking effect from April 2012.
- The total amount of benefit that can be claimed in a single household is to be capped to £26,000.

Tax credits

Tax credits were a new approach to the provision of cash benefits introduced by the previous New Labour government. They are income-related benefits, so means tested, and therefore selective or targeted benefits. Instead of being assessed and paid out by a conventional social security agency, however, they were administered by the tax authorities following the amalgamation of the Department of Inland Revenue with Customs and Excise, called H.M. Revenue and Customs (HMRC). There were three tax credits – the child tax credit, the working tax credit and the childcare tax credit. These benefits were designed to encourage people to take paid work rather than remain on benefits, in that they acted as a form of supplementation of wages. The child tax credit was designed to be a weapon in the government's attack on child and family poverty. Tax credit claimants complete a fairly lengthy and complex claim form: income is calculated over the year and the credits payable are assessed on the basis of that figure. There may appear to be advantages in having a single agency for handling taxation and benefit payment, but flaws in the current management of the scheme led to serious criticism due to problems of under- and overpayment resulting from the difficulty of tracking changes in people's financial circumstances as their incomes fluctuate, and hardship has been caused to some needy families as HMRC has clawed back overpayments. Tax credits represented a significant shift in the direction of targeted benefits away from universal benefits.

The pension credit, so-called, is not really a tax credit in the same way as the others, but a means-tested benefit for retirement pensioners like, but more generous than, income support. It replaced the minimum income guarantee in 2003 and is a revamped version of the means-tested supplementation that has always been available for recipients of the state retirement pension whose overall incomes were low enough to qualify. It is administered not by HMRC but by the Department for Work & Pensions (DWP). Again there have been recent changes to the provision of tax credits following the Welfare Reform Act (2012) and the publication of the DWP and DFE (2011) report: *A New Approach to Child Poverty: Tackling the Causes of Disadvantage and Transforming Families Lives*. The changes (HM Revenue and Customs 2012) include:

- The financial limits for eligibility of child tax credit have been reduced, effective from April 2012.
- There has been the removal of the over-50 element from working tax credit (allowing extra access to the credit for those aged 50 or over), effective from April 2012.
- Parents need to work at least 24 hours per week to qualify for working tax credit (previously this was 16 hours), effective from April 2012.
- The time for which people can backdate their tax credit claims has been reduced from 3 months to 1 month.

There are many more changes associated with public spending cuts and contributory benefits.

Contributory benefits

Among contributory benefits, the lion's share goes towards the huge retirement pensions bill. Incapacity benefit has historically taken a sizeable slice of the social security budget, hence the Coalition Government's efforts to reduce spending in that area. However, compared to the very large amounts spent on retirement pensions and incapacity benefits, the jobseeker's allowance and other contributory benefits, such as widowed parent's allowance and maternity allowance, take relatively small slices of the social security budget.

Who benefits?

Who benefits from all this expenditure on contributory and non-contributory benefits, representing an estimated £165.5 billion in 2012/13 (DWP 2012a)? If we examine this question in relation to the main recipient groups, we find that older people are the largest single category. Figures from 2011 show just under 13 million people receiving a state pension, with pension aged people accounting for 67 per cent of total DWP spending (DWP 2012a). Women are increasingly more likely to benefit from contributory schemes such as the state pension because of changes in their working patterns. For women the main change since the early 1980s has been a steady increase in numbers building up entitlement to contributory state pensions through NI contributions, as their participation in employment has increased (ONS 2012c).

While older people are the largest single group of social security beneficiaries, there are concerns about demographic change and future demands related to this for the provision of welfare. The Department of Health (DoH 2009) argue that, as a result of growing life expectancy, the need for care provision will significantly increase. The Department of Health (2009) predicts that by 2029 there will be 1.7 million more adults needing care and support and proportionately fewer people of working age to help pay for the funding of that care and support. Welfare costs then in this area are expected to rise significantly. The Office for National Statistics (ONS 2012c) suggests that public expenditure on state pensions and related benefits is projected to rise from 5.7 per cent of GDP in 2010/11 to 6.9 per cent in 2050/51. There are other changing trends associated with pension provision:

- People are also increasingly more likely to invest in employment-related private pension schemes, as shown by the total contributions to private pension schemes rising in real terms by 56 per cent between 1995 and 2007 (ONS 2009), which in effect serve to 'top-up' state pension payments; for some groups these will act as a buffer to age-related poverty (see later discussions). However, not everyone can afford to do this, some individuals do not have access to employment-based schemes and many employment schemes are seeing significant changes and reform that will reduce payments to recipients.
- Legislation has also been changing. The Pensions Act 2007 reintroduced the link between state pensions and earnings. In 2010 the government introduced the 'triple lock' policy guaranteeing that the state pension will be increased each year by average earnings growth, inflation or 2.5 per cent, whichever is higher. The 2012 budget saw pension provision change again into a flat rate scheme, effective from 2016, which aims to reduce dependence upon top-up benefits such as pension credit (Insley 2012).

However, while debates abound in the media about changing policy, economics and future provision, it is interesting to note that contributory benefits account for 54 per cent of total DWP spends in 2012/13, compared with around 70 per cent in the 1960s and 1970s (DWP 2012a).

In more general terms, government figures show that 'households in the bottom half of the income distribution tend to be net gainers from the tax and benefit systems while those in the top half pay more in tax than they receive as benefits' (Office for National Statistics 2012b). The overall impact of both taxes and benefits is that income is shared more equally between households (ONS 2012b). So the social security and taxation systems do act more like a 'Robin Hood' than a 'Sheriff of Nottingham'.

One way of looking at how far incomes are evened out by the tax and benefit system is to consider how much each group's income is modified by it. 'After all taxes and benefits are taken into account, the ratio between the average incomes of the top and the bottom fifth households (£61,400 and £15,200 respectively) is reduced to four-to-one. Cash benefits and direct taxes have the impact of redistributing income from richer households to those with lower incomes, thereby reducing income inequality' (ONS 2012b: 1). However, it is worth noting that the effect of indirect taxation is to modify slightly the redistributive effect, resulting in a lessening of the poorer groups' shares of 'final income'.

Figure 6.2 illustrates the overall effects of taxes and benefits on household incomes. This ranks the population in bands called quintiles (fifths) in terms of income, from highest to lowest, and employs the concepts of 'original' and 'final' income to demonstrate the impact of taxes and benefits. Figure 6.2 shows a clear redistributive effect, taking into account direct and indirect taxes, cash benefits and benefits in kind (such as health services and education).

This is even more apparent if redistribution is looked at from the point of view of *lifetime* earnings and contributions rather than from a single point in time. Reporting on income data for individuals over their complete lives, Hills shows that the 'lifetime poorest' receive 'somewhat more' than the 'lifetime richest' (2004: 197). These estimates include benefits in kind, such as the NHS and education, as well as social security.

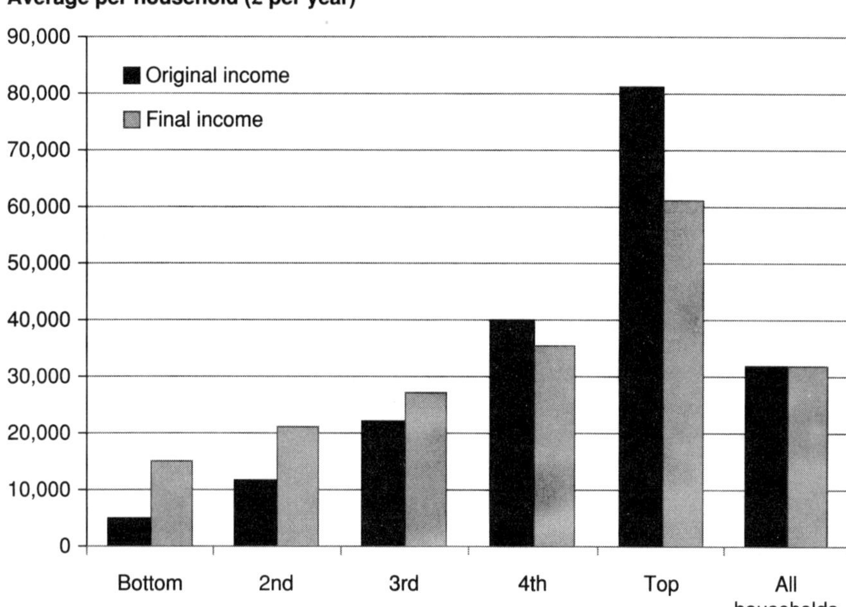

Figure 6.2 Original income and final income by quintile groups for all households, 2010–11
Source: ONS (2012b). Contains public sector information licensed under the Open Government Licence.

However, 'most benefits are self-financed over people's lifetimes, rather than being paid for by others. Nearly three-quarters of what the welfare state was doing in the late 1980s and early 1990s was like a "savings bank"; only a quarter was "Robin Hood" ' redistribution between different people' (Hills 2004: 197).

Hills shows that 'regardless of lifetime income, gross benefits from the state look much the same – around £200,000 per person (at 2001 prices), but also shows a clear redistributive effect, in that more of the receipts of higher income groups are "self-financed". What this means is that the better-off are paying more for the benefits they receive; the less well-off pay less – i.e., a higher proportion of their benefits involves some redistribution from the better-off' (Hills 2004: 196).

Again, this broad picture of 'who benefits' from social security and other forms of welfare provision must be qualified by a number of things. For instance, gender makes a difference, in that, 'on average, women are net lifetime beneficiaries from the system, men net lifetime payers for it' (Hills 1997: 21; 2004: 197). The question of how much an individual gains or loses over a lifetime is also affected by the generation or 'age cohort' they were born into. Those now in middle age will have to fund existing benefits and services throughout their lives – including, for instance, retirement pensions for those who are now old. But if the welfare system contracts in the future, withdrawing or effectively lowering the real value of pensions and social security benefits, they will not gain as much in their lifetimes as earlier generations or cohorts did.

These assessments of the redistributive effects of state welfare spending and taxation need to be placed in context. Inequalities of wealth and income have been growing within the UK for many years, and there are persisting inequalities in relation to health, educational achievement and so on. These result from a variety of causes, including growing inequalities in incomes from work and the growth of unemployment since the 1970s as well as other effects which can be attributed to globalization (see Chapter 4). The system obviously does not equalize in the sense of eliminating all inequalities. What can be said is that inequalities would be greater without the tax and benefit system. While the previous government's tax and spend policies have probably done something to slow down the rate of increase in inequalities, the current UK government is facing increasing criticism related to their policy approach, which is seen by many as one that will actually increase inequalities in the longer term. Policy is certainly important in relation to inequality, so complete Activity 6.3 to explore this in more depth.

Activity 6.3 Policy and inequality

- Outline as many UK government departments as you can. Visit the Gov.uk website and use the directory www.gov.uk/government/organisations to help you in completing this task. List the policy focus of these different departments, and some example policies. Think about how each of these departments can play a role in redistribution and the creation of equality, or how they may actually serve to increase inequalities.
- Think broadly how policies and how it may impact upon inequalities. For example, think about recent changes to education policy (changes to school-based exams) and the changes to fee prices in higher education. Use the Internet to search for media reports about these policy changes; what do they say about how these policies relate to equality?

Completing Activity 6.3 will have helped you to explore the complexity of state provision of services and how they function in relation to equality. Some areas of government provision are very clearly linked to poverty and inequality yet, despite this, income inequalities and poverty remain a significant problem within the UK.

Poverty and social exclusion

The sums spent on social security in Britain each year are so vast as to be almost unimaginable. For instance, the total annual budget of the DWP in 2011–12 was £151.6 billion, representing approximately 28 per cent of total UK Government spending (DWP 2012a).

However, these sums translate into small amounts for the individual or the family. For example, 2012–13 state pension rates are as follows: a single man or woman receives £107.45 per week, as does a married man, woman or civil partner (who qualify with their own NI contributions); this person's spouse or civil partner (using his wife's, her husband's or their civil partner's NI contributions record) receives just £64.40 per week. There is also pension credit, which as a benefit is aimed to top up income to weekly rates of £137.35 for single people, or £209.70 for those with partners (Directgov 2012b). There are, however, concerns that older people often do not claim their full benefit entitlement.

Significant increases in pensions and benefits for older people who are on low incomes have taken place in recent years. However, even these increases do not alter the fact that, when divided up between millions of pensioners and other benefit recipients, the huge amounts of money collected and distributed as social security become relatively small weekly sums for the individual household. There have also been some pension-related developments as a result of broader welfare reform already discussed earlier, the most significant change being that the default retirement age has been abolished. Thus, new legislation stops employers from compulsorily retiring workers once they reach the age of 65 (BBC News 2012d). This has implications for pension provision in that individuals may choose to work for longer and thus delay collection of pensions. However, it will not change the relatively small amounts of pension payment received at an individual level.

This provides the most basic answer to the question 'why does poverty persist in a society with a well-developed welfare system?' The sums paid to benefit recipients are simply too low to lift them out of poverty. However, to leave our discussion at this point would be highly unsatisfactory. In the first place, showing that social security benefits are 'too low' does not address the question of *why* – if they are too low – this is the case, or the question of how this state of affairs has come about.

Second, there are other causes of poverty than apparently meagre levels of state benefit. Some argue that many of those in poverty have brought their fates upon their own heads, that benefit levels are adequate enough and that the poor cannot manage their incomes very well. Others argue the opposite – that the poor are caught in poverty not through their own fault but as a result of economic forces they cannot control – for instance, a decline in job opportunities for people without educational qualifications or skills.

The question of why poverty persists therefore demands a fuller answer. The causes of poverty are complex, and there are many different faces of poverty. As some commentators have pointed out, 'There is genuine uncertainty about how poverty might be measured and about whether, indeed, it is possible to measure a single state called poverty' (Johnson et al. 2000: 112).

To begin to understand poverty, it is helpful to disentangle various concepts and ideas about the subject. This will then enable us to look in greater depth at the causes of both poverty and social exclusion, and at the role of social policy in dealing (or not dealing) with these problems.

- As a first step, it is important to separate – but also see the connections between – *inequality* and *poverty*.
- Second, the relationship between inequality and poverty helps to clarify the idea of *relative poverty* (that is, the theory that poverty in a highly unequal society can only be defined relative to what other people, or the majority, have). Definitions of poverty as 'relative' can be contrasted with the concept of *absolute poverty*.
- Third, poverty and social exclusion are overlapping states – that is, many people in poverty are 'socially excluded'. However, it is useful to separate these concepts. Not *everyone* who is poor is socially excluded, and some of the socially excluded are not poor.

Poverty and inequality

Inequality can be defined in various ways. One way of measuring the degree of inequality is to compare differences in income and wealth between the top, middle and bottom sections of society. The greater the difference between the top and bottom, the greater the degree of inequality.

Some have argued that poverty does not automatically increase as inequality increases. Thinkers on the political right such as Hayek (1944), Friedman (1962), Joseph and Sumption (1979) and Scruton (1984) have all suggested that inequalities are a natural and desirable characteristic of a free, capitalist society (see Chapter 2). If the better-off have incentives to increase their incomes and to amass wealth, so this argument runs, then the resultant economic growth and prosperity will benefit everyone, including those on the lowest incomes. According to this theory, there can be a society in which there are wide disparities in income and wealth, but in which those on the lowest rungs of the ladder live modestly, but not in poverty-stricken conditions.

One not-so-charming expression to illustrate this view is to call it a 'horse-and-sparrows' theory of reducing poverty. The more oats that are stuffed into the horse at one end (that is, the faster the economy grows and the more the rich benefit from this), the more horse droppings will come out of the other, for the little sparrows (the poor) to pick over.

Much the same idea has driven the development aid agenda since the 1960s despite criticism related to the effectiveness of this approach (see Chapter 4). Economists and development planners then thought that the best way to help the poor in developing countries would be to stimulate economic growth – and therefore employment and general prosperity – by giving aid to capitalist firms and business people, not directly to the poor themselves.

There are major flaws with this approach and not much evidence that the horse-and-sparrow mechanism actually works. Far from a trickle-down effect, whereby wealth amassed by people at the top of society permeates the lower levels to create general prosperity, most observers of trends in inequality have noted the opposite. Hills et al. (2010: 1) argue that 'Britain is an unequal country, more so than many other industrial countries and more so than a generation ago. This manifests itself in many ways – most obviously in the gap between those who are well off and those who are less well off'. Their report shows that both earnings and income inequality between any subgroups of the population was greater in 2006–7 than it was in 1968. Thus, inequality within the UK is increasing despite some long periods of economic growth. The story of substantial economic growth benefitting the rich but not the poor is one that can be evidenced on a global scale. The legacy of two decades of Conservative government (between 1979 and 1997), according to Denny (2000: 2), left Britain 'with the worst poverty record in the developed world'. The New Labour Government, 1997–2010, developed a range of social policy measures that attempted to tackle poverty and reduce gaps between the rich and the poor. However, it became clear in their early **tenure** that 'the disposable incomes of the poorest and richest decile groups [were] still edging apart' (Gordon et al. 2000: 8). The authors of this report by the Joseph Rowntree Foundation concluded that 'Evidence of the arrest or reversal of the divergent trend, while eagerly awaited, is not yet showing up in published survey data' (Gordon et al. 2000: 8). Meanwhile, the incomes of the richest tenth continued to grow.

The policies of the previous New Labour government did have a measurable impact on poverty, and especially child poverty, according to recent research. Child poverty fell by around one-seventh under the previous Labour government (Aldridge et al. 2011). The impact of their policies in relation to inequality generally is more ambiguous (Hills 2004; Hills and Stewart 2005; Stewart 2005). Thus the current government inherited a rather mixed picture, as follows:

- Child poverty had been significantly reduced, and was continuing to fall.
- The poverty rate for working-age adults without dependent children had risen to 20 per cent over the previous ten years.
- The pensioner poverty rate had declined to 16 per cent, which is around half the rate it was in 1997.

- Unemployment figures had continued to fluctuate. In mid-2011, six million people were unemployed, which is two million higher than in 2004.
- An increased number of households were in danger of fuel poverty (which has since has risen significantly).

The current Coalition Government is claiming to address child poverty through its reforms to the tax and benefits system, as well as employment policy. However, this has led to criticisms that they need to develop a more redistributive policy approach to tackle poverty effectively (Aldridge et al. 2011).

Relative and absolute poverty

In making any observations about poverty in the UK, we have to accept certain assumptions and conventions about the way poverty is defined. Does the UK really have one of the worst records in the developed world in failing to prevent poverty? How widespread is poverty in the UK, in fact? To answer questions such as this we have to remember that, as mentioned at the outset, poverty is not a single, identifiable 'thing'. There are two commonly accepted ways of defining it, and these view poverty either as a *relative*, or as an *absolute*, fixed measure.

One way of seeing as relative is to say that people who have incomes below half the national average are poor. The incomes of the poorer groups are defined *relative* to average incomes, or incomes in society as a whole. There are several disadvantages with this kind of relative measure. It might be comparatively easy to work out, but it is a fairly arbitrary one. Why 50 per cent of the national average income – why not define poverty as having an income of less than 60 per cent, or 40 per cent, or 33 per cent of the average? Also, as Gordon et al. (2000: 8–9) point out, a single statistical measure such as this, while convenient, is not 'based on independent criteria of deprivation or disadvantage; it does not relate to the needs of individuals, or to any agreed definition of what it is to be poor'.

Thus estimates of people's incomes that calculate whether they are getting 60, 50 or only 40 per cent of the average person's income are arguably providing us with information about *inequality* and *low income* rather than poverty. We cannot be certain that everyone whose income is below 50 per cent of the average is actually poor. At the same time, there might be some poverty among people whose incomes are above 50 per cent of the average. Householders who are buying their own homes, for instance, might be earning wages that are well above average but, because of having to make steep mortgage repayments, find that they cannot easily afford household essentials.

Johnson et al. (2000: 116) also show how calculating poverty by the half-average measure can be very misleading 'because it is very sensitive to changes in income levels among the richest people'. As they point out, incomes among the richest 10 per cent of the UK population increased very quickly in the late 1980s. This had the effect of significantly raising average incomes, so that 'measured "poverty" grew dramatically in the late 1980s, when unemployment was relatively low, but earnings growth at the top end was high'.

Similar problems of using the half-average measure of poverty also occur if benefit payments give people incomes that one year are just above the half-average figure, then the next year just below. Not much change will have occurred in the incomes of less well-off groups, but suddenly many more people will be recorded as living in poverty. As Johnson et al. conclude, the half-average measure is therefore purely arbitrary for this reason also, and 'can result in very large numbers of people being recorded as in poverty' (2000: 116).

Therefore, though poverty seems to be more common in Britain than in other comparable countries, the arbitrariness of the half-average indicator and other measures has the effect of throwing a cloud of uncertainty over the picture.

In order to better understand both the extent and nature of poverty in Britain, a number of researchers have spent a great deal of time and effort in trying to refine definitions of relative poverty. For example, in 1979 Townsend published *Poverty in the United Kingdom*, a huge book (longer than *War and Peace*, as one commentator observed). It did more than any other study in recent decades to stimulate debate about poverty and how social policies can address it. The breakthrough in poverty research that Townsend made was to build upon earlier ideas that it is not just lack of money or bare necessities that define poverty, but the lack of things that are widely *perceived* as necessary by society.

Thus Townsend developed a sociological definition of poverty, suggesting that it is an obstacle to people being able to take part in activities (such as watching television) that are customary in that society. He argued that it is possible to be objective about the things that are commonly regarded as necessities (for example, a television set), and thus objectively to define poverty as being deprived of those things. Townsend constructed a 'deprivation index' from a list of 60 items that he and his colleagues regarded as key indicators of a standard of living that would avoid poverty. The index included a wide range of amenities and activities relating to health, diet, social support, heating and lighting, housing conditions, clothing and so on. This list was then tested in surveys of the public to ascertain its validity. As Alcock (1997: 80) points out, the indicators included items such as 'the lack of a refrigerator, no holiday away from home in the last twelve months and the lack of a cooked breakfast most days of the week, all of which correlated highly with low income'. However, it is important to note that Townsend's overall measure of relative poverty was based on a *combination* of the deprivation index and incomes of households, not on income alone or simply on a measure of deprivation from commonly accepted necessities.

Townsend's masterpiece soon became the subject of controversy. Some argued that its definition of relative poverty was too generous. *Poverty in the United Kingdom* suggested that about 25 per cent of British households were poor, compared with the 7 per cent counted as poor according to official calculations (which equated poverty with being in receipt of means-tested supplementary benefits). Townsend's figure was regarded as an overestimate by many commentators. Official estimates of poverty might have been too low, but they raised the question of whether Townsend's estimate was too high.

Other questions about Townsend's influential study were raised by David Piachaud (1981), who did not question the concepts of relative poverty developed by Townsend but queried the validity of the deprivation index. Piachaud argued that much of the variation in deprivation scores reported in the study were 'merely due to diversity in styles of living wholly unrelated to poverty' (1981: 420). For instance, questions about whether the children of the family had had other children to play or to tea in the past four weeks, or whether the family had eaten a roast Sunday dinner, were more to do with lifestyle than with deprivation. Piachaud therefore concluded that, though people on low incomes would tend to score high on the deprivation index, there would also have been 'considerable numbers' of people on low incomes who would not be identified as deprived, as well as 'many with high incomes who score high on the deprivation index' (1981: 420).

These criticisms seem to have had a constructive outcome. Townsend and other social policy researchers went on to further improve the methods by which it is possible to identify the items that a majority of the population consider necessary, and thus – by implication – to discover what proportion of the population is deprived of these things. Major poverty surveys were conducted in Britain in the 1980s and 1990s (see Mack and Lansley 1985; Gordon and Pantazis 1997) and this research has continued to be built upon and extended by more recent studies. Globally poverty and related inequality are measured in a variety of ways, for example using the Human Development Index or, indeed, capability measures (see the work of Sen 1985, 1999). Assuming poverty is relative, complete Activity 6.4 to explore how need is defined socially.

Activity 6.4 Constructions of need

Do you agree that the following list of items are necessary to avoid both poverty and deprivation?

- damp-free home
- beds and bedding for everyone
- mobile phone
- attending weddings, funerals
- refrigerator
- warm, waterproof coat
- home computer
- television set
- toys (for example, dolls, teddies)
- celebrations on special occasions
- a meal in a restaurant/pub monthly
- three meals a day for children; two meals a day for adults
- freezer
- fresh fruit and vegetables daily
- hobby or leisure activity
- telephone
- washing machine
- car

1. Which of these are necessities of life and how, in such a context, can we define need?
2. See www.jrf.org.uk/publications/poverty-and-social-exclusion-britain for the full report detailing the findings from the UK Poverty and Social Exclusion Survey in 1999, which incorporates the views and perceptions of members of the public. Compare your own views to this.

Activity 6.4 will have helped you to understand that poverty is a complex, multidimensional phenomenon affecting different groups of people in different ways, and having different causes. Thus we can identify specific kinds of poverty in terms of the groups affected – for instance, child poverty, 'pensioner' poverty, urban or inner-city deprivation. Types of poverty can also be identified in terms of inability to afford certain things, such as fuel poverty, housing poverty or water poverty (which, in a developed society such as the UK, means being unable to afford a plentiful supply of water from a metered supply).

Given this complexity, together with nagging doubts about the reliability of relative measures of poverty, it is not surprising that absolute measures of poverty hold a certain attraction. Does not a single 'absolute' line of income, below which people or households can be counted as being in poverty, offer a much more scientific and objective measure than apparently wishy-washy relative definitions? Governments in other countries, such as the USA, clearly think so. The US federal government establishes a 'poverty line' of minimum income and regularly updates it. From this, numbers of households and individual people living in poverty, below the line, can be calculated. This information is used not only by federal and state governments to evaluate their anti-poverty policies, but also by critics of government policy and NGOs working to reduce poverty. The current global measure of absolute poverty is those who are living on less than US$2 per day.

The UK has no such official poverty line. However, there is one commonly used 'absolute' definition of poverty, in addition to relative definitions such as the half-average income measure discussed above. This is the definition of poverty as *having an income that is below the level at which means-tested benefits are payable.*

This 'absolute' measure is not particularly objective or scientific, however, because it reflects the government's *idea* of minimum income, or how much money the government of the day thinks it necessary to give individuals and families in poverty to live on. Yet there can be many people with incomes that are just above the official minimum level, but who are actually in poverty. Thus absolute definitions of poverty suffer from the same problem of arbitrariness that relative measures do. Who decides where the poverty line, or level of minimum income, should be set? Whose interests are considered when the calculation is made – those of the poor, or those of governments wishing to hold down social security expenditure?

The latter question implies that official interests always win out, and that by setting the minimum income and means-testing levels rather low, governments seek to underestimate true levels of poverty. However, an absolute measure based on receipt of state benefits can have the opposite effect. If governments extend eligibility for means-tested state benefits or take active steps to encourage take-up of existing benefits, this can have the perverse effect of simultaneously improving many people's incomes yet defining more people than before as being poor – because they are receiving means-tested benefits!

In summary, absolute measures of poverty – whether based on minimum income required, on whether a person or a family is receiving means-tested benefits, or on more complex indicators of income – cannot provide a problem-free, scientific alternative to relative definitions. As Burden (2000: 43–4) points out, an absolute measure has the attraction of providing an obvious and precise measure of poverty that can be debated publicly and can act as a clear guide to policy-makers wishing to address problems of low income. As he suggests, though, it is an arbitrary measure that can distort the picture of poverty rather than clarify it. An absolute measure also tends to focus attention on the poor as a separate group. This distracts attention from the broad pattern of inequality, and the idea that growing poverty in one section of society could be related to growing affluence in another.

Social exclusion

The concept of social exclusion, on the other hand, helps to highlight the idea that poverty and deprivation in one part of society are linked in some ways to what is happening in the rest of society. If social exclusion exists on a large scale, this might point to a failure of government to develop 'inclusive' policies that relieve deprivation and create opportunities for people to climb out of poverty.

But what is 'social exclusion' and how does it compare with definitions of poverty? As Alcock (1997: 92) notes, the term social exclusion began to enter social policy debates from the mid-1980s onwards. It became a highly fashionable term once the Labour Government of 1997 was elected. Social exclusion can often appear as a substitute term for 'poverty'. This is partly because governments tend not to like to admit to the persistence of poverty, or indeed the failure of policies to tackle it. New Labour used social exclusion, while the previous Conservative administrations led by Thatcher and Major preferred to discuss 'low income' or 'low income groups' rather than 'poverty' or 'the poor'. The current government's focus has moved away from the term social exclusion, although official views recognize the complexity of issues of poverty and related problems such as long-term unemployment. Therefore social exclusion as a concept does still hold value in broadening our understanding of poverty.

- First, concepts of poverty tend to focus on lack of *material resources* (chiefly money income, but also including other things such as lack of adequate housing). Social exclusion, on the other hand, focuses on the *relationship* (or lack of it) between the excluded individual, family or community and the rest of society. The 'socially excluded' have been pushed out by the rest of the community and therefore find it hard to take up opportunities to improve their situation. Material poverty and social exclusion often go hand in hand, therefore, but separating the two concepts allows us to recognize how some people might be socially excluded even when they are *not* poor or living on particularly low incomes. For instance, black people and disabled people experience high poverty rates, but some people in these groups are not poor. Nevertheless, they might experience social exclusion in the form of racism or discrimination and restriction of opportunities. However, as indicated above, these distinctions are blurred. Relative definitions of poverty – such as those used by Townsend and his colleagues – refer to poverty as being deprived not only of material resources, but also of opportunities to play a full part in society. They are, in effect, 'socially excluded' (see Townsend 1979; Gordon et al. 2000).
- Second, concepts of social exclusion tend to focus on lack of educational and employment opportunities. Thus policy in this area has rested upon efforts to get people into jobs, education or some kind of 'mainstream' activity in the community. This does not mean that social exclusion is *always* associated with unemployment, only that it tends to be seen this way. Poverty, on the other hand, is a concept that can be applied as easily to people in work on 'poverty wages' (the working poor) as to people who are unemployed or excluded from the labour market for other reasons (such as older people).
- Third, the policy remedies for poverty and social exclusion tend to emphasize different strategies or policies. Again there is overlap, but anti-poverty strategies have tended to stress the importance of bringing about *greater equality of incomes* and other material resources. If a whole community is poor, for instance, there might be a government strategy to put extra resources into that community, such as better-equipped schools, improved infrastructure, leisure facilities and so on. At a nation-wide level, poverty could be tackled by raising levels of social security benefits to raise the incomes of poorer people. Policies to combat social exclusion, on the other hand, have tended to stress *creating more opportunities* for poorer people so that they can improve their incomes themselves. This is where the Coalition Government aims to

make change; to create more equality of opportunity rather than stifling initiative. In practice, however, these are differences of emphasis rather than clear-cut differences. Many anti-poverty programmes in the UK – and particularly in the USA – have included efforts to stimulate enterprise, retraining and community involvement as well as trying to redistribute resources or improve income levels.

In summary, though the concepts of poverty and social exclusion overlap, there seems to be some merit in using the term social exclusion to identify new problems of deprivation and disadvantage. For instance Lawson (1995: 5) refers to the way that 'new poverty' has increased as a result of economic restructuring and changes in the job market. New kinds of social and economic insecurity have come about, leading to the exclusion of 'an increasingly vulnerable minority', for whom 'the prospects are a life more or less detached from the broader economic and social experiences of mainstream society'. Issues with the changing nature of employment and resulting poverty and exclusion have been recognized on a global scale.

People in poverty have commonly experienced social rejection and found their social status devalued, especially in a materialistic and competitive society. However, the point being made by authors such as Lawson is that two newer kinds of change are happening in the 'postmodern' world (see Chapter 14). The first is a widening of opportunity and significantly improving standards of living for the 'broad middle mass' of society. As a result, traditional class barriers and allegiances are weakening, together with other social divisions such as those of gender and race. But as these fragmenting processes occur and living standards improve for the affluent majority, this majority is less and less able to understand or identify with the minority, who are effectively excluded from taking up the same opportunities. The second kind of change, therefore, is a fragmentation of 'the poor' into increasingly isolated and vulnerable groups – for instance, older people on very low incomes, young unemployed people, certain groups of mentally ill and disabled people, young lone parents, and some sections of 'racial' and ethnic minority communities.

Therefore, although both poverty may be increasing it is not a shared experience or a common pattern of life as it might have been, for instance, in the days of high unemployment and economic depression in the 1930s. The challenge for governments in the twenty-first century will be to find ways of changing social policies to make them more flexible and able to meet the increasingly diverse needs of the fragmented groups that are both poor and socially excluded.

Conclusions

This chapter has discussed 'who gets what' from the welfare system. The focus has largely been upon economic benefits and costs. This is not to deny the importance of the social and political costs and benefits of having a well-developed welfare system. For instance, commentators on the right claim that an 'over-generous' or open-handed welfare system creates social costs or problems such as welfare dependency and laziness – or, more politely, 'work disincentives'. Supporters of a comprehensive welfare system, whether on the left or the right, would point to social benefits such as greater social stability and perhaps less crime. Indeed, Wilkinson and Pickett (2009) use a variety of global data to show that more equal societies do better in a number of ways such as having less crime and being more stable thus welfare provision may act to encourage better outcomes in the UK context.

These latter questions, important though they are, were not the main subject of this chapter. Discussion of the social effects of the welfare system – especially the connections between social policy, social control and poverty – is continued in the next chapter. However, restricting our gaze to cash or money benefits can give a rather narrow view of equality. As mentioned at the outset, conventional economics might miss the important contributions of labour or care provided 'free' by carers or family members.

In addition, as Powell (1995) reminds us, when earlier social theorists such as Tawney (1964) and Marshall (1970) defined equality in social policy, 'they appeared to be talking about equality of status, entitlement, universality and citizenship rather than the more demanding forms of distributive justice' (Powell 1995: 170). In other words, it would be a mistake to judge the welfare system solely according to the way in which it distributes cash benefits or other calculable outcomes, such as length and quality of medical treatments, or the number of educational qualifications gained.

There is something over and above these rather narrowly defined outcomes: a principle of equality that transcends class and other inequalities. The politicians and planners who established the welfare system after the Second World War were inspired by this idea of equality. 'Equality of entitlement' is a principle that one will be treated equally as a citizen when in need of a service, whatever one's earnings or station in life.

As we have seen in this chapter, the impact of the welfare system as a whole upon top-, middle- and bottom-income groups is mixed with some benefits serving to redistribute to those at the lower end of the income scale (ONS 2012b). However, those in the middle do significantly benefit in relation to health and education services. Social security, by far the most significant 'gatherer and distributor' of resources in the welfare system, funnels a net flow of money from better-off to poorer income groups. However, because of wider social and economic inequalities, this vital role of social security might be obscured. For one thing, tax reforms have lightened the burden of those on the highest incomes, while relatively high taxes have been levied on poorer groups, especially through increases in indirect taxation in recent years. However, it is important to note that people in poverty – one-parent families, older people, unemployed people – would be even poorer without the welfare and social security system. The social security system has not been able to prevent rising levels of poverty, or to curb inequalities, but it continued to be a 'Robin Hood' – albeit a rather old and arthritic Robin Hood. How far government changes have had a detectable impact on problems of poverty, and on the future of the welfare system as a whole in a number of social policy fields, are discussed in Chapter 14.

We need to bear in mind that there is a range of explanations for rises and falls in rates of poverty. Government actions alone do not determine the rate of poverty. It cannot be controlled like a tap, as if economic and social policies can either quickly increase poverty, or reduce it to a trickle in months. Historically, the sudden and rapid rise in UK poverty in the 1980s did seem to show the clear effect of Conservative policies. However, it is also true that underlying economic and social changes were encouraging the trends in inequality and poverty. These changes included change in the employment market leading to declining demand for unskilled and semi-skilled labour, which in turn leads to higher unemployment or lower wages for people in low-income social groups. Globalization can also have an effect, tending to depress wages because employers in other countries can produce goods more competitively. While New Labour made some effort to develop social policy to tackle income inequality and poverty, that administration still put its economic objectives before those of social policy, resulting in limited success in these areas. The current Coalition Government has embarked upon welfare reform, and economic changes to limit future spending thus the signs are that policies will attempt to construct a much more flexible, targeted and means-tested welfare system rather than try to revive the goal of creating a more equal society through a traditional welfare state of universalistic services and benefits.

Summary of key points

- There are many positive aspects to the welfare system. However, there are also controversial questions about how need should be defined and how to ensure entitlements and equality.
- The provision of welfare means that some groups of individuals gain, while others lose out depending upon the nature of contributions and the criteria upon which allocations are made.
- Welfare can be used to tackle poverty and social exclusion. However, the goals of welfare provision in Britain are now overshadowed by retrenchment and policies to reduce the size of the welfare 'cake'.

Key terms and concepts

disposable income
economic growth
external benefits
gross domestic product (GDP)
income:
  original income
  gross income
poverty:
  absolute
  relative
real increases (for example, in spending, wages or benefits)
redistribution
social security benefits:
  contributory
  non-contributory
  income-related
  non-income-related
  selective
universal
targeting
taxation:
  direct
  indirect
progressive
regressive

Suggestions for further reading

Barr, N. (2005) *The Economics of the Welfare State.* 4th edition. Oxford: Oxford University Press.

This is perhaps the best in terms of combining in-depth economic analysis with a comprehensive coverage of the welfare system. This fourth edition discusses the different parts of the welfare system such as cash benefits, the health service and education. The text argues that the welfare state exists not just to help the underprivileged, but also for efficiency reasons. The book is student friendly.

Bartholomew, J. (2012) *The Welfare State We're In.* London: Biteback Publishing.

This is a critical discussion of the welfare state, which poses the question of whether the welfare state has in reality done more harm than good. The author asks questions such as: Do welfare benefits cause unemployment? How and why does the NHS fail to deliver? Can state education ever be properly reformed? Does broken parenting matter? Is a low state pension better than none at all, and who pays for it? The book offers an alternative view to that discussed throughout the chapter in that suggesting that the welfare state undermines both the decency and kindness which first inspired it.

Castles, F.G, Leibfried, S., Lewis, J., Obinger, H. and Pierson, C. (2010) *The Oxford Handbook of the Welfare State.* Oxford: Oxford University Press.

The Oxford Handbook of the Welfare State is a large book detailing everything you need to know about the modern welfare state, through fifty chapters. The book explores the philosophical case for (and against) the welfare state. It provides historical analysis and looks at a whole range of issues that the welfare state embraces such as roles of parties, unions and employers; the impact of gender and religion; patterns of migration and changing public opinion; the role of international organizations; and the impact of globalization. The book covers pensions, health care, disability, care of the elderly, unemployment and the labour market. There are global comparisons, and debates about the global future of the welfare state.

Glennerster, H. (2003) *Understanding the Finance of Welfare: What Welfare Costs and How to Pay for It.* Bristol: Policy Press.

This is a readable and also an authoritative introduction. The book focuses upon resource issues in particular, which remain central to social policy debates today. The book explores the economic and political limits of taxation, markets and public expenditure as well as the economic case for the provision of public services.

Further suggestions

You will also find the annual publication *Work and Pensions Statistics* by the DWP extremely useful.

This source gives a breakdown of public spending on all the main social security benefits. It also provides helpful explanations of the purposes of each benefit, the rules governing eligibility and so on. Reports and policy documents from the DWP can be found at www.gov.uk/government/publications.

The Joseph Rowntree Foundation regularly funds social research in this area, and you will be able to find reports and research updates at www.jrf.org.uk.

The Coalition Government's overall programme for government contains useful information about planned changes and reform across all policy areas, including welfare and taxation. You can see the full programme and download the pdf file at www.direct.gov.uk/prod_consum_dg/groups/dg_digitalassets/@dg/@en/documents/digitalasset/dg_187876.pdf.

7 Social policy, politics and social control

Key learning outcomes

By the end of this chapter you should:

- be able to understand the ways in which welfare can serve as a mechanism of social control
- be able to identify and outline the complexities associated with welfare as a mechanism of social control
- be able to discuss the difference between direct and indirect social control in relation to the policy process and welfare

Overview of the chapter

Chapter 6 focused on economic issues and 'who gets what' from the welfare system. But that topic has social and political implications in that 'who gets what?' is also a way of looking at social inequality and the impact of government policy on social divisions. This chapter builds on these issues by continuing the debate about what impact social policy has on society. It focuses on the central question of how far social policies play a political function in terms of maintaining the social order and buttressing government power.

This chapter explores questions that are still much in debate today, such as did the gradual building up of a system of government-organized welfare in the twentieth century increase the state's control over us? Did it erode liberty and personal freedoms? In return for a certain amount of security, did the welfare state destroy both self-reliance and willingness to look after others? Or are such ideas misleading, and could the opposite be true – that only when there is generous state provision of education, health care and world-class social services can people be genuinely free and able to fulfil their potential to develop themselves and help others? This chapter addresses these questions and explores the debate about the connections between social policy on the one hand, and questions of social control, coercion and freedom on the other.

Social control and the rise of welfare

Where do your views lie in relation to welfare provision? The questions asked in the chapter overview might seem unnecessary to anyone who takes it for granted that social welfare is unequivocally 'a good thing'. Surely, if education, health and welfare services successfully meet most people's needs and alleviate social problems, the more that is provided the better? There is a case to be answered, however. Sometimes the welfare system does become more concerned with controlling us than with meeting our needs or respecting our rights as independent citizens. Commentators on both the political left and right have suggested that a bureaucratic state can, in the name of providing help, become paternalistic and insensitive.

But was this the main reason for the development of social policy and welfare services in the nineteenth and twentieth centuries? Was the state's growing concern with public welfare – for instance, public health, the welfare and education of children, better housing and so on – really motivated by a need to manage and control the population? If this theory is correct, it means that the actual welfare of the population was always secondary to governmental aims of maintaining order and political control. It also implies that, once political and social order can be maintained by other means than providing welfare – for instance, by cultivating consumerism or materialism – governments will be less and less interested in supporting the continued improvement and extension of the welfare state.

Before jumping to these conclusions, however, it is important to look at what history tells us about the development of welfare states. Historical experience suggests that the rise of welfare can be explained only by reference to a wide range of factors, not just attempts by the state to extend social control. Complete Activity 7.1 to explore the factors that influenced the development of the British welfare state.

Activity 7.1 Exploring the history of welfare

Use the Internet to view the short film 'Poverty and the Welfare State: Five Evils II' available on You Tube at www.youtube.com/watch?v=LvqYknY8pvA.

You may also find this film about welfare service creation of interest:

'The NHS: A Difficult Beginning', www.youtube.com/watch?v=-ywP8wjfOx4&feature=related. This is a longer programme, at an hour, but if you can spare the time then it is worth watching.

While watching these different stories of welfare creation, make notes about the complex range of factors that you can see were influencing the creation of the welfare state.

As Activity 7.1 has demonstrated, welfare creation was complex and underpinned by multifaceted factors including social control. In many analyses of the creation of the UK welfare state, industrialization in the nineteenth and early twentieth centuries is constructed as posing problems of social conflict and disorder. Sometimes governments saw the expansion of welfare benefits and improvements in living conditions for the working classes as ways of dampening down these conflicts, mainly by giving concessions or 'buying off' the strongest and more militant groups. However, the reasons for the development of welfare were complex and included a number of influences, as illustrated in Figure 7.1.

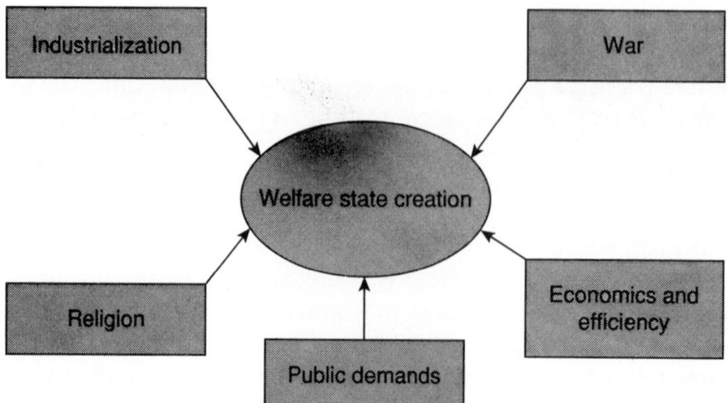

Figure 7.1 Influences on welfare state creation

- *Industrialization* occurred at different times, at varying speeds and in different ways in different countries, but broadly speaking the development of industrial society can be seen as perhaps the most important stimulus to the development of social welfare. However, different national governments responded in their own particular ways, according to the political and cultural traditions of each country and to the new needs of the industrial age – for instance, needs for more housing, sanitation and better education – and some highly industrialized societies (notably the USA and Japan) never developed Western-European-style welfare states.
- *War* between countries – at least preparation for military conflict – was sometimes as important a stimulus to improve social welfare as conflict and protest within countries. Governments began to see the connections between health, education and literacy and the building up of effective military strength.
- *Religious activity* and competition between different churches or denominations was sometimes as important as political conflict in promoting the growth of education, hospitals and charitable efforts to care for the poor. For instance, the role of charity and charitable institutions was particularly significant in Britain and the USA. And in the Netherlands, one reason for the high level of educational and welfare development was the determination of both Protestant and Catholic communities to develop their own systems of social support and welfare.
- *Economic efficiency* can also be seen as an important factor in the development of social policy. Governments and employers began to realize that public spending on health care, social insurance, education and other benefits resulted in a more productive and efficient labour force.
- *Public demand* for better public services and more education-led governments that were reluctant to develop social policies to consider doing so. Note that this explanation is not quite the same as the theory that governments decided to prevent general social disorder or political unrest through the cynical use of welfare improvements or concessions. Public demand for more social welfare was a reflection of the development of *democracy*. Once elected parliaments were in place, welfare and social policy began to develop to unprecedented levels, and this was more an unexpected, 'bottom-up' type of development than a result of 'top-down' policies imposed by paternalistic governments.

Thus welfare systems developed for a variety of reasons in each European country and in North America (see Jones 1985: 34–77 for a useful summary of the evidence).

Table 7.1 Ideological position and view of welfare

Ideological standpoint	Relationship between welfare and state control
Marxist approaches	Welfare is to serve the interests of capital: to keep a reserve army of labour (unemployed) ready for the economy and to train the labour force to be good workers (educational provision). Welfare policy is to maintain the status quo, partly by reducing excesses of inequality and exploitation.
Feminist approaches	Welfare serves to maintain and support patriarchal authority over women and the continuation of gender norms, hence policy is often based upon assumptions about women as carers and dependants.
Liberals	Liberalism begins from the viewpoint that every individual has rights. Generally, freedom is seen as important and liberals advocate less state 'interference' in preference to the market and voluntary action. However, the liberal model does support strong regulation to prevent one set of interests harming any other (e.g. control of environmental pollution).
Socialists	There are many forms of socialism, but in general socialists view welfare as positive in supporting collective security and well-being. Some social control and regulation is necessary to promote equality.
Conservatives	Conservatives believe in the importance of social order and the provision of welfare as a mechanism to support this. Welfare is secondary to overall social control and conservatives usually argue for a reduction in welfare provision, though some versions (e.g. 'compassionate conservatism') support welfare provision, especially targeted or selective benefits and services.

The development of welfare, and indeed contemporary provision, is viewed in different ways depending upon ideological standpoint, as Table 7.1 illustrates.

Table 7.1 shows contrasting views of the relationship between welfare and social control. Interestingly the variety of influences which led to welfare creation has also meant that the *scale* of such provision, and how far it was considered proper for the state to intervene in people's lives, varied considerably from country to country. Indeed, this remains the case today, with some countries intervening much more than others. For example, China's one-child policy serves to regulate the number of children that can be born; this decision is located within the private sphere in other countries.

Clearly, some explanations for the development of welfare during the industrial age fit some countries better than others. Economic development and the modernization of society in Britain during the nineteenth century were certainly strong influences (see Chapter 3). However, Jones (1985) concludes that political and social control factors, while by no means being the only ones, did play a leading part in stimulating the early development of social policy and welfare provision:

> There exists no discernible link between the level of economic development (indices of industrialization and urbanization) and the first introduction of social insurance measures designed to meet the needs of... the sick... the old, and the unemployed. It [was], if anything, the less developed of European societies which [proved] to be the most prompt in introducing social insurance... [There was] a tendency for traditional, patriarchal regimes to embark promptly – even prematurely – upon preventive social policy measures. (Jones 1985: 52)

Other observers of the development of welfare have also established this early connection between social policy and political control. A famous study entitled *Regulating the Poor: The Functions of Public Welfare*, by Piven and Cloward (1971), showed that federal spending by the US government on social welfare tended to increase where there had been civil unrest and inner-city riots. On the other hand, Piven and Cloward argued, growing restrictiveness in providing welfare and the introduction of stricter forms of means testing can be used by government as ways of not only gaining electoral support among the comfortable majority but also controlling or 'regulating' the poor. Social policies, in their view, have contributed to a process of **marginalization** of the poor. Given broadening social inequalities within Britain, the poor are marginalized in a number of ways. For example, in terms of:

- educational outcomes,
- employment statuses,
- levels of earnings,
- a lack of social mobility (see Hills et al. 2010), and
- area effects, where benefit claimants are heavily concentrated in deprived areas as a result of the links between place, poverty and disadvantage (see Lawlor and Nicholls 2008).

Furthermore, the poor are often subject to more state control than other groups. Hillyard and Percy-Smith (1988) have argued in their book *The Coercive State* that a wide variety of social policies, including social security and health service reform, illustrate a trend in Britain towards a more controlling and less democratic form of government than before. This is taking place, they suggest, despite a 'liberal rhetoric' or widespread assumption that government is based on democracy and that the actions of the state are legitimate. Much contemporary political discourse remains focused upon those who are poorer, who are continually constructed in negative ways. More recently Jones's (2011) book *Chavs* provides examples of the continued demonization of the working classes who, he argues, are stereotyped and criminalized through both the media and the political establishment. However, Hillyard and Percy-Smith (1988) are careful to point out that the growing power of the state is a complex phenomenon. It cannot be reduced to a single trend or example, because government – and people's experience of it – is multifaceted: 'In short, the state in its various roles may at different times, in different situations and for different people, be seen as benevolent protector or provider, impartial arbiter between competing interests, a minor irritant, or alternatively, as obstructive, intrusive, oppressive and coercive' (Hillyard and Percy-Smith 1988: 14).

Social policy and regulation

The term social control has negative connotations and is often identified with coercion, limitation of individual freedom, or disempowerment. Thus, some social policies have been heavily criticized for disempowering women such as those that limit women's rights to abortion, which is a highly emotive area subject to continuing debates. This is, however, too narrow a view. All social policy is 'social control' and who says 'social policy' is effectively saying 'social control'. In its most general sense, social control simply means some kind of collective regulation of individual or group behaviour or actions. Social control is not merely inescapable, it is arguably highly desirable. A society of any degree of size, complexity, internal differentiation and division of labour is inconceivable without some kind of social control. Any society which is sufficiently differentiated to possess some system of governance – that is, a state – is necessarily involved in social control of a formal kind. (Social control may of course be informal, as in the exercise of discipline over children within the family.)

A broader, more ideologically neutral concept which is roughly synonymous with that of social control is 'regulation'. In the previous chapter we noted Lowi's suggestion that a distinction could be made between regulatory, distributive and redistributive public policies and politics, or, more accurately perhaps, regulatory, distributive and redistributive aspects of such policies (see Lowi 1966; Blank and Burau 2004).

What aspects of social control or regulation would most of us, apart, perhaps, from a few anarchists, welcome and find highly desirable? The criminal law is one aspect of regulation or social control, as are many other areas of law. Law in general is clearly an instrument of social control – a device through which governments promote control of or over society. However, what is regulated and defined as criminal varies widely across societies. Some argue that it is those in the poorer sections of societies who are more likely to be subject to regulation via the criminal law than the ones in need of social control, such as better-off people who commit 'white collar' crimes. Legislation and regulations governing public, or preventive, health – clean water, sewerage, the collection and disposal of human wastes, communicable disease control, environmental standards, regulations governing food standards and purity, and workplace health and safety; legislation which restricts maximum hours of work; housing standards; the minimum wage; regulations governing public house opening hours; the National Curriculum; anti-discrimination legislation in relation to race, gender, age and disability; the law relating to the treatment of children; regulations governing the compulsory detention of the mentally ill – all these are examples of collective interference with individual freedom.

At a certain level, therefore, all politics and public policy are really regulatory, because distributive and redistributive policies can themselves be regarded as forms of regulation. Governments interfere with the freedom of individuals and free markets in all kinds of ways. The existence of the NHS providing health care that is 'free' at the point of use, for example, is an interference with free markets in health care and a form of market regulation. Sociologists have for many years discussed the ways in which social policy acts as a mechanism of social control, as Box 7.1 illustrates.

Box 7.1 Social policy as a mechanism of social control: sociological insights

- The works of Foucault (1977) and Donzelot (1980) examined the pivotal disciplinary role exercised by welfare and social work professionals/providers in controlling populations.
- Rose (1985), Garland (1985) and Squires (2006) outlined the complex relationship between those interventions pertaining to welfare and protection, and those pertaining to control.
- Scourfield and Welsh (2003: 400) argue that all forms of state welfare provision are forms of social control.
- Lianos (2003) also notes that all forms of organization necessarily involve control.
- Abbott and Sapsford suggest that 'it is now widely accepted that social workers are "soft policemen"' (1990: 120).

Indeed, in recent years extensions in some areas of the criminal law have been discussed in the context of increasing social control, particularly those aimed at those more visible in relation to public order (Anti-Social Behaviour Orders are one such example – see Donoghue 2008).

Too much control – or not enough?

Rather than social control being seen as the problem, there is mounting concern that, as welfare systems retract and social inequalities grow, increasing disorder will result. The problem could be a *lack* of social control. Gray (1995: 12), for instance, argues: 'What is less obvious is the role played by the new inequality in weakening the ties of community. Inequality has divided us, most palpably, in cities, where it has enforced a brutal segregation according to income and access to jobs. It has promoted an erosion of relationships of trust affecting most aspects of social life, alongside a precipitous collapse of public trust in institutions.'

Have you ever given consideration to the ways in which social inequality and a lack of trust can affect many aspects of life? Complete Activity 7.2 to reflect on this.

Activity 7.2 Exploring inequality

Use the Internet to visit TED Talks and to view the presentation given by Richard Wilkinson, 'How Economic Inequality Harms Societies' available at www.ted.com/talks/lang/en/richard_wilkinson.html.

What does Wilkinson say about the relationship between trust and levels of inequality? What might this mean in the context of social policy formation and social control?

There are some societies in which lack of trust has led to heavy-handed levels of social control. China, for instance, tightly controls access to the Internet and media reports. However, on the other side of the coin there are ways in which social control has arguably been a positive influence. For example, road traffic legislation and control have been linked to rates in accident reductions. Enforcing school attendance could also be described as positive. The positive side of social control becomes clearer if we use words other than social control or social order. Notice how Gray uses the words 'ties of community' and 'institutions' in the quotation above. If we put the words 'social control' in place of 'the ties of community' in the passage quoted above, and substitute 'the social order' for 'institutions', the meaning is more or less the same. Social control can lead to a social order that enhances welfare, security and trust. The difference between an ordered and a disordered society can mean the difference between being free to walk alone at night without fear of intimidation or violence, or not. It will also affect whether or not we have to pay a steep price for individual security (insurance premiums, alarm systems, house security and so on).

Note that these examples illustrate a contradiction. A social order which is rule-bound, in which there is effective law enforcement and where everyone is expected to conform also brings certain freedoms: chiefly, freedom from worries about crime or, more positively, a sense of belonging to a structured community.

Table 7.2 Social order and control in Singapore

Benefits of social control	Problems with social control
Singapore is one of the few large modern contemporary cities in which women can walk freely without serious worries of being attacked, and where street crime and burglary are still relatively uncommon.	The mass media, the universities and any potential sources of dissidence are subject to government surveillance and controls.
The state has a comprehensive provision of health care and education for all.	There are strict penalties for infringing rules governing everyday life, from personal dress and hairstyles to throwing litter.
Singapore is rated highly on the rule of law, control of corruption and government effectiveness by the World Bank (2004).	Some aspects of the political process, civil liberties and political and human rights are lacking (World Bank 2004).

One particular welfare system illustrates this contradiction very well: the city-state of Singapore. In Singapore, which is virtually a one-party state, the government suppresses free thought and political opposition to a degree. These contradictions are illustrated in Table 7.2.

Yet the key to understanding social control in Singapore is not just effective law enforcement and political repression, and an economy in which work is plentiful – in fact there have been threats to Singapore's strong economy in recent years – but also its social policies. Singapore has a comprehensive system of health and education services that buttress the social order and enhance **social consensus**, making the existing **paternalism** seem more acceptable than a nakedly repressive regime.

Does this mean that, in western market economies, social disorder and violent crime (Paton Walsh 2001) are attributable to cutbacks in the growth of welfare provision? Unfortunately, the answer may not be straightforward. Whether social policy maintains order or causes change is much debated. Depending on one's political and ideological viewpoint, the relationship between social policy and social stability can be seen in different ways.

- First, factors other than changes in social policy or cutbacks in welfare could be causing upheaval. For instance, social and geographical mobility; the break-up of old neighbourhoods, communities and extended family ties; the decline of stable employment opportunities (especially affecting young men); and changes in culture and social norms reflect, among other things, more individualistic approaches to life and greater tolerance of self-seeking or violent behaviour.
- Second, there is, on the other hand, an argument that 'over-generous' or openhanded social security policies have brought about increasing social disorder. Arguing from the political right, Murray (1994) suggested that in the period between the 1950s and 1980s social security benefits were both substantially increased in real terms and made easier to obtain. According to this argument, increasingly liberal welfare systems undermined work disciplines and subsidized the lifestyles of an underclass that is socially deviant and rejecting of authority. Family structures were undermined by welfare, which made single parenthood both more financially feasible and more morally acceptable. Many of these arguments are still visible within contemporary political discourse.
- Third, social welfare might be achieving the opposite of what Murray (1994) suggests. If social controls are weakening, it might not be social policies that are bringing

this about. Rather, social policies, despite many governments' attempts to curb the growth of the welfare system, are doing the opposite. They provide some (crumbling) social cement and some protection from the divisive effects of economic and cultural change. Thus, public sector provision in the UK has been argued by some to work as a supportive mechanism during times of financial difficulty.

Bearing these different perspectives in mind, we examine in this chapter *whether* or *how far* social policies have played, and might continue to play, a central role in buttressing the social order. The relationship between social policy and social control will be discussed in three main ways:

- at a political level,
- at an individual level, and
- at a local or urban community level (in the concluding section of this chapter).

Social policy and the political order

Social welfare and political control in historical perspective

One of the best-known examples of the political uses of social policy is provided by the history of welfare in Germany. In the late nineteenth century, Otto von Bismarck, the German Chancellor, introduced the first comprehensive national scheme of social insurance in the world. Thus Germany led the field in social insurance at the time, and Germany's insurance scheme had an important influence on social policy in other countries, including Britain. The leading UK Liberal politician, David Lloyd George, visited Germany and was impressed not only by the social benefits of the scheme but also by the political credit gained by the government. By 1911, the Liberal government had introduced the first social insurance scheme to Britain in the form of a National Insurance Act (Part I dealt with insurance against loss of earnings through sickness, Part II with unemployment insurance).

The German government's reforms brought in compulsory insurance for sickness, industrial injury and old-age pensions during the 1880s. These policies were developed before the vote was gained by the working classes and at a time when the government was trying to contain the pressures and demands of a rising trade union and labour movement.

Jones (1985: 50) is not alone in seeing early social insurance in Germany as very much a top-down set of reforms, and 'a means whereby an existing ruling elite endeavours to shore up and legitimize its position in the face of threatened . . . upheaval'. But this was not the whole story. As mentioned in the introduction, social welfare development occurred for a variety of reasons. In Germany, social insurance was provided at a comparatively early stage, partly because of long-standing traditions of paternalistically looking after workers and giving them some social protection (Spicker 1993: 136).

This protective, paternalistic attitude could itself be seen as a form of social control and of trying to preserve a traditional, semi-feudal order. However, Spicker (1993) argues that it also represented a genuine recognition of workers' rights and needs. To see the German reforms solely as a matter of veiled repression would be wrong. There were other autocratic regimes in the nineteenth century where nothing like the apparently progressive social insurance schemes in Germany was ever conceded to the workers.

Twentieth-century Britain: social welfare in the political order

Another point to remember is that while governments might try to use social policies to establish political control, this does not mean that they always succeed. Sometimes new social policies have an effect that is far from stabilizing.

In Britain, Lloyd George's social insurance reforms of 1911 initially led to more conflict and disorder than consensus and acceptance of government control (Lloyd 1993: 34–5). Opposition came from employers who resented having to pay towards employees' insurance cover. There was also some rather frivolous opposition among well-to-do employers, who played up outrage at the idea of having to lick insurance stamps to record weekly contributions for their domestic servants. More significantly, private insurance companies opposed the government scheme, fearing a loss of business, while even trade unions were sceptical about it. Better-paid manual workers' unions had already set up their own 'sick clubs' or medical insurance schemes, and resented the idea of government takeover or control. Finally, many doctors opposed compulsory health insurance because they feared growing state regulation of the work of the medical profession. This latter objection proved to be rather short-sighted, as many people could not afford medical treatment and, until the introduction of the NHS later on, some doctors found it hard to make a living. Earlier introduction of a full health insurance scheme in Britain would have swelled patient numbers and meant more business for doctors.

The willingness of Lloyd George and the Liberal government to struggle against all this opposition was significant. Despite the end result in 1911 being a rather modest and limited insurance scheme that only covered certain sections of low-paid workers, the reform showed that Lloyd George and the Liberals were strongly motivated to challenge many established interests.

Why were they prepared to do this, and to take considerable political risks in introducing the National Insurance Act? There is no doubt that political factors played their part. Liberal leaders were hoping to steal the thunder of a growing Labour Party movement by pushing ahead with social legislation. But there were reasons other than trying to retain electoral support. Lloyd George's motives were, at least in part, genuinely to help low-paid workers. There was a challenging, radical side to Lloyd George's campaign, and therefore it is hard to see the social policies of this time simply as a device to maintain party political control, or the status quo.

However, while social and economic reforms can cause controversy and disrupt the political order rather than cement it, at least in the short term, there is an argument that over a longer period social policies do have the effect of stabilizing society and reducing political conflict. What is the evidence for this?

In Britain, there have been some major 'leaps' in welfare development, illustrated in Table 7.3.

Historically, comprehensive and inclusive reforms stimulated as much political conflict and tension as stability, illustrating the complex relationship between political order and welfare provision. In the UK, a consensus on the continuation of a welfare state existed between the two main political parties between 1945 and the mid-1970s. A loose social contract between government, trade unions and employers emerged in the 1960s and 1970s, but there were always divisions on *how* social policy should be developed (for instance, with regard to education policy and comprehensive schools). Many divisions still remain within contemporary approaches to policy, with these even being played out in the governing Coalition. For example, the Liberal Democrats' election manifesto had a commitment to opposing increased tuition fees for those in higher

Table 7.3 Major leaps in welfare reform

Government era	Type of reform
Liberal reforms of 1906–14	Creation of a basic insurance scheme for workers as discussed above, despite much resistance.
Labour government's welfare state programmes from 1946 to 1951	The introduction of the NHS despite large-scale resistance from doctors, and the introduction of a comprehensive welfare state in the exceptionally consensual and socially disciplined atmosphere of the immediate postwar years. This has been argued to be an attempt to prevent social divisions returning. It was, in this way, a response to a *potential* rather than an *actual* threat of crisis and social disorder (Hennessy 1992).
Conservative reforms that began in 1979 but accelerated from the mid-1980s to the early 1990s	Mrs Thatcher's new-broom approach to social policy – while it was intended to win popular support as well as representing a hard-headed approach to government spending – received a very mixed reception and in the short term seemed to provoke conflict rather than develop a new consensus (Deakin 1994). The idea of competition to increase efficiency has continued to be used in UK social policy.
New Labour welfare reforms, 1997–2010	Increased spending in some areas, the development of new areas of provision in attempts to support those on low income and in poverty. This, however, was accompanied by increased emphasis on the responsibilities of citizens in relation to employment and tightening control in some areas of welfare provision. The private sector also became involved in welfare provision.
Coalition welfare reforms, 2010 onwards	Welfare retrenchment in terms of spending, linked to national debt and austerity measures within policy discourse. Promises of tighter control on some aspects of welfare, increased costs to some sections of society and in general public support for removal of those deemed to be dependent upon the system.

education but these have now been introduced. This increase in fees led to challenges to the social order in the form of protests and some associated civil unrest.

Marxist or 'political economy' views of the social order (see Chapter 7 for a discussion of this perspective) suggest that, although governments have proved willing to invest in large-scale welfare systems in order to stabilize the inherent tensions and inequalities of capitalist society, this will eventually lead to greater instability. This is mainly because welfare spending exacts too high a tax on private employers and may begin to make capitalist firms in high-welfare-spending countries uncompetitive.

At the same time, **welfare capitalism** cannot really do without an advanced welfare system. A welfare state:

- helps to regulate the labour market by absorbing the shocks of economic restructuring and redundancy;
- mitigates the effects of political crisis and questioning of 'the system' by giving capitalism a human face or an appearance of fairness and equal opportunity; and
- meets the needs of a capitalist economy for a labour force that is kept in reasonable health and is sufficiently well educated to keep up with new work technologies.

Although Marxist explanations such as these have given some insight into past connections between social policy, the political order and capitalism, more recent social policy trends in the UK and elsewhere cast doubt on their relevance today. A capitalist economy's need for a well-maintained traditional welfare state might not be as great as suggested. For example, the 'Thatcher experiment' demonstrates that previously unthinkable levels of unemployment could be allowed to occur, together with relatively radical reforms and pruning of the welfare system, despite protest and resistance. Thus, despite threats to political and social stability, governments can not only survive but even prosper electorally.

Britain and other examples

Significant welfare reforms are under way in the UK (see Chapter 6), so we do not yet know what their impact will be or whether they will unleash unmanageable political and social tensions. If so, new forms of social policy might be needed to help to restore the political and social order.

Social policy is not always used as an effective tool to promote equality and fairness, and thus maintain social stability. Despite some social policy innovations and anti-poverty measures New Labour's first term in office (1997–2001) revealed a cautious approach. Social inequalities continued to widen (Dilnot 2001), violent crime increased (Paton Walsh 2001) and, as Islam and Mathiason (2001: 1) point out, 'Investment in hospitals, schools and transport infrastructure sunk to its lowest sustained level since the Second World War during Labour's [first] four years in power'.

Interestingly, the general election campaigns of 2001 and 2005 focused on the various political parties' commitment to restoring public services, particularly in health and education. At that time it seemed that the tide of public opinion might be swinging towards wider acceptance of the need for better public services, and for more direct taxation to pay for them. However, in broad outline the second and third Labour Governments' agenda for public services and social welfare showed more similarity with the market-style reforms of previous Conservative administrations than a determination to introduce clearly pro-welfare and pro-public-sector policies. This pro-market approach has been strengthened by the Coalition Government. There is a strong determination to reduce the costs of public services and to cut back on service provision and levels of benefit despite protests about the changes to tuition fees and the NHS. While some aspects of these changes have led to more unrest, the changes have been made anyway. Arguably, both general discontent with government and specific dissatisfactions with health services, education and other public services are more likely to increase as a result of following this kind of policy. However, much depends on other factors. The state of the economy and the public's sense of satisfaction with their incomes play a key part, as do constantly rising expectations of what the education, health and social services should be able to deliver. Interestingly the Coalition has pushed for research in the area of well-being as a measure of progress, suggesting that a broader approach is needed that moves beyond economic measures to understand what matters to people (Bentley and Churcher 2010).

One way of assessing future prospects in the UK is to consider the impact of welfare reforms in other countries, though comparisons are always difficult because distinctive and different political conditions affect outcomes. However, one particularly telling example is provided by New Zealand's experience of radical cutbacks to its welfare state in the 1990s.

New Zealand had built up an advanced welfare state that was in many ways the forerunner of the British model, and 'by 1938, New Zealand had the most comprehensive social security system in the world' (Walker 1994: 17). However, two governments (first a Labour government, then a National Party (conservative) government) brought in drastic social policy changes. These included selling off the entire stock of public housing, together with cuts in housing benefit. A new tax was introduced to claw back the retirement pension from all but low-income pensioners. The reforms also included the ending of 'free' health care and the introduction of new means tests for access to health services, plus reductions in unemployment, single parent and widows' benefits of between 10 and 25 per cent.

However, the New Zealand example demonstrated that welfare cutbacks and restructuring can go a very long way before there are anything like completely unmanageable political tensions or conflicts. The 'cementing' role of social policies in maintaining the political order, though important, might not be absolutely crucial. Other ways of maintaining political order – in particular, a greater reliance on policing and the criminal justice system – might to some extent replace the role of social welfare, as discussed in Chapter 5.

Finally, though, we should remember that the relationship between social policy and the political order varies greatly between countries. In France in 1995–6, for instance, a great deal of political instability (including nationwide strikes and protests) was triggered by proposals to trim the country's huge social security budget and introduce welfare reforms. And, more recently, proposals to cut spending and reform welfare have led to widespread civil unrest, general strikes and riots in both Greece and Spain (BBC News 2012f, 2012g). These examples of political conflict and disorder *before* welfare cutbacks or proposed changes in regulatory policies have begun to bite are different from the New Zealand case, where these things happened after cutbacks began to bite.

Social control and individual freedom

So far we have considered social policy and social control at what might be called a political or institutional level – that is, the ways in which social order and control might be affected by government and by changes in welfare institutions. We have seen that both the introduction of social insurance (as in Germany at the end of the nineteenth century) and severely pruning the welfare state (as in New Zealand) can have important consequences for the social order.

However, changes in policy and their impact are an individual matter as well as being changes that are played out on the wider political stage. Social control involves a relationship between individual human beings and the various social and political institutions that make up the individual's world. But what does 'social control' in this sense actually mean? Perhaps two examples might help:

- social control that is *directly* coercive, such that an individual's autonomy or freedom is deliberately and obviously suppressed; and
- social control that is *subtly* oppressive and which encourages people to fit into accepted social roles, or suppresses their individuality in less obvious ways.

Social welfare and coercion

Those who are in a controlling position in the field of welfare – for instance, professionals and practitioners in health and welfare services – might tell service users that what is being done for them is 'in their own interests'. However, an objective appraisal might reveal that control operates to benefit the service provider or the administrator of a policy more than the user of services.

Not surprisingly, most of the criticisms of directly coercive control occurred when long-stay care in mental hospitals and other kinds of residential institution was much more common than it is today. Ken Kesey's fictional *One Flew Over the Cuckoo's Nest* (1962) – later dramatized and made into a feature film starring Jack Nicholson – and a study by Erving Goffman of **institutional care**, *Asylums* (1991), had a telling effect upon attitudes among professionals as well as the general public towards 'over-control' in long-stay institutions.

Kesey and Goffman both tried to show not only that patients in mental hospitals are restricted in their freedoms, losing civil liberties and their rights as citizens, but also that institutional control seeks to change behaviour and identity in a malign way, disabling individuals and making them more dependent than before.

The 'liberal critique' of social control in institutions helped to pave the way for the development of community care policies and the widespread closure of long-stay facilities (see Chapter 12). Despite the development of community care, however, abuses of power and 'over-control' in residential settings still occur. There have been many recent examples of such abuse within residential care and in hospitals (BBC News 2012a, 2012h).

Nor is the directly coercive approach restricted to health services or personal social services. Since the early 1990s there has been a renewed interest in government in finding new ways to deter undeserving claimants and to prevent social security fraud. In the USA, for instance, welfare reforms introduced by Bill Clinton's administration consolidated tougher approaches to welfare claimants that had begun earlier on. President Clinton's reforms introduced strict time limits to the receipt of benefits, after which all government help is withdrawn.

In the UK nothing quite as strict as this has yet been introduced. However, the trend in Britain is also towards a more directly controlling approach in benefits policy, a move that began in the early 1990s (Dean 1991: 180; Spicker 1993: 108), which has continued and is still evident within contemporary Coalition Government reform. It was also developed by the Labour Government in 2001, through the Welfare Reform Act, which was designed to detect and curb welfare fraud. Similarly, Coalition Government policies are an attempt to show greater willingness to suspend benefits where fraud is suspected and the greater likelihood of prosecution in cases of benefit 'fiddles'. The tougher approach is also clear in the ways that successive governments have encouraged claimants to find work. And it can be seen in the policy of making receipt of benefits conditional upon taking up employment training, and, in the USA, in the introduction of workfare policies. As Spicker (1993) observes, the prospect of 'workfare work' (together with the possibility of parents having to place their children in substandard childcare facilities while at work) becomes a deterrent against claiming.

Welfare reform in the USA is an important example to consider because US social policies have been an influential model for British politicians and decision-makers. Both Labour and Conservative politicians have been keen about learning from US experiments to try to change the behaviour and attitude of welfare recipients. The underlying ideas, language and terminology of American reforms can be seen in UK social security and welfare reforms. Complete Activity 7.3 to explore this in more depth.

Box 7.2 Learning from the USA?

- US evidence on the impact of welfare reforms is mixed. For instance, Horowitz (1995), in studying a federal-government-sponsored project to assist teenage mothers, found that some professional helpers relied heavily on a coercive, controlling approach. In seeing their task as 'making responsible citizens' out of people who are over-dependent on welfare, these workers demanded submission to authority from the teenage mothers. They wanted to see what the professional workers defined as 'changed attitudes'. The results of this type of intervention were, in some cases, the opposite of what was required. Welfare dependency was increased while self-esteem and independence were reduced. Other professional workers, however, genuinely fostered a more independent outlook among teenage mothers and helped them to make their own decisions.
- Britain is similar to the USA in that moral concerns about single parenthood and fears about the welfare system creating dependency, strongly voiced by many politicians and the media, have helped to create a social climate in which a more directly coercive approach to control is encouraged. However, this does not mean that such a coercive, controlling approach will always be used – it will depend on the way any particular project is staffed and run.

Activity 7.3 Moral panics and the need for control

Stanley Cohen, in his study *Folk Devils and Moral Panics* (1987) first used the term 'moral panics'. He defined these as an episode of anxiety about threats to the values and principles that are upholding society. Cohen emphasized the role of the mass media in contributing to these panics. Some argue that moral panics arise when there are economic crises. So in the wake of the current economic crisis, use the Internet to access media reports and discussions of welfare to identify some groups that you could label as contemporary folk devils.

1. List the groups that you think are folk devils.
2. List some examples of negative labelling.
3. Consider your own viewpoint in relation to Cohen's ideas: what are your beliefs? Do you believe that these groups are seen as folk devils or are there other reasons why they are picked out for attention in the mass media?
4. As a final insight, visit this website and take the CHAV test: http://chavstest.com/quiz/index.php. Read the questions carefully and think about how these reflect negative labelling. Are Chavs still seen as 'folk devils'?

Activity 7.3 will have helped you to explore labelling and how it is part of social control. Despite concerns about some social groups, and associated negative labelling, social security fraud and undeserved claiming should clearly not be ignored. There is a substantial amount of unjustified claiming. In 2010–11 overpayment of benefits due to fraud was estimated to have cost £1.2 billion (NAO 2012). This results not only in a loss of resources that could be better used elsewhere but also in an undesirable degree of welfare dependency among claimants, as well as general cynicism and disillusion with the welfare system. Nor is it sufficiently convincing to make the point that losses from the public purse through dishonest tax evasion are greater than social security fraud, therefore the latter is excusable. Two wrongs do not make a right, even if the tax evasion wrong is of a much bigger size.

A more relevant point, perhaps, is that while a degree of control and a fair system for checking eligibility are clearly needed, the recent policy shift towards a tougher stance on social security carries with it dangers of excessive or punitive control. It could represent the growth of a kind of 'policing' of personal and family life that is unacceptable in a free society.

One way in which this 'policing' and additional supervision of people's lives has been justified is in relation to the underclass debate mentioned in this and earlier chapters (see Chapter 2). Murray (1994) and others on the political right drew attention to the supposed threat posed to the social order by the emergence of an underclass, and the need to take a more restrictive approach to the provision of social benefits, housing and other forms of welfare to people in poverty. However, since the late 1980s – when conservative opinion was preoccupied by worries about the underclass – there has been disagreement about whether such a group exists. Even if it does, it is not certain that social welfare plays the role in trapping people in an underclass that Murray suggests. The term underclass is less frequently used in political circles now, although it is still mentioned on occasion such as in the aftermath of the 2011 riots with rioters labelled as 'feral underclass' (Wilson 2011).

However, assuming that there is an underclass, there has also been debate about the causes of underclass formation. Is an underclass created by cultural causes (the values and lifestyle of a criminal, 'work-shy' group who reject society) or structural factors (lack of opportunity, and people being excluded from the labour force as a result of economic change and high unemployment in run-down areas)? How specific groups of people are viewed and described is therefore affected by our ideological position (see Table 7.4).

Table 7.4 Views of the underclass, ideological position and policy approaches

Ideological position	View of the underclass and control
Political right	The underclass is a way of life that can be altered because it is based on individuals' choice to live irresponsibly, according to unacceptable values and unwillingness to work. This is the main reason for 'getting tough' on social security.
Political left	The underclass is the result of lack of opportunity, and people being excluded from the labour force therefore more employment, training opportunities and support are required.
New Labour	Combined both types of explanation in their policies on social security and welfare dependency, through the terms 'social exclusion' and 'the socially excluded'. Implemented policies that were both supportive of some groups, such as those engaging with employment, and more punitive for those who ignored their responsibilities. Those who did not engage were viewed as in need of reform; the attitudes and outlook of those claiming benefit needed to be changed, and claimants had to be re-educated.
Coalition Government	View many as dependent, and stress the need to be tough and reduce welfare dependency for those who are lazy, feckless and irresponsible. While not using the term underclass, Coalition Government ministers still emphasize the need to be tough and to control certain individuals.

In Chapter 8, the question of how far government policies in these areas of employment and social security are directly controlling or coercive in this way will be further discussed. What can be concluded here, though, is that there has been a clear trend since the early 1990s towards increasing regulation and restriction of welfare benefits. New Labour policy attempted to lessen dependence on the state and to reduce the state's role in our lives. However, their social policies steadily increased the importance of means testing and selectivity of benefits, and the Coalition Government's reform has continued in much the same vein (see Chapter 6).

Social policies and indirect control: the examples of age and other social divisions

As well as direct forms of control we also need to consider the ways in which social policies and social welfare might be thought to have *indirectly* controlling effects. To illustrate this, the examples of age divisions in social policy will be discussed. Other examples, such as the indirect ways in which social policies might maintain gender divisions, or disadvantage disabled people, are also important.

One way of detecting the impact of the more subtle or indirect forms of social control is to observe the impact of *ideas* and *beliefs* on particular groups. For instance, Thompson (1998) outlines the various ways in which prevalent stereotypes and myths oppress disabled and older people. They are often seen as incapable of participating fully in decision-making or in shaping policy. Welfare practitioners and professionals are prone to think of older and/or disabled people as dependent, needy and as victims of tragic circumstances (the decline of health in old age, or the 'tragedy' of disability).

These dominant assumptions can subtly (and sometimes not so subtly) reinforce the idea that it is only younger and non-disabled people who can legitimately take decisions on behalf of, or make policy about, the welfare of older and disabled people. Often, these ideas are so powerful and such common currency that many people who themselves are older and/or disabled will share them, or at least be reluctant or unable to challenge them.

The term oppression is helpful in understanding this. As Thompson (1998: 10) suggests, oppression can include any action or degrading treatment that denies people their citizenship and human dignity. It can take the form of obvious coercion, such as mental cruelty or physical abuse. However, the kinds of oppression we are about to look at are not so obvious, and often are all the harder to challenge because they might exist in an atmosphere of co-operation between those who provide health and welfare services and those who are provided for.

This is illustrated very well by the example of state pensions for older people. The state retirement pension is a key example of the way a welfare benefit can become a form of social control.

When the first state pension was introduced in Britain in 1908, it was very popular. Millions of older people saw it as a liberation from worries about the Poor Law and 'going on the parish'. Yet the first state pension was not a large amount and was restricted to people over the age of 70. As average life expectancy for most people was *below* 70 years in the early twentieth century, and many would die before they qualified for it, the state pension was not quite the generous innovation it might have seemed to begin with! In an age of individualism and of expecting people to fend for themselves, however, it was seen as a generous policy for the state to commit itself to giving a regular – if very small – income to older people.

Also, the first state pension was seen very much as a *gift* – because it was a *non-contributory* benefit (see Chapter 6) at that stage. Any older person who qualified (they had to be means tested and on a low income) received the pension without having had to make insurance contributions earlier on.

Thus we can see in this early example of social policy the contradictory effects of welfare. The first pension was both liberating and oppressive. It was liberating because it provided a small income and a little independence for every old person who qualified for it. It was oppressive and controlling, however, in that it was a form of welfare provided as a gift for which people were expected to feel grateful. It was not at that stage a benefit that people had earned through insurance contributions. Above all, it began a trend towards marking out old age as a distinct phase of 'retirement', in which people would increasingly be expected to adopt a passive, dependent role in society.

At the time the first pension was introduced, about two-thirds of men aged 65 were still in paid employment (and only a small minority of women, young or old, were in full-time paid work). Admittedly, much of this work was a necessity. Without a pension to look forward to, many men had to carry on working – possibly until they died – simply to make ends meet, and despite increasing infirmity. Nevertheless, the positive side of this was that 'retirement' did not really exist then in the same way that it does now. Old age was seen as a distinct – if typically short – period of life, but it involved roles at work and in the family and community.

In the 1930s, the proportion of men still in work after their 65th birthday had fallen to one-third. By the 1950s – following the Beveridge-inspired reform in 1946 of the contribution-based state retirement pension, first introduced in 1925 – the proportion had shrunk yet further, to just a few per cent of 65-year-olds. As Phillipson (1982) has argued, this represents the *social construction* of a phase of life. Old age is not simply a 'natural' stage in which the ways we behave or the ways we are seen by others are determined by the physiological or biological processes of ageing. Later life, according to Phillipson and others (see, for instance, Johnson and Slater 1993), is also a social experience very much influenced by social expectations and economic pressures.

This can also be illustrated by the further development of the pensions system. By 1946, when a National Insurance Act implemented Beveridge's reform of the state retirement pension (see Chapter 3), pensionable ages were set at 60 for women and 65 for men (they had been the same for both men and women – 65 – until 1940). That momentous step from 'middle aged' to 'old' and from 'employed' (or employable) to 'retired' was based on a rather arbitrary, socially defined dividing line. Not only that, but also a more significant condition was introduced. From 1946 on, older people could not get the state pension unless they 'retired' and gave up work. This institutionalized the idea of old age as a 'pensioned off' and workless phase of life (Walker 1990: 59). The notion of older people being excluded from work (with its connotations of being made valueless) became an entrenched idea. It has remained as a defining characteristic of the status of older people even though the retirement condition was abolished in 1989.

Are perceptions in this area changing? Contemporary policy changes now mean that older people are expected to work for longer, with the age of eligibility for state pensions being increased for both men and women in the UK. From December 2018 the state pension age for both men and women will start to increase, to reach 66 by October 2020 (Directgov 2012b). Will these policy changes result in wider attitude changes in relation to widespread views surrounding old age? Complete Activity 7.4 to explore this area more.

Activity 7.4 Old age as a social division

Use the Internet to access the website www.bbc.co.uk/programmes/b01kjt7k. Here you will find a range of information and documentary programmes related to ageing. As a starting point listen to the radio programme 'You and Yours: Working when I'm 65'.

1. What does this programme tell you about age as a social division?
2. Do older people wish to work?
3. What barriers still exist for those who wish to remain in work?

There is a range of related links on the BBC website so explore these too. Now reflect upon how the UK social policy changes will affect you and those that you know when you are older. What are your views?

While there are changes afoot to extend working life, it remains the case that historically social policy has indirectly been an instrument of social control and, according to Phillipson (1982), an integral part of a capitalist market economy's construction of the 'redundant' status of old age and 'retirement'.

Similar patterns can be observed in other areas of welfare. As with the state pension, being entitled to certain 'special' benefits and services that are targeted towards a particular group is a mixed blessing. On the one hand, such welfare benefits are genuinely helpful and needed. People need pensions, and they need a range of social services. They can be in the form of free or subsidized transport (for example, bus passes), specially designed accommodation (for example, **sheltered housing**), or domiciliary and community services (for example, 'meals on wheels', **day centres**). They also include cash benefits such as special one-off allowances for older people, which echo the gift-like nature of the first state pension.

On the other hand, the more that the welfare system creates 'special' services and benefits for older people the more likely it is to assist in the process of marking out later life as an 'unfortunate', needy or dependent phase of life. The 'concessions' that are provided to people when they reach retirement age are a subject of humour. Jibes such as 'Have you collected your bus pass yet?' illustrate the rather pointed ways in which people remind each other of age divisions. They also illustrate the way in which a stereotype of ***welfarism*** can be applied to older people and to the status of old age. Proposed Coalition Government policy may, however, mean that some of these special provisions are removed in the future.

Welfarism does not only devalue the status of older people. As Thompson (1998) points out, it can also be the basis of patronizing attitudes towards disabled people and other marginalized groups such as people with mental health problems. In all these cases, being dependent on welfare is seen as the defining characteristic of such social groups.

A number of shocking revelations of the maltreatment and routine abuse of older people in hospitals and other situations have been made (see BBC News 2012a, 2012h). These cases show that the distinction between 'indirect' and 'direct' social control can be rather artificial. In practice, the connections between prejudice and action, or discrimination, are close. The neglect and abuse of older people in the health and social care system are reflections not only of economic or staffing crises in an over-stretched health service, but also of an underlying culture that has given us a set of negative perceptions of older people.

Therefore, as we have seen, social policy and welfare services have a dual impact. On the one hand, welfare services and benefits are – despite their limitations – often protective and helpful. On the other, they mark out certain groups such as older people as 'special' or marginal. This reinforces a dependent, devalued status. A similar dual impact of social policy has been observed in relation to gender divisions, and in particular with regard to women's independence and social position, which has led to widespread criticism of such policy from feminists.

The development of a welfare state undoubtedly helped women in many ways – for instance through the introduction of general benefits such as the retirement pension and unemployment benefits, and special benefits such as widows' pensions, maternity benefit and child benefit. At the same time, however, the way in which these benefits were introduced in the 1940s helped to reinforce a dependent status for many women, as Box 7.3 illustrates.

Box 7.3 Gendered social divisions and the role of social policy

- By building on certain assumptions about marriage and the family role of women, social policies have often reinforced a traditional 'breadwinner' role for men and a domestic role for women.
- The system worked on the assumption that women would be economically dependent on men and that they would play a less important role than men in the job market (see, for example, Lewis 1983; Dale and Foster 1986; Pascall 1986; Hallett 1995).
- The Beveridge committee's plan for social security assumed that most married women would not continue in full-time paid work. Early social security policy therefore assumed that it was right for married women's security to be determined by their husbands' contribution records. Married women could not claim important benefits as independent citizens in their own right. This has changed now, however.
- While some argue that the social security system is built upon 'a male model of employment patterns requiring full time and continuous employment' (Wyn 1991: 108), recent reforms have attempted to encourage women into work. However, gendered assumptions about responsibilities means that women remain disadvantaged (Pascall 2008).

Despite the evidence that the social security system can be oppressive, however, there is another side to the story. Income support and benefits of other kinds, though providing only a basic income, may nevertheless give a degree of independence to some women's lives. This 'modicum of independence', suggests Wyn (1991: 109), might 'enable women to get out of dangerous relationships with men'. So while life on social security can hardly be said to be liberating in the full sense, it might give a degree of freedom to women wanting to set up their own households or control their own resources.

Taken to an extreme, this is the argument put forward by Murray (1994) and others on the political right – that social security policy has been a key element in weakening traditional family norms and in creating the acceptability of single parenthood. However, this argument does not have to be pushed to the extreme to show that the effects of social security benefits on people's lives are contradictory. They have mixed effects. As we have seen, social security rules bring disincentives and controlling effects. The take-up of benefits by lone parents has increased very significantly since 1990 but the low levels of income on benefit are hardly conducive to a free or liberating lifestyle.

Nevertheless it is true that, without social security, a certain amount of freedom would be lost. If there are decisions to freeze or reduce a benefit – such as the Coalition Government's decision to introduce a cut-off to child-benefit provision based upon levels of earnings – then there are often many objections, including from those who defend women's rights. Britain's relatively ungenerous welfare system does not provide as good an example of the effects of social security and other policies on gender roles as some other west European countries where provision in areas such as maternity benefit, and child and family policy is much more extensive. For example, Sweden, though it has undergone welfare reforms and has slightly reduced the scale of some welfare benefits and services, is still one of the most generous and comprehensive examples of a welfare system that is designed to help women. This is especially so in the case of policies which are meant to ease women's re-entry to work and support them in the task of balancing family and paid work responsibilities (Summerskill and Hinsliff 2001).

Interestingly, Swedish women's participation in the labour force is much higher than in Britain. However, despite this the apparently liberating family and child-care policies in Sweden seem to have subtly confirmed traditional gender roles. A lot of Swedish women continue to work 'long' part-time hours rather than full-time, whereas – because of traditional gender roles – relatively few fathers work part-time or share parental leave equally with mothers. Given the persistence of these values and of gender roles, it is not surprising that the generosity of the welfare system gives little incentive to women to work full-time and perhaps pursue a career to higher positions.

In this way a generous and enlightened welfare system can be seen to be subtly reinforcing the social order and its established gender divisions. But this is not an argument for reducing support for parents who work. Nor does the Swedish example prove that social policies that strongly support women will *inevitably* reinforce traditional gender roles. Swedish policies provide many positive outcomes for women – the opportunity to enjoy a protected standard of living while being involved with childrearing and paid work. The point is rather that social policies that try to bridge the worlds of work and family seem to have a mixture of effects, both liberating and controlling.

Is social control through policy always negative?

A view of the social order as something that can genuinely help individuals to develop, or that will encourage the social integration of individuals and minority groups, suggests that social control can be benign. The educational process can be used as an illustration. Learning to read, for instance, involves mastering the rules and conventions of language in written form – the shapes of the different letters, how words are spelled, the rules of grammar and punctuation. The parent who reads with the child and points out these rules and understandings is in a way exercising 'social control', though usually in an enjoyable and flexible way. Nevertheless, in pointing out where the child has misread a word, or by gently correcting mistakes and guiding the young reader back to the text, the parent is controlling the situation and the child's learning. Of course, this may be done well or badly. With too much control and too little enjoyment, the young child may well reject the parent's help.

Later, at school, the same principles apply. To make progress, children need a certain amount of control. The tasks they work on must be sufficiently exciting and interesting, but the classroom environment must also be relatively calm and secure. Equally, the school itself will need to be well run. Thus social control exists at a number of levels: individual, group and institutional.

Presented in this unproblematic way, social control *can* be seen to be working in the individual's best interests even though individuals – for instance, young children – may not realize the benefits of being controlled. Control that leads to independence of the individual is genuinely liberating. The child is guided into reading, but eventually becomes an independent reader who is free to explore a wider world of books or the Internet.

The problem with this definition, however, is that social control is not always completely in the best interests of the person being controlled. There is the question – raised at the very beginning of this chapter – of whether the welfare system, being part of government and the state, is more concerned with controlling us than with our welfare (for instance, by restricting demand for good-quality services by telling us what we 'really' need). Control involves paternalism and, in its most paternalistic forms, will make it difficult for individuals to exercise their rights.

Conclusions: can social policies bring benign control?

Social policies have brought benefits to people and even a measure of liberation. However, critics of the welfare system on the political right have argued that welfare – especially social security – can become too controlling and can easily interfere in people's lives in negative ways. To radical critics of welfare on the left, the traditional welfare state was shot through with sexist assumptions about the roles of men and women, and continues to foster ageist definitions of older people and patronizing attitudes towards disabled people as dependent and redundant.

In trying to reach your own conclusions about the role of social policy in the social order, you might find it helpful to review the main strands in the argument outlined at the beginning of this chapter. The welfare system can be seen either as maintaining and supporting the social order and accepted means of social control, or as undermining and weakening the foundations of existing society. But it is quite likely that different parts of the welfare system play different roles and have different effects from each other. In total, the welfare system probably performs *both* functions – simultaneously supporting some parts of the social fabric but causing change and a weakening of traditional social bonds in other respects, as this chapter has continually illustrated.

First, the point has been made in this chapter that it might not be fair to view social control in an entirely negative light. Indeed, there are some positive definitions of social control that have been discussed, such as education. Yet the problem of paternalism remains, and debates continue in relation to social policy as a benign mechanism of control.

A number of examples and trends in social policy illustrate the complexities associated with social control through the policy process. As discussed in this chapter, there has been a noticeable change in British social policy – beginning with the Conservative administration before 1997, New Labour until 2010 and now vigorously pursued by the Coalition Government – towards a 'tougher', more restrictive approach towards welfare claimants. Also, the emphasis of social security policy is now much more upon the goal of getting claimants into paid work, where this is feasible (see Chapter 9 for further discussion of employment policy). As pointed out above, this can be seen as a positive goal, and being encouraged into work will often be in the interests of people, but it has increased the danger of creating a society in which 'the state knows best what's good for you'.

In other respects, though, some legislation protects rights and freedoms and allows individual citizens to challenge government institutions that are too controlling. For example, the Human Rights Act 1998 has led to many challenges to state control in some controversial areas such as prisoners' rights to vote (see Chapter 5).

In addition to this Act there have been other significant steps in advancing human rights by introducing legislation that helps people to challenge unfair discrimination or to win access to services or facilities that they have a right to use – for instance the Disability Discrimination Act 1995 (although this has been criticized for applying the 'medical model' of disability: see Casserley 2000). Despite their limitations, the Human Rights Act and the Disability Discrimination Act provide positive and potentially very helpful means for people to challenge 'the coercive state' discussed by Hillyard and Percy-Smith (1988). Also, as Stainton (1994) points out with reference to the needs of people with learning difficulties, there are ways – even without relying upon anti-discrimination legislation – to give more respect, choice and freedom to users of welfare services. Policies that aim to empower recipients are discussed later (see Chapter 12).

Therefore the prospects for 'benign' social control and for greater openness, freedom and democratic participation in providing and running welfare services are mixed. On the one hand, we are witnessing – especially in the field of social security and employment – a tendency towards more 'top-down' control and paternalism. In other respects the advent of equality legislation acts as a counterbalancing influence to 'the enormous growth of the power of public and quasi-public bodies over the lives of individuals' (Wadham and Mountfield 1999: 4).

It is likely that the question of how far social policies are either liberating or oppressive will only be resolved with any certainty by studies of specific policies or the particular social groups or individuals affected by those policies. Far-reaching 'radical' criticisms of the nature of society, social control and 'the oppressive welfare system' might not be as helpful, because – as we have seen in this chapter – the relationship between social policy and social control is complicated and contradictory.

Summary of key points

- Social control is inextricably bound up with the provision of welfare and social policy because social welfare often functions to regulate specific groups of people, as well as providing benefits.
- Social control is not always negative. Many would agree that in education, for example, it can be positive for many individuals, depending on how it is applied.

Key terms and concepts

Chavs
coercion
ideology
marginalization
oppression
social consensus
social contract
social control
stigmatization
underclass
welfare capitalism
welfare dependency
welfarism
workfare

Suggestions for further reading

Alcock, P. (2006) *Understanding Poverty.* 3rd edition. London: Palgrave Macmillan.

This book provides a readable and succinct overview of social security policy that also has much to say about the nature of social control. The book is a very useful introduction to the field covering the context of poverty, definition and measurement, social divisions and poverty (including gender, racism, age and disability) and the policy framework.

Bernard, M. and Phillips, J. (eds) (1998) *The Social Policy of Old Age.* London: Centre for Policy on Ageing.

This book critically reviews social policy developments as they have affected older people since the creation of the welfare state. It covers traditional policy areas and issues, and it offers perspectives on how policy might develop to meet more successfully the demands of an empowered older population.

Hillyard, P. and Percy-Smith, J. (1988) *The Coercive State.* London: HarperCollins.

This book surveys a wide range of policy areas (including examples such as the 1988 reform of the NHS) to show that in many respects the welfare state has become much less democratic and accountable over the years. It provides useful historical context for understanding contemporary changes.

Jones, O. (2011) *Chavs: The Demonization of the Working Class.* London: Verso.

This book focuses upon middle-class contempt towards working-class people and explores the ways in which they are regarded and labelled by right-wing commentators. Controversial but insightful, the book is worth reading in relation to the power of labels and continued social divisions within the UK.

Piven, F.F. and Cloward, R. (1993) *Regulating the Poor.* 2nd edition. New York: Vintage.

This is a classic study of the link between welfare and social control. It still deserves to be read, especially with hindsight and as a way of understanding the subsequent assault on the welfare system by conservative politicians in the USA and Britain in the 1980s. This is a classic social science analysis examining welfare state change and associated social control.

Roulston, A. and Prideaux, S. (2012) *Understanding Disability Policy.* Bristol: Policy Press.

This book explores disability policy within a broad social policy framework, which includes a focus upon welfare. Looking at social security, social support, poverty, socioeconomic status, community safety, official discourses and spatial change, the authors explore disabled people's opportunities. The book also examines changing official and academic constructions of disability and their implications for social policy in the twenty-first century.

Spicker, P. (1984) *Stigma and Social Welfare.* London: Croom Helm.

This book explores the relationship between stigma and social welfare. It is available free through a creative commons licence and can be located at www2.rgu.ac.uk/publicpolicy/introduction/books/stigma.htm. Paul Spicker continues to write extensively in relation to welfare and so his later books may also be of interest, such as the 2007 *The Idea of Poverty* (Bristol: Policy Press), which covers definitions, measurement and understandings, on occasion being controversial.

Yeandle, Sue (ed.) (2008) *Policy for a Change: Local Labour Market Analysis and Gender Equality.* Bristol: Policy Press.

This book explores a range of questions that are relevant to this chapter, including: Why is part-time employment such a popular but economically damaging choice for women? What barriers still limit women's horizons and narrow their aspirations? It explores women's employment and related policies, and pervasive myths about women and work are examined.

8 Who makes policy? The example of education

Key learning outcomes

By the end of this chapter you should:

- be able to understand the ways in which education policy illustrates different models of power
- be able to identify and outline the complexities of government decision-making, using changes in education policy as an example
- be able to discuss the recent policy changes in education being made by the Coalition Government

Overview of the chapter

In Chapter 7 we explored a general question – how far is social policy an agent of social control? In this chapter we continue the theme of power and control through an examination of educational policy. Social policies are always the result of the exercise of power in some way. Governments might introduce policies without much consultation with those outside the narrow circle of elite politicians and their advisers (in which case we may refer to policies that are imposed from the 'top down'). Or policies might be the result of a lengthy political process that sometimes involves a lot of conflict among politicians and various pressure groups outside government. Recent educational reform and policy changes have resulted in conflict and widespread debate about the long-term effects of the policy changes. This chapter explores these changes and associated controversies, and continues the debates started in Chapter 7 in relation to the connections between social policy on the one hand, and questions of social control, coercion and freedom on the other. Power within the policy-making process is also critically discussed as a starting point for this analysis. However, the chapter is not intended to give a comprehensive overview of education policy in the UK; rather, it will use key developments in education as illustrations of the way policies and decisions are made, in order to examine how democratic the policy-making process is.

Power and democracy

Not all policy-making is surrounded by intense controversy or conflict between different groups in society. First, 'top-down' or imposed social policies might be widely accepted without opposition either because they are seen as beneficial or good policies in themselves or, in a 'paternalistic' welfare state (see Chapter 6), because it does not occur to most people that they should, or could, be able to participate in the decisions made about their welfare. Much of the legislation and policy-making that created the British welfare state in the 1940s could be seen this way (see Chapter 2). Second, new social policies might emerge from a democratic process of discussion, or consultation between government and people, without highly divisive conflict. As a rule, though, democratic involvement in policy-making entails heated debate, disagreements between groups who see things differently from each other, and eventually some trade-offs or compromises.

Where policy-making is less democratic, governments are able to develop policies that suit their own interests before those of the general public or the people who are going to be most affected by the new policies. Thus it is highly important to be sceptical about *why* any given social policy has been introduced, and how far the power of central government will be enhanced or reduced by it. This is because some policies are made not only for the 'official' reasons that are stated by government – for instance, to improve social welfare or educational services in some way – but also because they have been designed to promote the power of government (and the political party that runs it). For instance, as will be discussed later in this chapter, a series of reforms to education in England and Wales have much reduced the power of local authorities over schools and, according to some, have increased competition and social exclusion in secondary education through the break-up of the comprehensive school system in England.

Thus it is crucial to make a distinction between the two roles, or 'faces', of a policy. One role of a social policy is to try to make an improvement in human welfare or to develop services (which it might or might not do very effectively). The other role – often as equally important as the first, at least to those who draft policies – is to enhance the power of the political leader, government department or minister responsible for the policy. In extreme cases, where the political motivations of government and rival political parties become increasingly blatant, the policy in question will come to be seen as a 'political football'. In other words, it will have become more important for a government or for an opposition party to score points over their rival, or to try to switch the direction of policy to suit their particular ideology, than it is to have thought about the pros and cons of the policy itself. Housing policy (see the conclusion of Chapter 11), for example, has been described as a 'political football'.

In summary, then, there are two introductory points to make about the relationship between social policy, power and the role of government.

- First, there is a distinction to be made between policies that are, on the one hand, drawn up and imposed by government without much discussion or democratic input and, on the other, policies that have been shaped by a more democratic process of negotiation between interest groups, or of participation and 'grass roots' involvement.
- Second, there is the question of how far policies are developed in the public interest. In education, for instance, will a new policy actually benefit children's learning or respond to parents' wishes for a better education system? Or is the new policy designed primarily to promote the power and reputation of a governing party (thus enhancing its prospects for re-election) or the 'government machine' as a whole (civil servants and advisers, as well as politicians)?

This chapter will use education policy as an example to examine both these points. Therefore you should have gained, by the end of this chapter, some knowledge of recent developments in educational policy.

Government and state

In education, as with all major public services, government and state play leading roles in shaping the system. However, what is meant by 'government' and 'state' is not always obvious, and first some basic definitions are needed (see Table 8.1).

Table 8.1 Defining government and state

Term	Definition
Government	Involves an intricate web of relationships among: • a Prime Minister, ministers in cabinet, and political advisers who form the core of central government policy-making in the UK • senior civil servants and government ministers who work out the details of important policy changes • parliament and the government of the day. The UK government at Westminster must manage legislation in the House of Commons and House of Lords. It must deal with challenges to its policies from opposition MPs and sometimes from MPs in the government's own party. Government must also respond to select committees
The state	This includes: • public servants: for example, teachers, and Department for Education civil servants who administer and implement policy • local government (elected councillors and local government officials) and other local bodies (for example, school governing bodies) • quangos (quasi-autonomous non-governmental organizations), which are set up by central government to supervise and/or fund a particular function or task. For instance, the Office for Standards in Education (Ofsted) is headed by a Chief Inspector of Schools and is responsible for supervising arrangements for assessing the quality of schools and teachers

Government shapes policy, but what actually happens on the ground is often determined by the effectiveness of civil servants at the national level, or by the amount of co-operation with central government departments shown by local officials or by professionals such as teachers.

Government and state are sometimes partners and sometimes rivals in creating and implementing policies. However, they are far from being the sole influences on policy. Many other things constrain the hands of government and state: for instance, the *economic cost* of a policy and the public money available, the *political acceptability* of a policy and the legacy of *previous policy decisions*. Even a government strongly committed to change will often find it extremely difficult to alter existing policies or the ways in which policies have been decided in the past.

Key interest groups (for example, business interests or parents' lobby groups) might also have enough power either to block a policy or to amend it, or to put new issues on the *policy agenda*. This last term refers to the way in which some issues gain leading importance in national life while others do not, or slip off the agenda after a period of being in the limelight. There are differences of opinion as to what is of pressing importance. Therefore, it would be wrong to think of the policy agenda as a single list of priorities that everyone agrees upon. However, it is a useful concept. It helps to understand which issues the government wishes to place at the top of the agenda and which at the bottom, while pressure groups such as parents' representatives may have different priorities. Complete Activity 8.1 to explore how issues get on the policy agenda.

Activity 8.1 Jamie Oliver and the school dinners campaign

In 2005 Jamie Oliver, a celebrity chef, launched a campaign called 'Feed Me Better' as part of a Channel 4 documentary series. The campaign was about improving the quality of school meals. It prompted much media attention, political discussion and subsequent policy change.

Use the Internet to view the following websites to read more about the campaign:

- Jamie Oliver's blog and discussion of the issues: www.jamieoliver.com/news-and-blogs/news/school-food-campaign-latest
- BBC news report about a school meals review following the campaign: http://news.bbc.co.uk/1/hi/education/4551421.stm
- A recent BBC news report (2011) in which Jamie Oliver criticizes current nutritional standards: www.bbc.co.uk/news/education-15888059

Now make some notes on the following questions:

1. How was Jamie Oliver able to get the issue of school food onto the policy agenda? Reflect upon changing patterns of obesity, political interest in the issue and willingness of the government to listen.
2. What policy changes were made as a result?
3. Were the policy changes that were made sustainable?

From exploring this issue in Activity 8.1, you should have realized that Jamie Oliver was just one actor among many who helped to raise awareness and achieve policy change in relation to one aspect of educational provision. Naik (2008) argues that Jamie Oliver did not put school meals on the policy agenda. However, he and the media together helped to both promote and develop policy within this area. This facilitated wider acceptance of the changes though some children rejected the changes to school meals and some groups of parents also opposed them. A change of government has, however, resulted in a change of policy in this area, and less support and funding for improvements to school meals. This is an illustration of changing power dynamics in the policy process.

Models of power: understanding how decisions are made

In order to make sense of what has been happening in education, or in any area of social policy, it is helpful to compare different views or models of how policies develop. No single model or theory will perfectly account for every policy and its outcome. To understand the policy process satisfactorily we need to combine a number of models.

The democratic pluralist model

The **democratic pluralist model** is probably the closest to popular and 'common-sense' views of how government *should* act and how policies *should* be made in a democratic society. However, partly as a result of widespread publicity about leading politicians' alleged manipulation of evidence put before parliament (for instance, before and after the second war in Iraq), and about abuses of power and privilege by politicians, many people's trust in the idea that decisions are made democratically, or that politicians are accountable to the people, has been eroded especially in the wake of recent and ongoing expenses scandals. This loss of belief in democracy has arguably been demonstrated by decreasing turnout at general elections. For instance in the election of 2005 the lowest turnout since 1919 was registered, and less than half of young voters (aged 18–25) bothered to vote. However, the 2010 UK election saw a significant increase, with the numbers of voters rising by over 2m people to 29.6m, when compared to the 2005 turn-out (Walton 2010).

While public disillusionment with politics and politicians is often said to be growing in the UK, this does not mean that the democratic model, or view of how politics works, is completely worthless or outdated. Arguably, there is at least *some* democratic input into the policy-making process in Britain, and politicians are *held* accountable to the democratic will to some degree.

However, it is impossible to resolve the argument about 'how much' democracy we have, or how democratic policy-making is, without defining democracy itself. For instance, if we were to define a democracy as a community in which everyone had an exactly equal say, and in which power was shared absolutely equally between all individuals, then no large-scale societies or political groups would qualify as 'democratic'. This ideal does not, and cannot, exist in its purest form.

Thus a realistic definition of democracy does not necessarily entail complete equality of power or an equal say in policy-making. This point was made by Dahl (1961) in a classic study of how politicians and other power-holders operated in an American city. He concluded that there are clear inequalities in democratic politics – certain business interests and pressure groups are much more powerful than others, for instance. These arguments are frequently repeated and evidenced today in relation to the American political context. However, a political system can be regarded as sufficiently democratic as long as electors and democratic parties have the final say.

Similarly, in British politics, some individuals and groups are clearly more articulate and better resourced than others, and for a variety of reasons will have more say over policy than poorer and marginalized groups. In a **parliamentary democracy** the people's representatives (MPs) are supposed to be able to speak from their own point of view and according to their own consciences; MPs are not supposed to be delegates who simply report or mirror the opinions of their constituents. In any case, constituents' views are often difficult to summarize, as opinion on many key issues is sharply divided.

In practice, MPs are often more constrained by party discipline than by their own consciences or views. Their behaviour in the House of Commons usually reflects the instructions of party leaders and 'party whips' (MPs who act as organizers to make sure that their fellow members follow the 'party line' and vote accordingly). However, when a governing party is divided over certain key issues these constraints might be loosened. At these times it is possible for opposition and dissent to grow within the governing party's own ranks. This will lead to a fuller, more democratic debate about the contentious policies being fought over. Also, the democratic model holds that general elections guarantee the accountability of governments to the public. A government that persistently ignores the wishes of the people can expect to be thrown out of office when the next general election is held.

Finally, the democratic pluralist model suggests that governments are held in check because power is widely diffused in society beyond government and parliament. For instance, decisions about education will not be made by government acting alone. According to the democratic model, a plurality of groups or a number of voices will have their say. These may include bodies such as business leaders and associations (the Institute of Directors and the Confederation of British Industry are two leading examples), teachers' associations and unions, parents' lobby groups, and religious organizations.

A government that ignores powerful vested interests and pressure groups will, according to this model of power, quickly lose its authority and be forced to back down on policy decisions. This suggests a picture of policy-making as a constant contest between government and major social institutions and groups. Government might initially set the agenda, but must constantly respond to demands from the social groups and economic influences that surround it.

The elite control model

The **elite control model** suggests that elite groups of various kinds combine to run all the major government institutions, with relatively little accountability to anyone outside their own exclusive ranks. 'Democratic' institutions exist: for example, relatively unfettered mass media, elections, parliaments and individual rights to express oneself. However, as a result of a combination of skill, experience and monopolizing key leadership positions, it is always members of elites who have the decisive influence or the authoritative voice in these supposedly democratic institutions.

Elites are rather different from each other in terms of what they do and what their first priorities will be. There may be some conflicts of interest among civil service, political, military, business and professional elites. However, a theory of elite control suggests that top-ranking members of leading professional, governmental and business organizations will tend to be drawn from the same social backgrounds, to have gone to the same elite schools and universities, and to share a similar culture. Bonds of family and kinship will also tend to tie them together. Even if some have risen into the elite from non-elite backgrounds, they will have been safely incorporated into the exclusive club. Thus, despite their differences, members of elites will tend to pull together to make sure that they retain overall control of policy decisions.

This model would suggest that the blueprint of the 1940s welfare state was the work of a government elite. A tiny influential group worked out what would be in the best interests of the masses and proceeded, in the postwar period, to implement their wartime plans. Barnett (1986) contends that this civil service elite of 'Whitehall mandarins' was both high-minded and left-leaning in its aims and political values.

Whether or not Barnett is right about the way in which the welfare state was created (for further comment, see Deakin 1994: 36), this example raises the interesting point that elite control need not necessarily result in policies that are fashioned according to the narrow self-interest of the elite itself. The NHS, for instance, is largely the product of conflict and power struggles between a political and a medical elite (see Klein 1995; Box 8.1), and arguably remains such a product in light of recent policy changes (see Chapter 10).

Box 8.1 Example of elite policy-making

Historically the birth of the NHS was a difficult power struggle between doctors, many of whom were not in favour of it, and politicians of the time who wished to create the service. The politicians 'won', though only after conceding to many issues to the medical profession. Recent reforms of the NHS (see Chapter 10 for more detail) have resulted in similar struggle between those working in the service and those in politics, with many NHS staff and users arguing against the proposed changes (Campbell 2012b).

The political economy model

The **political economy model** rests on rather different assumptions from the first two. Basically, both the democratic pluralist and elite control models pose the question 'which groups are in control?' Are policies shaped primarily by democratic institutions and groups or are they determined by elites?

A political economy perspective, on the other hand, draws more attention to the underlying economic system and how the political system interacts with it. The economic systems that prevail in almost every country in the world are now openly capitalist market economies of one kind or another – even China, which, though retaining a one-party communist political structure, has become the fastest-growing capitalist or market economy in the world.

Thus the basic idea of a political economy perspective is that social policy will tend to be shaped by the needs or demands of a market economy. This includes education policy. The political economy view of power asks in what ways government spending on education is influenced by the needs and demands of business and industry. For instance, the drive to cut employers' costs by reducing the burden of taxation might influence government to restrain public spending on all public services, including education. But this factor could be balanced by some employers' pressure on government to increase education spending, especially in areas such as improving literacy and numeracy or the use of new technologies, in order to lift the levels of skills and productivity of the school-leavers or university graduates they wish to recruit.

Although a political economy perspective emphasizes the needs of the capitalist system as a whole, it also has implications, like the first two models, for the question of who controls or dominates policy-making.

In many respects, the political economy model comes close to the theory of elite control. As it suggests that most major policy decisions are subject to the backing of 'big business' or capitalist interests, it is a short step to saying that government and civil service elites interlock with business elites (leaders of City and financial institutions, and of manufacturing, retail and other commercial organizations). The political economy model can be equated with Marxist views of a class-structured society in which a ruling class controls policy and makes most, if not all, the big decisions (see Box 8.2). The way in which this control is actually exercised is a matter of debate among Marxists, who disagree with each other about how directly or openly government and state are manipulated by ruling class interests (Ham and Hill 1993: 35).

Box 8.2 Example of the political economy model of policy-making

The Coalition Government has significantly reformed the landscape of Higher Education since starting in office. Their introduction in England of higher-rate variable fees to be paid by students, and an associated reduction in government funding for institutions followed the Browne Report and the subsequent 2011 White Paper, *Putting Students at the Heart of the System*. These changes have introduced a quasi-market at the heart of the system (Callender 2012). The political economy model helps us to understand these developments in that we can see how higher education institutions – universities and colleges – are being transformed into businesses selling 'products' (qualifications) to 'consumers' who pay fees for them. A political economy view of society and social policy suggests that such gradual 'marketization' of services comes to be accepted by the public as natural, rational and a common-sense approach – in other words, we come to accept ruling class ideology; the alternative, which would be a return to publicly funded services not run on commercial lines, will increasingly be seen as 'unrealistic' and impossible.

Despite these differences, however, Marxist perspectives share a common view that it is the underlying political–economic system that shapes policy, rather than the particular elite groups, political parties or leaders that happen to be in power at a given time. There may be shifts of power within the ruling class, they argue, but the system as a whole will tend to perpetuate gross inequalities of wealth and power. These inequalities now have international dimensions as the globalization of trade and capitalism concentrates wealth in fewer and fewer hands, and in huge international business corporations (see Lansley 2011). This in turn creates the potential for growing conflict between the haves and have-nots – between those who control policy and the mass of people who have to deal with the consequences of government decisions that tend to favour the rich and powerful.

The background: education and Conservative policies of the 1980s and 1990s

In this section the development of education policy before the Coalition Government came to power in 2010 will be discussed. The aim, as stated at the beginning of the chapter, is not to summarize every change in education but to analyse the *process* of change – in particular, how and why certain decisions were made, and what this tells us about the democratic nature (or otherwise) of decision-making in Britain. You may find it helpful to reflect on the three models of power, outlined in the previous section, as explanations of the way in which education policy developed historically and, in particular, at the turning point of a landmark in policy, the 1988 Education Act.

In 1987, a Conservative government was elected to power for a third term in office under the leadership of Mrs Thatcher. Some changes in education policy had already been introduced in the period 1979–86 by Mrs Thatcher's previous administrations (for instance, a 1980 Education Act strengthened parents' rights to preferred places for their children in state schools). However, Mrs Thatcher's third term in office represented a long-awaited chance to bring radical organizational changes to all the main welfare state services, including education.

A common element in Mrs Thatcher's government's strategy for overhauling the public services was the introduction of an internal market. As far as schools were concerned, this meant a new approach that would result in competition among local state schools to attract and retain pupils. The theory was that with greater freedom to choose between different schools in the locality, parents would 'reward' what they saw as the better schools by trying to get their children enrolled in them. Meanwhile the schools with a poorer record would experience falling enrolment. They would thus be confronted with a strong incentive to improve the educational performance of their children in order to make themselves more attractive to parents.

As 'money follows the pupil' – that is, each school receives a set amount per year for each student it enrols – the aim was therefore to develop a *market-like* system of state education to reward the better-achieving schools with more money, and thus more teachers and resources. At the same time, the discipline of the market – as demonstrated by declining student numbers and less money every year – would force the poorer schools to improve their performance.

Whether an internal market in education would work in the way just outlined was (and still is) hotly contested, and debates still rage about the use of markets in public services. The Coalition Government's approach is one in which competition, a central aspect of the internal market, remains central to their policy approach (BBC News 2011a).

Some of the drawbacks of introducing market-like competition in education are discussed later in this chapter, and they have implications for the wider question of whether internal markets achieve the desired effects in *any* public services such as the NHS and social services.

However, at this point it is sufficient to note that Mrs Thatcher's government in 1987 was about to press ahead with some gradual, but in the end very significant and far-reaching changes to the way education and other public services were going to be run. Their strategy for change included not only the introduction of internal markets in public services, but also:

- challenges to the traditional power and status of professional groups such as teachers,
- a weakening of the power of local authorities,
- the setting-up of quangos or central government agencies to regulate and inspect services,
- emphasis on 'consumer choice' rather than democratic accountability in the public services.

The changes that any government makes are often underpinned by their ideological view, the economic circumstances they face and their view of the purposes of education. Now complete Activity 8.2 to explore the Coalition Government's educational goals.

Activity 8.2 What is education for?

Use the Internet to access YouTube and the speech 'Michael Gove MP – What is Education For?': www.youtube.com/watch?v=mrzFEyt8MvE.

1. Make some notes as you are listening; do you agree with the Education Minister's view of the purpose of education?
2. Can you identify the links between these views and changes in the education system that are being made?
3. His talk supports the value of some subjects, schools and universities more than others: is this elitism? What are your thoughts about this?
4. Overall, what are your thoughts about his focus upon examinations and the importance of specific subjects such as maths and sciences?

While the Coalition Government is now introducing educational reform, you need to understand historical educational changes in this area to see that much of this reform is not significantly different to previous changes; rather, it reflects incremental change.

The 1988 Education Act

This Act was a very significant landmark. It introduced many important reforms to schools in England and Wales, and it paved the way for the development of the internal market in education referred to in the previous section. The 1988 Act set the policy agenda in education for the 1990s – not only for Major's Conservative Governments (1990–2 and 1992–7) but also for the Labour Government from 1997 to 2010 as well as the current Coalition Government. Table 8.2 demonstrates this.

The lessons of the 1988 education reforms: how policy was made

The 1988 reforms were extremely important in terms of what was to change in the classroom, how children and older students were going to be tested and what they would learn. At the same time the reforms were important not only because of the scale of the change but also the *way* in which the new policy was introduced.

Central government appeared to be awarding itself many additional powers to run state education, and this provoked a great deal of controversy, especially among educationalists and the teaching profession. But it had also done so in a way that had apparently involved little consultation with the general public and little involvement with the teaching profession or with local authorities.

This is not to deny that the case for some educational reform was strong. The argument for a National Curriculum, for example, had been accepted in educational circles well before 1988. Also, significantly higher numbers of British young people were leaving school with few or no qualifications compared with most other European countries. In the past, there were demands from employers and other groups for testing and for setting national standards of school attainment in literacy and numeracy. While these changes were implemented during the 1980s, employers have recently shown that they still remain unsatisfied with the current education system and the types of students that are 'produced' in relation to their skill sets (BBC News 2012c). Historically, too, in the teaching profession there was pressure for devolved management from local authorities to schools, another trend which has continued (see Table 8.2).

The significance of the 1988 education reforms lies less in the basic ideas, which were not particularly original, but more in the ways those ideas were interpreted and put into practice. There were three main features of the education reform process – first, the speed with which changes were introduced; second, the lack of consultation or consideration of alternatives; third, the degree to which the reforms centralized power.

There was little warning before the general election in 1987 that the sorts of changes outlined above were going to be unleashed in the education service. Broad proposals for change were released by the government shortly beforehand, but not with enough detail to spell out the full implications, as is often the case with any policy reform. Thus a democratic model of power – a view of policy-making that is based on ideas of consultation and participation from all sides – offers little insight into the origins of the education reforms of 1988, or the early stages of the policy. This is equally true of policy changes being made today, with the Coalition Government approach being criticized because, despite offering the opportunity for online consultation where people

Table 8.2 Historical and contemporary educational reforms: Conservatives and the Coalition Government

1988 reforms	**Current reforms**
The removal of many of the powers of local education authorities (LEAs) over the running of schools, and handing over of most of the responsibilities of school management to head teachers and school governing bodies. This was a new policy of local management of schools (LMS). It applied to all secondary schools and most primary schools (over a certain size). Every state school was now required to manage its own budget and plan its own development, including staffing. The money to run each individual school was still to be funnelled through the LEA, with the school itself deciding how to spend it.	The Coalition Government has extended this reform in England; individual head teachers will now be freed from central and local government policies so that they are able to make decisions at a local level. These decisions will also mean that they can determine their own curriculum, the length of the school day and even the times of lessons (Valentine 2011).
School governing bodies were to have elected parent governors and nominated teacher representatives, as well as other members representing the local authority and local businesses or community organization, to strengthen their voice.	Parents in England again have increased power and control in some areas: for example, they can set up free schools. However, in some areas parental power is reduced: for instance, they have less power to oppose the creation of academies.
The introduction of a National Curriculum and School Attainment Tests (SATs) for all children at the ages of 7, 11 and 14.	SATs are remaining within the education system following a review in 2011, although are subject to minor reform from 2013: for example, there will be a greater focus on each child's progress throughout the year, rather than just review of a one-day snapshot of a test. The Coalition Government is also reforming the examination system, and will change the GCSE approach with new examinations being taken from 2017, in which there will be an increase in what is required to achieve a pass.
The creation of a new category of grant-maintained schools – basically, independent state schools. These were to be funded directly by central government rather than via the LEA. This funding formula gave an incentive to schools to opt out of LEAs. The Act stipulated that parents had to be balloted about any proposals for a change to grant-maintained status, and that a majority of those who voted had to be in favour for the change to be agreed by the Secretary of State for Education.	This policy was extended under the New Labour Government, who created the Cities Academy school programme (see later in this chapter). The Coalition Government has extended this by: • removing local authorities' power to veto a school becoming an academy, • removing parents' and teachers' legal rights to oppose plans, and • allowing schools to 'fast-track' their applications to become academies.
Drawing on a US policy experiment ('magnet schools'), the Act launched proposals for a new range of specialist schools such as city technology colleges that were to be jointly funded by government and business. This new kind of secondary education was to be provided in the best-equipped and best-staffed environment possible.	Drawing upon Swedish policy, the Coalition Government has created a programme of free schools; schools that are free from local government control but which are still monitored and funded by central government.

could offer their ideas for policy development, the government simply rejected ideas for change and implemented its original planned policies (Groves 2010).

Debates also continue about the influence of business interest in policy development. However, there is not much evidence to support a 'business power' or political economy explanation for the 1980s reforms. Mrs Thatcher's government may have professed an understanding of the needs of business and enjoyed close attachments with business leaders, but the specific ideas on how to reorganize education came from a small political elite, not from sustained discussions between government and industry or business groups.

Business interests perhaps worked more as a background explanation of the forces influencing government at the time. As discussed above, some business opinion laments the relatively low standards attained by British school-leavers and the way this reduces Britain's productivity and competitive edge. Therefore the education reforms of 1988 would have been regarded favourably both by business and government if they looked like policies that could raise standards with relatively little increase in expenditure.

The strongest interpretation, however, is that the political elite leading government was motivated first and foremost by ideology. Many of Mrs Thatcher's policies began in this way. There was a tendency to push innovations from the top downwards, although in many cases this was tempered by political pragmatism and caution. In the case of education, it was the lack of consultation with education representatives outside government that underlined the impression of policy-making by a tight circle of top people in government: the Prime Minister and her policy advisory group, and selected Cabinet ministers. No Green Paper or consultative document was issued to air the government's broad plans for the education system. The 'elite control' model seems to be particularly powerful as an explanation of the genesis of this important policy.

One element of the reforms – the idea of allowing secondary schools to opt out of the local education system – was a particularly good example of the way policy was created at the very top level of government. This policy was created 'on the hoof'. Mrs Thatcher suddenly launched the idea in the 1987 general election campaign 'to the surprise of her colleagues'. She predicted, in a stirring speech, that 'opting out would be as successful as council house sales in liberating families from socialism' (Carvel and MacLeod 1995: 15).

The education reforms were very quickly drafted after the general election by Kenneth Baker, the Education Secretary, and by top civil servants. The late Nicholas Ridley, a former government minister, is quoted as saying that they were 'hammered out in . . . no more than a month' (Gilmour 1992: 167). It was these quickly drafted plans that became law shortly afterwards.

The government at that time enjoyed a large majority in the House of Commons. When a government has a small majority – or is part of a Coalition Government, as is currently the case – it is more likely that proposed legislation will be subjected to scrutiny and amendment. This is especially the case if the government is divided and if its supporting MPs must be placated with concessions or changes to a Bill. Proposed legislation for the UK must go through a series of stages in parliament at Westminster before it becomes law and government policy (see Figure 8.1).

In the case of the Education Reform Bill, however, the government's original plans as set out in the White Paper (see Step 4 in Figure 8.1) survived virtually intact to the final stage of legislation (see Step 12). This occurred despite widespread concern that the Education Reform Act 1988 gave too many new powers to central government and, in so doing, raised serious constitutional issues. However, the British system allows a Prime Minister with a safe majority to push a legislative programme through parliament, using it more or less as a rubber stamp.

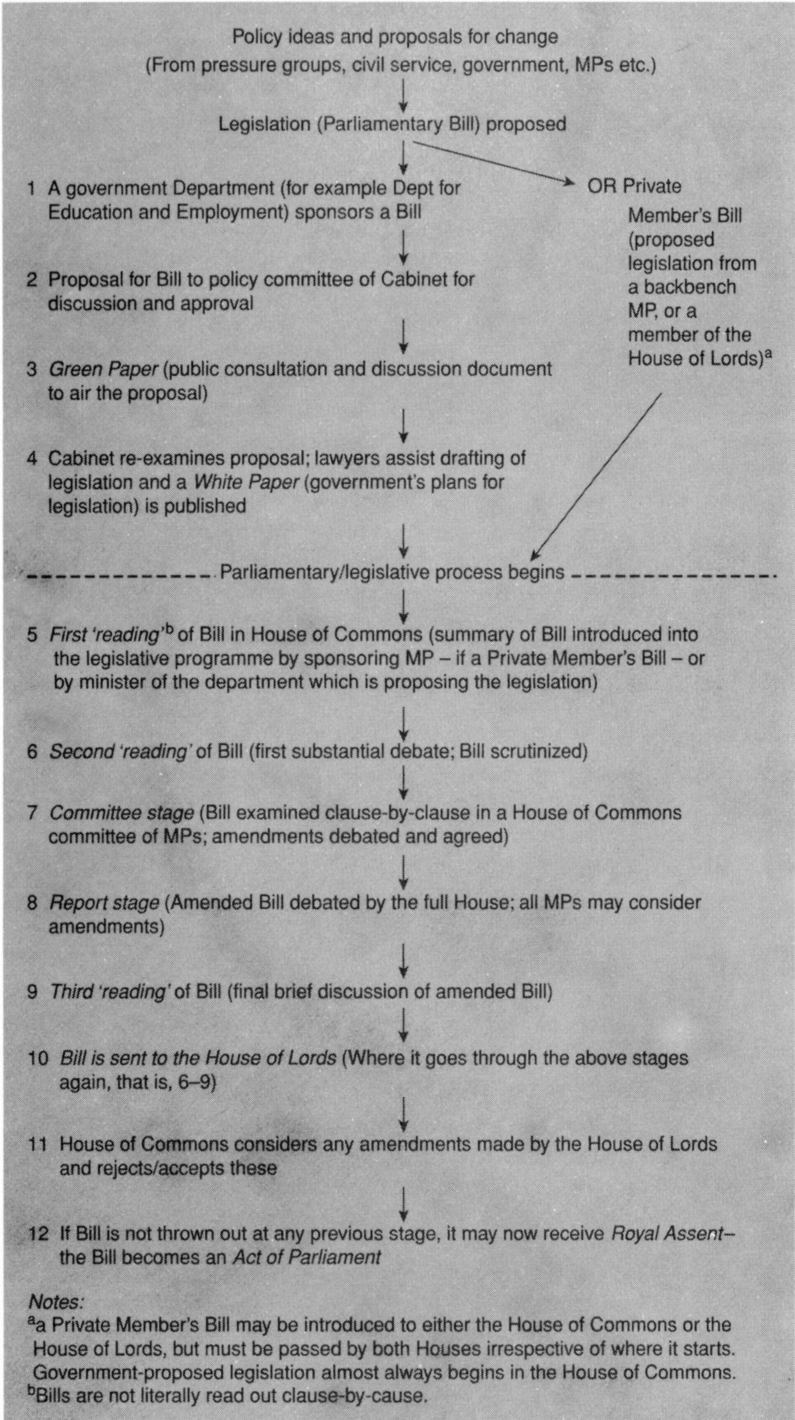

Figure 8.1 Policy-making and the legislative process at Westminster

Interestingly, the Coalition Government's ability to push education reforms through in this way has been much more limited. For instance, the government has successfully developed its plans to expand the number of free schools, but in other areas has had to greatly amend or withdraw its proposals, performing several 'U-turns' on such matters as the introduction of baccalaureate qualifications in England to replace GCSEs, and the removal of coursework assessment at A-Level.

In other democratic systems (for example, in the USA), there are more checks and balances between different legislatures (Senate and Congress). The role of the president in both the USA and France is a very powerful one. But, unlike the British prime minister, a US or French president may be forced to govern with a majority or near majority of representatives from opposition parties.

Both of these examples – and many other western countries – have written constitutions. In most cases this gives a more significant role than in the UK to supreme courts, whose role is to test whether a government's actions and policies are lawful within the constitution. In the USA, Supreme Court decisions can effectively amend or block government policies.

In contrast, the 1988 legislation on education highlights the way in which policies can be steam-rollered through parliament, however hotly they are debated by opposition MPs. The House of Lords may also find flaws in proposed legislation and seek amendments, but the second chamber's powers are circumscribed and it cannot permanently veto legislation or insist on changes. Comparisons can be drawn here between the process in which the latest NHS reform was achieved (see Chapter 10).

It is for these reasons that Gilmour (1992: 187) argues that the British system is best described as a 'plebiscitary democracy' rather than a parliamentary democracy. A plebiscite is a one-off vote of the people, as in a referendum or general election. Having made one key decision, the electorate hands all power to a ruling elite. Now complete Activity 8.3 to explore this idea in more detail.

Activity 8.3 British democracy in action

Do you agree with the statement that Gilmour makes when he says that, in the UK, the electorate having made one key decision (to give power to a particular group/party) then hands all power to a ruling elite?

1. To help you reflect on this statement consider this – prior to coming to power the Liberal Democrats promised to abolish tuition fees in higher education. This was clearly stated within their manifesto. However, once they gained power as part of the Coalition Government in 2010, they changed their approach and supported the introduction of higher fees.
2. You can use the Internet to explore this issue more; use your searching skills to find news reports about this as well as academic debate and discussion.
3. Now think about what this example illustrates when you apply Gilmour's statement to it.
4. You may also wish to reflect on the way in which the Coalition Government gained power – did the British electorate make the decision to hand all of the power to a coalition?

In education policy, as we have seen, the way in which the legislation for the 1988 reforms was created and pushed through Parliament seems to bear out Gilmour's criticisms. But what does the development of education policy *since* the 1988 Act tell us about the nature of policy-making in Britain?

Implementing the historical Conservative reforms

A policy is not just a piece of legislation or a static list of written objectives and guidelines. As stated at the very beginning of this book, policies *develop* once the implementation process starts. Although the initial stage – the creation of a policy – is interesting, it is the further development of a policy in the 'real' world that makes the study of social policy particularly fascinating. Policies are living things – and a policy becomes what is implemented in practice as well as what is written down in formal or legal terms. Sometimes social policies are successful. This means that they actually achieve what they were designed for, or at the very least they are successfully implemented in a way that fits with the government's initial plan or vision. Sometimes, though, policies are less successful. The troubles experienced by the Conservative Government in trying to implement the 1988 Act illustrate this. In this case the power of central government was challenged by professional groups (teachers), and by other groups and interests at the local level and outside central government. Box 8.3 illustrates the barriers to implementation faced by the Conservative Government.

Box 8.3 Barriers to implementation

- First, significant numbers of teachers began to resist certain aspects of the National Curriculum. With low morale related to pay and working conditions teachers began to refuse to set SATs. The boycott spread widely in 1993 and, as Ranson and Travers (1994: 224) observed, what began as a protest over ill-prepared tests 'became a general dispute about the national curriculum, testing, and ... using information from the tests to create national league tables of school performance'.
- Second, the secondary school 'opt out' policy made very slow progress. In the first few years, only a handful of schools in England and Wales applied to opt out. In Scotland the policy did not take off at all. By 1995, the total of grant-maintained schools (those that had opted out of their LEA) was still little over a thousand.

The example in Box 8.3 is particularly illustrative because it modifies the 'elite control' view of policy-making. In this case, the teachers were not able to create a new policy but they were able as a professional pressure group to challenge and obstruct government power. However, we must remember that, though the schools' 'opt out' policy progressed at a snail's pace, the Conservative Government was successful in pushing through the main framework of the 1988 Act. An internal market was introduced into every level or sector of education, the National Curriculum was implemented, SATs became an institutional part of the education process in England, if not Scotland and Wales, and far-reaching reforms in the funding and inspection of education were carried out. These were the foundations of the new education policies that were inherited by both Labour in 1997, and the Coalition Government in 2010.

Centralizing control: the New Labour educational legacy

After its first election victory in 1997, the Labour government announced that 'education, education, education' was to be at the top of its policy agenda. The decision to announce that education would be a priority reflects the strong emphasis in New Labour ideology on providing opportunities for individuals to better themselves. This ideology carries with it the assumption that it is more important to equalize *opportunity* – the chance to do well and to enjoy individual success – than it is to equalize *outcomes* such as incomes, standards of living or levels of education. Thus the reverse side of this coin is that New Labour philosophy accepts that marked inequalities in achievement and outcomes are inevitable. This is a contrast to the more socialist or social democratic ideas of 'Old Labour'. New Labour is guided by the belief that lack of resources does not itself explain failure. As Toynbee and Walker (2001: 47) suggested, New Labour's ideology stressed the point that 'it is not so much resources as attitudes and organization that explained poor school performance'.

Thus the Labour approach to education, while branching off in some new directions, reflects a degree of continuity with 1980s education policy in a number of ways, as illustrated in Table 8.3.

Table 8.3 Areas of historical policy continuation under New Labour

Policy aims 1988–97	Continuation (from 1997)
The creation of different kinds of secondary school.	Emphasis continued on creating different kinds of secondary school and justifying the gradual break-up of the comprehensive school system – a process that has come to be known by the ugly term 'de-comprehensivization'.
To develop individuals' school achievement and create more opportunities.	Similar emphasis was placed on the belief that individual effort, merit and striving can overcome social disadvantage.
To direct policy from the centre and impose it on local authorities.	A strongly interventionist central government imposed its agenda, and centralized control of the education system.

Thus, as Table 8.3 shows, there was a strong continuation of previous policy as New Labour:

- did not dismantle the education reforms made in 1988. As mentioned, this meant that the internal market and the idea of competition between state schools were retained.
- did not aim for a return to the 1970s Labour policy of developing a common or comprehensive secondary school for everyone.
- did not significantly increase government expenditure on education in its first term, 1997–2001 (see above, and Toynbee and Walker 2001: 48). However, in its second term in office (2001–5), the government did increase education spending in real terms by 5.4 per cent annually.
- did not abolish grammar schools and other forms of selection in other types of school.

Some changes were made, and it remains important to understand these because some of these have similarly continued under the Coalition Government. Table 8.4 highlights changes made by New Labour and the areas in which the Coalition Government have similarly continued policy developments.

Table 8.4 Historical and contemporary educational reforms: New Labour and the Coalition Government

New Labour reform	Coalition Government reform
A variety of policies were implemented to improve teaching standards in schools. The government could impose central supervision for failing schools. In some areas where education was judged to be failing, local authority management of schools could be handed over completely to private sector companies.	Plans to implement a new curriculum by New Labour were abandoned by the Coalition. SATs, however, remain. The concern with standards also remains, though the plans for an English baccalaureate have been abandoned as a result of lobbying from business interests and employers.
In October 2005 the government published plans to turn all local authority secondary schools in England into independent trust schools. Schools can be independent trusts, able to appoint their own governing bodies, take charge of their own assets and, within certain guidelines, set their own admissions policies.	This policy has continued in the form of free schools that can be completely independently run. Based upon the Swedish model, this approach has been linked to the ideology of the Conservatives as it can be seen as part of their broader plans for privatization.
Part of the government's strategy for more specialized schools was the development of city academies. These are secondary schools intended to replace existing schools in urban areas where there is social disadvantage and low educational achievement.	These plans have continued and academies and the Coalition Governement has made this process easier. For many this means that the process of centralizing the control of education as started in the 1980s has continued.
In higher education, the government rejected an advisory body's recommendation of a 'graduate tax' to fund student maintenance and tuition fees. It abolished free tuition and passed the Teaching and Higher Education Act, which requires students to pay tuition fees.	The Coalition Government extended the cost of fees, and transferred the majority of the cost of higher education to students, arguing that this puts students at the heart of the education system, allowing them choice (Callender 2012). However, changes were made to the method of paying tuition fees in England. Instead of having to pay 'up front' or at the time of study, as before, students will now have to pay fees over a longer period after graduation – in effect a disguised 'graduate tax'.

Labour's policy continued to centralize power in many ways, as the Coalition Government has also done. Most of the examples of policy in Table 8.4 show central government placing a much heavier, more interventionist hand on local affairs than used to be the case. Even where central government seems to be delegating management to local schools or trusts, the effect is likely to reduce at the community level the role of locally elected representatives and parents in running schools. This can be seen, for instance, in the policy to develop 'city academies'.

Academies

New Labour's programme to develop this new type of secondary school was, historically, a controversial issue. New Labour planned to stimulate the development of 200 city academies by 2010, though by the end of 2005 only 17 had been opened. These new schools cost twice as much to build, on average, as a comprehensive school of similar size (Curtis 2005). Central government meets almost all the cost of building each new academy (approximately £25m) while the individual sponsor or sponsoring organization that undertakes to run the school contributes £2m. In return, the sponsors of academies are given almost complete management and financial control over their institutions. They are free to choose almost all of the academy's governors and the senior management team. They enjoy a lot of influence over the ethos of the school (this might be a Christian ethos, for instance), the curriculum and teaching methods. Sponsors who have so far come forward to run city academies include a mixture of wealthy businessmen, some of whom own groups of private schools in the UK and in other countries, philanthropists and voluntary sector organizations, and evangelical Christian groups (Taylor 2005).

The city academy programme shows how New Labour wished to step into local areas to create independent state schools. The academies cannot charge fees, but in many other respects are intended to model themselves on independent private schools. They are state schools but stand outside the main system of secondary schools. In this respect they also stand outside the local system for ensuring democratic accountability: the locally elected councils and their LEAs. It is important to remember that the initial aim of the city academy programme was to replace schools that were performing very poorly in socially deprived inner-city areas, so it would have been surprising if some of the new academies had not encountered significant problems at the start. However, neither a review of city academies by a private firm, Pricewaterhouse Cooper (PwC), nor other investigations of the programme found convincing evidence that the first batch had made a significant difference to examination results or to broader measures of educational achievement. There is evidence that some academies have been diverting their students from studying GCSE subjects to the vocational GNVQ, in order to boost their standing in school league tables (Taylor 2006).

A highly critical study conducted for England's Local Authorities Association concluded that the city academy programme was 'hugely expensive' and 'unproven' in terms of transforming failed schools (Smithers 2005). Similarly, a Parliamentary Select Committee in 2005 found that while patchy educational improvement could be detected in city academies, progress in low-achieving, inner-city schools *not* in the city academy programme had been significantly *greater*.

The lesson to be drawn from this seemed to be clear: while educational opportunities and achievement can perhaps be lifted by heavy investment and dramatic improvements in a few selected academies, a more general and better rate of improvement can be sustained by spreading the extra resources more widely across inner-city schools. Despite this evidence, the Coalition Government has continued to drive forward the creation of academies since coming to power, with The Academies Bill successfully passing through parliament in 2010. There are, however, some slight changes when comparing Coalition Government policy in this area to that of the previous government (see Goodwin 2011), in that

1. the academy model is to be applied as the universal school type rather than just as an option,
2. the rationale for academies is different: it is not about a radical fresh start for the Coalition Government; rather, it is about shifting the focus to excellent schools – those that are outstanding, and
3. the new academies will also no longer have an obligation to follow the National Curriculum.

However, despite these changes academies, though they are run by their sponsors as independent trusts, remain the creatures of central government. They are part of a wider, central government strategy to greatly reduce the role of the local authorities in education that began in the 1980s and continues to the present day.

Restructuring education: radical reform or piecemeal change?

While the Labour government claimed to be a very active, interventionist government intent on introducing sweeping reforms from the centre, the overall impression given was one of *piecemeal reform* – that is, an approach that introduces change bit by bit, or in small steps. Labour education policy before 2005 did not seem to be directed by one 'big idea' or one major piece of legislation, such as the previous government's Education Reform Act 1988.

In education there were some minor departures from Conservative policy such as the abolition of the assisted places scheme – a programme developed by the last Conservative administration to subsidize private school places for children of ability who could not afford them. However, as shown earlier, Labour worked to gradually extend, rather than to reverse, the internal market-oriented reforms of the education and welfare system introduced by Mrs Thatcher's government in the 1980s. Similarly this has been the case so far with the policies being implemented by the Coalition Government.

Did the current proposals for educational reform under the Coalition Government mark a decisive shift from this gradual approach? Tables 8.2, 8.3 and 8.4 have already drawn out several areas in which policy reform can clearly be seen as a continuation of long-standing piecemeal change. The Coalition Government too appears, at the time of writing, to be retaining the bulk of the New Labour approach to education in England by focusing upon standards and league tables: 'There are no indications of any serious challenge to New Labour's centralised standards agenda which, if anything, is further reinforced by Coalition policies' (Goodwin 2011: 422). Similarly, early years education policy has seen little change. There will be a continuation of free childcare for all 3- to 4-year-olds for 15 hours per week, and this entitlement will be extended to 2-year-olds from disadvantaged backgrounds. Sure Start funding has been capped, and the government is introducing payment by results for Sure Start Centres. There are some other areas of change being introduced by the Coalition Government that are less of a continuation of historical policy change (Gillard 2010):

- In the context of the harsh spending cuts being implemented across all public services, education too has faced drastic budgetary changes. It is clear that the economic and political environment in which the Coalition Government is implementing change is a very different one from that New Labour experienced in its previous terms (Goodwin 2011) though overall the education budget has not been significantly reduced. At the time of writing, the Department for Education was being asked for savings of just 1 per cent over the four years of the spending review (Paton 2010). Budget cuts have been implemented as follows (Gillard 2010):
  - The schools rebuilding programme has been cancelled. Some building projects will go ahead, but the few allowed to continue will face significant reductions in their available budget.
  - The Playbuilder scheme instituted by New Labour has also been scrapped; this was a programme to support the creation of new community playgrounds across England.
  - The School Food Trust has been subjected to budget cuts and now has charitable status.
  - The National Healthy Schools Programme has also been cut. It was established in 1999 to promote a whole-school and whole-child approach to health (Valentine 2011).

- The Coalition has scrapped the quango responsible for curriculum development: the Qualifications and Curriculum Development Agency (QCDA). The government has instead received advice about the curriculum from TV presenter Carol Vorderman, who headed a task review of mathematics (*Guardian* 2011) – a step which received some criticism.
- There have been changes to provision for families on lower incomes as follows:
  - A planned extension of pilot schemes in which free school meals were provided to those from low-income families has been scrapped.
  - The Educational Maintenance Allowance has also been scrapped; this was provision created under New Labour to support those from low-income families in continuing on to further education.
  - The Coalition Government has created a pupil premium in which schools are now to be given extra funding for children who are from disadvantaged homes. This is argued by some to plug the gap left by the savings required as a consequence of the Comprehensive Spending Review (Paton 2010).
- A new Education White Paper was published, entitled *The Importance of Teaching in 2010*. This focused on the implementation of a new curriculum, the development of academies and raising teaching standards. Changes to examinations were envisaged, with a move away from a modular GCSE structure to one in which pupils take a final examination. Critical commentators (Gillard 2010) argue that the paper offers policy discourse about freeing teachers from constraints and external control but in reality enforces more centralization and control.
- Changes to higher education fees in England have already been mentioned. However, New Labour promised additional university places (20,000 in total), which the Coalition cut to 8,000. Thus, student numbers have been reduced and universities were threatened with fines if they did not comply (Gillard 2010). Student numbers have reduced by 17 per cent according to some measures (Morgan 2012), and there are concerns that universities are failing students from poorer backgrounds (Shepherd 2011).

The new reforms have received criticism from the Labour opposition. However, it is clear from the analysis offered in this chapter that the Coalition Government's policies on academies, free schools and university tuition fees are mainly extending the policies that were first implemented either by Conservative governments before 1997 or by New Labour after 1997.

Policies for the future?

So far we have briefly examined a number of recent policies on education to show that there are several key features or themes in the way that policies have been made under the last three British Governments. One unifying theme, as mentioned earlier, is a strong determination to run education (in England) from the centre, by the Department for Education, rather than reviving the more decentralized form of educational administration through the local authorities that used to prevail. A second theme is that most of the education policies implemented since the 1980s have been more 'right wing' than 'left wing' irrespective of the party in power.

The right-wing nature of many New Labour policies on education has been illustrated in this chapter: for instance, in the reforms of student loans and the financing of higher education, in the policy of bringing in private companies to run 'failing' state schools and LEAs, and in wanting to replace (in England) the old-style comprehensive school system with a more diverse system.

As this chapter has shown, this pattern of more right-wing policies has also continued under the Coalition Government. How strong or effective the influence of the Liberal Democrats in government is very questionable, at least as far as education policy is concerned. This is especially the case in relation to the Liberal Democrats' willingness to break their election promise not to increase tuition fees for higher education. Their voice has been strangely silent in the policy-making process. It may have been the case that the Liberal Democrat proposals around tuition fees were never realistic and that the party never had any intention of abolishing them even before they entered government (Wilson 2012). For some commentators, the Liberal Democrats simply serve to prop up the current Conservative policy direction (Gillard 2010). This does not mean that every single aspect of educational policy since 1980 has lacked left-wing, or pro-poor, policies. The New Labour expansion of, and subsidies towards, preschool childcare and nursery facilities, for example, showed that the government has genuinely attempted to improve opportunities among social groups that have hitherto been seriously disadvantaged. Indeed, there has been the introduction of a pupil premium by the Coalition Government with similar goals. Similarly, in higher education, the introduction of another government watchdog, the Office for Fair Access (Offa) to monitor the numbers of students from state schools and from low-income home backgrounds in every university, together with penalties for universities that do not recruit a sufficiently diverse range of students, showed some commitment to 'left-wing' goals of equality. The point, however, is that these latter policies were somewhat overshadowed by the more dominant right-wing policies to push ahead with the development of an internal market in education, and with a more competitive, selective approach to schooling than would have prevailed if the comprehensive secondary education system had been maintained (as it has been, largely, in Scotland and Wales).

The effectiveness of these changes is open to debate. A recent survey of British educational standards highlighted many underperforming schools and showed that children's chances of getting into a good school are effectively a 'postcode lottery' (Metro 2012). Whether the proposed examination reforms will lead to overall improvements is also currently in debate. There are questions about value for money in relation to higher education, with the cost of going to university estimated to be £53,000 per student when completing a three-year degree programme (H. Smith 2012). For some these changes are about power and control, too. Collini (2011) argues that the new approach to university funding is creating a rigged market, and that this is amounts to a gamble with the British university system. The gradual privatization of universities is ideologically consistent with a right-wing approach.

The effects of all of these policies remains to be seen, but given that school leavers and university graduates face fewer opportunities in relation to job prospects and high levels of youth unemployment (Gant 2012), and yet young people are much more likely to be armed with A-Levels and degree qualifications than in the past, the prospect of the rapid devaluation of qualifications is very real.

The future of educational delivery is also one which needs consideration given fast-moving technological development. Many higher educational institutions are introducing online delivery of courses, and this is an area where policy development may occur within schools in the future. Complete Activity 8.4 to expand your knowledge of this area.

Activity 8.4 Exploring online learning

Use the Internet to access TED Talks (www.ted.com/talks); listen to the talk 'Daphne Koller: What we're learning from online education'

1. Watch Daphne Koller discuss the opportunities that online education can offer for those currently excluded from current systems; do you agree with her points?
2. Do you consider yourself to be one of the lucky ones given that you are studying within higher education?
3. How realistic do you think her vision of free education for all is?
4. What is your ideological standpoint in relation to this – do you agree that education online should be provided in this way? If not, then what are your objections? (You might want to consider the point about the devaluation of education qualifications made above.)

The development of online learning is an interesting area for future consideration within policy circles as a potential area of change. Transformation so far has been focused upon more traditional concerns, but these changes remain significant. Indeed, if the Coalition Government's plans for a transformation of schools into a more diverse, less comprehensive system are fully realized then this will represent a large-scale, far-reaching change. In the long run, a 'piecemeal' approach to making changes is not necessarily the same as making only small-scale or modest changes. Over a longer period, perhaps a decade or more, a series of relatively minor changes and innovations can amount to a fundamental change, as this chapter illustrates. At the same time, such change can 'creep up' on the public if it is introduced through inexplicit policies, or policies that do not openly state what the wider strategy of government is.

This brings us back to the question of how policies are formed and developed. In the concluding section we will examine which of the three models of power ('democratic', 'elite control' and 'political economy' models) throws most light on the way government makes policy.

Conclusions

Recent education policy provides an intriguing example of how policies are implemented in Britain and of who makes the key decisions in the first place. As we have seen, what sense we make of the education reforms of 1988 and subsequent policy on education under New Labour and the Coalition Government depends on our views about democracy and the role of government.

First, the idea that policy-making is a democratic process would appear to have little value as an explanation of the origin of the education policies that have been discussed, whether these are the policies introduced as a result of the 1988 Education Act, or more recent policies such as the development of city academies and free schools. All the specific proposals for change in education, and in many other policy areas, seem to come from the prime minister at the time, and her or his closest advisers and ministers (Gilmour 1992; Deakin 1994; Woodward 2006).

This point about the way the key decisions are often made at the very top of government (rather than emerging from democratic discussion in Parliament, or as a result of consultation with experts and the general public) also applies to 'non-decisions'. These are crucial decisions not to take a particular course of action. In education, a striking example of the exercise of prime ministerial power (not discussed above because it has become a 'dead' issue) was the fate of a radical plan to transform the content and assessment of education for students aged 14–19: the Tomlinson Report of October 2004.

Sir Mike Tomlinson, a former Chief Inspector of Schools and a respected educationist, had been asked to head a committee to examine how the education system for 14–19-year-olds could be modernized. He produced a plan which met with broad approval in the educational world, including the top universities such as Oxford and Cambridge. Hodgson and Spours referred to Tomlinson's suggestions as 'a carefully constructed consensus for a unified and inclusive diploma . . . built up over months of consultation' (2005: 4). But, as soon as the report was published, Tony Blair made it clear that whatever was agreed about the radical proposals for the new diploma in England, the 'gold standard' A-Level examination would not be scrapped (Smithers et al. 2004). This announcement effectively scuppered the Tomlinson proposals immediately, because retaining A-Levels under the umbrella of the new diploma would have undermined the status of any other qualification, and especially vocational (work-related) courses.

Does this example, and the other examples of 'top-down' policy-making made earlier, completely invalidate the idea of democratic influences on policy? There are two dangers in reaching this conclusion. The first is that a democratic model does not rule out the idea that power is concentrated in government. It would be naive to expect every policy to reflect grassroots opinion or consultation with pressure groups. As Dahl (1961) concluded, a pluralistic democracy in the real world works on the principle that central and local government are in control. The point is that, in a democracy, government is accountable to the people at election time, and also (especially in the USA) to the courts.

Thus, a different conclusion would be that the governments under Thatcher, Blair and the current coalition have only been acting as any government does in a parliamentary democracy. Government may run ahead of the public will in education matters, but it remains open to the electorate to reject governments and their associated educational policies. Does this mean that a democratic model provides an accurate view of policy-making in Britain after all? Unfortunately, neither is this the case. Such a conclusion would also be unsatisfactory.

A democratic model, although it does allow for the idea of government playing a lead role, nevertheless portrays political leaders and institutions as relatively open to 'outside' or pressure group influences *during the process of policy-making*. According to Dahl (1961), interest groups should be able to influence government decisions *before* they are finalized. However, the education reforms of the 1980s were introduced with little or no consultation. As will be recalled, only the vaguest references to the education reforms were made in the 1987 election campaign, and when government put forward its proposals in 1988 it did so without going through a consultative (Green Paper) stage. Similarly, there were only the vaguest hints during the 2001 election campaign of the government's firm intention to expand the roles of specialist secondary schools and of the private sector in education. This occurred again at the next general election, when Labour only mentioned their long-term plan to 'de-comprehensivize' secondary education, and to replace the standard comprehensive schools with a more diverse system of independent school trusts, in veiled terms that did not spell out the alternatives to the public. Finally, the decision to reject the Tomlinson proposals for the reform of 14–19 education was reached without any consultation with the teaching profession or with education pressure groups. Given that the coalition entering government in 2010 was the result of a long protracted set of talks with other political parties, educational reform was again not clear, although for many the current reforms appear to be driven by the Conservatives rather than the Liberal Democrats.

The tendency of governments not to disclose before elections what they are intending to do lends weight to wider concerns about the health of democratic institutions in Britain today (see, for instance, Hutton 1995; Rawnsley 2001). These concerns throw additional doubts upon the value of a democratic model as a way of really understanding how decisions are made. In education, we have seen how control by democratically elected local councils has been eroded in a number of fields. Key functions (funding, running schools and colleges, delivering local education services such as transport) have been taken over by other centralized bodies, by school governing bodies that meet in private and by private sector companies. In sum, there is a strong argument that the trend towards ever more centralized government, combined with the weakening of local democracy, has put increasing amounts of power into the hands of a small political elite of decision-makers. This has been particularly noticeable when one political party is dominant in the House of Commons (as with the Conservative Party in the 1980s and with Labour between 1997 and 2005) and when the prime minister can be relatively unconcerned about opposition from other political parties or from rebels in the ranks of the governing party. Despite this, however, it would be wrong to jettison the democratic explanation of policy development altogether. MPs, even those who belong to the governing party, have the right and the freedom to oppose legislation proposed by the government, as the case of the defeat of the Conservative proposal to change the boundary system in the UK in relation to voting, which led to heated debates in parliament and opposition from some Liberal Democrats. Changes were not made as a result. In addition, even if the government has a free hand to decide *what* is to be done, *whether* it is done and *how* are rather different matters. As we saw at the implementation stage of certain policies discussed in this chapter (for instance, opposition by teachers to aspects of the National Curriculum), a pluralist – if not fully democratic – model can help to explain how policies are modified and adapted after they have been launched, or legislation passed.

On balance, then, a reliable or accurate picture of policy-making depends on the simultaneous use of two or three theories of power and politics, rather than exclusive reliance upon one. An emphasis on the power of elites might be particularly relevant for analysis of the 'corridors of power' and the early stages of policy formation. But it might be necessary to incorporate ideas about pluralistic politics and democratic influences when looking at the local level or at how policies are received at the grassroots.

The third, political economy model of power, as discussed earlier, points to the underlying economic and political influences on policy as a way of analysing why particular policies were adopted and others were not. There are contradictory pressures to hold down taxes on business and to limit social spending by government (as the Coalition Government is clearly doing, drawing upon the Comprehensive Spending Review, 2010) and yet also to develop a more productive workforce through better training and *more* spending on certain types of education.

As we have seen in this chapter, the winning side in this tug-of-war was initially the pressure to keep down public expenditure, including spending on education. The proportion of Britain's resources devoted to education changed very little during the 1990s, and even fell slightly during Labour's first term in office, 1997–2001. However, during its second term in office, 2001–5, the other side of the tug-of-war gained a lot of ground, as government spending on education (and on related services and facilities, such as child-care and preschool or nursery provision) increased significantly. While the Coalition Government has made some cuts to services and provision, the education budget has remained relatively unscathed compared to many other areas of public service provision. Part of the historical impetus for New Labour's financial commitment to education was undoubtedly a genuine drive to widen opportunities for children and to improve the quality of educational services. A political economy perspective reminds us, however, that an additional reason for the extra spending on education can be found in the 'business case' for it. For the UK to remain a competitive economy in global markets, it is imperative that the education system be able to produce a sufficiently well-educated and adaptable workforce. However, there are strong reasons to question whether the UK's education system has received enough investment over the past few decades, and whether it is sufficiently good at retaining enough young people in the kinds of education and training that help to boost productivity.

Thus, as mentioned in the earlier section on the Conservatives' education reforms of 1988, the political economy view of power might be better in helping us to interpret the general direction of policy, such as trends in government spending on a service such as education, rather than in understanding specific policy changes. For instance, the whole idea of developing an internal market in state education seemed to be inspired by a strong belief among politicians in the value of incorporating business methods and competition into the state sector. But the specific policy to do this did not result from a clear set of demands from business leaders or those representing financial interests. This analysis is also true of the reform to higher education funding recently implemented, although the review that led to it was led by Lord Browne, who has a background in business. His proposals were also criticized for not being based upon any research evidence (Callender 2012) and therefore are also related to political and ideological beliefs.

The importance of political leaders' beliefs about what ought to be done illustrates another way in which the political economy perspective is useful. It can help to show us how changes in a capitalist or market economy change ideas and the expectations we have of government and the public services. The Conservatives' education reforms show how we have gradually become accustomed to certain ideas about privatization, the introduction of an internal market in public services and competition between service providers. Arguably, it is now seen as more 'natural' and 'common sense' than before the 1980s' reforms for there to be competition between schools for students and funding, or that getting private sector bodies to run schools is likely to provide the best administrative solution – even though there is often evidence against this and ongoing debates about how effective this policy approach has been. As the business of running schools becomes less and less obviously a public service, people will be more likely to turn to their school's governing body, or the local consortium or company running education in their area, than government. It is for this reason that central governments in the future might not be as damaged in elections or lose as much popularity as might be expected as a result of crises or failures in the nation's schools.

However, we cannot explain any of these problems or the education reforms discussed in this chapter unless we recognize the importance of elite control in UK policy-making. The reasons for the elite's ability to formulate and direct policy are a matter of debate, but it is likely that Britain's traditional class divisions in education play a large part. Political elites, whether of the left or right, are reluctant to bring change to a selective and elitist system that suits them very well. Thus, compared with the view that policy-making is basically democratic in Britain, an elite control model seems to better explain the formation of education policy. Despite differences in matters of detail, both New Labour and the Coalition Government's policies on education closely resemble those of the 1980s Conservative Government. This bears out the contention that, while the UK is a parliamentary democracy, any change of government at election time largely has the effect of exchanging one political elite for another that has broadly similar aims and interests.

Summary of key points

- UK education reform in the 1980s represented a radical change in the direction of social policy in this area. The change has since travelled in the same direction irrespective of the government in power and their political and ideological standpoint.
- Educational policy, and the ways in which it has changed in recent years, demonstrates the ways in which power can be understood within the policy-making process, with policy in this area clearly linked to social control and power dynamics.
- The analysis in this chapter shows that the political elite dominate in decision-making within the British policy-making arena, and this is the most appropriate framework for understanding the operation of power dynamics within this context.

Key terms and concepts

democratic pluralist model of power
elite control model of power
implementation
parliamentary democracy
political economy model of power
policy agenda

Suggestions for further reading

Ball, S. (2008) *The Education Debate.* Bristol: Policy Press.

This book offers an analysis of the flood of government initiatives and policies that have been introduced since the early 1990s, including Beacon Schools, the Academies programme, parental choice, Foundation Schools, faith schools and teaching standards. The book explores this raft of policy interventions and critically evaluates them within the context of social policy. A useful introduction to the field of educational reform.

Ham, C. and Hill, M. (1993) *The Policy Process in the Modern Capitalist State.* London: Wheatsheaf Books.

This book remains one of the best and more readable texts on the nature of policy-making and models of power. The book sets the scene and remains an invaluable guide for students to the main theories drawn from political economy, sociology and political science. The book details how and why some policies come about, why some policies do not see the light of day, and why many fail.

Lukes, S. (2005) *Power: A Radical View.* 2nd edition. London: Palgrave Macmillan.

Though written primarily for a sociological and political science audience, this book has many applications in social policy. It is a classic, and this second edition contains more material, including discussion about the contributions of Michel Foucault. It remains an important reference point within social and political theory.

Tomlinson, S. (2001) *Education in a Post-Welfare Society.* London: McGraw-Hill.

This book provides an overview that is both extremely informative and readable, including thorough discussions of key policy issues such as education and equity (class, gender and 'race'), education and the economy, and New Labour's record on education. It also includes a succinct discussion of the development of education policy in England and Wales since 1944.

9 Work and welfare

Key learning outcomes

By the end of this chapter you should:

- be able to understand the ways in which work is a central component of people's welfare and therefore a key issue in social policy
- be able to identify and outline the historical connections between work and welfare
- be able to understand some key changes in current policies on work and welfare

Overview of the chapter

Work is, will be, or has been a central part of most people's lives. The kinds of work we do, how much we earn and where we work play a very important part in defining who we are. Not surprisingly, therefore, work strongly affects a person's welfare. Work might be deeply satisfying, or stressful, or mundane and boring. It strongly influences our psychological welfare in various ways. The amount of money earned and the amount of time spent earning it constrain the choices we can make. At a personal level, the quality of the food we eat, whether we can easily take part in leisure and sporting activities, enjoy the holidays we want, and have a satisfactory home are all likely to be strongly influenced by the jobs we have. Similarly, health, education and social security are all affected by work and income, and by changes in employment patterns. This chapter therefore explores the relationship between work and welfare, starting out with an examination of the historical relationship between the two. We will then examine the central importance of work as a social policy issue today. The chapter then turns to a critical examination of the approach being adopted by the Coalition Government.

Historical connections between work and welfare

Historical connections between work and human welfare are deeply rooted. Concerns about well-being at work can be traced back to the nineteenth century or even before that. For instance, the Factory Acts that were passed in 1833, 1844 and 1847 limited the hours per day that children could be expected to work (Fraser 1984). The aim was to protect children from being exploited under the harshest conditions in factories and other hazardous workplaces. Eventually, child labour was abolished as elementary schooling became commonplace.

Another example of the historical relationship between work and welfare can be seen in the development of trade unions in the pre-welfare-state era. As unions and workers' associations grew in importance, many established a wide range of benefits and services for their members. These included social facilities and leisure activities, holiday schemes, insurance against the cost of sickness or funeral expenses and other welfare benefits. Trade unions and professional associations retain an important function in managing occupational pensions, and in negotiating a wide range of concessions and benefits for their members – for instance, in health, vehicle and travel insurance. Some commentators argue that trade union power is dwindling, however; historically, trade unions were associated with the Labour Party. Most union leaders supported Ed Miliband's campaign to become the leader of the party in 2010, for instance.

Work: an object of social *and* economic policy

Given the historical connections between work and welfare, it is surprising to realize that, traditionally, social policy as an academic subject seemed to downplay employment policy or ignore it altogether. Most university courses in social policy used to focus on the 'five great social services' (see Chapter 1) – education, health, housing, personal social services and social security. Employment policy was often left in the shade. Similarly, the first edition of this book did not contain a separate chapter on work – an omission remedied in the second edition.

There is now a lot of interest in employment policy and its connections with social welfare, especially in relation to certain groups in society such as school-leavers and the section of young people who have difficulty finding worthwhile jobs. Media reports frequently focus on the lack of employment opportunities for young people. The previous Labour government's approach to employment policy and its various 'welfare to work' programmes also undoubtedly stimulated interest in this field because their approach placed work centre stage in social, as well as economic, policy. This focus has also remained important for the Coalition Government, as will be shown later.

However, it remains the case that there is still something of a mental divide between the world of employment – often associated with the realities of making a living, of commerce and the private sector – and the world of social policy and welfare. The latter is more often associated with care, protection and with the problems of people who cannot work.

The conceptual divide between economic policy – including employment policy – on the one hand, and social policy on the other, can be traced back to the development of the state after the Second World War. Unlike other European countries, the British approach to planning the economy and the welfare system ran on two rather separate tracks.

Beveridge's plans in the 1940s for a universal system of social security assumed that there would have to be full employment after the Second World War. It was seen as essential to have as high a number of (male) workers in jobs and contributing to the system as possible, to keep it solvent. This was part of a **Keynesian strategy** that involved managing public spending in ways that would maintain full employment and economic growth. However, despite the postwar recognition that the success of the welfare state rested on the economy, and vice versa, not as much was done in Britain as in other welfare states to dovetail economic and social policy.

In France, Germany, Sweden and other countries, a more *corporatist* approach (see Chapter 3) led to planning the economy and the welfare system together. The **main link** between the two was work. Thus, in a country such as Germany or Sweden, wages were never thought of in isolation from social benefits, even in the private sector of employment. Negotiations between employers, unions and government led to agreements on pay, the amount of tax and insurance contributions to be levied by government, and the level or value of social benefits (for example, child benefits or family benefits). Sometimes unions were willing to moderate their wage demands if government did not increase taxes, or if social benefits could be raised.

In the UK, this idea of a firm social contract between employers, employees and government never developed to the degree that it did in most of the major north European countries. Employment policy, wages policy and economic development were seen mainly as 'economics' issues in the UK and as separate from 'welfare' issues.

There were attempts by the Labour government of the 1970s (1974–9) to encourage trade unions, the major employers and government to work together to reach agreements on wages, prices, taxation and social benefits. However, the lack of a corporatist tradition and the conflict-ridden state of **industrial relations** in Britain meant that none of these agreements held.

Arguably, Labour lost the general election in 1979 mainly because it was perceived as a government that had failed in its attempt to manage industrial relations, or to weld together any lasting agreements between trade unions and employers. Mrs Thatcher, who led the Conservative government that replaced Labour in 1979, abhorred any policy that smacked of government 'interference' in the labour market, or of any attempt to engineer agreements on wages, prices and social security through a corporatist approach. Consequently the 1980s were the decade in which the Conservative government dismantled Labour's mechanisms for bringing trade unions, employers and government together to discuss economic and social policy. The impact of these changes still remains significant today. Trade union power and influence were cut down drastically. Government firmly turned its back on consensus politics and on policies to integrate economic and social policy.

Now that old-style corporatism is also being dismantled in Europe, it is very unlikely that the UK will ever develop such integrated policies for managing the economy, employment and social benefits. The trend begun by Mrs Thatcher (and continued by New Labour and then the Coalition Government) is now in the opposite direction, towards the deregulation of employment conditions and wage bargaining between employers and employees that is free of government influence or control. However, there is still a considerable gulf between the employment policies followed by countries such as France, Germany and Sweden, and employment policies in the UK.

Does work equal welfare?

First, it is necessary to explore in a little more depth the connections between work and welfare. While it is one thing to safeguard welfare *at* work (for example, through health and safety regulations) or *after* working life (for example, through the provision of pensions), it is another to claim that *work itself* is beneficial and enhances human welfare. Clearly, everything depends on the work in question. Heavy manual work for a pittance in degrading or hazardous conditions is one thing; well-paid work in a bright, pleasant office is another. However, even though work varies widely and different working conditions have different welfare implications, some claim that work generally has positive effects on people. Research commissioned under the New Labour government brought attention to the importance of work as a means of welfare, for instance the research by Dame Carol Black (2008). Complete Activity 9.1 to explore this in more depth.

Activity 9.1 Work and Health: The Black Report 2008

Carol Black, National Director for Health and Work, was commissioned in March 2007 by the Secretaries of State for Health, and for Work and Pensions, to conduct a review of the health of Britain's working-age population. This was about increasing understanding of the health of working-age people and the impact this has on government, the economy and society.

1. Use the Internet to explore the report – you will be able to find the full report easily using a search engine.
2. Read the executive summary (and more if you wish, but the report is lengthy).
3. Make some notes about the key points of the report.
4. What does the report say about the relationship between work and health?
5. What are your views about the recommendations set out by the report, and, given the time that has now passed, do you think that there has been significant policy change in this area?

In completing the first activity in this chapter, you will have begun to explore and learn about the complex relationship that exists between work and health. This poses difficult challenges for policy-makers especially as, in reality, most people find that work has a mixture of positive and negative effects on their lives, illustrated in Table 9.1.

Table 9.1 The ways in which work influences individual lives

Work as a positive influence	Work as a negative influence
• Being in work generally means that people's *incomes* are higher than they would be if they were unemployed or dependent on someone else. It has been shown that incomes have a very direct effect on health and education. Rates of illness and illiteracy are much higher in areas where unemployment and poverty are common. Children are more likely to thrive and to develop to their full potential in households that have good, or at least adequate, incomes.	• Is work always good for us, either in terms of income or other benefits? There are some important exceptions to the principle that getting a job or staying in employment is always beneficial. First, some groups choose to leave full-time employment (e.g. via early retirement where possible), suggesting that, when it is possible to make a choice, some people expect their welfare and general satisfaction with life to be better when not employed. Second, poverty is not restricted to people out of work. Having a job does not guarantee a higher income than being unemployed, despite the introduction of a minimum wage.

(continued)

Table 9.1 The ways in which work influences individual lives (*Continued*)

Work as a positive influence	Work as a negative influence
• Employment promotes *social inclusion*. Unemployed people are more likely than those in employment to be socially isolated and excluded. On the other hand, being at work tends to get people involved in friendships and community life. Traditionally, getting a job after leaving school was a very important transition that marked maturation from adolescence to adulthood. However, changes to the structure and types of employment mean that this is no longer the case (see Robertson Elliot 1996).	• *Work does not necessarily promote social inclusion*. In fact, the opposite might occur if a **dual labour market** develops. This means that there are broadly two types or 'sectors' of work available. First, getting a job in the formal employment sector does not always require a lot of educational qualifications or a high level of skills, but there is a formal selection process. Second, there are jobs in the 'informal' sector, in which the work is more often available on a casual or temporary basis than in the formal sector. Typically, jobs in this sector are low-paid and often mean working irregular hours, or during evenings, nights and early mornings. Employers might do little or nothing to safeguard the welfare, pension or health rights of employees. Disproportionate numbers of women, disabled workers, black and ethnic-minority workers and other disadvantaged groups are found in temporary, part-time and insecure employment of this type. A dual labour market therefore acts as a mechanism for *excluding*, rather than including, some groups.
• There is also an argument that work promotes *psychological well-being*. This can come from two main sources. First, work brings social contacts and involvement, and through these we find and develop our identities. A second source of psychological welfare could be the work itself. This is most likely to happen when the work is intrinsically satisfying, skilled, challenging or worthwhile. However, it could also occur even when there are some strongly negative aspects to the work if the individual draws some satisfaction from being able to hold down a difficult job or overcome its hardships.	• *Work can cause unhappiness, alienation and psychological stress*. There are several major causes of these kinds of problems. Work remains an alienating, dehumanizing experience for significant groups of people. As a result of constant changes in the technologies of mass production, much work has been deskilled and reduced to a series of fragmented, monotonous tasks. Work can also make us ill from accidents, pollution, absorption of hazardous chemicals and other substances, noise and repetitive strain. • *For some, problems arise from overwork as much as the work itself.* Workers in the UK on average have to spend significantly more hours at work each week and have fewer holidays than their counterparts in western European countries. Also, job insecurity – the real or perceived threat of redundancy – adds to feelings of dissatisfaction and stress. Finally, conflicts between the demands of work and home – particularly those experienced by lone parents, or by those caring for ill and frail relatives – can exacerbate levels of stress.

Employment policy options

As illustrated in Table 9.1, most people find that work brings a mixture of positive and negative influences on their welfare. For instance, an employee might find that they are in a work group that is both supportive and fun to be with, and that the work itself is fairly interesting. In the same job they might suffer from repetitive strain injury and discover that their leave entitlement is less than they anticipated.

However, the fact that the impact of work on human welfare varies considerably from individual to individual should not blind us to some of the broader patterns and inequalities in employment that exist. This applies particularly to the 'stark contrasts' that have been observed in both the amount of unemployment and the quality of jobs available in different parts of the UK (see Bennett 2000: 678–9). Box 9.1 illustrates some of the gender inequalities evident within the contemporary UK workplace

Box 9.1 Gendered inequalities in the workplace (BBC News 2010a)

- Women tended to have lower hourly rates of pay in general when compared to men.
- While pay differences are narrowing between full-time working women and men, there are still significant gaps between part-time workers.
- Women in the public sector tend to earn more than those in the private sector because gendered pay gaps in the private sector are starker.

The gender issues identified in Box 9.1 are just one example; there are also pay gaps between people who live in the north of England compared to the south (BBC News 2010a), and many other inequalities. Thus persistent inequalities and problems in the workplace pose two policy questions for government.

First, if work has mixed effects on people's welfare and in some cases might have strongly negative effects, should employment policy concentrate on simply getting as many people as possible into jobs as quickly as possible? This kind of strategy would focus on stimulating *demand* for workers. It is the kind of policy that makes it easy for employers to hire workers. For instance, employers can be given a government subsidy for every unemployed worker who is taken onto the payroll. Another aim would be to reduce the amount of regulations governing pay and conditions that employers have to abide by. The main goal of this sort of policy is to reduce the number of people officially counted as unemployed, and not to look too closely at the sorts of work that people are more or less firmly pushed into.

A second approach to employment policy rests more on improving people's prospects of employment by enhancing and upgrading their skills and general employability. This kind of policy concentrates on what has been termed the 'supply side' of the labour market – that is, the supply of labour and the quality of the people (as demonstrated by their skills and capabilities) available for work. In this approach there is more emphasis on people's long-term employability and success in staying in work than on the short-term goal of getting them any job as quickly as possible.

Before looking at the kinds of employment policy that have been introduced in recent years, we need to see the government's efforts in the context of the labour market – that is, the basic characteristics of working patterns and the labour force in the UK. Only then can we fully assess the value of recent employment policies, and how far they represent worthwhile efforts by government.

The context: work and unemployment in the UK

In the year 2012 there were 29.58 million people in employment aged 16 and over (ONS 2012a). In other words, they could be counted as members of the labour force in the sense that they are in paid employment. There were 2.51 million unemployed people, who again are members of the labour force because they are available for work (ONS 2012a).

The employment rate for men aged from 16 to 64 was 76.5 per cent for July to September 2012, while the corresponding employment rate for women was 66 per cent. The media have spent much time reporting about unemployment rates because of the economic recession. Unemployment is a problem in many countries and concerns about unemployment are not unique to the UK:

- In 2012 the unemployment rate for the European Union (EU) was 10.6 per cent of the **economically active** population for September 2012.
- The EU country with the highest unemployment rate was Spain, at 25.8 per cent.
- The EU country with the lowest unemployment rate was Austria, at 4.4 per cent (Eurostat 2012a).

Now complete Activity 9.2 to explore the ways in which an individual's work status is measured.

Activity 9.2 Exploring the measurement of employment status

1. Use the Internet to access YouTube at the following address: www.youtube.com/watch?v=Fze4o0bBfcw&lr=1.
2. Listen to the talk called 'Explaining employment & unemployment & inactivity'.
3. This talk explains how the figures you have just read about are compiled specifically in relation to the ONS approach.
4. ONS compiles lots of other data about the labour market – explore the website to learn more about the labour market trends being discussed in this chapter. See www.ons.gov.uk/ons/index.html.

Since the middle of the twentieth century there have been very significant changes in the composition of the labour force, as well as in the nature of work itself and the main types of jobs that are available. The main changes have been in the *age and gender composition* of the labour force. For instance, in the past almost all men used to work right up to the standard retirement age of 65. In 1971 over 95 per cent of men aged between 60 and 64 were economically active, but now this situation has been reversed, with a large majority of older men being outside the workforce. In fact the economic activity rate among all men has been in decline since the 1970s. This is explained partly by increases in the numbers of men taking early retirement after the age of 45, and by an increase in the number claiming that either disability or long-term illness prevents them from working. However, given changes in retirement policy (see Chapter 6), these trends may again be changing and, in the future, older people in general are likely to work for longer.

Over the same period the total of women who are economically active increased dramatically, from only 10 million to 13.6 million (ONS 2001: 77).

These very marked increases can be explained only by the long-term trend for women to take up paid employment, either full-time or part-time (over 16 hours per week). In the 1950s and before that, a large majority of women were engaged in domestic work in their own homes, and relatively few combined this with part-time paid work. Interestingly, just because women are working more does not mean that they do less housework (Yapp 2012). Therefore, despite women closing the gap in economic activity rates between themselves and men, informal unpaid activity such as housework is still often 'gendered'. Despite the increased numbers of women working in the UK, the situation has not reached the near-equal rate of men and women in paid work that prevails in Sweden and other Scandinavian countries. Women's participation in the labour market has increased across Europe, with the proportion of women not working falling from 40 to 35 per cent between 2000 and 2010, while the share of men outside the labour force remained almost stable (Eurostat 2012b)

Thus the rise in British women's rate of participation in the workforce is impressive but, to put it in context, we must note that many more women than men work part-time, as can be seen in Table 9.2.

Table 9.2 Employment status by sex in the UK, 2011 (thousands)

Employment status	Males	Females	All
Full-time employees	11,223	7,078	18,301
Part-time employees	1,504	5,178	6,682
Self-employed full-time	2,310	550	2,860
Self-employed part-time	484	606	1,090
Total	15,521	13,412	28,933

(ONS 2011b)

These gender differences in rates of full-time and part-time work partly explain other gender inequalities in the workforce. As many more women than men are in part-time work, it is not surprising that their total earnings are considerably less than men's. Also, the discrimination against part-time workers that can occur when opportunities for promotion or training are considered means that women are more likely than men to be held back in their career development.

However, not all of the gender inequalities in pay and promotion can be explained by women's much greater involvement in part-time paid work. There are also significant differences in the types of work that men and women tend to do. While many men work in the service sector of the economy (which includes jobs in catering, hotels and leisure services, welfare and care services, retail, and clerical and administrative jobs), a higher proportion of women do so. Conversely, significantly more men than women work in construction, transport and manufacturing.

Traditionally, service-sector jobs have been more often part-time, less valued and lower paid than jobs in manufacturing and related areas of the economy. The tendency for men to be in jobs that are seen as suitable for them, and for women to be steered towards traditionally 'feminized' occupations, has tended to underpin and maintain pay inequalities between men and women. Discrimination against women employees, whether or not they are working alongside men, is also a strong factor in holding down women's pay.

While the pay gap has continued to narrow in some areas, Toynbee and Walker (2001) suggest it will probably continue to narrow in the future, but only slowly and more as a result of market forces than government attempts to equalize pay between men and women. This is a significant point because the labour market is far from static and, whatever happens to pay inequality, there will undoubtedly be further changes to the working roles of men and women. For one thing, the number of jobs in manufacturing is in long-term decline. Men have found it increasingly difficult to get work in occupations that they used to rely on. An increasing proportion of men will have to take jobs in the service sector and, like women, may have to adapt to working 'flexible hours' or in part-time jobs.

This brings us to another facet of change in employment, because there has been an increase not only in part-time and flexible working but also in the number of temporary jobs. As will be recalled, this has raised concerns about whether a dual labour market is developing in the UK, and whether this is going to lead to a lot more job insecurity and **casualization** of work contracts in the future. For instance, there has been concern in recent years about the practice of imposing 'zero hours contracts' on employees – a kind of piecework whereby the worker is paid only if there is work to be done in a given time period or part of the working day.

The evidence on the spread of casual work contracts and job insecurity in the UK is mixed, with some commentators arguing that 'flexible' working leads to casualization, zero hours contracts, job insecurity and worsening working conditions for a growing number of people (Citizens' Advice Bureau 1998). Others argue that there are widespread gaps between perceptions and reality in relation to the contemporary job market (Doogan 2009). Doogan argues that 'new' capitalism has created an ideological offensive, a form of domination in which fear and anxiety are used as tools to create compliance among the labour force. This implies that the labour force *potentially* has much more power than is realized. Doogan's (2009) argument holds weight in that in some respects the UK's workforce remains a relatively stable one.

Change is evident in working practices and growing the expectations of employers that their employees will work longer and more flexible hours. As James (1998) suggests, depression and mental stress are on the increase. This is only partly because of an objective increase in workload. Subjective attitudes to what are perceived to be the growing pressures of work are also significant – in particular, the stress of trying to combine the emotional demands of parenting with the demands of work (James 1998: 149).

Employment futures

Given the many changes to the labour market, future trends have been analysed in order to offer insight to policy-makers who are concerned with the direction of policy in relation to employment, skills and careers. Wilkinson and Homenidou (2012) highlight several likely future projections in the UK labour market in the period up to 2020:

- Recovery from recession will be slow; the UK economy will probably generate around 1.5 million additional jobs by 2020.

- While the number of people available to work is projected to rise significantly, labour market participation rates are expected to fall slightly, because of the ageing population.
- Private services are expected to be the main source of employment growth.
- Most employment growth will be in higher skilled, white-collar occupations, while there will be a continued decline in employment in semi-skilled manual roles.
- The demand for skills as measured by formal qualifications is projected to rise.
- The southern part of England is predicted to see significantly more rapid employment growth than the devolved nations and the northern regions of England.

The report has very little to say about unemployment; however, the story of unemployment is crucial within policy-making.

The story of unemployment

Any understanding of work and policies to stimulate employment would be incomplete without some knowledge of *un*employment. In the past, there have been mixed trends in rates of unemployment.

Perhaps one of the best-known periods of high unemployment in the UK and other countries was that of the Great Depression of the 1930s. It was during the early 1930s in particular that existing unemployment insurance schemes struggled to provide enough benefits to the millions of people who had been thrown out of work. For this reason Pierson (1991: 116) and other commentators believe that the 1930s became a seedbed for the development of the welfare state after the Second World War. Political leaders expressed a common wish never to return to the days of high unemployment and poverty that were experienced in the 1930s. As mentioned earlier, Beveridge insisted that full employment would have to be a central plank in the development of an adequately funded system of social security and health care.

Whether as a result of government policy or the inevitable upswing in economic activity that came with postwar reconstruction, full employment – at least, for men – became a reality during the three decades that followed the end of the Second World War in 1945. This was the so-called 'golden age' of the welfare state. Among all those who were counted as economically active, unemployment stayed below 3 per cent of the labour force until 1975.

From the mid-1970s on, however, the rate of unemployment began to rise. Between 1976 and 1986, it rose from 5 to almost 12 per cent of the workforce. The steepest rise took place in the early 1980s, during Mrs Thatcher's first period in office. Her government abandoned the economic strategies used by previous Labour and Conservative governments to assist struggling industries and to use public spending to stimulate employment. As a result, unemployment soared and government expenditure on unemployment and social security benefits also rose very substantially.

At the time, there was concern not only about what seemed to be a reckless economic strategy but also about the impact of high unemployment on the 'social fabric' of the UK. For instance, by the end of the 1970s, unemployment in Northern Ireland had risen to what then seemed an astronomical 9 per cent of the labour force – three times the typical rate in the UK before 1975. It was said at the time that, if unemployment in the rest of the UK were to reach such a high level, there would almost certainly be some kind of profound social crisis. Within two years, however, a 9 per cent rate of unemployment had become the *lowest* rate to be found in any of the UK's regions – the south-east of England. Thus the steep rise in unemployment in the 1980s did not result in the predicted 'melt down' of the social order. However, concerns about unemployment being the cause of declining social welfare and poorer health are still being voiced. And even though complete social breakdown was avoided, unemployment and associated changes in the labour force did bring momentous social change. The 1980s are associated with the first great shake-outs of labour to take place since the 1930s, and with the sharp decline of traditional heavy industries and coal-mining as large-scale employers. The Conservative Government of the 1980s decided to tough out the inevitable confrontations with the trade unions. In the ensuing struggles between organized labour and government, the threat of unemployment played a key role. Grudgingly, the trade unions had to accept government-imposed reforms of labour relations and new controls on strikes.

It would be wrong to conclude, however, that Mrs Thatcher's government was unconcerned about the political implications of high unemployment. Considerable government effort was devoted to reducing the official rate of unemployment. Critics argued that much of this was an exercise in recategorizing unemployed people as economically inactive so that they would no longer appear in the official statistics as unemployed. However, the Conservative Government of the 1980s did make vigorous efforts to develop job creation and training schemes, particularly to reduce the unemployment rate among young people. This was in one way surprising, because the government was also strongly committed to a policy of non-intervention or laissez-faire in the job market.

As Figure 9.1 shows, unemployment between the 'Thatcher' and 'Major' years of 1988 and 1994 and the 'Blair' year of 2004 was more than halved for men and almost halved for women. More recently, as the graph in Figure 9.1 shows, unemployment increased between 2007 and 2012, with the steepest rise occurring between 2008 and 2009, following the financial and economic crisis of that year.

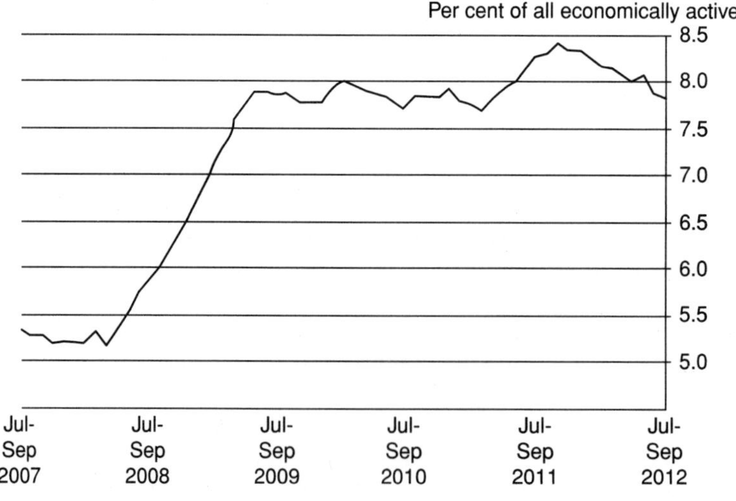

Figure 9.1 Unemployment rates (aged 16+) 2007–12
Source: ONS 2012a. Contains public sector information licensed under the Open Government Licence v1.0. www.ons.gov.uk/ons/rel/lms/labour-market-statistics/february-2012/statistical-bulletin.html.

In sum, a historical perspective shows that the ability of government to manage employment, to link work to welfare issues or reduce unemployment is very dependent on the health of the economy and the **business cycle**. This point should be borne in mind in the next section, which reviews the impact of various government policies on employment and unemployment.

Current employment policy

As mentioned at the beginning of the chapter, the previous New Labour government 1997–2010 made work the centrepiece of its policies on social welfare. The government tried, with varying degrees of success, to break down the division between policies on welfare and social security on the one hand, and employment on the other. In attempting to 'get people off welfare and into work', it developed an *active* **labour market policy**. This amounts to a set of government strategies to actively intervene in the job market. Government aims to forge partnerships with employers, not only to stimulate the creation of more jobs but also to encourage more efficient employment of workers, using detailed measures to match individual people to jobs.

Adopting an active labour market policy meant that the government committed itself to the principle that no one who is able to work should be left out of the labour market. The aim is to improve people's welfare through employment. Government policy was trying to ensure that both individuals and families were better off financially, and could obtain benefits (notably tax credits) through being employed, rather than by obtaining benefits through being unemployed.

Although Britain's recent active labour market policies do not yet match those of Sweden and other Scandinavian countries, they do represent a step towards a system in which it is assumed that almost everyone's 'gateway' to social benefits and full citizenship is through getting a job. In Sweden, for instance, strong efforts are made to integrate into the workforce as many disabled people as possible, so that benefits for disabled people can be channelled through employment. Likewise, parental benefits – for instance, an insurance scheme that pays for parental leave from work – are obtained through employment.

Under New Labour, Britain's active labour market policies developed in two directions: first, various New Deal schemes were introduced in order to reduce unemployment and improve both the skills and general employability of workers, and especially of young people. Second, a variety of policies to *improve the conditions and welfare of people already in work* were implemented. Table 9.3 compares the policies introduced by New Labour to those of the Coalition Government in relation to getting people into work.

Table 9.3 shows that an element of compulsion was introduced into New Labour's active labour market policy; an element that has since continued. This raises important questions about compulsion in employment policy. On one side, any attempt by the state to compel people to change their personal behaviour and appearance can be seen as an infringement of personal freedom, even if as a result people are 'encouraged' into jobs. But, on the other side, there is practical evidence that the more coercive approach of the New Deal worked better than previous policies with people who are demotivated and have been unemployed long term. Hasluck (2000: 372), for instance, points to evidence that there was a relatively positive view of the NDYP among young people who were involved in it.

Table 9.3 Historical versus contemporary workfare reforms: New Labour and the Coalition Government

New Labour	**Coalition Government**
The New Deal The New Deal for Young People (NDYP) began full operation in 1998 and was supplemented by other employment schemes – New Deals for the long-term unemployed, for lone parents, for disabled people and for workers over 50 years of age. In implementing its New Deal philosophy, New Labour tried to bring about an active labour market approach to employment policy. As Hasluck (2000: 370) points out, the New Deal was supposed to be different in trying to offer 'help that is tailored to the needs of individual job-seekers'. This policy approach represented both the 'caring' and 'controlling' strands of welfare discussed in Chapter 7. Claimants who refused to take an available job, or refused training, faced having their benefit stopped for 14 days, rising to a month if they continued to turn down all of the options they were offered. One of the principal aims of the New Deal was to reduce social exclusion as well as to promote sustained employment.	All existing welfare to work programmes that the Coalition Government inherited have been ended and instead there now exists a single welfare to work programme for every individual categorized as unemployed. The Welfare Reform Act 2012 (DWP 2012c) introduced a wide range of reforms which aim to make the benefits and tax credits system fairer and simpler by: • creating the right incentives to get more people into work, • protecting the most vulnerable in our society, and • delivering fairness to those claiming benefit and to the tax payer.

There were many questions asked about the effectiveness of this approach; in particular, did it actually help people to obtain work or create many jobs given its context within a period of unbroken years of economic growth (see, for instance, Elliott 2000)? Was the New Deal scheme cost-effective (Toynbee and Walker 2005: 61)? Did the scheme get people into work (Hasluck 2000: 371)? There is a range of mixed evidence about New Deal, and similar questions are also being asked about current Coalition Government approaches. Arguably, whether or not the New Deal policy had been introduced, the overall size of the labour force would not have been much different from what it is today. However, as a result of this New Labour approach, employability has been placed centre-stage and the principle established that as many people who can work will be helped by government to do so. The Coalition Government has stressed the importance of:

- reducing barriers to work,
- helping people into work, and
- ensuring that benefit provision is conditional on willingness to work (DWP 2012a).

The Coalition Government has also started the process of re-assessing individuals in receipt of incapacity benefit so that their readiness to work can be determined. Those found to be able to work are now moved from incapacity benefit onto jobseeker's allowance. These changes have caused significant debate about the ethics and fairness of the system, particularly as the government has employed a private company called Atos to

Activity 9.3 Welfare to work

1. Use the Internet to explore recent policy changes in terms of welfare to work as an approach. Start with the DWP website to read about the changes from the perspective of the government. Then search the Internet for news reports and media discussion related to the changes.
2. From what your search found, what can you conclude about the welfare to work programme? Is it effective? If there are problems, what are they? For example, as a starting point consider some the problems that arise when paying private companies to get people back into work.

   What is your own view about welfare to work and the use of private companies?

conduct the assessments (McCartney 2011). Now complete Activity 9.3 to explore the impact of the changes.

Other policies – the welfare of people in work

While the New Deal and other similar schemes represent new ways of getting people into jobs, recent employment policy has also concentrated on the welfare and incomes of people who are already in paid work. The main employment policies that have developed in this direction are as follows.

Employment relations

Under the previous New Labour government an Employment Relations Act was passed in 2000. This legislation was enacted partly to satisfy the requirements of EU law following the British government decision to sign up to EU social legislation in 1997. It established new rules governing the recognition of trade unions and of employee rights (such as the right to be consulted by large employers about major decisions concerning the future of the firm or business). It also reflects a requirement by the EU to regulate working time. It is now illegal for employers to require their employees to work for more than 48 hours per week – though a number of occupations are exempt, and professional and senior management employees can also be exempted through voluntary agreements to work longer hours. Another important element in this legislation was the introduction of new 'family-friendly' rights concerning parental or family leave from work. For instance, for the first time fathers have been given the right to take (unpaid) parental leave following the birth of a child. Family leave includes the right of parents of young children to take time off for family emergencies. Statutory maternity leave has been increased; an employee can take up to 52 weeks' leave no matter how long they have been with their employer, how many hours they work or how much they are paid, and the qualifying period (the time that the mother has to be in work before being able to claim this right) has been reduced. However, there have been concerns about workers' rights since recent Coalition Government changes mean that employers are now able to terminate employees' contracts in an easier way. Policy changes mean that the employment tribunal system has been changed, rights to compensation have also been amended and redundancy rules again changed (Newton Dunn 2012).

Tax credits

Various kinds of tax credit were also introduced under the New Labour government in order to raise the incomes of people who were in work but on low incomes. These were an important part of the previous government's 'welfare to work' policy and the drive to eliminate the 'poverty trap'. The most important of the tax credits was the working families tax credit (WFTC), launched in 2000 to replace family credit, a social security benefit that had been inherited and continued by the former Conservative government. WFTC was an interesting and significant development because it was managed by the Inland Revenue, as part of the tax system, not as a benefit to people in work from the DWP. It represented the growing importance of the Treasury in shaping social policy in the UK.

By 2001 WFTC was supplementing the incomes of approximately 1.5 million families, paying on average an extra £24 per week more than such families would have obtained from family credit (Toynbee and Walker 2001: 21). Other kinds of tax credits were also introduced. WFTC was replaced in 2003 by child tax credit and working tax credit for working people on low incomes – the former being much more important. These tax credits are effectively targeted, means-tested benefits paid through HMRC and designed to 'make work pay'. Child tax credit in particular was an important means of channelling resources towards families with children and was a component of the previous government's strategy for tackling child poverty. The government also introduced a disabled person's tax credit, which helped employed people who became disabled and was intended to encourage such people to stay in work.

While the Coalition Government has kept this system of tax credits, there have been a number of changes (see HM Revenue and Customs 2012):

- lower income limits for eligibility
- the number of hours that couples need to be working to qualify has changed
- the time-period in which tax credits will be backdated has declined from 3 months to 1 month.

Minimum wage

A minimum wage was introduced in 1999. New Labour's announcement of its minimum wage policy met with a great deal of controversy, with objections from both the trade unions and business. Trade unions and other groups representing the low paid argued that the minimum was set too low (it was introduced at only £3.60 an hour for the full rate).

The rate has, however, been steadily increased since its introduction, and this remains the same under the Coalition Government. Table 9.4 illustrates the different rates and increases in the minimum wage.

Table 9.4 Minimum wage (£)

Year	21 and over	18 to 20	Under 18	Apprentice*
2012 (current rate)	**6.19**	**4.98**	**3.68**	**2.65**
2011	6.08	4.98	3.68	2.60
2010	5.93	4.92	3.64	2.50

*This rate is for apprentices under 19 or those in their first year.

Source: Gov.UK 2012. Contains public sector information licensed under the Open Government Licence v1.0. www.gov.uk/national-minimum-wage-rates.

Business leaders strongly opposed the introduction of a minimum wage because of the cost to employers, and their argument was that wage increases for the lowest paid would price some people out of jobs. In a buoyant job market and a period of economic growth, however, this proved not to be the case – there was no evidence that introducing the minimum wage led to higher unemployment. On the contrary, in periods of economic growth, raising the lowest paid people's incomes to a minimum level leads to increases in spending, more economic activity and thus more employment. Despite the recession and increased rates of unemployment, as well as a change of government, there has been little change in this area.

Part-time workers

New Labour also introduced legislation to protect the interests of part-time workers. As with the Employment Relations Act 2000 and the introduction of more 'family-friendly' employment policies, this policy represented the influence of EU social legislation. The UK government had to implement the EU's part-time working directive, which meant that part-time workers are now entitled (on a pro-rata basis) to the same rights to holidays, parental leave, sick leave, pensions and other social benefits as full-time workers. The UK has a relatively high proportion of part-time workers, compared with most European countries except, for instance, the Netherlands. Therefore, this measure is a significant change because it adds considerably to employers' costs, but also lends stability and security to a workforce that has experienced some problems of job insecurity and 'casualization'. Given the EU directive, again there has been no policy change in this area from the Coalition Government.

Conclusions: in whose interests is employment policy?

When New Labour gained power in 1997, they implemented policies that were quite different from previous Labour policies on work. Under Blair's leadership the Labour Party severed many of its historical links with the unions. Reform of the Labour Party constitution and the introduction of a 'one member, one vote' system for electing the leadership removed much of the direct, block-vote influence trade unions had had on party policy and the selection of a new party leader. Their focus upon welfare to work as a social policy approach was a radical shift, and interestingly it has been continued under the Coalition Government. The importance of work is now central to social policy, particularly when examined alongside the welfare changes that are also being made. Welfare now is frequently linked to work. Individuals are now expected to demonstrate inability to work as proof of their eligibility for welfare. Given these changes, we can ask the following question: is employment policy designed primarily with the welfare of employers in mind rather than that of the workers and unemployed people?

This question assumes that employers' and employees' interests *must* be in conflict with one another. But can pro-welfare employment policies – in some respects at least – be beneficial to both sides of industry, and do they necessarily favour one side's interests at the expense of the other? That employment policy can serve both the interests of labour and business would certainly be the current Coalition Government's claim. However, given the hours that people work and the large divides in earnings found within the UK, questions are frequently asked about the importance of work, as well as work–life balance.

Explore the idea of work–life balance by completing Activity 9.4.

Activity 9.4 The idea of work–life balance

In the UK, many people work long hours, and the media has recently reported that the recession has worsened this trend as people are concerned about their job security. While work is arguably beneficial for health in numerous ways (see earlier in this chapter), there are caveats to this. Use the Internet to access TED Talks (www.ted.com/talks) and to find the talk by Nigel Marsh called 'How to make work-life balance work'.

1. Listen to the talk.
2. How far do you agree with the views of the speaker?
3. Have you experienced any work–life balance problems or observed any among your friends or relatives?
4. How might social policies help to ensure a better work–life balance in future?

Given that finding a balance between work and family life is a serious issue, the evidence needs to be weighed carefully to judge whose interests are being served by recent employment policy. First, as Bevan (2000) shows, there are grounds for accepting the argument that 'family-friendly' employment policies of the kind Labour introduced and that have so far been continued under the Coalition Government (for instance, limits on working time, parental leave, incentives to employers to improve childcare facilities) are also in the interests of business. There is not always a conflict here, despite some costs to business, because 'family-friendly' policies do not only benefit employees, they also lift productivity because employees are more satisfied, and better able to work productively, when conflicts between the demands of work and family are reduced. Also, business firms are more likely to retain valued and skilled workers with children, and to attract productive workers with family commitments when they implement 'family-friendly' policies.

Second, as the example of the minimum wage shows, there is not necessarily a conflict of interest between having this policy and making profits or sustaining economic growth. The USA, a country devoted to free-market capitalism and minimal state control of business, nevertheless has a minimum-wage policy. For the reasons discussed previously, a minimum wage tends to increase employment opportunities and general economic growth rather than acting as a burden on business.

Third, there are more general signs that employment policies have benefitted both business and the majority of people in work in Britain. Previous New Labour policies apparently delivered full or near-full employment and increased average wages to in excess of £20,000 for the first time. Increases in prosperity led to higher consumption and sales and thus greater market opportunities for business. To this can be added the effect of tax credits and benefits in lifting the incomes of low earners. There is thus a strong case for concluding that New Labour successfully followed employment and economic policies that have benefitted the workforce as a whole, as well as business interests. However, while the first two terms of office were relatively positive for New Labour, the third term saw a changing economic picture linked to recession on a global scale. Thus unemployment increased, as did the cost of living, and the Coalition Government inherited a different picture of employment rates and a less stable economy. Therefore while there have been some areas of continuation of policy, as this chapter has illustrated, there have also been reductions on spending that have affected welfare provision (see earlier chapters) and attempts to stimulate growth in order to increase employment opportunities.

The Coalition Government, when compared to New Labour, has also focused much more upon the needs of employers rather than employees. Under New Labour, employees gained a lot more than employers, and sometimes at employers' expense. However, recent Coalition Government policy to support business and to simplify the process by which individuals can have their employment terminated is arguably beginning to reverse this trend in some specific areas.

And despite the range of employment legislation enacted by New Labour – for instance, the Working Time Directive, the minimum wage, various kinds of tax credit, parental leave and holiday entitlement – the end result is still a relatively lightly regulated, flexible labour market. Countries such as France, Germany and Sweden have retained – despite some changes towards flexible employment policies – a more tightly regulated approach to labour relations. Comparisons between different countries' employment policies and their impact on employees' welfare can be misleading, however. While British workers' job security might not be protected by legislation as fully as workers in other European countries, we have seen in this chapter that job insecurity in the UK is not as widespread as is often believed.

On the other hand, if unemployment and job security are taken out of the picture, there is little doubt that some key aspects of workers' welfare are less well looked after in the UK than in other leading European countries. As mentioned earlier, British employees work longer hours, have fewer holiday entitlements, a lower minimum wage (compared to France), fewer training opportunities, less paid parental leave and poor childcare facilities for children of working parents, compared to the European norm. Lack of affordable childcare remains a particularly persistent problem. The Coalition Government has pledged to create more childcare places for 2-year-olds (Parkinson 2012), but this is a targeted approach for those on low incomes and does not remedy long-standing issues such as lack of flexibility for parents who work outside office hours or the lack of availability of specialist provision for disabled children.

The employment prospects and welfare of disabled people are particularly poorly protected in the UK. According to a report by Burchardt (2000), not only do disabled people in the UK find it more difficult to find employment in the first place – even when qualified for the job – but also they are much more likely than other workers to lose their jobs within a year of starting. Employed disabled people are likely to have significantly lower earnings than their non-disabled peers, even when comparisons take account of age, qualifications and occupation.

Burchardt (2000) suggests that, though disabled employees face particular problems of discrimination and poor protection of their interests at work, their problems are shared with other groups in society that face economic exclusion. The position of disabled workers is representative of wider problems of inequality and discrimination in the labour market.

In sum, therefore, the UK has not witnessed the kind of economic and employment policies under New Labour, or the Coalition Government, that would have led to significant change in the labour market. Most observers of recent employment policies would argue that they tilt more towards employers' interests than employees' and reflect both new Labour and Coalition Government overt aims to be pro-business governments. Where employers' and employees' interests in improving employment conditions seem to coincide, there have been small but significant steps towards improved welfare at work.

Summary of key points

- UK employment policy saw changes in approach under New Labour that have largely been kept, so far, by the Coalition Government.
- Employment policy is now increasingly focused on welfare to work; it aims to support people back into employment and encourage individuals to seek employment, using sanctions in some cases.
- Employment policy tends to favour employers' interests first and employees second, though there have been some significant gains for employees.

Key terms and concepts

active labour market policy
business cycle
casualization
deregulation
disposable income
dual labour market
economic activity and the economically active
full employment
Keynesian strategy/policy
recession
social exclusion

Suggestions for further reading

Parker, S. (2013) *The Squeezed Middle: The Pressure on Ordinary Workers in America and Britain.* Bristol: Policy Press.

This book examines changing pressures on the working population. While costs of living are rising, average wages are not. Policy-makers have assumed that as economies grow so then do wages. However, lessons from both America and the UK show that this is not the case. The book focuses upon analysing the impact of different policies on those on low to middle incomes, to draw lessons from America.

Rogowski, R., Salais, R. and Whiteside, N. (eds) (2013) *Transforming European Employment Policy: Labour Market Transitions and the Promotion of Capability.* Cheltenham: Edward Elgar.

Since the mid-1990s, there have been changes in the focus of European employment and social policy. This book gives an analysis of this, looking at employment policy as a form of governance, and the new forms of policy delivery and audit which accompany it. The book is useful for providing understanding of the European context in which UK trends around individual and collective capabilities are embedded.

Shildrick, T., MacDonald, R., Webster, C. and Garthwaite, K. (2012) *Poverty and Insecurity: Life in Low-Pay, No-Pay Britain.* Bristol: Policy Press.

This book explores the changes in employment trends in the UK in recent years in examining the relationship between social exclusion, poverty and the labour market. The book critically examines long-standing and dominant views about 'the workless' and 'the poor', by exploring close-up the lived realities of life in low-pay, no-pay Britain. The book analyses if work is really a route out of poverty as so many policy-makers suggest. It is based on qualitative, life-history research with a 'hard-to-reach group' and draws upon these experiences to illustrate the features of contemporary working life for many UK individuals.

Vickerstaff, S. (2012) 'Work and Welfare', in J. Baldock, N. Manning, S. Millar and S. Vickerstaff (eds), *Social Policy*. 4th edition. Oxford: Oxford University Press.

This chapter provides an overview of employment policy and welfare, reviewing recent UK policy changes in this area in a reader-friendly manner. Other chapters in this edited collection will also be of interest in relation to the broader scope of this book.

Vickerstaff, S., Phillipson, C. and Wilkie, R. (eds) (2011) *Work, Health and Wellbeing: The Challenges of Managing Health at Work*. Bristol: Policy Press.

This book explores the complex relationship between health and work in the context of demographic change. Given the aging population, policy-makers need to enable people with health issues to continue working. This book explores how work participation in middle and later life can be improved.

10 Are professionals good for you? The example of health policy and health professionals

With Lynsey Warwick-Giles

Key learning outcomes

By the end of this chapter you should:

- be able to understand the ways in which health policy and the roles of health professionals are inter-related
- be able to identify and outline the advantages and disadvantages of the NHS
- be able to discuss the recent policy changes being made by the Coalition Government in health policy

Overview of the chapter

This chapter will explore the relationship between health professionals, health policy and medicine. The chapter will once again focus upon power within the policy process, but will also examine the power that the professions wield in their work. Consider some personal situations in which you have been treated by a health professional such as a doctor, dentist, nurse or an expert with particular skills such as a physiotherapist. For example, think about reclining in a dentist's chair. The dentist is hovering above, ready to administer a local anaesthetic. Although anticipation of pain might be uppermost in your mind, there may be some other thoughts: how effective will this course of treatment be? How much will it cost, and who will be paying? If you have to bear most of the cost, is this fair and can you afford it?

Although you may be concentrating on how to get through the next 15 minutes, other thoughts may flit across your mind: what are your impressions of the equipment or 'technology' used by the dentist? Who paid for it? How considerate or friendly is the dentist, and how good are they at finding out what you need? When and where did the dentist receive training, and do you have confidence that they will not hit a sensitive nerve?

The more we reflect on personal experiences such as this, whether with a dentist, a nurse, a doctor or a therapist, the more we come to realize that what happens – the outcome of the course of treatment – is not simply the result of an individual professional treating an individual patient. Individual outcomes are also affected by broader factors, including policy. This chapter will explore a range of these factors, including:

- *government policy*: for instance, how much treatment and what kinds of treatment, if any, will be provided 'free' at the point of use for patients? How does this affect our willingness to use health services?
- *technology*: what have advances in the 'tools' available (medical equipment and techniques, drugs and other therapies) done to change our experience of medical treatment, of going into hospital or going to the dentist's?
- *the 'market' in health care*: is demand for health care and for particular treatments – whether through the NHS or on a private basis – high or low? Are doctors, nurses, radiographers or speech therapists in short supply? How difficult was it for you to obtain an appointment with the practitioner, and were you placed on a waiting list?
- *the professions*: are medical professionals and practitioners such as dentists able to dictate the level or quality of treatment given to patients? Are they able to insist on certain professional standards of treatment, or are they sometimes forced to provide cheaper, short-term remedies?

These are just four major types of background influences on the relationship between the medical professional and the user of health services. They show that professionals alone do not determine outcomes. Professionals themselves operate in a world of constraints, costs and opportunities. However, this chapter, in addressing the fundamental question 'Are professionals good for you?' will focus on the role of the professional as a key actor in social policy. The examples in this chapter are taken from the field of health, but some of the lessons about professional power and influence that we may learn from them can be applied to other parts of the welfare system. For instance, in the personal social services, probation, housing and planning, education and training, similar questions can be asked about how much trust should be placed in professionals and practitioners. How much freedom of action and responsibility should they be given to make policy, or to provide services as they see fit?

The chapter will also examine the NHS as a service, as well as looking at the ways in which recent changes are likely to impact upon both health care and health professionals.

Health, illness, modern medicine and health policy

The wider social and economic influences on what happens to us in the doctor's surgery or the hospital are reflected in government policy. What the government can afford by way of health services, the rising cost of drugs, what the public expects from health services, developments in medical technology and many other factors including ideology (see earlier chapters) all contribute to the shaping of health policy. This in turn will constrain what an individual doctor, dentist or nurse can offer.

However, health policy is not solely something to do with medical experts or health services. Of course, medical treatment may enhance health. Unless a decaying tooth is filled it may be lost, leading to other problems and poorer dental health. Sometimes, however, treatment may actually make no difference or, even worse, may adversely affect health. **Iatrogenic diseases** are those that result from medical intervention or from medical complications following treatment.

In general, health and illness are decided by many factors other than individual treatment. Dental health, for example, is much affected by diet and lifestyle (for example, how much sugary food we eat, and how often) and by **preventive health policies** such as fluoridization of water supplies, something which has had a very marked effect on reducing the incidence of tooth decay in children.

In sum, 'health policy' can be defined in two ways – either as:

- government efforts and policy to improve health through the health services and medical treatment; or as
- any government activity that affects health and illness, not just the activities of the Department of Health (DoH), the NHS, health professionals or other health services.

The second, broader definition of health policy shows that it is related to many other policies: for instance, taxation of sales of tobacco, or the effectiveness of regulations on air and water pollution, the safety of food and of the working environment.

Health, illness and poverty in developing countries clearly illustrate how health and illness are often more influenced by policies in other fields than health services. Agricultural and food policies, for instance, may have a much greater impact than health care on children's life expectancy if they succeed in stimulating the production and distribution of nutritious local foods. Similarly, economic or agricultural policies to increase the production of cash crops can have the effect of raising the cost of locally produced foods and thus threaten balanced diets and the health of children in the poorest families.

In Britain, another example is the introduction of the compulsory wearing of seat belts in motor vehicles. Although this is classed as transport policy, it has had clear health benefits by reducing the number of deaths and injuries in car accidents. Now complete Activity 10.1, which will help you to reflect upon the areas of policy that can influence health.

Activity 10.1 Policy sectors and health effects

1. Outline as many UK government departments as you can. If you are finding this difficult use the Internet to explore the range of departments that exist.
2. List the policy focus of these different departments, and some example policies. For example, think about transport, education and housing as starting points.
3. Think about how the policy sectors that you have identified and their associated policies may impact upon health. For example, think about anti-poverty policies such as the UK winter fuel payment to older members of society. How might this policy influence health?

Completing Activity 10.1 will have helped you to understand that health outcomes are related to more than just health policy. Another example of the connections between environment and health can be seen in research on inequalities in health. The publication of the Black Report (Townsend and Davidson 1982) detailed a social gradient in terms of health outcomes within the UK, showing that large differences exist between the social classes, genders and ethnic groups in terms of health outcomes (see Graham 2000). For example, those in the lowest social class are more likely to die in any age group, irrespective of gender or ethnicity. The risk of mortality increases progressively as we move down each rung of the social class ladder. Furthermore, the lower social classes are also more likely to experience higher levels of morbidity or ill-health. There is now a large body of evidence to demonstrate that similar health inequalities exist across the world, as shown by the World Health Organization (see the Commission on the Social Determinants of Health 2008). Higher rates of illness and death in some sections of the population are clearly linked to social and environmental factors and, faced with these problems, the impact of health services and modern medicine is limited. There is evidence that suggests that only 25 per cent of the health outcomes of a developed population is attributable to its healthcare system (Harrison and Macdonald 2008).

This is perhaps even more the case because concerns about health and the role of health services often neglect the less visible or glamorous preventive and environmental services. *Curative* services and the work of doctors, nurses and other specialists in front-line medicine succeed in gaining a lot more public attention than *preventive* services, as illustrated by strong interest in medical dramas such as the American series *House* or the BBC's *Casualty*. However, the chief role of curative health services is to deal with illness or injury that has already occurred. Curative services play an insignificant role in improving general health. Arguably the contribution of the less glamorous, behind-the-scenes preventive services can be much greater, though even here their contribution can be overestimated; social and environmental factors are the main determinants of health and illness.

Health promoters – that is, agencies that focus on social and environmental policies, such as the Framework Convention on Tobacco Control and the Kyoto Protocol on Greenhouse Gas Emissions (Labonte 2010) – therefore focus upon the importance of prevention. Recent UK healthy public policy included the 2008 smoking ban introduced by New Labour and the minimum pricing unit on alcohol by the Scottish Government in an attempt to tackle binge drinking and reduce alcohol-related illnesses and health problems (Higginson 2012).

To sum up, the assumption that health services and health professionals play a major part in making people healthy must be seriously questioned. There are many key challenges to health that policy-makers are faced with and many of these fall outside traditional health care. Many of these challenges are on a global scale (see Box 10.1).

Box 10.1 Challenges for global policy-makers that affect health

- economic instability
- social inequality
- population changes such as increased numbers and the movement of people
- demographic change, especially the ageing population
- environmental challenges such as climate change
- civil conflict, war and terrorism

The challenges highlighted in Box 10.1 all impact upon health, and are globally significant (see Chapter 4 for more discussion of the global policy environment). Nationally too, policy-makers need to tackle problems such as inequalities, and the broader determinants of health. This has been recognized within the policy-making arena recently albeit to a limited extent.

For example, in the *Healthy Lives, Healthy People* White Paper (2010), the Coalition Government focused upon public health and the need to create a 'wellness' service. The Coalition Government also discussed the need to encourage individual behaviour change for health benefits. There is now a Behaviour Change Unit located in the Cabinet Office, in which a behavioural insights team frequently offers advice and analysis in relation to a wide range of areas. The Coalition Government has also discussed the concept of 'nudging', as illustrated in Box 10.2.

Box 10.2 Nudge as a form of behaviour change

Nudge has emerged from America and is based upon the idea that positive reinforcement and/or *suggestion* can influence the motives and decision-making of groups and individuals alike, at least as – if not more efficiently than – direct instruction, legislation or enforcement (Thaler and Sunstein 2009).

The Coalition have debated the use of Nudge as a mechanism to improve health; we can be nudged into making healthier choices such as eating better, and exercising more without the need for the government to introduce new legislation or more heavy-handed approaches.

The idea of using Nudge led to much debate about its effectiveness. There is so far a lack of evidence and the concept has been criticized as being theoretically weak. However, it appeals to government because it is low in cost and is an example of the 'smaller state' approach (Brown 2012).

Despite the recent focus on public health, the work of health professionals remains important and can contribute to improving quality of life when people have fallen ill. In relation to more serious illnesses, there have been remarkable improvements in medical treatment. Advances in keyhole surgery and in anaesthesia, to give just two examples, have enabled operations to be performed on very old patients, for whom some treatments (under general anaesthetic) would formerly have been too risky.

Modern health services therefore face a set of priorities and needs which are entirely different from those of 100 or even 50 years ago. **Acute illnesses** or life-threatening (mainly infectious) diseases have been replaced by long-term or **chronic illnesses** or conditions as the more prevalent forms of illness: examples are rheumatoid arthritis, multiple sclerosis, diabetes, asthma and various forms of mental illness. Death is now often preceded by relatively long periods of disability. Medical services and treatments may assist with the control and management of symptoms, but they can rarely cure these diseases. Despite this, as Busfield (2010) points out, people still expect cures. Other sociologists have written about increasing **medicalization**; the process by which problems formerly not seen as medical come to be seen as illnesses in need of treatment by the medical profession.

The health professions: too much power?

A number of sociologists and other critics of the medical profession have put forward the idea that it does indeed have too much power over policy and patients. But to justify this argument, somewhat different explanations have been put forward (see Box 10.3).

Box 10.3 The power of medicine

- Feminists suggest that the rise of the medical profession has provided a vehicle for medically trained men to exercise power over women. For example, Donnison (1988) shows how professional men began to gain control of midwifery from the eighteenth century onwards.
- Illich (1990) argues that the medical profession has become an exploitative and disabling influence on society. It has sought to capitalize on patients' vulnerability by making them ever more dependent on medical solutions for their ills (in the form of drug-based treatments, surgery and hospitalization) when, according to Illich, the solutions lie more in a basic change to healthier ways of life and patterns of consumption.

However, we do not have to put all the blame on the shoulders of doctors to conclude that much of what doctors are expected to do is inappropriate to our needs. As Kennedy (1980: 641) put it, 'We have all been willing participants in the creation of a myth' of modern medicine, 'because it seems to serve our interests to believe that illness can be vanquished and death postponed until further notice'.

Thus the medicalization of social problems – the tendency to seek medical solutions to socially influenced ills such as depression or sadness, unemployment and redundancy, poverty and isolation – could be part of society's response to deeper or more fundamental changes.

De Swaan (1989) suggests that the medical profession does not so much set out to dominate society as fill a void by responding to a growing demand for the medicalization of people's problems. He gives other examples of the ways in which decisions and policies have become increasingly 'medical' in recent decades. For instance, medicalization can be observed in decisions about offenders and whether they should be 'treated' rather than punished or simply kept in prison. It can also be seen in the use of medical advice in assessing the income support needs of disabled people and in the increasing use of medical checks in employment, recruitment and the world of mortgage and life insurance (de Swaan 1989: 1167).

Another illustration of the medicalization of the social world is suicide and self-harm. Self-harm is committed by many thousands of people each year. It includes not only those who end their lives but also those who disable themselves, sometimes permanently, as a result of drug overdoses or other actions. However, some think that the government's confidence in the medical profession's ability to deal effectively with these problems is misplaced. As Taylor and Field (1997: 147–8) suggest, in the case of suicide and self-harm the influence of a medical approach to these problems may be more likely to make them worse than better.

These examples illustrate the limitations of modern medicine. However, a balanced view must recognize that the influential role of doctors is partly the product of social demands and pressures. These include consumer demand for medical solutions to personal and social problems, for new medical treatments and the development of medical technology. There are many examples of health consumerism within contemporary western society, including that of health tourism (Box 10.4).

Box 10.4 Health tourism

- Health tourists are consumers of healthcare services who search for treatment in countries in which they are not residents.
- People now engage in health tourism for various reasons: long waiting lists and high costs of elective treatments such as cosmetic surgery at home, and affordable long-distance travel.
- Arguably, health tourism only benefits a small number of people, draws resources away from public health care and distorts health services in the countries catering for tourists (Davies 2010).

Thus, changes in relation to expectations and medical consumption are responsible for the continued power and status of the medical profession. Yet if the medical profession were all-powerful, the status and role of doctors would be broadly similar in every society. However, as de Swaan (1989) suggests, the position of the medical profession varies considerably in relation to the health services of different countries, together with the amount of power or influence it has over health policy.

In fact, the status and power of the medical profession also varies over time. This can be demonstrated by the changing role of doctors in Britain's health service. In recent years there has been a lot of upheaval and reorganization in the NHS and this has significantly affected the status and role of doctors and how much control they have been able to exercise over health services. Recent policy changes by the Coalition Government also indicate changing power dynamics within medicine. The roles of the nursing profession and of other healthcare practitioners and professionals have also been much affected, not only in relation to their work with doctors but also in terms of their general position in the NHS and in the wider society.

In the remainder of this chapter, we shall look first at how and why a crisis in the role of the medical profession has developed in recent years, and how public confidence in the competence and ability of doctors to provide adequate standards of medical care has been badly dented. Second, we shall look at key aspects of current health policy and at recent health service reforms to examine how far they are likely to succeed in addressing the crisis in health care. Is current health policy likely to generate greater confidence in health services and health professionals?

A crisis of confidence in the medical profession

There are several important signs of a growing crisis of confidence in Britain's medical profession and in the ability of the NHS to provide effective healthcare treatment. One of these is a steep rise in the number of dissatisfied patients who claim to have been harmed by faulty medical practice and a corresponding rise in the cost of settling claims of medical negligence. A 2012 report by MPs showed that the NHS is facing a

£15.7 billion bill to settle a rising number of clinical negligence claims, and that the figure had increased by more than 10 per cent in a year (Wardrop 2012). However, recent Coalition Government changes may mean that claims decrease because, as part of broader spending cuts by 2015, legal aid will no longer be available for clinical negligence cases (with a few exceptions that come under human rights legislation) (Rix 2011).

However, not all the increase in willingness to take legal action against the medical profession is a result of an objective decline in professional standards. Perhaps just as many mistakes in medical practice were made in the past. In more recent times, several factors have lessened a traditional reluctance in Britain to challenge medical opinion and practice. These factors include the exploration of medical errors and dilemmas in 'popular television series [such as] *ER*, medical diagnoses on the internet and a climate where complaints against all public services are encouraged' (Sherman 2001: 4).

But it is important to stress that the current crisis of confidence in medical expertise has not been caused simply by the spread of increasingly well-informed and disillusioned public perceptions of doctors or greater willingness to challenge medical authority. It seems as though the traditions of secrecy and professional autonomy that used to hide the true scale of medical error are being removed (Boseley 2000a; Gibbs 2000). A more objective picture can now be seen – a picture that can be pieced together by various public inquiries and reports that have followed in the wake of tragic cases of professional incompetence and wrongdoing. The UK media also play a part in reporting these stories, and fanning public outrage. Table 10.1 offers numerous examples of recent medical error and malpractice.

As the examples in Table 10.1 show, trust in the medical profession to manage itself has been dealt a severe blow. There are other more recent high-profile cases that again are adding to this lack of trust. Complete Activity 10.2 to explore some more recent examples of malpractice.

Activity 10.2 Malpractice within the medical profession

1. Use the Internet to explore the following two examples of medical malpractice: Mid-Staffordshire Inquiry (Francis Report) and the case of Colin Norris.
2. What details did you read about these cases from your Internet search?

What do these cases tell us about the medical profession?

When considering the significance of these examples of medical error, malpractice and discrimination, it is important to remember that most medical treatments are carried out satisfactorily. More than this, many contrasting examples of medicine and nursing could be found to demonstrate high levels of care and professional commitment. For every rare case of a doctor or nurse who is allowed to continue killing or at least risking the lives of patients over a long period of time there are many more who are dedicated and professional – but who make an occasional mistake. One of the main problems of health policy has been to discover a way of safely monitoring the work of medical professionals without excessive central control and regulation, and without further undermining the professional credibility of medical staff.

Table 10.1 Examples of medical error and malpractice

Example	Detail
The Shipman case	Harold Shipman, a general practitioner (GP) in Manchester, was found guilty of murdering 15 of his women patients. He is suspected of killing many more – possibly as many as 250. This case showed that there was no central checking system or established procedure for analysing the unusual pattern of sudden deaths that took place for years in Shipman's practice.
The Elwood case	James Elwood was a consultant at the Swindon and Marlborough NHS Trust when, in 1999, staff at the hospital where he worked decided to review 400 of the cervical smear tests that he had analysed and taken treatment decisions about. This first check showed a serious mismatch between the test results and the problems being presented by patients at the outpatient gynaecology clinic. A wider check of his cases (Gibbs 2000) revealed misdiagnosis across Elwood's medical career. Some patients had received unnecessary treatment for cervical and other forms of cancer while others were shocked to discover that they still needed cancer checks – and in some cases urgent treatment. This case shows not just that one doctor's actions might have been harmful, but also that there had been a failure of the professional system to systematically check the work of individual practitioners.
Heart surgery at Bristol Royal Infirmary	There was an inquiry into the deaths of babies in Bristol Royal Infirmary between 1984 and 1995 following heart surgery. It was found that the two surgeons who carried out this work had continued even though they should have known that the survival rate of the babies they operated on was significantly worse than at other hospitals (Kennedy 2001).
Inadequate regulation of locum doctors	In 1998 Darren Denholm, a 10-year-old boy, died during what should have been a routine tooth extraction. Dr Evans-Appiah, a locum doctor who had trained overseas and was registered as a dental anaesthetist, administered a general anaesthetic but made serious mistakes in doing so – and as a result caused the death of the patient. He was found guilty of 17 charges of malpractice in October 2000 (Boseley 2000b). Incredibly, Dr Evans-Appiah was allowed to continue working after the death of Darren Denholm and made further mistakes. This example illustrates not just individual failure to meet professional standards but also a failure of the NHS to adequately regulate the work of a large number of locum doctors, upon whom the health service is heavily reliant in certain areas.
Ageism in medical practitioners' and nurses' attitudes to patients	This is a rather different point from those made above. However, it has also dented public confidence in doctors and other healthcare workers. Older people (aged over 65) make up over half of all hospital patients. Therefore the discovery of widespread ageism in the health service has extremely important implications for treatment and quality of care. A recent report by Robert Francis in response to an official inquiry in Mid-Staffordshire highlights the importance of quality of care, as discussed later in this chapter.

Flaws in service delivery

A key problem in this respect is deciding how far the professional doctor or nurse has been personally responsible for flaws in health care and how far problems have resulted from shortcomings in the health service.

For instance, healthcare trusts differ in their willingness to pay for expensive drugs and to provide them free to their patients. Campbell (2012a) demonstrates that 'seriously ill patients with life-threatening rare diseases are being denied vital drugs because of a postcode lottery across the NHS'. The media frequently report on the existence of 'postcode prescribing'. These issues are continuing to occur despite the setting-up of a national body, the National Institute for Health and Clinical Excellence (NICE), which is designed to regulate the treatments that are available free of charge under the NHS and to bring equality of treatment between different areas. Controversy has arisen in relation to many of NICE's decisions to restrict the use of such drugs for treating Alzheimer's to those with a moderate form of the condition (Jack and Timmins 2006). Another much-publicized case was that of Ann Marie Rogers, a sufferer from breast cancer, who failed initially, and then succeeded, in her attempt to use the courts to force her local primary care trust (PCT) to fund the prescription of the anti-cancer drug Herceptin (Tait 2006). The PCT's refusal to allow prescription of the drug was a clear case of 'postcode rationing' in that funding for the drug was available in more than a dozen other areas (Jack 2006; Tait 2006).

Problems arose because health authorities and trusts have differed from each other in their spending priorities. Therefore in the past a consultant might wish to prescribe a certain drug or treatment but knew that the health trust would not pay for it. Now, medical professionals might be involved in the decisions made at local level about which treatments should be provided to patients, but nevertheless might not have as free a hand to prescribe expensive or unusual treatments as many patients and members of the public assume they have. Consequently, some of the crises of confidence affecting healthcare professions originates not so much in the failings of the professions themselves as in local variations in the NHS system for deciding which treatments are to be 'free'. Also, there is a general pressure on the NHS to limit spending on expensive treatments. The way in which decisions are now made is in the process of going through change, with the establishment of Clinical Commissioning Groups in which GPs will be able to decide which services and treatments to commission. This means that doctors have more power than before, in some senses. However, this will not necessarily lead to a reduction in the existence of postcode prescribing or rationing.

A similar point can be made about public concern over waiting lists. Waiting times become a problem for doctors, nurses and other healthcare workers because they are the front-line staff who must explain to anxious or angry patients why delays in treatment are occurring. They also have to take hard decisions about which patients should have priority in the queue. As a result, the waiting list and waiting times have become another factor that can undermine the status and respect generally accorded to the medical and nursing professions. While many discontented patients might continue to respect hard-pressed medical staff and blame a faulty healthcare system for delays in treatment, some might not – the individual consultant or doctor will be blamed for the delay. For instance, this can occur because of delays some patients have experienced in obtaining a first appointment with a consultant (patients who have not been seen by a consultant are not officially on a waiting list). In 2004 the DoH established a new target for maximum hospital waiting times of 18 weeks, to be reached by 2008. The average wait should, however, be only 9 or 10 weeks. It was intended that the 'clock' for waiting times should start ticking from the date of a GP's referral of a patient to hospital, not when the hospital consultant put the patient on the list (Toynbee and Walker 2005: 12). However, recent reports have suggested that the number of NHS patients waiting longer than 18 weeks to be seen at hospital has increased for the first time in a year between 2011 and 2012 (Smith 2012).

In addition to dealing with disquiet or discontent about variations in treatments available and delays in obtaining treatment, medical professionals must also cope with other strains in the NHS. For instance, there have been mounting concerns about dirty hospitals; almost 43,000 patients in the past year caught a life-threatening superbug (strains of bacteria that have developed resistance to antibiotics) while in hospital (Gregory and Myall 2012). There has also been public concern about second-rate dental treatment for NHS patients and about breaches of confidentiality when medical records of patients have been released inadvertently by administrative or medical staff.

Thus there are many concerns about the quality of health services in the UK. As we have seen, some of these concerns are being expressed because of objectively poor standards of care – for instance, waiting times, discrimination against older patients, dirty hospitals. Rising concern can also be explained by subjective factors or changing public attitudes. There are rising public expectations of what the health service should be able to provide, and greater public awareness of what the latest medical treatments can achieve. Conversely, people are also increasingly aware of the limitations and flaws in modern medical practice. Either way, medical professionals are increasingly exposed to challenges to the traditional basis upon which their status and authority depended.

Medical and nursing professions in the development of the NHS

To understand professional power and its influence on health policy more fully, we need to consider how the health professions – and especially doctors – were incorporated into the NHS in the first place. Understanding the choices that were made in the 1940s about the kind of health service Britain was to have throws light on the choices and dilemmas facing us today about what kind of health service we want.

The introduction of the NHS after the Second World War represented one of the more radical and socialist policies in the Labour Government's welfare state programme. The NHS Bill put before Parliament in 1946 proposed sweeping changes, but it also entrenched medical professional power in various ways. With the NHS, Britain was given a health service in which the GP was to act as a gatekeeper to specialist care or hospital treatment. The patient firstly had to convince the GP that they were a 'suitable case' for further treatment before accessing other services.

Also, the NHS contract hammered out between the medical profession and the government in 1948, when the health service began to operate, was to make GPs *independent contractors* to the NHS, not *salaried employees* of the health service. This deal was struck mainly to protect the professional independence of family doctors. Therefore Britain developed a health service in which a key role – acting as gatekeeper to other services – was to be played by professionals who saw themselves as a somewhat independent and separate group. Britain did not develop an integrated service of salaried doctors in which GPs, specialist doctors, the hospitals and community or preventive health services worked closely together. Now complete Activity 10.3 to explore the history of the NHS in more detail.

Activity 10.3 The history of the NHS

1. Use the Internet to access the following website: http://news.bbc.co.uk/1/hi/health/7462013.stm.
2. Here you can read about the 60th anniversary of the NHS, as well as its beginnings. Scroll down the page, and go to the 'from the archive' section (on the right-hand side); click on the link and then you will have access to a range of footage about the beginnings of the NHS.
3. Select the historical clips that interest you most, but do watch 'Stuffing their mouths with gold', which details the resistance of doctors to the NHS at the outset.
4. What does the footage tell you about the power relationships between doctors and the NHS at the beginning? Do you think that this has now changed?

Despite the range of problems with the NHS and the frequently negative media stories that are featured in relation to the service, there are advantages to the provision. The next section discusses both the advantages and disadvantages of the NHS.

The advantages and limitations of the NHS

Despite the issues with the creation of the NHS it became a justifiably popular institution. The concept of free health care for everyone enshrined certain values of equality, fairness and compassion. Thus the NHS became a defining characteristic of the British way of life, much as the BBC and other national institutions did in postwar society. More than one commentator described the NHS as 'the sacred cow of British politics'. Others, such as the former Labour Secretary of State Barbara Castle, have described the NHS as a 'church'; the implication of this sort of label is that the system has value over and above the value of the medical care provided and the reductions in illness and disease that result. In the words of Rudolf Klein, 'the NHS was seen to have a moral, as well as a scientific, mission' (1993: 137).

Despite the positive aspects of the NHS, the British public has always had worries about its performance in relation to specific issues such as waiting lists. However, until recently public opinion in the UK has tended to endorse and approve the original design. Other countries' health services were usually compared unfavourably with Britain's NHS, especially on the point of the main virtue of the NHS – 'free' health care for everyone, whatever their status, provided according to need.

In the last few years, though, growing concern about the effectiveness and safety of treatment provided by consultants and medical professionals, as discussed earlier, has fed deeper unease about the drawbacks of having the kind of health service that Britain introduced in 1948. Both the advantages and limitations of the 'NHS design' for health services are summarized in Table 10.2.

Table 10.2 The advantages and disadvantages of the NHS

Advantages	Disadvantages
Easy access to services: it is straightforward to be able to access a GP if you are registered. Accident and emergency services are also accessible, as is basic treatment in walk-in centres.	Queuing for, and rationing of, medical services. Access to 'free' services might be a good thing but, unless medical facilities and staffing are increased to keep up with demand, it leads to the formation of long waiting lists or to lengthening waiting times for ambulances and emergency treatment. Medical professionals often have to take hard decisions about which patients are to be given priority, and are thus accused of 'rationing' medical services.
Universal coverage: everyone is able to gain access.	The universally available family doctor service can act more like a barrier slowing access to other services than as a link promptly facilitating access to specialist services.
Equality and economy: the service is equitable as all can access it, and as the GP is the most frequently used service, the service remains economical, as GPs serve as gatekeepers to the more expensive specialist services.	The quality and effectiveness of the NHS are patchy. Survival rates after treatment for cancer, for instance, vary widely from one district to another. In practice there is often a two-tier health service, with world-class treatments and highly effective specialists in some areas and second-rate treatment in others.
The NHS avoids the commercialization of health care: the use of NICE (discussed earlier) means that approval of new treatments and drugs is decided by a panel, who review evidence.	Until recently, the UK has managed to spend significantly less of its national income on health services than comparable countries have. As already mentioned, economy and cost containment are advantages of the NHS system. However, this is also a drawback. As discussed earlier in the chapter, the strains of running a health service with a minimum of resources are now glaringly obvious, especially as evidenced by delays in obtaining treatment, and poorer outcomes after treatment when compared with outcomes in other European countries (e.g. rates of death from cancer).
Professionalism: in 1948 the government gave the medical profession a very free hand and a lot of power to run the health service. In particular, consultants were given the largest say in deciding on how medical services should develop in the hospitals, and they took the key policy decisions about spending priorities. This brought some benefits to the NHS and encouraged the development of leading medical research in certain specialisms.	Professionalism: this has distorted the development of health services. Often, facilities were developed more in line with consultants' professional interests and the more glamorous, high-prestige areas of medicine (for example, heart surgery) than with healthcare needs in the surrounding community. Public health services and geriatric medicine, for instance, tend to be neglected. Also, giving the doctors a great deal of power and responsibility in running the health service added to the problem of lack of accountability in the NHS, and has fostered an atmosphere in which the medical profession can be seen as acting in a high-handed or arrogant way.

The health professions and health service reform

Concern about the limitations of the NHS is not new and in one way or another has been expressed ever since the NHS was brought into being (Klein 2006). Because both the medical profession and the NHS have traditionally enjoyed a lot of public respect, however, governments have been wary of introducing any fundamental changes.

Policies perceived as supportive of the NHS are often described as vote winners, such is the popularity of the service among the public. Even Mrs Thatcher's Conservative Government, inspired by the 'radical' ideas of the pro-market, anti-welfare-state right, did not dare to attempt a root and branch privatization of health services in Britain.

On the other hand, a succession of important reforms to the structure of the NHS have been introduced since 1974. While the history of the NHS is effectively the history of both development and change, since the 1980s the pace of change and reform has quickened, reflecting government concern about public dissatisfaction with the health service and questions about the effectiveness of the medical profession. Recent change in the health service prompts the question of whether the power of the health professions is as strong as it was.

For instance, a key reform was introduced at the end of Mrs Thatcher's period in office – the NHS and Community Care Act 1990. Well before this major change was introduced, policy thinking had been shaped by an influential report (DHSS 1983) on the need for management reform in the NHS. Sir Roy Griffiths – an independent adviser to the government and chief executive of Sainsbury's supermarkets – wrote this report (not to be confused with Griffiths's later report on community care – see Griffiths 1988).

Sir Roy's 1983 report paved the way for a great deal of internal change in the structure of the NHS during the 1980s. It introduced the concept of the *general manager* – a powerful role which Griffiths had envisaged as leading and controlling the competing interests of the various professional groups in the health service (doctors, nurses and the various therapeutic professions).

Doctors were to face further changes in the way in which hospitals and the health system as a whole were to be run. The most important change was the introduction of an internal market into the NHS – the main purpose of the NHS and Community Care Act 1990.

As a result of this legislation, the existing administrative structure of the NHS was broken up. Rather than the DoH funding each health authority according to a complicated formula based on health needs in the area and patients' use of services, a market system of funding meant that money was supposed to 'follow the patient'. Just as with other public services that were subjected to market reforms by the Thatcher and Major governments, the health service was divided into groups of 'purchasers' and 'providers' of health services. Health service providers (for instance, hospital trusts) were expected to compete to provide their services, with the aim of increasing efficiency and awareness of the costs and benefits of NHS services. While this may seem a long time ago, the legacy of these concerns about efficiency and effectiveness have remained at the forefront of NHS reform, and the NHS has continually been restructured since Thatcher. It was reconfigured under New Labour and is once again in the process of significant change following recent Coalition Government reforms.

While the internal market system introduced into the NHS in the 1990s by the Conservatives was formally scrapped as a result of Labour Government reforms after 1997, New Labour had subsequently shifted its position on the NHS, at least in England, if not in the rest of the UK, in ways which can be seen as a return to aspects of the regime established by the Conservatives after 1991. There may appear to be little point in examining the details of the Conservative reforms or the degree to which they actually succeeded in meeting their aims. The verdict of evaluative research is a mixed one (Le Grand et al. 1998; Ham 2004: 44–7). The Conservative reforms were inherently hard to evaluate for various reasons, not least because the plans were modified in the process of implementation and afterwards. Also, the effects of the reforms are hard to disentangle from the effects of other policy changes occurring at the same time. It is worth bearing in mind the view of observers like Rudolf Klein that, in relation to NHS reform, 'implementation is all' (Klein 1998: v).

In many respects the Conservative 'blueprint' was watered down. By 1996 and the last Conservative White Paper on the NHS, not much apparently remained of the original conception of a market-driven, competitive system in which the preferences of the healthcare consumer/patient shaped developments (DoH 1996; Ham 2004: 50–2). It has been argued that professional medical power was not seriously dented by the management and market reforms of the 1990s, even though doctors have had to cope with a great deal of change.

This is because, it has been suggested, some doctors came to have more, not less, power over their patients as a result of the internal market. There was, for example, the danger of 'cream-skimming' by some GPs – that is, deterring the more costly, chronically ill patients from registering with their practices and attracting the healthier, less costly ones (Robinson and Le Grand 1994), and although the internal market was meant to give consumer choice to the patient, in practice it was usually the GP or specialist doctor who chose which hospital or treatment the patient was to be referred to. Thus money tended to follow the choices made by doctors, on their patients' behalf, rather than following the patient as an independent consumer. Increasing numbers of doctors became experienced in the new style of management (Hunter 1992). Instead of being frozen out of vital decisions by non-medical managers, many began to adopt new strategies to protect their professional dominance.

The conclusion of one observer, reflecting other findings, is, however, that 'the change in behaviour and culture was nevertheless tangible . . . the separation of purchaser and provider responsibilities altered the organizational politics of the NHS leading to changes in the balance of power both within the medical profession and between doctors and managers' (Ham 2004: 46–7).

The NHS and the medical profession in a new era of uncertainty: the legacy of New Labour

One of New Labour's main objectives when elected in 1997 was to make significant improvements to British people's health. In line with this objective, the health services were to be rebuilt. The government put forward its plans in a White Paper, *The New NHS: Modern, Dependable* (DoH 1997). At the same time, though, the government was also determined to restrain public expenditure to the targets outlined by the previous Conservative administration. This meant, in effect, that – as with education policy – the government's health objectives in its first years in office were addressed without a significant injection of extra money.

The emphasis was on achieving change through yet further reorganization and redirection of resources within the NHS, rather than on improving the facilities, staffing and resources available to the health service that were inherited from the Conservatives. In fact, however, the NHS (like education) was relatively generously treated during the first term of the Blair government in comparison with the rest of the public sector (Ham 2004: 61–2; Glennerster 2005: 286).

New Labour increased NHS funding while in office, having been stung by comparisons on health spending between the UK and other western European countries, which in the majority of cases show that Britain had been spending significantly less per head on health services. Having made strong public commitments to improving health services, the government felt it had to meet its promises or suffer increasingly damaging electoral consequences. Also, there is a genuine impulse in government circles to change the priorities of health policy by, for instance, bringing greater attention to connections between the environment and health, and reducing some of the stark inequality in disease between poorer and better-off groups in society.

During Labour's 10 years in power the emphasis on quality and performance continued. While it was true that significantly more money was channelled into the NHS, the government tried to follow a policy of releasing extra money only if certain conditions were met, and improvements in performance achieved. There were aims to develop a more 'patient-centred' NHS as well as the strengthening of procedures to make doctors, nurses and other health service groups more accountable to bodies that supervise and stand outside the NHS. This had important implications for the issues of professional power, competence and freedom to run health services, as discussed earlier.

Following the publication of a White Paper on *The New NHS* in 1997, and various other consultation documents, wide-ranging health reforms were discussed in parliament, leading to the passing of a Health Act in 1999. This Act, together with other legislation, brought about certain key changes in the NHS and its relationship with professional groups, which are summarized in Table 10.3.

Table 10.3 Health policy under New Labour: the impact on health professions

Area of change	Impact upon professional role
The internal market in the NHS was replaced by a policy of encouraging co-operation and partnership between all care providers.	Different professional role – partnership working needed.
Labour built on and expanded some Conservative changes by making all GPs 'fundholders'.	GPs have more financial power and responsibility.
New Labour committed themselves to the idea of a 'patient-led' NHS, to the expansion of patient choice and, in principle, to a greater devolution of decision-making responsibility to lower levels in the system.	Patients are officially seen as important and having rights; in many senses this challenges traditional medical authority.
New Labour policies began to change doctors' contracts with the NHS with the introduction of 'modern' contracts for GPs and hospital doctors linked to improvements in care.	Performance monitoring of professionals: less independence and more governance for GPs and hospital doctors.
Restructuring resulted in other changes in budgetary control with newly created Primary Care Trusts (PCTs) becoming budget holders.	More devolved and localized financial power but this was not in the hands of GPs – it was managed by PCTs.
There was more central regulation and inspection of the health service with standards monitored by NICE, and the Commission for Health Improvement (CHI).	More monitoring, and therefore less independence and further governance.

Table 10.3 shows the impact of New Labour's health reforms. The Coalition Government also brought about a radical restructuring of the NHS, which in turn has had a profound effect upon the role of the medical profession and other health practitioners.

The Coalition Government's approach to the NHS

In response to the social and demographic factors identified earlier, such as higher expectations of the health service, an ageing population and the changing nature of disease, the Coalition Government has begun large-scale reform of the NHS. The need to reduce costs underpins much of the Coalition Government's drive to reform the service. It is also based on the Conservative ideology that focuses upon the importance of markets, choice and competition, as well as the Liberal standpoint that democracy needs to be devolved to a more local level. The government's approach aims to 'free NHS staff from political micromanagement . . . drive up standards, support professional responsibility, deliver better value for money and create a health nation' (Coalition Government 2010). Across the world, governments attempt to provide health care in a context in which they have to balance the goals of such provision while containing spending (Beland and Wadden 2012). Rationing of services remains an important component of contemporary policy-making, despite it being a very difficult task. Complete Activity 10.4 to explore rationing in more depth.

Activity 10.4 The difficulties of rationing

1. Use the Internet to listen to the following Moral Maze debate 'Rationing the NHS'– available at www.bbc.co.uk/programmes/b01p0s0v. Given that spending in the NHS is increasing year on year and that budget cuts are occurring in all other public services, this programme debates how much longer we can afford the principle that treatment should be based on need and be free at the point of delivery.
2. What is your viewpoint about this? Do you agree that care should be rationed for those with life-style diseases? What might be the problems of implementing this in practice?

The White Paper *Equity and Excellence: Liberating the NHS* (DoH 2010a) outlined the new structure of the NHS in England, including the abolition of Primary Care Trusts and the introduction of GP Clinical Commissioning Consortia (GPCC). GPCCs will consist of a number of grouped GP practices working together to commission the majority of healthcare services (excluding primary care) for their local population. GPCCs will be provided with a budget for secondary care services, and be expected to work alongside local authorities to ensure that their communities' needs are being met. Each area will have a newly established Health and Wellbeing Board (HWB), which will be local authority led, charged with setting the overall strategic direction for health and social care. Another body was also introduced: the NHS Commissioning Board (NHSCB). The purpose of the board is to ensure that GPCCs are meeting their communities' needs as well as staying out of financial risk. In addition, the NHSCB will be responsible for commissioning primary care services and some specialized services. Alongside these changes, local public health services are being transferred to the local authorities to be supervised by a new national-level co-ordinating body called 'Public Health England' (PHE). Furthermore, all NHS trusts now have to become foundation trusts (which have more independence in financial and managerial terms) by 2013, and will be financially regulated.

Given the extent of these changes, there was understandably public outcry and considerable opposition from the health profession. It was because of this outcry that an official 'pause' in the legislative process was called by David Cameron and Andrew Lansley (the Secretary of State for Health at the time) (DoH 2011a). The 'pause' was referred to as a time of 'listening', where people could raise their concerns about the proposals and current policy changes. After the 'pause' a number of amendments were made to the initial proposals (DoH 2011b). GPCCs were to now be referred to as Clinical Commissioning Groups (CCGs) with wider memberships including a nurse representative, a secondary care doctor and two lay members. The reason for the amendments was to ensure that there were other medical groups being represented within CCGs and to answer charges that they would be too GP-dominated.

It is unclear at the time of writing how these reforms will work in practice, as GP commissioning has not been done on this scale previously. There have been smaller examples of these kinds of changes in the past with GP Fundholding (1991), Total Purchasing Pilots (1995) and Practice Based Commissioning (2004). The difference with all these schemes is that they were voluntary, so it was up to GPs whether they wanted to take on the commissioning role rather than it being imposed. All of these schemes identified some areas in which GP commissioners were able to bring about improvements in services. However, there were also some drawbacks, such as increased managerial costs, local diversity (Klein 2010) and a tendency to focus upon the needs of practice populations rather than the needs of the population more widely (Mays et al. 1998). Thus how these latest organizational upheavals in the NHS will affect the delivery of services and patients' health in the longer term is uncertain. One thing is clear, however: from 2013, doctors in England faced one of the most fundamental reforms to their role in the NHS since 1948.

The impacts of this significant policy change have yet to be felt but it is clear that once again health professionals will face changes to their role in many ways; time will tell.

Conclusions

As mentioned at the start of this chapter, professionals – though given enormous responsibility in many situations – themselves operate in a world of constraints and uncertainties. In addition to the ethical and moral choices professionals are called on to make, there are the constraints of government health policy, the cost and feasibility of providing services, and so on.

Therefore, while health professionals can easily become too dominant or may be expected to have the final say in resolving a dilemma, it would be wrong to portray the medical profession as an all-powerful group which always acts in a single-minded, unified and self-interested way. The medical profession is not a homogeneous group. Also, the other health professions (for example, nursing and the various therapies, such as physiotherapy) have always been divided in their attitudes towards health policy, as shown by the history of the NHS and in arguments between them and doctors about recent health reforms.

Another point to be underlined is that, despite the attention drawn to the shortcomings and flaws of health professionals in this chapter, there are many altruistic, caring and public-spirited professionals. Nor is it true to say that professional interests are always narrow, or self-seeking, or against the public interest. Often, the professional approach benefits the patient, and the interests of the professional and the patient coincide (for instance, in raising standards of post-operative care, or investment in medical research that leads to treatment breakthroughs).

However, in promoting a curative approach to medicine which downplays the economic, social and environmental causes of disease, the professional tradition in medicine inevitably draws doctors and other health professionals into supporting a health system that does relatively little to improve health. If all health practitioners were suddenly removed from society, and if every hospital and doctor's surgery were to be closed, their absence would hardly be noticed in terms of the amount of illness or the death rate. What *would* be noticed, of course, is a great deal more pain, discomfort and uncertainty. The health professions and health services play a very important role in managing illness, but a much less effective role in creating or maintaining health.

Despite the limitations of modern medicine, government policies to improve health still place a lot of emphasis on the role of the medical and nursing professions, and much of the debate about health policy focuses on the health of the NHS rather than upon health itself, despite the Coalition Government policy recently putting more emphasis on public health and innovations such as 'nudge' to bring about behaviour change.

Nevertheless, it is still true to say that the bulk of investment in 'health' is in mopping up illness, and in trying to improve the performance of the NHS in this respect. This is particularly the case in health because of the size and dominance of the NHS. Changing the direction of the NHS, and of health policy in general, has sometimes been compared to steering a 'super-tanker' – drastic actions might be taken on the bridge and in the engine room, but with apparently little effect until some time later.

Thus it is never easy to reach firm conclusions about either the future of the NHS or the long-term effects of changing government policy on the role of the health professions. What signs are there, if any, that the Coalition Government's agenda of reforming the health service has eroded the traditional power and status of professional groups? Arguably, current reforms are not reducing professional control over health services, but rather are increasing it, with the extension of budget holding and the power to make decisions about care needed within an area. Set against this is the loss of professional freedom and ability to look after patients that GPs will experience when they become more involved in health service management. Those who do not become so involved are likely to have to cede some power and influence to non-medical managers of commissioning groups. In addition, some control of the NHS from the centre (the Department of Health) will continue, and doctors will therefore have to satisfy new regulations and inspection of their work by national monitoring bodies. On the other hand, there are severe limits on the reforms that can be implemented without doctors' co-operation and, just as the government's plans to introduce the NHS in 1948 depended on winning over the doctors, so do the Coalition Government's plans for health service reform and improvements in health services.

As pointed out at the beginning of this chapter, professional power and status depend to some extent on the 'scarcity value' of an occupational group. By and large, doctors have retained their monopoly and control over health services, despite the encroachment of new procedures to assess and monitor their work. The government cannot afford to alienate the doctors too much, and it is desperately trying to boost the numbers of medical students and reduce the number of working doctors who leave the profession every year. A growing number of GPs, especially women in their late twenties and thirties, now want to reduce their working week to part-time hours to meet child-rearing or family responsibilities. Specialists and consultants are also in short supply.

Thus, for this and the other reasons mentioned above, the medical profession is likely to retain much of its power over health services and health policy. There is little evidence in today's NHS of a fundamental shift in the balance of power towards the patient. There are signs that patients are becoming more questioning and are prepared to be more critical of doctors than they used to be. But despite such apparent readiness to challenge traditional professional attitudes, the policy-making and administrative machinery is simply not in place to give patients an effective voice at the *policy level* of the NHS.

Whether professionals are good for us – the initial question – is therefore decided upon mainly by the non-elected organizations that scrutinize the quality of health services and by the medical profession itself, rather than by the people who use health services or their representatives.

Summary of key points

- While health is determined by many broad factors, much health policy tends to focus upon illness services such as the provision of health care. This is despite evidence that health services as treatment focused simply do not address the many causes of ill-health.
- Social change has brought a wider range of influences on health policy. Changing public expectations and media reporting have highlighted the flaws in service provision, but despite this there has not been a fundamental shift in public support for the NHS or the power and status of the medical profession.
- The history of the NHS is a history of constant reform. These reforms have received opposition from the medical profession, yet throughout these changes the medical profession has retained much of its power and influence over the running of health services if not the overall design of the NHS.

Key terms and concepts

acute illnesses
chronic illnesses
curative medicine
hypothecated taxation
iatrogenic disease
internal market
medicalization
outcome
preventive health policies/services

Suggestions for further reading

Buse, K., Mays, N. and Walt, G. (2012) *Making Health Policy*. 2nd edition. London: Open University Press.

This is a comprehensive and practical text which provides a clear introduction to health policy analysis. The book provides an overview of the theoretical base of the field with a range of real-world examples drawn from different settings. The book is an excellent introduction but one that also addresses complexity within the field.

Kennedy, I. (1981) *The Unmasking of Medicine*. London: George Allen & Unwin.

This is a classic historical study of the changing nature of disease and the limited role of medicine. Despite its age the book is an excellent critical analysis of medicine and the medical profession. The book examines power, professionalism and ethics within the medical profession and while many changes have taken place since its publication such as increased patient involvement, it still remains an excellent read.

Klein, R. (2010) *The New Politics of the NHS: From Creation to Reinvention*. 6th edition. Abingdon: Radcliffe Publishing.

This book is an excellent introduction to the NHS, assuming no prior knowledge, and detailing the political history of the NHS from 1948 to the present day. It examines the way in which successive governments have tried to deal with the problems associated with a centralized healthcare system, specifically the tensions between central control and local responsiveness, and between managerial influence and medical autonomy. In doing so it also examines the role of different actors in the healthcare policy arena: political parties, professions, consumers and interest groups. Indispensable.

McKeown, Y. (1979) *The Role of Medicine: Dream, Mirage or Nemesis?* Oxford: Basil Blackwell.

Another historical critique of medicine. This book demonstrates the author's fundamental belief that medicine is ineffective. Although not the first to argue this scenario, the author discounts most human agency in the modern decline in mortality.

Walmsley, J., Davies, C., Hales, M. and Flux, R. (eds) (2012) *Better Health in Harder Times: Active Citizens and Innovation on the Frontline*. Bristol: Policy Press.

This book examines changes in the way in which patients engage with health care in the context of shortcomings in clinical care and patient experience, funding cuts, and concerns about service levels and standards. This book explores new ways of living and working with long-term conditions, new approaches to service redesign, use of information technology, leadership, co-production and creating and accounting for quality.

White, K. (2009) *An Introduction to The Sociology of Health and Illness*. 2nd edition. London and New York: Sage.

This is a clear accessible and comprehensive introduction to the sociology of health and illness. The book highlights how becoming sick and unhealthy is a consequence of the social, political and economic organization of society. It outlines the role and functions of medical explanations of disease, showing how an appreciation of the dynamics of class, gender, ethnicity and the sociology of knowledge challenges medical power.

Utopias and ideals: housing policy and the environment

Key learning outcomes

By the end of this chapter you should:

- be able to understand the way in which housing policy has developed historically
- be able to identify and outline the advantages and disadvantages of housing policy
- be able to discuss the recent policy changes being made by the UK Coalition Government in relation to housing policy

Overview of the chapter

This chapter will explore the history of housing policy to provide you with an overview of developments in this area, and then it will illustrate more recent changes being made under the UK Coalition Government. Of all human needs, shelter is one of the most fundamental. But housing is also important because it can give the sense of security that stems from bonding with 'home'. Satisfactory homes help personal development and also help people to develop roots: a fusion of personal identity with place, neighbourhood and family. Establishing a home of one's own can also give a sense of responsibility and achievement. Not least, the economic investments that people make in their homes represent important goals of status and success. But these are not necessarily selfish: many people are motivated to own and improve their properties in order to pass them on to their descendants.

Given the deep significance of the home in the human psyche it is not surprising that government policies on housing are subject to a lot of commentary and criticism. The same can be said of any policies that affect people's ability to purchase a home. Indirectly, there are important housing implications, for instance, in the government's ability to manage the economy. This will affect economic growth and employment prospects in particular regions, which in turn might affect the chances of young people being able to find well-paid jobs and to purchase homes of their own. Similarly, economic policies have effects on interest rates (which are set by the Bank of England, independently of government), which in turn determine the cost of borrowing and therefore of mortgages to purchase houses. Another example of 'non-housing' policies which nevertheless affect housing are those on the 'green belt' around urban areas, and whether house building should be allowed in environmentally protected or 'green' areas.

Yet despite the strong importance attached to housing, it is also an example of welfare and human needs that for decades government has been tiptoeing away from. As will be explained in this chapter, the notion that government should be directly involved in building housing on a large scale, renting it out and controlling the housing market in various ways was once widely taken for granted. The 'welfare settlement' established at that time included an assumption that the state would play a growing part in providing and managing housing, and the welfare state promised a society in which everyone had a right to good-quality homes whether or not they wanted to purchase them. In the general elections of the 1950s and 1960s, the Conservative Party was as anxious to boast about its record in building record numbers of council houses, when in government, as Labour was.

However, housing is now – and always has been to a considerable degree – an area of welfare in which the *market* is far and away the most important means of settling who gets what, or how needs are to be met. The other four of the five great social services (health, social security, education and personal social services) are increasingly being run on market lines. However, they are still basically public services and most people's needs for education, health care, social security and so on are still being met from public funds and not solely according to what they can personally afford, as is mostly the case with housing. Therefore, a focus on housing provides an important test of how well or badly the market serves people's needs. It is also an example of welfare in which, if anything goes wrong, government is being held less and less accountable as time passes. The dominance of the market in housing suggests that there is little scope in this area of welfare for dreams and ideals – surely, if the market decides almost everything, money considerations override all others? As will be discussed in this chapter, the history of housing in Britain suggests that this point is only partly true. In the past many idealistic plans of housing philanthropists or state planners to provide better housing for ordinary people were 'anti-market' attempts to break the chains of market forces, and to make 'ideal homes' affordable. However, pro-market housing policy can also be inspired by dreams and ideals. For instance, Mrs Thatcher's housing policies in the 1980s were strongly affected by the aspiration of home ownership for virtually everyone, and the dream – shattered by the property crash of the early 1990s – of a housing market in which everyone would gain and no one would lose. The more recent economic crisis that started in 2008 has also impacted negatively upon home owners, with some in negative equity, increased repossessions, stagnating prices and a static market in which buying and selling is more difficult for many. This is without mentioning the issues associated with purchasing homes and the unaffordability of home ownership for many young people.

In this chapter we shall examine these and other kinds of housing utopias and ideals, together with the inevitable disillusion and reassessment that follows them. In some cases, housing ideals are connected to wider visions, involving dreams of ideal communities and environments. Although space will not permit detailed examinations of these broader ideas, it is important to see housing in its context. Social planners in the past, and those who want to develop new kinds of housing today, link policies for better housing with policies for better (for example, 'greener' or more sustainable) environments and communities. This focus upon sustainability is continued today in the work of many planners.

Before returning to these broader questions near the end of the chapter, however, we need to examine definitions of housing policy in more detail.

Housing policy: definitions and significance

'Housing policy' refers to a wide range of government action. It covers any government actions, legislation or economic policies that have a direct or indirect effect on housing. These might include policies affecting supply of housing, house prices, tax policies affecting house purchase, housing standards and patterns of **tenure**. Housing is of special significance to the study of social policy for a variety of reasons, as illustrated in Box 11.1.

Box 11.1 Why housing is of special significance in the study of social policy

1. Housing illustrates an area of welfare in which the market is more or less supreme. Studying housing therefore allows us to see what the strengths and weaknesses of the market are, in terms of meeting people's needs.
2. Housing is an area of special interest because it highlights the complex nature of needs and how need could be defined. 'Having a roof over your head' is an attractively simple but insufficient definition of housing needs. To define either housing or being homeless properly, we have to use concepts of quality and autonomy
3. Housing is intimately connected with a wide range of other welfare issues such as health. According to historians of public health (see, for instance, McKeown 1979), housing policy, along with other environmental improvements such as the introduction of effective sanitation, did more to improve health and life expectancy in the nineteenth and early twentieth centuries than anything achieved in medicine or health services. Poor housing conditions are still with us, however, and the effects of damp, poorly heated homes on health can still be observed.

Housing is important to the study of social policy for the reasons illustrated in Box 11.1. To take the issue of housing need, for instance, study of this area throws light on the problem of **homelessness**. If someone has a roof over their head but lives in a severely overcrowded dwelling which is hazardous to health, arguably they are not adequately housed and are therefore homeless. Similarly, there is an argument that adults who have virtually no independence or autonomy in their dwelling are homeless: for instance, if such a person does not have any say in when they can use the space or rooms in the dwelling. People living in hostels, residential institutions or 'bed and breakfast' accommodation might fit into this category, and could therefore be regarded as homeless. Consequently, official statistics on homelessness should be treated with caution, because it is in any government's interests to use narrow definitions of homelessness and to present it as a manageable problem that they are dealing with effectively. Official definitions of homelessness are likely to concentrate on categories of people who live on the streets or sleep rough more than upon the larger group without adequate homes.

Housing policy is also related to inequalities and social divisions; local housing policies might either be able to prevent the development of 'sink' housing estates, where people on low incomes and experiencing high rates of joblessness are concentrated, or they might have few resources to be able to prevent them developing. For similar reasons, local housing policies might contribute to either a heightening or a lessening of racial tensions. In 2001, for instance, there were serious outbreaks of violence and property damage in northern English towns such as Oldham and Burnley. Tensions between the local white and Asian communities were exacerbated by their effective segregation into different territories and areas of housing; conflict and street fighting erupted when each side thought that the other was invading 'their' territory. The UK media often highlight stark contrasts in types of housing conditions, with the existence of contemporary gated communities serving to segregate those who are more advantaged. This has been a longstanding problem in many countries including the UK. Complete Activity 11.1 to explore this in more depth.

Activity 11.1 A brief history of UK housing policy

Use the Internet to watch the following very short clips about housing policy available at the BBC Learning Zone website.

1. Access www.bbc.co.uk/learningzone/clips. Use the search box to find and watch the following clips:
   - Clip 5270: 'Housing from 1930s to the Present Day'
   - Clip 7024: 'How was the lack of housing and poor slum conditions solved after World War 2?'
   - Clip 3845: 'Housing - Right to Buy scheme'

   You can also enter 'housing' into the search box to give you wider results.
2. Compare the state approach to housing policy historically to the current approach, in which there is less state involvement. What does this tell you about the changing direction of housing policy?
3. What are the implications of these changes in housing policy in relation to inequalities in access to adequate housing?

Completing Activity 11.1 will have helped you to understand that there are many social divisions related to housing. For example, they are evident between home owners and those who occupy **social housing**. One study in Bradford found that 'the Pakistani and Bangladeshi communities, although forming close on one-fifth of the city's population, occupy only 2.24 per cent of council housing and 8.4 per cent of other housing lets' (Wainwright 2001: 6). The high rate of owner-occupation among the Asian communities is partly an expression of preference – there is a history of many in the Pakistani community, for instance, preferring to buy houses rather than rent. However, there is also a fear factor – few families in the minority communities wish to move into the predominantly white **council housing** estates in Bradford. Local housing policies have not succeeded in combating racism in council housing allocation, nor have local authorities been able to reduce the minority communities' fears of racial abuse, vandalism and crime – the reason 'repeatedly given for Asian families turning down offers of empty houses on "bad reputation" estates' (Wainwright 2001: 6).

This is not to say that housing policy alone could solve every problem of poor health, racial conflict or social deprivation, but it is true that, more than in any other area of social policy, decisions made in housing policy have a directly territorial impact. Visible, spatial inequalities can be either lessened or accentuated, as illustrated by the gulf between run-down council estates and spruce, security-conscious housing developments for the affluent. Recent analysis demonstrates the continuation of British spatial inequalities, which include housing. Dorling and Thomas (2011) provide a geographical analysis of spatial inequalities that permeate Britain today, showing areas that have the highest rates of unemployment, areas experiencing high residential repossessions, differential crime rates across areas as well as comparisons in well-being and environmental differences. There is also a geographically broader evidence base that highlights area effects in relation to global inequalities, and these broad divisions affect housing opportunities. Marcuse (1993) argues that cities have been divided since the industrial revolution. He outlines differential types of housing evident in contemporary western societies (see Table 11.1).

Table 11.1 Divided cities with differential housing

Type of division	**Description of the division**
Luxury housing	• Often not really part of the city. • Those at the top of the social, political and economic scale live in these places. • Includes gated communities, which exclude those seen as less socially desirable.
The gentrified city	• Sections of the city occupied by professional/managerial groups.
The suburban city	• Housing occupied by skilled workers and mid-range professionals. For example, places in the outer city or apartments near the centre.
The tenement city	• Housing occupied by lower-paid workers, which often includes rental properties and social housing.
The abandoned city	• This is housing left over for the poorest sections of society such as the unemployed, excluded and homeless.

Adapted from Marcuse (1993)

Given the segregation that exists, the social divisions associated with housing and the frequently cited issues of lack of affordable and adequate housing for many, social policy within this area remains a significant challenge.

Housing utopias and ideals

First, to put recent changes in perspective, it helps to look at how housing has been the subject of utopian plans and ideals for a long time. Therefore, in this section we consider the main landmarks in the development of housing policy. Three broad phases of 'housing dreams' and ideals can be discerned in recent British history. Table 11.2 illustrates these developments.

Table 11.2 Historical phases in housing policy

Time period	Historical phase of policy
Nineteenth century and early twentieth century	• 'Model housing' schemes such as the Bournville estate built by Cadbury in Birmingham were like beacons in a sea of squalid, overcrowded accommodation for the masses. • Most of these schemes were the result of **industrial paternalism** – enlightened employers building good-quality housing for their workers – but some were associated with charity and with efforts to provide 'decent' accommodation for people in poverty.
1918–1960s	• Housing ideals were much affected by concepts of **social engineering**. The idea of planned new towns and 'garden cities', for instance, pre-dates the First World War, but became influential in housing policy and the design of suburban housing in the 1920s and 1930s. • This phase of idealism encouraged socialistic ideas about housing, including the ideal of mixing together people of different social classes. In practice, examples of such social engineering were few and far between. • This period in housing policy was one in which the idea of local councils as providers of housing (through rented council housing) was strongly endorsed by Conservative as well as Labour governments.
The period after 1970	• The market and home ownership became more central to housing policy than before. • Mrs Thatcher's governments of the 1980s were chiefly responsible for widening the base of home ownership in Britain, but the percentage of people in council housing had already reached a plateau before 1979 (see Figure 11.1). • The policy of selling council houses to tenants had existed before Mrs Thatcher came to office. However, sales were small until 1982 when the policy gained momentum (Forrest and Murie 1988: 110).

Figure 11.1 shows how the base of home ownership was increased following Thatcher's Right to Buy Scheme.

From philanthropy and self-help to social engineering

Although housing standards were generally very poor in the Victorian period, housing did gradually improve as the nineteenth century progressed and as large numbers of working people became better off than before. Further, although much housing was squalid, conditions and types of housing varied.

In both rural and urban areas, there were isolated but significant attempts by employers, philanthropic organizations and the growing number of 'respectable' working-class families to improve housing. Each of these groups had somewhat different housing ideals and aims (see Box 11.2), though they shared a common determination to bring about greater security of tenure and a healthier environment with better sanitation.

Victorian **philanthropy**, industrial paternalism and workers' self-help failed to provide enough low-cost homes for the mass of working people by the time the First World War broke out in 1914. Also, only a small number of council houses were built before

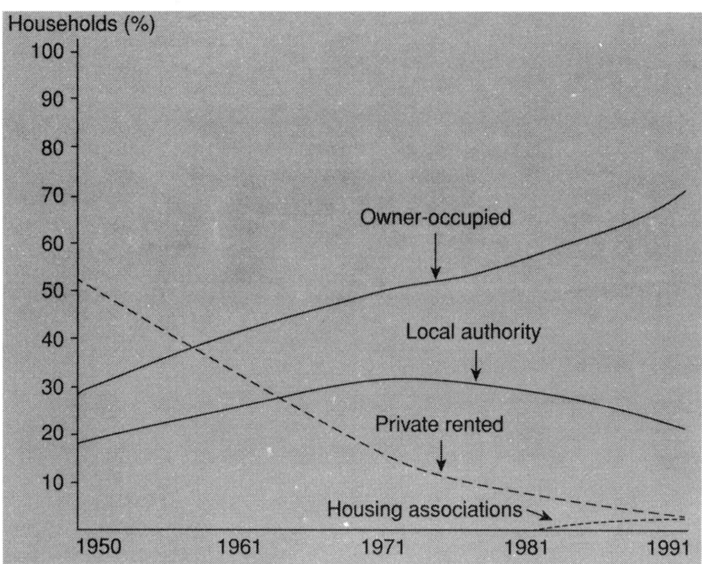

Figure 11.1 Housing tenure in Great Britain, 1950–91 (adapted from Balchin 1995: 6)

1914. However, local authority housing was to become the main solution for trying to reduce the housing shortage between the wars, when 900,000 council homes were built.

The period from the end of the First World War in 1918 to the 1970s can be regarded as the heyday of state intervention in housing. Even though market forces continued to dominate the housing sector, and home ownership increased dramatically during this period, there was widespread agreement that the market alone could not satisfactorily provide enough housing of acceptable quality.

More than this, there was a revolution in ideas about housing and the environment. Individualistic British notions of laissez-faire and letting people find their own housing solutions remained strong, but they were challenged by new ideas about architecture and planning. These ideas suggested that, in an ideal world, the state could plan everyone's housing needs and design an environment in which social divisions could be minimized.

Such ideas came from a variety of sources. Before the First World War, Ebenezer Howard – a radical liberal thinker who advocated a new kind of urban living – developed the concept of the garden city. He had worked in Chicago in its pre-skyscraper days and had been impressed by the idea of a decentralized city in a spacious landscape. Howard believed that new towns could be built in the countryside of Britain; people could collectively own common facilities such as schools and workshops, for which they would pay a common rent, and they would be free to build their own houses in planned green spaces.

Similarly, after the Second World War, the idea of building new towns and outer suburbs in green open spaces continued to have a strong effect on British planning and housing policy. In the 1950s and 1960s, a succession of new towns appeared in England and Scotland. These, along with 'outer ring' housing estates, were usually part of a policy of clearing away inner-city substandard housing and 'decanting' people to environments which were seen by planners as infinitely better than those they were uprooted from. Notions about ideal housing have changed over time, as Activity 11.2 illustrates.

Activity 11.2 Ideal housing environments

Use the Internet to watch the following very short clips about housing policy available at the BBC Learning Zone website.

1. Access www.bbc.co.uk/learningzone/clips. Use the search box to find and watch the following clips:
   - Clip 7440: 'The Ideal Housing Estate?'
   - Clip 6267: 'The city of tomorrow: sustainable housing in Sweden'
2. What do you think is the ideal housing environment to meet the contemporary demands of society? Is it about affordability, sustainability and equality or do you have an alternative vision?
3. If you were a policy-maker where would you start in terms of tackling current housing challenges within the UK context, balancing ideals and budgetary constraints?

Contemporary housing policy focuses upon regeneration. Historically, however, slum clearance was a major focus for those making housing policy. The major task of slum clearance and rehousing fell to governments after the Second World War. Between 1945 and the end of the 1960s, the twin ideals of state intervention in housing and government planning of the environment reached full bloom. The percentage of households in public rented (council house) homes rose from 12 to 31 between 1945 and 1971, while the percentage in private rented accommodation plummeted from 62 to 17 over the same period (Malpass and Murie 1994: 73). However, owner-occupation rose from a quarter to a half of all households, and this represented a flowering of the private housing market as well, albeit greatly helped by government intervention through tax relief to mortgage payers. Ideas about ideal housing and the purpose of housing have evolved over time; Box 11.2 provides some historical context.

Box 11.2 Octavia Hill (1838–1912)

Octavia Hill can be seen as one of the key founders of modern social work, as well as a pioneer of housing policy and management. The daughter of a middle-class but not particularly well-off family, she concentrated on trying to find housing solutions for slum-dwellers and the very poor. This involved social casework and developing a relationship with families as well as finding them housing.

She hit upon the idea of developing an organization to *manage* rented properties that could be let to 'deserving' poor people in need of accommodation. Property owners handed over management responsibility to Octavia Hill's scheme, which guaranteed them a fair financial return and which was staffed by middle-class women volunteers who collected rents and supervised tenants and properties.

Owners could be assured that their properties would be well looked after, thus encouraging them to let to people from the poorest backgrounds. Otherwise, landlords were reluctant to let rooms to the poor. Usually, high rents were charged for inferior accommodation and, as a result, tenants at the bottom end of the rented accommodation market tended to 'flit' or default on rent.

After the opening of Paradise Place in Marylebone in 1865, Octavia Hill's housing scheme spread to include a large number of properties in London. Although it only ever reached a minority of people in need, it was an imaginative breakthrough in providing basic accommodation for poor families. However, her scheme was far from being 'pro-poor'. Its philosophy was governed by rather authoritarian ideas about how the behaviour of the poor could be improved. Tenants were expected to follow the advice of their social superiors, the volunteer women who called to collect rents and to instruct them how to conduct their lives.

Hill's philosophy did not challenge the economic principles of the housing market. She opposed the idea of using charity to help poor people with their rents, or of subsidizing the cost of housing in other ways. Octavia Hill was against the early experiments with subsidized council housing in London in the 1890s, for example (Malpass 1984: 35).

If Hill's philosophy meant that a poor family had to struggle to pay rent for a single room (and, according to Hill's standards, one room per family was usually 'adequate'), then this was quite proper in a market system and the only way to develop independence in the poor. On the other hand, Hill wanted a fair housing market with legislation to guarantee basic standards. She successfully lobbied parliament to improve housing: for example, through the Artisans' and Labourers' Dwellings Improvement Act 1875. However, Hill's views of the causes of poverty remained fundamentally individualistic and moralistic, and these perspectives were clearly evident in the stance she took as a member of the Royal Commission on the Poor Laws (1905–9).

The Conservative governments of the 1950s continued the council house-building programme and were especially active in this respect between 1951 and 1954, but after 1955 they put a higher priority on encouraging private builders to meet general housing need. Gradually, local authority council housing came to be seen as the sector in which poorer households would be *re*housed, and which was to carry the burden of slum clearance in the 1950s and 1960s. As Malpass and Murie (1994) point out, the official standards governing council houses were lowered after 1953, and council housing began to be seen as of significantly lower status and as having less appeal than privately built homes.

This was also the case during the period of Labour government in 1964–70, when owner-occupation was endorsed as the favoured form of housing tenure for the majority. However, Labour began a crash programme of public sector house-building, rehousing and slum clearance for the inner cities. Tower blocks and large housing estates were thrown together with great haste, while long-standing urban communities in inner cities were bulldozed to make way for new roads, open spaces and shopping centres.

The pace of public sector house-building at this time, combined with local government corruption in some areas and the patchy implementation of quality controls, meant that many problems were laid down for the future. Many of today's problems of leaking roofs, inadequate ventilation and corroding concrete date from the 1960s' and 1970s' rush to build cheap public sector housing. Poor building standards were matched by ill-conceived designs for housing estates. In many cases, either warren-like 'concrete jungles' were built, or bleak wastelands that are poorly serviced with shops and other community facilities. The impact of housing policy in this time period has left a negative legacy that remains a challenge for the current Coalition Government.

The triumph of market ideals: housing policy in the 1980s and 1990s

The 1980s saw the tide turning against the ideas of social engineering and planning that had come to dominate housing policy. In practice both Conservative and Labour governments *before* 1979 had increasingly looked to the private market as the main supplier of housing, despite differences of emphasis between the parties. But it was the housing policies of Mrs Thatcher's government after 1979 that marked a decisive change in policy ideals and assumptions. Planning restrictions on the sale of land would be eased. No longer would council housing remain as a major player on the scene. This kind of housing would be increasingly **residualized** (see Box 11.3).

Mrs Thatcher's housing policies went with the grain of public attitudes and aspirations (Cole and Furbey 1994), which in Britain – and particularly in England – favour owner-occupied housing for the reasons mentioned at the beginning of this chapter.

However, the housing policies of Mrs Thatcher's government included a lot more than encouraging owner-occupation through council house sales. Other pro-market changes were brought in, such as the decontrol of rented accommodation. For instance, the Housing Act 1980 introduced shorthold tenancies (giving landlords the right to evict tenants after a contracted period of between 1 and 5 years) and 'fair rents', a new procedure through which former rent controls were abolished and landlords could more easily charge higher rents than before. The aim of these policies was to stimulate the private rented sector by offering greater incentives to landlords. But there was also continuity, as in the policy (popular with people buying their homes) of continuing to give tax relief on mortgage repayments.

Box 11.3 Residualization

This is a useful concept in social policy. It refers to a process whereby public services are increasingly used by a 'residual' or excluded minority of poorer people, rather than by the community as a whole. Two-tier services or facilities develop, with the better-off majority using private sector services (including housing) which they or their employers pay for. Poorer families and individuals are left with public welfare services which, because the middle-class and better off working-class families no longer use them, tend to become run-down, poorly funded and socially stigmatized. If council accommodation is becoming a residual category of housing, for example, this would mean that a certain stigma would be attached to living on a council estate – it would be a sign of social exclusion and downward social mobility.

Above all, though, it is the 'right to buy' legislation that Mrs Thatcher's administration is most remembered for in the field of housing. The Housing Act 1980 gave both council tenants and some housing association tenants the right to buy their homes. As far as council tenants were concerned, this law gave substantial government discounts on the price of homes as an incentive to buy. These were discounts of between a third and a half of the property's market value, depending on the tenant's length of tenure. Local authorities were required to provide mortgages of 100 per cent for buyers.

Another Housing Act, in 1985, extended the powers of central government to force local authorities to sell council accommodation to tenants. Similarly, the Housing and

Planning Act 1986 forced the pace of council house sales by increasing discounts to buyers and by making it easier for whole blocks of housing estates to be sold off (see Malpass and Murie 1994: 106).

The Housing Act 1988 sought to break up further what was seen by Conservatives as a 'municipal monopoly' of council estates. This Act not only gave individual tenants the right to choose another landlord, such as a housing association, but also introduced a policy of large-scale voluntary transfers (LSVTs) of council estates from local authorities to housing associations or even to private landlords. These policies were attempts to privatize 'problem' council estates – those which were particularly run down and where very low market prices for accommodation made it difficult to purchase or sell, under the former 'right to buy' legislation. These policies have continued and mean that much social housing is now not in local authority control.

The 'right to buy' legislation and the other policies to transform large council housing estates were aimed at stimulating market solutions to Britain's housing needs. As such, they have been contrasted with the former mentality of social engineering and state planning which had held sway over housing policy. However, in some ways Mrs Thatcher's policies were also examples of social engineering, if by this we mean a paternalistic use of the state to bring about changes on people's behalf that are seen as beneficial for them. It was not as though Mrs Thatcher's government simply relaxed local authority control over housing and let the market run free in the private rented or owner-occupied sectors. Rather, pro-market ideals and solutions had to be brought about – engineered – by all kinds of government incentives such as discounts to council house purchasers.

The most immediate achievement of this state-directed and state-subsidized market was an explosion of sales of council houses and housing association homes, which resulted in the proportion of properties rented from local authorities in Great Britain (i.e. UK minus Northern Ireland) declining from 30 per cent to 19 per cent of the total housing stock between 1979 and 1997 (Ford 2003: 144). Selling off government-owned assets (that is, council housing) on a large scale, promoting goals of individual ownership and gain, and enlarging the role of the market, were all hallmarks of the 'Thatcherite' approach. In retrospect, housing policy in the 1980s now stands out as the area of social policy in which these ideals or goals had their most marked effect. Accompanying this trend was an increase in the overall proportion of owner-occupied dwellings, from 56 per cent in 1970 to 67 per cent in 1997 (Ford 2003: 144, Table 8.1).

By the early 1990s, however, the housing market was in serious crisis. It suffered from an economic hangover, following the 'wild party' of property speculation and booming house prices in the 1980s. House prices fell steeply and, at the same time, interest rates set by building societies for first mortgages rocketed. This represented a crippling increase for some first-time buyers, especially as tax relief on repayments was being pared down and many had taken out large mortgages to buy houses at inflated prices. These issues have recently been seen again following the 2008 global credit crisis and associated national recessions, and while there are some differences – for example, British interest rates have been kept low by the Bank of England – there are many similarities between contemporary housing issues, and those seen in the 1980s and 1990s.

Whether or not governments are wholly responsible for bringing about such outcomes in the housing market, the effects of the booms and of government housing policy in the 1980s, and more recently in the 2000s, show very mixed results from the pro-market and privatization dreams of that period. Some notable problems associated with this policy approach are as follows:

- A rising rate of house repossession, as a growing number of householders experienced mortgage repayment difficulties (Cassidy 2012).
- A cutback in the number of new houses being built, as the construction industry faced an uncertain future. Easton (2012) argues that there is a lack of affordable homes being built in the UK, with building declining significantly. In 2009/10 54,000 affordable homes were built. In 2010/11 this fell to 49,000, and in 2012 there were fewer than 16,000.
- The spread of negative equity, which is indicative of market failure. Negative equity occurs when house values fall so steeply that house-buyers face having to pay back a loan or mortgage that is greater than the current market value of the property. Barrow (2012) illustrates difference in levels of negative equity in the UK. Many more homeowners in the north are in negative equity (8.5 per cent), than in the south (3.3 per cent).
- Disappointing performance of the private rented sector.
- An increase in homelessness. A number of social trends combined to increase homelessness: high rates of divorce, separation, family conflict and break-up. Arguably there would have been a rise in homelessness whatever kind of government had been in power or whatever housing policies had been implemented. However, a range of policies introduced in the 1980s do seem to have contributed to the rise in homelessness and the number of people living in temporary accommodation Rogers (2012) shows that homelessness rates are increasing in England as a result of the economic downturn, rising joblessness and soaring demand for limited affordable housing. In 2011 there was an increase of 44 per cent in households who were homeless after repossession. These trends are likely to continue in the wake of benefit changes, as well as changes in public service provision (see earlier chapters).

This brings us to the more general question of what the outcomes were of Mrs Thatcher's policy of council house sales. By 1994, the number of dwellings rented from local authorities had fallen to its lowest level since 1963 – about one in five of the then 23.7 million dwellings in Great Britain (CSO 1996: 176). However, this shows not only the enormous impact of the Conservative Government's housing sell-off policy but also that the rented public housing sector did not completely disappear. Despite the haemorrhage of sales, it remains a substantial sector, accounting for almost 5 million homes. Such a large sector is bound to include wage earners and younger households, not just a residual minority of older people, or unemployed people and those dependent on social benefits.

Although people who live in local authority housing cannot be portrayed as a 'housing underclass' or as a completely residualized group, however, there has undeniably been a *trend* towards residualization as a result of selling off council accommodation. Between 1983 and 1990 the proportion of 'economically inactive' people in Britain increased from 32 to 38 per cent. But among council-house heads of household the proportion was already much higher (50 per cent in 1983) and increased at a faster rate to 61 per cent in 1991 (GHS 1983: Table 6.9; 1992: Table 3.31). In other words, during the period of maximum council house sales, the people 'left behind' in council accommodation were increasingly those out of work or older people. Over the same period, the proportion of skilled manual people as householders in council accommodation fell from 24 to 15 per cent, another indicator of residualization. Council housing is now only rarely the type of home occupied by skilled, higher-paid working-class people. Above all, the drastic reduction in the amount of low-cost council housing seems to have had the most significant effect in that it took away opportunities for young people and others facing family difficulties to find affordable accommodation.

Opponents of the council house sales policy pointed to what they saw as the negative consequences – for instance, the cost to the public purse from sales which, far from saving public expenditure, have added to it (Balchin 1995: 166). The cost of giving tax relief to first-time buyers with mortgages cancelled out the gains from house sales and from cutting back council house building. Further, it should not be forgotten that large subsidies had to be given out to make purchases feasible for low-income families.

In terms of the social effects, critics of council house sales point to the 'creaming off' of better council houses by purchasers. It is mainly the more popular two-storey houses with gardens that have sold well, and this makes it increasingly likely that poorer families with young children must be housed in the unsuitable accommodation that is left, often in high-rise blocks. Communities also face break-up, according to the critics, because families who have purchased their homes trade up for a better house elsewhere and leave the neighbourhood.

But whether selling council housing inevitably has these effects is a matter of debate. Much seems to depend on the type of area and community in question. For instance, an interesting study of council housing and the African-Caribbean community by Peach and Byron (1994) showed that black tenants often experienced racial discrimination in the allocation of council accommodation. They were more often given flats rather than houses, or accommodation on the least-favoured floors or parts of tower blocks, compared to white tenants. Despite this unequal treatment, however, the research showed that a surprisingly high number of African-Caribbean council tenants were interested in the right to buy. Furthermore, those who had bought their council homes were found to have improved their position in the community and their well-being. In other words, the right to buy policy had not excluded the African-Caribbean community or led to further residualization of black tenants in council-owned accommodation.

An important exception to this finding was that single Caribbean women with dependent children *were* more likely to be in inappropriate, council-rented accommodation. For this group, the option of purchasing their home was likely to be unrealistic or difficult. However, Peach and Byron conclude that, for this community as a whole, householders who purchase their flat or house are more likely to stay in the neighbourhood and to seek improvements in the local area. Rather than contributing to the break-up of community life and rapid turnover of residents, the right to buy policy in this example showed that it had helped to stabilize the local community.

This finding about one minority community could have implications for everyone living in council estates. 'Since it is the more economically able and entrepreneurial who buy', Peach and Byron (1994: 381) suggest, 'it could be argued that the act of purchase ties them to the locality more strongly'. As they also point out, the opposite has been found to be the case in 'housing projects' (social housing) in the USA, where all tenants must be receiving welfare payments to qualify for housing. The experience there has been that, as no accommodation is sold, anyone who 'makes good' and improves their income is automatically ineligible for housing and has to leave.

The African-Caribbean example is important because it shows the dangers of generalizing about the longer-term effects of 1980s and early 1990s housing privatization. While there are clear trends towards residualization, or the concentration of poor, socially excluded and unemployed people in rented council accommodation, this is far from being a universal phenomenon. However, increasingly there is stigma associated with living in social housing across the UK. Complete Activity 11.3 to explore the idea of stigma associated with type of housing further.

Activity 11.3 Social housing as a stigmatizing environment

Use the Internet to search for discussion and media reports about the stigma associated with social housing in the UK. As a starting point you can access the suggested links below, which discuss the issue of stigma and social housing:

- *Guardian* discussion, 'The Stigma Enigma': www.guardian.co.uk/society/2005/jan/05/societyhousing.thinktanks.
- Joseph Rowntree Report, 'Challenging images: housing estates, stigma and regeneration': www.jrf.org.uk/publications/challenging-images-housing-estates-stigma-and-regeneration.

1. What does reading about stigma and social housing tell you about dominant opinions of social housing?
2. Have you ever considered your own opinions?
3. How do you think that social policy in this area has contributed to these views?

More history: housing under New Labour – a forgotten dream?

Dreams and utopias, it will be recalled, are the underlying theme of this chapter. Until recent times, housing policy seemed to be directed by large-scale plans and strong ideological preferences – 'dreams' of a better way to live, and hopes of solving Britain's housing shortage. 'Old' Labour in the 1960s realized ambitious plans to tear down old inner-city housing and build modern, publicly owned tower blocks and whole new towns to replace it. And in 1979, Mrs Thatcher's radically different housing policy – to sell council homes on a large scale – was widely trumpeted and quickly implemented.

By contrast, housing under New Labour since 1997 became a low-profile public issue. As Kemp (1999) points out, Labour's 'silence' about housing policy in 1997 was striking, and 'Apart from a few specific manifesto commitments . . . it was not at all clear what Labour's housing policy objectives would be, nor what instruments it would use to pursue them' (1999: 134). Toynbee and Walker (2001) agree, citing as evidence Labour's avoidance of the issue of the large numbers of new homes that were needed in the UK during their time in power. The Barker report, commissioned by the Treasury in 2004, demonstrated the lack of investment in British housing and the existence of what is in effect a housing shortage (Toynbee and Walker 2005: 134, 260).

The significant point here is that the New Labour government 1997–2010 shied away from the issue of housing shortages rather than devising a plan or opening up a public debate.

To say that New Labour's approach to housing and to related environmental issues seems to have been low key is not to say that the government has *no* policy at all. Nor is it to suggest that large-scale plans and dreams of solutions to Britain's housing problems are always 'a good thing'. As shown above, the ambitious plans contained in previous governments' housing policies have gone sour in various ways.

New Labour's modest policies are summarized in Table 11.3.

Table 11.3 Summary of New Labour's approach to housing policy

Area of housing focus	**Policy**
General policy in this area	• A laissez-faire approach to housing for the majority of the population. Provision of new housing was left largely to private developers and companies, and the government sought to steer housing development, at arm's length, to so-called 'brownfield' sites (land formerly used for industrial or other urban uses such as housing, but now vacant or derelict). • Continuation of policy in which housing is seen as less and less of a government responsibility. • Home ownership regarded as the preferred and dominant tenure.
Public and social housing	• Here there was a continuation of the Conservative policy of transfer of ownership. Transfers were to registered social landlords, Private Finance Initiative (PFI) schemes, or local housing companies (LHCs). • Policy discourse was about increasing responsiveness and widening choice and access, moving away from the traditional bureaucratic housing allocation procedures of local authorities. • New Labour also attempted to reform social sector rents to make them fairer and more affordable, and to resolve inherited dilemmas over the marketization of rents and the linked issue of extent of assistance via housing benefit (Ford 2003: 156–7).
Regeneration	• New Labour made a particular point of trying to connect housing policy to its other policies to improve the quality of life in poorer neighbourhoods and socially excluded communities. • A bewildering variety of local initiatives and community development projects were launched in order to co-ordinate housing improvement with other efforts to upgrade public services such as education and health care, and to reduce crime and vandalism. • Kemp (1999: 135) highlighted New Labour's preoccupation with 'rundown council estates' and policies to ensure that 'housing played its part in combating "social exclusion" and in contributing to urban regeneration'.

Overall New Labour continued following a market approach to housing, as determined by the previous Conservative government. This appeared to work relatively well because of the generally positive economic conditions experienced during the late 1990s and early 2000s. Interest rates had declined to their lowest levels since the 1960s, unemployment had also declined to a low level and, as the real incomes of the majority had risen steadily since the mid-1990s, all these favourable economic trends stimulated house purchases and home ownership. House prices rose by 60 per cent between 1995 and 2000, but because of the reduction of interest and mortgage rates this did not lead to the scale of debt problems and repayment difficulties seen in the early 1990s. For some, however, the market did not work well. While the 'affordability crisis' of the early 1990s in housing was mainly among people who could not afford to keep up repayments on their mortgages, in the early years of the twenty-first century it is becoming a problem of those who cannot afford to buy a house to begin with. The problem is particularly acute in London. Consequently, the capital is experiencing severe problems in attracting or retaining public sector workers on average incomes (cleaners, nurses, police officers, teachers, transport workers) who cannot afford the available housing. Similar problems are occurring in other parts of south-east England, as well as in rural areas and exclusive city areas outside this region.

These problems show that supply of low-cost housing is a vital part of any housing policy aiming to meet the needs of the population as a whole. As Toynbee and Walker (2001: 179) point out, about a third of the new homes to be built in the south-east to meet the huge anticipated rise in demand for housing will need to be affordable – that is, 'built by councils or social landlords'. The lesson of history is that the market alone cannot be relied on to meet such needs very well.

However, there was not a return, under New Labour, to policies that favoured the idea of continuing with local authorities as the main providers of social housing. New Labour continued during their time in offering to transfer council housing stock to registered social landlords (RSLs) – that is, non-profit-making housing associations. The government also provided central funds in order to assist local authorities to set up 'social' companies to run housing estates. These new-style companies were allowed to raise money in the open market to finance house repairs and upgrade the surrounding environment. Financing was provided partly by banks and building societies and, though tenants will have a voice in the management of the new housing companies, they have been criticized by traditional Labour supporters as 'backdoor privatization' (Hetherington 1998).

However, Labour policy did accept that there was a need to improve housing for people who could not afford to purchase it and who remain in rented accommodation. Blair's first administration allowed £800 million to be released from the capital receipts local authorities had gained from earlier sales of council housing (the former Conservative administration had prevented local authorities from using this money). These funds were used partly in order to pay for the repair and renovation of the existing stock of local authority housing and also to fund a modest increase in new social housing. However, overall lack of substantial investment has left a negative legacy in relation to the condition of some social housing provision.

As noted in Table 11.3, a dominant theme of New Labour policy thinking was the idea of social exclusion and a concern with mitigating it. A stark manifestation of social exclusion in relation to housing is homelessness. However, New Labour did not perform well at dealing with homelessness, which increased because of a decline in the number of available social sector lettings (Office for National Statistics 2005: 141).

New Labour did, however, seriously focus upon neighbourhood renewal, emphasizing area-based strategies and the need for 'joined-up' approaches to urban renewal. ('Joined-up'-ness was of course, like 'social exclusion', another significant New Labour slogan or mantra.) One policy product related to this approach came in 1999, when the government launched its 'New Deal for Communities' (NDC) programme for 17 of the poorest estates, and this was followed by a second round that brought the total of communities involved to 24 in the year 2000 (Atkinson 2003: 165). The NDC programme made funding available for its various projects. Money for community regeneration was also made available for the first three years from the Single Regeneration Budget, a fund, introduced by the Conservatives in 1994, that succeeded the former urban programme. This money (available until 2000) could be used for a wider range of purposes than it could under the urban programme, and the Single Regeneration Budget was used to fund the large variety of community regeneration projects. This source of funding was replaced by the Neighbourhood Renewal Fund in 2000, as a result of the Comprehensive Spending Review of that year, as well as by NDC funds (Atkinson 2003: 165).

There was also a separate flow of central government funds to local authorities and registered social landlords to maintain and improve their social housing stock – and this might be seen as 'housing' money rather than 'community regeneration' money. These two sources of funding were substantially increased (an extra £5 billion over the three years from 1999 to 2002) by New Labour (Kemp 1999: 142), as part of the government strategy to increase spending on selected public services such as education and health.

Therefore it would be wrong to conclude that New Labour has paid only lip service to the principle of improving social housing or of putting public money into local communities. In 1999, a Local Government Act, in addition to giving local authorities the freedom to spend gains from the sale of council houses (as mentioned above), required local authorities to promote the well-being of their communities. Thus, not only did the government devote a lot of energy and considerable amounts of money to its efforts to remove the causes of social exclusion and disadvantage in selected areas but also it succeeded in being innovative in the way social problems and needs are being thought about. For instance, previous governments had not developed quite the same links between housing policy, community development and local networks to provide or improve social care, as New Labour aimed to do (for an examination of these policies, see Barr et al. 2001).

Although new ways of tackling social deprivation and social exclusion on housing estates were developed, however, critics of New Labour point to a number of limitations to their 'community regeneration' strategy. First, at the same time as the government developed community regeneration, restrictions on both the amount of housing benefit and the eligibility of claimants to this benefit were introduced. Consequently some socially disadvantaged groups - for instance, young tenants on low incomes - argued that they were no longer able to afford rising rents. Second, any policy that targets particular kinds of community is bound, to a greater or lesser degree, to be a piecemeal, selective one. As a result, New Labour policies in this area were vulnerable to the charge that used to be laid at the door of community development projects in the 1970s, that they were only palliative policies - a substitute for more effective, universal policies to reduce poverty and to improve people's environments.

Finally, even if regeneration and housing improvement policies do begin to work in selected areas, their very success can lead to contradictory outcomes. This is because reducing the jobless rate, improving people's incomes and raising their aspirations leads to the out-migration of the more successful members of the community. At last they can escape the run-down estates and poor housing in which they have been living. Therefore, while community regeneration efforts might make a real difference to the lives of a considerable number of people, they are less likely than might be imagined to fundamentally change the neighbourhoods in which they are applied. Whether these are inevitably the results of community regeneration and development, however, will depend partly on the kind of community that is involved in the project, and how far local people identify with it and want to remain there. Also, the long-term effects of community regeneration will also depend on the type of resources that are developed. For instance, developing a credit union, childcare services or co-operative food purchasing are examples of community resources and services that make life easier and encourage people to stay in their local areas.

The Coalition Government approach

The Coalition Government inherited a very different economic situation compared to that of New Labour's early years in power, as previous chapters have already discussed. There was a global 'credit crunch', and the UK was facing recession and significant problems with the banking sector which were restricting the ability of people to either keep up their mortgage payments or, in the case of people wishing to buy property, to find banks willing to lend to them. 'Rising unemployment, economic recession and shortages of credit sent the housing market and house-building into crisis' (Murie 2012: 62).

In terms of the housing policy legacy, significant problems also remained. There is little doubt that as a result of a lack of capital investment – especially in the large, run-down council estates that still exist in parts of the English Midlands and northern England, Wales and Scotland – social housing is becoming even more unattractive and 'residualized'. It is not only the condition of the housing but also the image or reputation of social housing and housing estates that is deteriorating. There is a growing problem of 'unlettable' houses and blocks of flats, affecting not only the older 1960s properties but also council housing stock that was built relatively recently, in the 1970s and 1980s. Therefore, both central government and social landlords face a sharp dilemma. Is it worth spending millions of pounds on improving houses in certain areas when there is a strong possibility that they will still have to be pulled down?

In addition, New Labour's policies, despite being innovative, did not tackle the structural, deep-seated causes of both social exclusion and housing problems. Page (2000) showed that resources still did not get through to social housing estates on a sufficiently large scale to reverse a two-decade period of decline towards poorer services and a poorer physical environment. Public services provided by local authorities have been kept on a tight budget since the late 1970s and this, together with a lot of internal restructuring and reorganization, has left them poorly equipped to make sudden improvements in areas of social housing. And, while extra money was provided by New Labour, critics add that the rate of increase was little different from that added to the housing and environment budgets by the previous Conservative administration (Kemp 1999).

So what is the Coalition Government approach in the area of housing? Table 11.4 summarizes the current UK policy direction.

A recent housing issue being examined by the Coalition Government is that of the empty homes that are available in Britain. Similar to other policy areas (see Chapter 8 about education) the government commissioned a celebrity to explore the problem, George Clarke. Complete the final activity of this chapter, Activity 11.4, to learn more about this.

Activity 11.4 Britain's empty homes

The government has commissioned a review into the empty homes across the country. This review was led by George Clarke.

1. Use the Internet to access the following site – George Clarke and Partners http://georgeclarke.com.
2. Go to George's empty homes manifesto, which he delivered to the Coalition Government, http://georgeclarke.com/2012/11/george-clarkes-empty-homes-manifesto-delivered-to-government-today.
3. Watch the video called 'The Great British Property Scandal' available through this website.
4. Now take some time to reflect upon social policy in this area: is it working? Do you agree with George's viewpoint that empty homes should be 'recycled'? If you were a policy-maker, what would you do to resolve the empty house crisis?

Table 11.4 The Coalition Government and housing policy

Area of housing focus	Policy
General policy in this area	• Housing strategy published in 2011 stated that boosting construction was necessary for the economy and housing opportunities (HMG 2011). • The agenda that followed the publication of the housing strategy is, however, a continuation of previous laissez-faire policy approaches. Home ownership seen as the goal for all, thus the introduction of home bonus and first buy schemes. • The Coalition Government strategy also does not offer any response to failings highlighted within the private rental sector in terms of the poor management of properties and the lack of security for tenants (Murie 2012). • The Coalition Government is continuing to reduce the role of the state in housing but has allocated an extra £400 million pounds to kick-start private sector house-building that has already stalled. • The Coalition Government has reformed planning laws with the aim to simplify these in support of increased house-building. • Welfare reforms are affecting housing policy. Housing benefit reforms are being implemented, with caps introduced and the overall budget available to fund this benefit being reduced (Murie 2012). Housing benefit was also reduced in 2013 for recipients living in accommodation judged to be too large for them – the so-called 'bedroom tax'.
Public and social housing	• There is change in this area related to localism and flexibility. The Localism Bill 2010 included changes to legislation meaning that local authorities now decide who is eligible for social housing. • Increased flexibility in terms of tenure means that poorer families are more at risk of being forced to move if their circumstances change (Murie 2012).
Regeneration	• The Coalition Government is focusing upon economic growth as the primary mechanism for regeneration. • Devolution of responsibility (see Chapter 13 for detailed discussions of devolution). The Coalition Government has decentralized decision-making to lower levels – to individuals, public service professionals, neighbourhoods, communities, local authorities, and local institutions – expecting them to come up with solutions that meet the needs of their own localities (UK Parliament 2011). • Local Enterprise Partnerships have been created in many areas. These are described as a mechanism by which local communities and businesses are given the opportunities to support both economic growth and regeneration in their areas by addressing the particular barriers to growth they face (UK Parliament 2011). • The Coalition Government's focus is upon enterprise rather than regeneration per se.

Government policy related to empty homes has yet to be outlined. While the implications of the other Coalition Government changes are yet to be felt, some commentators such as Murie (2012) argue that where social segregation has been increasing, it is likely to be further increased as a result of these new policies. Furthermore, he concludes that the current Coalition Government policy approach is not likely to resolve the challenges that are being experienced within the UK housing sector, and that rather new problems are being created for the next generation.

Conclusions: housing and the environment in a postmodern society

No other aspect of social policy in the UK reflects dramatic change in quite the way that housing does. Alcock (1996: 36) describes housing as 'a kind of policy football – first kicked one way and then another'. But while this is historically true, the housing policies of the dominant political parties have converged since the early 1970s. There has been convergence towards the idea of the private market being the dominant way of providing housing, and of owner-occupation being the desired type of tenure for all but a few. Any real differences in approach have been more a matter of emphasis or the speed with which governments have implemented policies such as the sale of council housing.

Currently, the Coalition Government's broad policy on housing differs little from that of the preceding New Labour administration. There have been some changes in legislation (welfare cuts that will affect those in receipt of housing benefit and an increased localism agenda), but no reversal to a policy of planning on the grand scale.

Demand for additional housing has increased in recent years, and this seems likely to continue. Yet despite the need for more housing, government policy is not being used to tackle this issue, or to deal with the intense conflicts that will inevitably arise when housing shortages become even more critical.

A number of social trends are combining to put additional strains on the housing market and to increase the need for extra dwellings. They include a high rate of divorce, separation and family break-up, increasing mobility and the need to move to realize job opportunities, and an ageing population in which more very old people will survive in their own homes than they did in the past. At a time when the population needs an ever more flexible supply of housing to meet the rapidly changing family and work demands of a postmodern society, the inflexibilities of the market system are becoming particularly evident.

For instance, house prices have become prohibitively expensive in some parts of the UK, and especially in London, with the result that young house purchasers are being excluded from the market. There is a knock-on effect in terms of rising demand for private rented accommodation, which then encourages steep rises in rents. In turn, demand for rented social housing has escalated, with the result that tens of thousands of people in London, for instance, are on long waiting lists for social housing and are living in very inadequate temporary accommodation. This temporary accommodation may also be outside the capital (Butler and Ferguson 2012). Recently three London councils were considering moving at least 150 homeless families claiming housing benefit 130 miles away to Derby and Nottingham because of the lack of adequate housing available in their areas (Mullholland et al. 2012). This illustrates the point made above, about the problems some local authorities have in trying to let unwanted social housing, while others are struggling to combat a growing housing shortage.

There are even signs that, in areas such as inner London, where the demand for affordable housing is very high, some council estates are losing what has been unfairly termed their 'piss-and-pitbull' image (Bennett 1996). In the year in which English Heritage listed 67 council estates or tower blocks for architectural merit, Bennett adds, 'there are signs that certain council blocks are becoming coveted places to live. By way of purchasing or letting schemes, council flats are socially mobile as never before.'

While such trends might remain a mainly 'London phenomenon' for the foreseeable future, they do indicate a deeper swell of changes in attitudes to housing that will come to affect housing policy in the near future. On the one hand, as suggested by the above examples, there is a growing search for more flexible housing alternatives, especially among the young. On the other, there appears to be a growing concern with environmental aspects of housing.

Among architects, designers and environmental pressure groups there is growing concern with how to apply 'green' principles in housing – for instance, with the ways in which house design could be improved to limit energy loss and emissions of greenhouse gases. There is also concern about the environmental sustainability of local communities and the need to improve public transport, cycle paths and footpaths. This is seen in new developments that consider their environmental impact. For instance, plans for an eco-village on the outskirts of Plymouth were recently approved by the city council. The development will consist of 91 homes that are ranked as the highest category of energy-efficient housing (BBC News 2012b).

In some ways, environmental and green objectives may conflict with other policy objectives – for example, those related to fuel poverty. Policy in recent years has recognized that older people particularly need to maintain an adequate level of heat in their homes. However, this policy is not consistent with 'green' objectives if, for instance, home insulation is not carried out. In concluding this discussion of housing policy, therefore, it is important to note how the problems experienced by low-income groups in particular kinds of disadvantaged communities – inadequate transport, limited employment opportunities, a neglected physical environment and sub-standard housing – are all inter-related. If the trends of the 1980s and 1990s continue, the marginalization of the poor in these socially excluded communities will continue to be a marked feature of British society. Current Coalition Government policy may well serve to increase these trends in polarization related to social housing and council estates. However, it is also worth noting briefly that housing problems can also be severe among people who are on low incomes but who are owner-occupiers rather than tenants in social housing. A study by Revell and Leather (2000), for instance, found that almost a third of homes in England, Scotland and Wales need urgent repairs. Consequently, a significant number of houses in Britain are in poor condition, having problems of dampness, inadequate insulation, weather-proofing, heating and sanitation.

Therefore, while the majority of people in the UK are relatively well housed, neither the housing market nor government housing policy has served the minority very well. This minority includes poorer owner-occupiers as well as some of the groups renting private and social housing.

Summary of key points

- Current housing policy has followed the same direction since the 1970s irrespective of the government in power. However, a momentous change is taking place: the steady expansion of owner-occupation since the 1970s seems to have halted, with many younger people now unable to buy their own homes or obtain mortgages to do so. Consequently, the private rented sector is making a dramatic comeback to the housing scene in Britain.
- The state is reducing the responsibility that it takes for the provision of social housing, is relying upon the market and is promoting the ideal of home ownership for all. Recent Coalition Government policy is yet to be evaluated but is likely to increase polarization of provision and create further problems for the future.

- Social change means that there are new and different policy influences on housing policy than in the past. Trends such as increasing numbers of single-person households and an ageing population mean that housing requirements have changed and that more homes are needed.
- There is a well-documented shortage of adequate and affordable homes for many people within Britain, and polarization of housing provision. Sharp inequalities exist between those who can afford to purchase their own home and those trapped in social housing or other rented accommodation.

Key terms and concepts

autonomy
council housing
homelessness
industrial paternalism
marginalization
philanthropy
postmodernism
residualization
social engineering
social housing
tenure

Suggestions for further reading

Hanley, L. (2007) *Estates: An Intimate History.* London: Granta.

This book is the history of social housing written by someone who has lived in social housing. It provides an interesting historical analysis of the creation and development of estates, links changes in estates and perceptions of them to the broader policy context, and offers the reader an interesting insight.

King, P. (2010) *Housing Policy Transformed: The Right to Buy and the Desire to Own.* Bristol: Policy Press.

This book explores the right to buy, often described as the most controversial housing policy of the last 30 years. Unlike many other books that focus upon the costs of the policy and its negative impact, this book discusses the right to buy on its own terms. It explains how the policy links with a coherent ideology based on self-interest and therefore provides the reader with an alternative interpretation of this policy approach.

Lowe, S. (2011) *The Housing Debate.* Bristol: Policy Press.

This book examines the way in which Britain has emerged as a home-owning society and the implications of this, for example, how houses are used not just as a home but also as an asset. The key debate in the book is an examination of whether social policy and people's homes should be so closely connected, especially given the volatility of housing markets.

Lund, B. (2011) *Understanding Housing Policy.* 2nd edition. Bristol: Policy Press.

This book explores the major housing problems in contemporary Britain as well as the effectiveness of policy approaches in dealing with them. The book explores the political processes involved in the construction and delivery of housing policies; discusses theoretical perspectives, policy development and implementation, housing and social justice; and includes an assessment of the impact of New Labour's housing policies as well as discussion of the policy orientation of the Coalition Government.

Tallon, A. (2013) *Urban Generation in the UK.* 2nd edition. London: Routledge.

This book provides an accessible and critical discussion of urban regeneration in the UK. It analyses policies, approaches, issues and debates in the contemporary context as well as looking at historical agendas. The New Labour period of urban policy as well as the urban agenda and regeneration policies of the Coalition Government are both discussed. Student-friendly and readable.

12 Community and social care

Key learning outcomes

By the end of this chapter you should:

- be able to understand how policies on community care developed historically
- be able to identify and outline the positive developments and drawbacks of different community care policies
- be able to discuss the recent policy changes in community care made by the Coalition Government

Overview of the chapter

Imagine whisking someone forward in time from the late 1940s to today. Though many things in the welfare system would be vaguely familiar – NHS funding crises, for one – a puzzling change would be heated debates about something called *community care* or social care. 'What or who is a *carer*?' the 1940s' person might wonder (the rather specialized meaning of this term appeared well after the 1940s – see Bytheway and Johnson 1997). They would be similarly puzzled over terms such as 'continuing care', and even 'community' itself, for what exactly is a 'community' service – a service provided by local government, or perhaps by central government through a Ministry of Community Care? This chapter therefore explores the development of community care and associated policy in this area.

Our visitor from the past could also be forgiven for being puzzled by holes in the net of 'caring' services. They would be able to catch up with newspaper and television reports on 'community care scandals', including sad stories of mentally ill people who have harmed themselves and others when released into 'the community' with inadequate support. Talking to a sample of older people, our visitor would be astonished to discover that a considerably lower percentage of people would be 'going into a home' in their old age, compared to the 1940s. They would be told that, even if they wanted to do this, so many residential and nursing homes have closed in recent years that, in some parts of the UK, it is almost impossible to find a place. Instead, older people in daily need of care and help with 'daily activities of living' are supposed to be able to receive it at home from a range of service providers organized by the local authority. To find that this network of **domiciliary care** services had grown up in the community since the 1940s would be surprising enough to our time-traveller. But even more surprising would be the news that, in some areas, older people in need of these services would be expected to pay relatively high charges for them and, because of the cost, would be able to afford only a limited amount of **home care**. This chapter explores the issues associated with standards of care, funding and the many contemporary challenges that are evident within the community care system.

If our visitor had read George Orwell's *Nineteen Eighty-Four* (written in the late 1940s), they could be forgiven for thinking that something Orwellian had happened to the social services. Our visitor might think that a Ministry of Community Care was presiding over the opposite, community neglect, just as a Ministry of Love was overseeing perpetual war and political repression.

If our time-traveller from 1948 did form this impression, would you wish to reassure them that things today are not quite as bad as they might seem? Or would you argue that, in your view, community care policy and its successor, social care, represent one of the most glaring failures of the welfare system set up in the 1940s?

It is these opposing points of view, and what we would decide to tell our imaginary person from the past, that are the focus of this chapter. At the end you should be better able to decide how far social care policies have succeeded in reaching the goals set by government and other interested parties. As with other areas of social policy, we shall find that conclusions are 'messy' – inevitably so, as judgements partly rest upon political values and the evidence is conflicting. However, an informed view is possible and can be developed in two ways. First, we can examine the way in which community and social care have been *implemented* in Britain. This means looking at what type of care reforms were brought in and what the implications were, for both carers and the cared-for, of the market framework that was designed for service provision. Second, we are able to assess *outcomes* of the community care reforms in the 1990s, and finally the development and likely outcomes of more recent and current policies on social care, with significant proposed reform by the Coalition Government. A little more historical background is necessary, though, to understand more fully these two main aspects of community care.

The development of community and social care

The Victorian legacy: care in institutions

Although the language and the social conditions have changed a great deal, today's debates about social care reveal an age-old tension. What are the benefits, to society at large and to the people who are the objects of care and control, of **residential care** or institutional solutions on the one hand, and 'community' solutions on the other?

The main difference between now and 'then' (the nineteenth century) is that policy since the early 1960s has been to *deinstitutionalize* care and to rely increasingly on the community. In the nineteenth century, the main aim was to build institutions and to separate paupers, the destitute and those judged to be either mad or morally wayward from the rest of 'respectable' society. As we saw in Chapter 3, however, a large majority of those who received help under the Poor Law system did so outside Poor Law institutions. The sheer expense and organization involved in putting everyone who needed help into institutions thwarted the Victorians' aim. By the same token, one of the main causes, if not *the* cause, of **deinstitutionalization** and the modern policy of community care was the cost savings that resulted from closing residential care institutions (Scull 1984).

At the beginning of the twentieth century, a much higher proportion of those in need of care were in institutions, compared to the proportion today. Today many in need of care prefer to stay in their own home. However, demographic changes mean that the need for care will increase in the future because of the ageing population and changing household composition.

By mid-twentieth century, geriatric medicine emerged as a specialty, there was a boom in hospital building and, with the coming of the NHS, older frail people were more likely to be hospitalized than in the past and less likely to be placed in workhouse-type accommodation. Earlier chapters discussed the workhouse, which was effectively the only option for 'care' for individuals who had no other means of support. Complete Activity 12.1 to consolidate and review your knowledge.

Activity 12.1 The workhouse as institutional care provision

Institutional care in the UK originally developed out of the workhouse and poorhouses that were established under the Poor Laws.

Use the Internet to go to www.workhouses.org.uk.

- Explore the links on the left-hand side of the website home page, Old Poor Law and the New Poor Law (found under 'Poor Laws').
- You can also find the location of poor houses according to area – have a look for workhouses in an area that is near to where you live now.
- Explore the other areas of the website that interest you.

1. From your exploring and reading, what did you learn about life in the workhouse?
2. Is the history of institutional care in the UK positive?
3. What do you think are the challenges for policy-makers in providing institutional care?

As you will have learned from Activity 12.1, the conditions of workhouses were far from ideal, and the system of institutional care began to change as time moved on.

The 1950s and 1960s: deinstitutionalization gains momentum

With the medicalization of problems of ageing came the pressure to reduce length of stay. Hospital and nursing care are expensive, and in the medical world older people began to be labelled as 'bed blockers'.

There were parallel trends in other areas of care, such as psychiatric medicine and hospital care for mentally ill people. In fact, as the welfare system developed in the 1950s and 1960s, a number of factors worked together to put increasing pressure on residential and hospital care. First, there was mounting concern about spiralling increases in public spending on welfare, which still remains today. Second, the costs of residential care were rising particularly rapidly. Third, there were worries about the demographic and economic outlook (rapid increases in numbers of very old people combined with a slowing down of economic growth). And fourth, there emerged a strong critique of the negative and controlling aspects of residential and long-stay hospital care, as exemplified by liberal sociologists such as Goffman and critics of psychiatry (see Chapter 7).

Such critics of institutions had a point. A series of well-publicized scandals about abuse of older people and children in residential homes and revelations of the brutal degradation of people with learning difficulties and mentally ill people in hospitals seemed to bear out the oversimplified view that residential care is always a bad thing. Such scandals have also recently re-emerged, with the British media illustrating horrendous treatment of disabled people in homes, and older people in hospital settings. Historically these scandals meant that supporting those in need of long-term care to live freely in the community began to be seen as the best policy in almost all cases.

As Scull (1984) concludes, this consensus emerged during the 1960s. Both liberal or progressive opinion on the one hand and conservative opinion on the other could agree that, on the grounds of either human liberty or saving money, residential institutions of all sorts should be closed down. It is possible to trace the development of this thinking, and of community care as the alternative, in a number of official studies of policy and in significant pieces of legislation, as illustrated in Box 12.1.

Box 12.1 The development of community care

- The Mental Health Act 1959 sought to establish community care for the mentally ill and this led to a significant reduction in long-stay hospital facilities.
- In 1963, the Conservative Government produced a White Paper on the development of community care (Ministry of Health 1963), though an incoming Labour government in 1964 did not follow this up with legislation.
- In 1968, local authorities were required (under the Health Services and Public Health Act) to provide a home help service to older people.

Some of these policies led to improvements in services. Governments did not cynically close institutions solely in order to save public money. There *are* strong reasons for concluding that the needs of those who are frail, ill or disabled can usually be better met with help in their own homes, or in some other community setting. However, nothing like a concerted policy on community care emerged in the 30 years after the welfare state was born. Although the benefits of well-organized community care were acknowledged, the priority was more to close institutions than to divert substantial resources into personal social services for community care. As one indication of this, for instance, many local authorities never managed to provide home help services on the scale required by official targets before 1980 (Tinker 1981: 101–6).

Finding ways of getting health and social service departments to work together at the local level to plan, pay for and provide community services proved to be difficult – despite the introduction of joint financing arrangements in 1976 (Challis et al. 1995: 10). This underlined the point that health authorities in particular were concerned more with shifting the 'burden' of long-stay patients or residents than developing a flexible policy of community care.

Thus, as a result of these attitudes, a basic idea that all institutional care is bad became firmly entrenched policy. However, with the closing down of many of Britain's Victorian asylums and other long-stay facilities, quite a lot has been lost as well as gained. Take Bill Bryson's memory, from 1973, of the effects of a large mental hospital – now closed – on an affluent commuter area near London, for instance. It offers a different perspective on both patients and local residents:

> What lent Virginia Water a particular charm back then, and I mean this quite seriously, is that it was full of wandering lunatics. Because most of the residents had been resident at the sanatorium for years, and often decades . . . most of them could be trusted to wander down to the village and find their way back again. Each day you could count on finding a refreshing sprinkling of lunatics buying fags or sweets, having a cup of tea or just quietly remonstrating with thin air. The result was one of the most extraordinary communities in England, one in which wealthy people and lunatics mingled on equal terms. The shopkeepers and locals were quite wonderful about it, and didn't act as if anything was odd because a man with wild hair wearing a pyjama jacket was standing in a corner of the baker's declaiming to a spot on the wall or sitting at a corner table of the Tudor Rose with swivelling eyes and the makings of a smile, dropping sugar cubes into his minestrone. It was, and I'm still serious, a thoroughly heartwarming sight.
>
> (Bryson 1996: 80–1)

The 1980s: 'community' and 'care' redefined

Bill Bryson's sketch of the relationship between a local community and a large mental hospital show us that the boundary between 'community' life and 'residential' or institutional life can be blurred. Unless inmates are incarcerated in prison-like conditions, there is bound to be a degree of interaction between the two. This point is important, because it is all too easy to assume what is meant by the respective terms 'community' and 'residential' care, when in fact their meanings are problematic. Box 12.2 explores the meanings associated with community and residential care.

Box 12.2 Definitions of community and care

- In the 1992 study by Knapp et al. of 28 community care pilot projects, for instance, living in the 'community' is assumed to mean anything except long-term hospital care. Thus 'community' care in this study included residential homes, **sheltered housing**, hostels, staffed group homes and home care (foster) placements (Knapp et al. 1992: 342).
- Parker (1990: 11) notes that in a Department of Health and Social Security (DHSS) consultative document of 1977, *The Way Forward*, 'The term "community" covered a range of provisions which included community hospitals, hostels, day hospitals, residential homes, day centres as well as domiciliary support.'
- In the 1980s policy came to define community care in a different way. The new policy was to aim for care by the community (primarily through family and neighbourhood support) in partnership with the state, rather than care in the community (the provision of state-run services to people in their homes or nearby).

These significant changes in policy occurred partly because the trends noted earlier were still at work: that is, concern about rising numbers of very old people coupled with a lack of resources, and so on. However, the 1980s in Britain ushered in additional pressures to find cheaper alternatives, not only to institutional care but also to expensive personal care delivered by the social services to people at home. These influences are illustrated in Table 12.1.

Table 12.1 Influences on the development of community care

Influence	Impact
New Right thinking about welfare	• As discussed elsewhere in relation to the health service (see Chapter 10), Mrs Thatcher's government emphasized certain pro-market priorities and goals. These included privatization, seeking value for money in government expenditure, setting up market-style arrangements for purchasing and providing services at the local level, and treating users of social services as consumers. • These goals were woven into the two most influential government reports on community and residential care in the 1980s, the Audit Commission (1986) report and the Griffiths (1988) report.
Increased costs from public spending	• In 1979 the cost to the public purse of subsidizing older people's use of private residential homes was only £10 million. By the mid-1980s this figure had increased alarmingly to £500 million per year, and by the end of the 1980s it was approaching £1000 million per year. • As the Audit Commission (1986) and Griffiths (1988) soberly reminded everyone, this open-handed subsidy had created 'perverse incentives' not to develop community care alternatives which, as well as being cheaper, would as likely as not be a better form of care.

The Audit Commission (1986) and Griffiths (1988) reports succeeded in convincing government and the social services community that there had been an unplanned drift into providing too much residential care. This perception took hold despite the findings of another government report (Firth 1987) showing that the overall provision of residential home places for older people (by private, local authority and voluntary sectors) had *not* risen very much in the 1980s in proportion to rising numbers of people aged over 75.

Therefore, the impression that large numbers of active older people, well able to support themselves in their own homes, were moving into private residential care at public expense was wrong. Actually, Britain has long had a comparatively low proportion of people in residential care, and there is now an argument for expanding residential accommodation. As Wistow et al. (1994) show, the ratio of beds in residential homes to older people (aged over 75) was static in the 1980s, mainly because local authority provision shrank dramatically relative to the growth of the independent sector (the private and voluntary sector homes combined).

Johnson (1999) reminds us that, in the UK in 1980, local authorities provided nearly two-thirds of all the places in residential care for older people, and the private and voluntary sectors provided about a fifth each. By 1995 the private sector was providing well over half of all the places, while local authorities were providing only just over a quarter, and the voluntary sector less than a fifth (Davies 1999: 84). This, as Davies points out, represents a rapid privatization of social services, not in the sense of a sell-off of government institutions but more in terms of a rapid replacement of state-provided services with private sector ones.

As far as organizing community care more effectively was concerned, the Audit Commission (1986) report and especially the Griffiths report (1988) were very influential in shaping government thinking about how to reform the funding and provision of care services. Their influences are clearly apparent in the government White Paper *Caring for People: Community Care in the Next Decade and Beyond* (DoH 1989), which prepared for the legislation of the NHS and Community Care Act 1990.

At the time, the Griffiths report was seen by some as ideologically biased and, despite its neutral and fair-sounding language, more concerned with finding cheaper solutions to the problem of social care than with human welfare. Such criticisms had some justification, but Wistow et al. (1994: 5) remind us that Griffiths was 'not entirely unsympathetic with the views of those critical about the adequacy of funding'.

But while the Griffiths report did show a concern that community care provision should be 'needs led' rather than entirely dictated by financial considerations, there was a failure or an unwillingness to spell out the full social costs of community care. Box 12.3 illustrates some of the social costs of policy development related to community care.

Box 12.3 Inequity in community care

- Policy made bland assumptions about family support when, according to some research, an unequal burden of care often falls upon women in families. Qureshi and Walker's (1989) study of patterns of care in a sample of families in Sheffield showed that female relatives are more frequently expected than men to cut down or leave paid work to perform a wider range of care tasks. Other studies demonstrate that men also care and are often forgotten about in such a role (see Arber and Gilbert 1988).
- There are many inequalities in the provision of care between households. Those who live alone are much more likely to receive home care services than people who live with others. This is the case even though there are substantial numbers of people living with a spouse or family who have greater needs than some of those living alone.
- Officially, every individual in need has a right to be assessed in their own right, but in practice 'community' care assessments usually put family circumstances before individual needs. Thus the care plans for two disabled people with identical needs will often be quite different if one happens to live with family while the other lives alone.

Box 12.3 underlines a significant point about the government's definition of community care and expectations of care by families. According to this definition of community care it is only right that the family should be asked to step in to provide help wherever possible, while care funded by the state is targeted on people living alone. However, the problem with this view is that it can lead to situations in which unfair assumptions are made about the willingness or ability of carers to provide sufficient support. Caring also has a significant impact upon those who perform this role. Complete Activity 12.2 to explore this further.

Activity 12.2 Thinking about emotional labour

Carers often are over-worked and isolated, lack support themselves and find that as a consequence of caring that their own health suffers. Community care policy has thus had negative implications for many individuals who care, and whose emotional labour remains undervalued.

The negative consequences of caring are now more frequently discussed and many organizations exist to provide support to carers, as well as advocating for policy change.

1. Use the Internet to visit some of the organizations that support carers such as:
   - Carers UK: www.carersuk.org
   - Princess Royal Trust for Carers: www.carers.org
2. What is your view about the provision of care: should it be funded by the state? What are the limitations of social policy in relation to providing care? Do you think that families should take responsibility entirely? What would the implications of this be for you, if you had to provide care for a family member on a full-time basis?
3. Consider what happens in countries where there is no coherent social policy in this area. Use the Internet to search for information about other countries and their approaches.

The second learning activity of this chapter should have illustrated to you that carers have needs too – an important point that is mentioned again in the next section.

The community care reforms: implementation and outcomes

The NHS and Community Care Act 1990 can be portrayed as a new version of an old tune: how to save money by replacing expensive institutional care with cheaper alternatives. However, it has transformed the landscape of care and the personal social services, mainly because it made sure that a market system would operate throughout. The changes made from 1993 onwards (implementation of most of the 1990 Act was delayed until April 1993) still structure the social services and were retained by New Labour – though Labour also introduced further changes.

This Act was at least partly a genuine attempt to rationalize a system for co-ordinating services that previously had been far too poorly co-ordinated. The main changes brought about by the NHS and Community Care Act 1990 were as follows.

- It was the first attempt to treat community care as a distinct entity and to bring comprehensive change to this area of social policy. Above all, the Act was supposed to bring the social services and the NHS together under one umbrella – a co-ordinated set of services that would focus on care in the community.
- The core aim of the Act was to give people the choice, wherever possible, of being cared for in their own homes.
- Local authorities were required to draw up care plans for their areas. These plans were to include an overall assessment of clients' needs irrespective of the facilities or resources actually available. Assessment was supposed to be client-led or needs-led.

- The Act brought a full change towards the introduction of an internal market in social services. The community care reforms required local authority social service departments to act mainly as the purchasers of care services (though local authorities were to continue to provide services where it was not possible to find other providers, or where people with the highest levels of dependency were involved).

Thus, as in the health services, a **purchaser–provider split** was introduced, with local authorities being responsible for ensuring that care needs were being addressed and purchasing services accordingly. A diversity of other agencies, either private (for-profit) or voluntary (non-profit) increasingly fulfil the role of providing services and engaging in face-to-face work with service users and their families.

Sometimes the phrases ***welfare pluralism and mixed economy of care*** are used to describe these arrangements, as the following example illustrates. Gertrude is 91 years old. She lives alone and has recently had a fractured elbow, following a fall which required hospital treatment. Following hospital treatment, she has now returned home. Five spheres of welfare contribute to Gertrude's care, as illustrated in Figure 12.1.

However, it would probably be more accurate to view the changes brought about by the 1990 Act as the introduction of a ***social care market*** (Wistow et al. 1994: 2). This is because the whole picture has been changed, rather than parts of community care

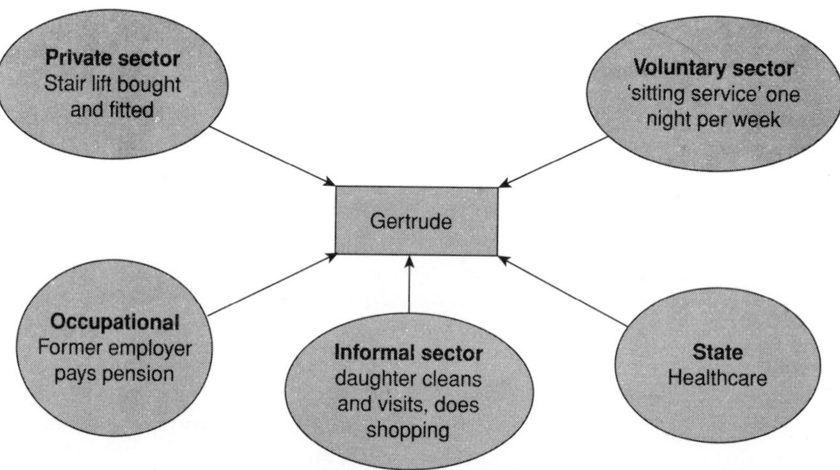

Figure 12.1 The mixed economy of care

remaining as islands of publicly run services. *All* services provided in the community, including local authority services, are now thought of in market terms.

Another central aim of the community care reforms was to establish **care management**. Care managers' responsibility is to draw up tailor-made 'care packages' for individual service users. The care manager is someone who will set targets and priorities, deciding who will get a service and what the aims of service provision are. These decisions are said to be based upon need, but as earlier chapters have illustrated defining need is a complex and difficult process (see Chapter 2). They are supposed to plan and manage the delivery of services to avoid duplication, or inefficient overlaps in services, or gaps in provision of care.

Another key change to be brought about by the 1990 Act was the return to local authorities of the power to decide who will receive state-supported long-term care in institutional or residential settings. No longer were people able to claim social security benefits directly to pay for private residential home fees. Only those who are judged to be in need may enter a private or voluntary sector home at public expense. Other financial changes are currently being made (see later sections in the chapter) but prior to these, the 1990 Act had introduced a system that gave local authorities an incentive to place people in private or voluntary sector homes rather than in their own residential institutions. Where residents' incomes fell below the means-tested level and they were to be given support by the local authority, local authorities could recoup some of the 'hotel' (board and lodging) costs – but only if the residents were in private and voluntary sector homes. If local authorities' own homes were used, from 1993 the local authority had to meet the whole cost ('hotel' and 'care' costs) if the resident was unable to do so.

Thus the residential care market was rigged in favour of the private sector. This meant that the government was able to claim that it had not 'pulled the plug' on support for private home owners, who had previously been able to count on a steady flow of publicly (DSS) funded residents into their homes. The abruptness of the government's change of policy was also lessened by the decision that people already receiving social security payments for fees in 1990 could continue to do so under the old arrangements (that is, direct payment from the DSS).

Outcomes of the community care reforms: the early years

Two main impressions of the early years of community care stand out. The first was the lack of any clear public endorsement or popular acclaim for the policy. If the new community care arrangements were successful, they were a very quiet success. Lack of public support for community care was also seriously weakened by isolated cases of attacks by dangerous mentally ill people on others. Though few and far between, these cases tragically resulted in deaths and injuries, both to the patients themselves and to unsuspecting members of the public. They caused headline news and public dismay about the ways in which dangerous patients had been discharged from hospital without any firm arrangements for managing their care or monitoring their behaviour.

The other main impression was of widespread dissatisfaction with the gap between the official rhetoric of community care as a needs-led policy and the reality of stringent controls on the resources available for home care and other community services. As deinstitutionalization gained pace in the 1990s, local authority social service departments were faced with rapidly rising bills for services to people who would have previously stayed in hospitals (and whose care would have been met by the NHS) or other long-stay institutions. As a result, they had little choice but to ration provision to service users, mainly older people, who had previously been eligible for a range of domiciliary services such as meals on wheels, lunch clubs and home care at relatively low cost Box 12.4 provides an example of the effects of these policy changes.

Financial constraints on local authorities and the effects of a social care market meant that many individual service users faced increased charges for home care and other services as the community care reforms took effect. Charges present a particular hardship to older people whose incomes fall just above the level at which they are eligible for

Box 12.4 Policy changes and the example of Gloucestershire County Council

Gloucestershire County Council sent out a standard letter withdrawing services from a block of service users (Thompson and Dobson 1995). In a high court case in 1995, five pensioners won a test case on this action and, as a result, local authorities may no longer cut community care services indiscriminately. However, the court judgment also ruled that local authorities 'can and ought to take resources into account both in the assessment of need and the provision of services' (Thompson and Dobson 1995: 20). As a result of this and other test cases affecting local authority responsibilities, local authorities must honour existing decisions to provide community services once needs have been assessed. However, if an authority is faced with a shortfall in resources, it is quite within its rights to re-assess individuals' needs and withdraw services, even though it is forbidden to send out a standard letter to whole groups, as in Gloucestershire.

social security assistance. An older person looking after a severely disabled spouse, for instance, might have to struggle along with a minimum of home care because a few more hours of help each week would be too expensive.

Other aspects of community care reform caused concern in the early years. For instance, there was a major concern that the goal of providing consumer choice from a variety of providers was not being addressed. The new community care policy seemed to put more consumer power in the hands of care managers and their superiors than in clients' hands. This shortcoming paralleled the health reforms, and the way in which they led to GPs and other doctors making 'consumer' choices on behalf of the patient, rather than patients themselves. These choices also may be limited under the constraints of existing services and welfare provision. Complete Activity 12.3, which will illustrate the difficulties of meeting the needs of those requiring care, and the implications of being a carer.

Activity 12.3 should have helped you to explore the complexities of care provision, and the implications for those involved in caring. Under the 1990 Act consumer complaints procedures were instituted by social service departments enabling individuals to complain in relation to care. However, these procedures vary in their effectiveness and still have a long way to go before they are even known about by the majority of service users (Dean and Hartley 1995).

Activity 12.3 The lived experience of care

Use the Internet to access and watch the following short video clips, available at www.bbc.co.uk/learningzone/clips:

- Clip 5624: Community Care for the elderly
- Clip 5623: Meeting older people's health needs
- Clip 7334: Caring for a Wife with Alzheimer's

1. From these clips what do you see as the most significant issues with the provision of care?
2. Is current policy meeting the complex needs of the many people requiring care?
3. What do you think will be the issues in social care that will challenge future policy-making?

Also, being able to make individual complaints about existing services is not the same as being able to participate in policy-making or in decisions about changing the direction, approach or content of services. Involvement of service users in planning community care in the early 1990s was minimal, according to Henwood (1995a).

However, government rhetoric about consumer choice and empowerment set up certain expectations and demands in the public mind, and interestingly is being repeated in Coalition Government policy at the time of writing. As the pressures on community care resources increased significantly after 1993, these demands and contradictions in the policy had to be managed largely by local authorities. To many older people, for instance, the levying of relatively high charges for community care services represented a betrayal of welfare state values, and a withdrawal of care that many had supposed would be provided free at the point of use.

While conflicts over lack of resources and charges for services represent important issues, though, it is possible in some ways to overstate the amount of change directly brought about by community care policy in the first few years of implementation. As Henwood concluded, community care reforms brought greater flexibility in service provision and 'perhaps an improvement on past practice', though two years after implementation the changes were 'still only marginal' (1995a: 18). The reformed system resulted in mixed results, as Table 12.2 illustrates.

Table 12.2: Community care policy outcomes

Individuals affected	**Outcomes**
Carers	• The Carers' National Association (Warner 1995) reported disappointment in carers' experiences of the reformed system of community care. • A Carers' National Association survey in 1994 showed that only 13 per cent of carers had received a separate assessment of their needs (Brindle 1995). • Many reported that they had never seen or had an opportunity to discuss a written assessment of the person they were caring for. • In general, carers did not appear to be treated as equal partners in the process of making decisions about community care plans. • Overall, the severe financial problems that local authorities faced from the outset hindered any substantial improvements for carers.
Care managers and other service providers	• In one survey of 600 care managers, Marchant (1995) found mixed attitudes to the community care reforms rather than widespread disillusion or collapse of morale. The survey also found evidence of considerable levels of stress among care managers as a result of budget cuts and financial restraints. • The survey also showed an increase in administrative work as a result of the implementation of the community care reforms. Stress results not only from form-filling but also from the restriction in opportunities for helping people in the direct, personal way that many social service employees had joined their profession to do.
Partnership working	• Henwood (1995b) noted some improvement in joint working between social service departments and health authorities. • Significant difficulties in managing care across the health and social care divide remained, however. This was especially so where hospitals had increased pressure on community services by altering discharge policies without telling social service and community health agencies. • Problems also remained in the negotiations between community health service providers and home care providers on the matter of 'who does what' when caring for people in their homes.

Overall, as Table 12.2 demonstrates, the reforms introduced some new complications and showed up the differences between the health and social services in their skills and cultures. These were patently too deeply entrenched to be transformed by a few years of community care reform, and the early stumbling blocks to 'joined-up working' were to prove to be of lasting significance. Therefore, the reforms shifted costs and responsibility in relation to the provision of care, affected all of those involved in providing services and of course had implications for those in receipt of care.

Social care and social services after 1997: New Labour and the Coalition Government; continued policy directions

The New Labour Government of Tony Blair elected in 1997 inherited the institutional framework for social care just described and continued with it. However, Labour did attempt to put their own stamp on policy. Social care, or community care, and the social services saw a large number of new initiatives. Changes under the New Labour Government included:

- New arrangements for the joint working of social and healthcare services and the provision of social care in the community through care trusts.
- The development of a social services performance framework and a new emphasis on standards of care.
- A *divergence* of policies in England, Scotland and Wales on paying for residential care and care in nursing homes.
- A shake-up of the regulation and training of social workers.
- Measures to give service users a greater say in the delivery of services – for instance through the development of the 'direct payments' scheme introduced by the Conservatives. This allows users of services or their carers to apply to their local authority to be paid directly for the services they need; they then take responsibility for engaging and paying for home care or other services themselves.

There were other important changes to the examples mentioned above, and a stream of reports, guidance and training packs from the Department of Health on a host of topics in the area of social care. Labour's key focus was about modernizing social services.

Modernizing social services

Labour's thinking on social care was contained in its White Paper of 1998, *Modernising Social Services* (DoH 1998a), one of a number of policy statements in the health and social care field that appeared early on in the government's first term. This identified and listed a number of problems with Labour's inheritance and expressed a commitment to dealing with these. Most of these problems – abuse and neglect of vulnerable adults, poor interagency co-ordination, service-led rather than individualized needs-led provision, territorial inconsistency in eligibility and care standards, inefficiency – were of long standing and even predated the Thatcher and Major governments.

New Labour's policy continued with the broad framework for community care built by the Conservatives in the NHS and Community Care Act 1990. The 'social market' was retained, and there was no attempt to return to the days when local authorities were the main providers of social care. The trend towards privatization of social care simply continued.

Labour preferred to talk about 'social' care rather than community care and, after election to power in 1997, portrayed the Conservatives' approach to community care as a discredited one. But on balance New Labour policies tried to shore up an inadequate community care system rather than replacing it with a different approach. Despite the policy discourse and rhetoric, therefore, the inherited framework of values and broad policy goals was maintained. In fact social and community care is an area of social policy which, arguably, exhibits a higher degree of party-political consensus than any other. Thus, it should not be surprising to read that the Coalition has continued in a similar vein although they have been faced with a different economic situation.

Social services expenditure

This actually increased under New Labour, with Frank Dobson, then Health Secretary, announcing that an extra £700 million would be spent on care services from 1998 until 2001. Though this was a substantial increase it represented only about one-fifteenth of the total (between £10 billion and £11 billion) spent annually on community care and social services, and was seen as disappointing and inadequate by mental health charities such as the National Schizophrenia Fellowship (Brindle 1998).

Moreover, this extra money was directed towards an increase in the number of beds in secure units for mentally ill people rather than to care 'in the community'. The strategy included assertive 'outreach teams' with new legal powers to detain mentally unstable people thought to be a risk to others. Much of the impetus for this policy came from public concern about the killings of Lin and Megan Russell in 1996 by Michael Stone, a man with a personality disorder previously considered untreatable and highly dangerous, who had been discharged from hospital to live in 'the community'. Concerns such as these are still prominent in current debates about failures in community care.

The prime concern of government was, some argued, less focused on finding the right mix of services for mentally ill people or others in need of care than on public safety and the government's credibility. Organizations defending civil liberties, for instance, were concerned about the new legal powers brought in by government to enforce treatment of people with mental disorders (Brindle 1998). Others were concerned about the purse strings that came with the extra money, because central government was to retain control of a substantial amount of the additional £700 million.

Expenditure on social care is substantial, and this level of spending coupled with the economic problems of the country has resulted in the Coalition Government revisiting the costs of this provision. At the time of writing, the Coalition Government was indicating that changes will be taking place, but was yet to provide full details.

Regulation, monitoring and inspection

The theme of increasing regulation and supervision of local services from the centre was continued by New Labour in the Care Standards Act 2000. This legislation was a product of the 1998 *Modernising Social Services* White Paper's concern to establish national, common standards in all branches of social and residential care (DoH 1998a). At this time, the Waterhouse report (2000) on long-term physical and sexual abuse of young people in residential homes in North Wales in the 1970s was being prepared. This report recommended improvements in the inspection of children's homes and young people's residential units, some of which had been 'hidden' from effective supervision in the local authority care system.

The main change brought about by the Care Standards Act 2000 was a separation of *inspection* of social services (which had formerly been in the hands of local authorities, but with independent checks by the Social Services Inspectorate) from their *provision* by local authorities and other bodies. The Act introduced an independent watchdog, the National Care Standards Commission, which is responsible for inspection of social services in England. There are equivalent bodies in Northern Ireland, Scotland and Wales (see Chapter 13). The Care Standards Commission works through local and regional offices and conducts inspections of social services for children and child protection, private and voluntary health care (for example, in nursing homes), home care and residential care services for older people, and services for adults with disabilities and other needs.

The 2000 Act also set up a General Care Council in England – again with equivalents in the other countries of the UK. These regulatory councils oversee the education and training of professionals (social workers) and other care workers, deal with matters of professional misconduct, and apply a code of conduct. This measure reflects – among other things – government concern about the abuse of young people and other service users in care and has tried to establish a new framework for making sure that serious abuse and inefficient supervision are reduced to a minimum.

The need for improvement in the supervision of social and community health services was underlined in the same year as the Care Standards Act by the tragic case of Victoria Climbié – a young girl who was brought to live in London, via France, from the Ivory Coast. Victoria was murdered after months of physical abuse and mental torture by her great-aunt, Marie-Thérèse Kauao, and Carl Manning, Kauao's partner. However, the lesson of this case seemed to be not only that tougher regulation of social and health services is required, but also that inadequate levels of staffing, support services and the organizational capacity of the local authority (in this case Haringey, in London) are also key to a full understanding of failures in care. There were many other reasons for the failure to detect and take action against the terrible abuse that Victoria suffered, such as a failure of the health practitioners who treated the girl to follow up her case. But the fact that the social services department in Haringey was very stretched in terms of staffing and the supply of experienced social workers seems to have been a crucial factor.

There have been some more recent disappointing reports of mistreatment. Carter (2012) details the investigation of mistreatment and neglect of elderly patients at a residential nursing home in Lancaster. Similarly, there were many other reports of abuse that emerged in the media, and some shocking video footage of instances of mistreatment.

Given the spending cuts that have been made by the Coalition Government and the implications that this has for staffing and other resources there is a strong argument that the confidence and morale of social services workers will continue to decline, and that cases such as this, tragically, may not remain a thing of the past. Relatively low wages and salaries in social services and social care work deter would-be employees. But in addition, and perhaps more important, is the perception that this type of work means having to carry the can for the local authority or other employer, in a work environment where there is insufficient support and where services are often inadequate.

Reduction in funding of social services may result in lack of adequate support. However, tougher regulation and better training of social services staff might make a difference, though quick results are unlikely. Social care covers a disparate range of services managed in different ways and by many different agencies, and the total of workers employed in providing social care is huge.

The Coalition Government has made some amendments to community care policy in this area, as part of the Health and Social Care Act 2012. However, these amendments do not represent a significant change to previous regulatory arrangements.

Funding of long-term care

From the beginning of the 1980s to the end of the twentieth century, the availability of 'free' or publicly supported long-term care services in a person's own home was increasingly restricted to those in most need or people on low incomes. And once the system of direct payment of residential care fees from the DSS was abandoned at the end of the 1980s, a rising number of older people faced more stringent rationing of 'free' residential care by local authorities.

This is partly because many more people now have substantial savings than used to be the case in the past. More own houses and other property above the value of £23,250, which is currently the cut-off point above which those going into residential care or using other care services have to pay their own costs in full. Those owning property or capital less than this threshold were subject to means testing, which assessed the contribution that they had to make. The problem of having to sell one's house to pay for care was a very politically sensitive issue for governments that have traditionally stressed the virtues of home ownership and the individual's right to keep their property (see Chapter 11). This issue also touched the political nerves of both main parties because of the anomaly of residents of nursing homes having to pay for their nursing care. If a person is treated as a 'patient' in NHS facilities, all health and nursing care is provided free. But while one person could receive free NHS care, another with very similar needs but in a different location could be asked to pay the steep monthly fees of a private nursing home, which would not come under the NHS umbrella.

New Labour set up a Royal Commission to investigate the whole question. While some argue that this was a stalling device, the Royal Commission on Long Term Care, headed by Sir Stewart Sutherland (1999), did rethink the problematic distinction between health and social care, and re-label both as 'personal care'. The report also made a distinction between personal care on the one hand and, on the other, the living and housing costs to be met when disabled or older people are receiving long-term care (whether in their own homes or in residential or nursing homes). The recommendations from this were that all personal care costs should be met free of charge for everyone, irrespective of their incomes. However, the government rejected the Commission's main proposals. They claimed that the costs of providing free personal care to everyone who needed it, whether in their own homes or a residential setting, might be manageable in the short term, but in the future would represent too great a burden on the taxpayer and the welfare system. Significantly, however, the independence now enjoyed by the Scottish Parliament, as a result of devolution, allowed Scotland to decide to introduce a policy of paying for the long-term personal care costs of everyone in need (see Chapter 13).

The thorny questions of trying to determine what exactly 'nursing' care is, how it differs from 'social' or 'personal' care, and how much nursing a particular individual needs, were not solved but rather thrown into the limelight by this policy. Similarly, the Coalition Government recognized the need for reform in this area and tasked an independent body, the Dilnot Commission, to develop a plan to fund the spiralling costs of social care in later life. Given the issues discussed throughout this chapter, the report unsurprisingly called for urgent reform and made several recommendations. Complete Activity 12.4 to explore this report in more detail.

Activity 12.4 Exploring the Dilnot Commission

- Use the Internet to access www.dilnotcommission.dh.gov.uk. Here you can read the full detail of the recommendations provided by the report.
- Now use the Internet to search for media discussions, analysis and debate related to the report and the recommendations – what are the issues associated with this? Are the recommendations positive in relation to reforming the social care system?

The key recommendations of the report (as you should have read in activity) are as follows:

- Individuals' contributions towards their social care costs should be capped. After the cap is reached, individuals would be eligible for full state support. At the time of writing, the plan is to cap the amount an individual will have to pay at £75,000.
- The means-tested threshold, above which people are liable for their full care costs, should be increased.
- National eligibility criteria and assessments should be introduced to ensure greater consistency when examining need for social or personal care.
- All those who enter adulthood with care needs should be eligible for free state support immediately, rather than being subjected to a means test.

These reforms are justified as being a mechanism to develop a fairer system of care. The King's Fund (2011) offered a commentary about the Dilnot Commission recommendations as follows:

- The proposals to cap individual liability for the costs of care and to raise the upper threshold for the means test were described as positive in that they are an improvement when compared to the current system and will mean that people in every income group would be better off.
- The recommendation to align the assessment of disability benefits with the adult social care system, so that people experience a simpler and more streamlined service, was seen as an 'admirable goal'.
- The proposal to set national criteria for eligibility in relation to social care was also seen as positive as a way of reducing 'postcode lotteries' in funding social care.

The King's Fund (2011: 4) concludes by stating that 'The coalition agreement stated that the government understood the urgency of reforming the social care system. A year on, the need for reform is even more pressing. Where they have failed in the past, politicians from all parties must now seize the best opportunity in a generation to ensure that people can access the care and support they need in later life. With the number of over 85s set to double over the next 20 years, the question is not whether we can afford the Dilnot proposals but how can we afford not to.'

The health and social care divide

Labour sought to deal with the long-standing problem of divided health and social care responsibilities, which we have already referred to. Legislation in 1999 (Health Act) and 2001 (Health and Social Care Act) attempted to establish a framework for co-ordination. The latter marked a determined step by the government towards a unification of health (NHS) and social services (local authority) organizations. The aim was to provide a coherent framework of community care through the formation of care trusts. The Act also carried forward the government's intentions to provide 'free' nursing care.

These reforms received criticism at the time (see Morris 2003: 216) and arguably were not effective in tackling the health and social care divide. Ham et al. (2012) argue that the current health and social care delivery system has not been able to keep pace with the population's needs and expectations and that furthermore the policy tradition of incremental changes to existing models of care are not enough to address these challenges.

The Coalition Government has, however, continued with incremental reform. Their approach to funding is that of personalization and the use of personal budgets in which direct payments are made to those who need care. The aim of this approach is to provide individuals with more flexibility in how the services that they need are provided. Thus, some money now goes directly to individuals rather than social care services in order to facilitate greater choice and control as well as decision-making. The policy of direct payments began under the previous New Labour administration. The Coalition Government published a White Paper, *Caring for Our Future: Reforming Care and Support* in July 2012, and this committed to the use of direct payments for those living in residential care. Direct payments were already being used for those in receipt of community care as part of the personalization agenda.

The Coalition Government also introduced the Health and Social Care Act (2012), which includes some references to social care reform. However, much of this has been eclipsed by the key changes brought about by the restructuring of the NHS. Some minor improvements in care for specific groups such as older people might take place, but without improved funding this is unlikely (King's Fund 2011).

The future of social care

Whether the Coalition Government that gained office in 2010 is destined to be the one that finally solves the puzzle of how to bring together the distinctive sectors of health and social care, and forces them to work together effectively, is doubtful. The lessons of history demonstrate that integration will depend partly on better funding of the social care side of the equation. However, since the public spending climate has become much less favourable, there is evidence that current financial deficits among some NHS commissioners and providers are undermining social care provision. Scepticism has been expressed about the extent to which genuinely 'joined up' working between health and social care can be realized, given the apparent prioritization of the NHS and acute care.

Conclusions

You will recall that at the beginning of the chapter you were confronted with the idea of someone visiting us from the 1940s – someone who would be rather confused about the terms 'community care' and 'social care'. This person would want to know whether policies on 'care' and social services had brought genuine improvements or not. How far is 'care in the community' an ideological cloak masking a reduction in government commitment to public welfare services?

First, the balance of evidence discussed in this chapter suggests that, despite government rhetoric about community care being a needs-led policy, it is in fact resource-led. This does not mean that we should point the finger only at recent policy as a way of explaining why community care has become a way of saving public money. The history of community care from the 1950s onwards shows that there are long-standing pressures to deinstitutionalize care and to limit government commitments to providing services to people in their homes. More recent financial problems and demographic changes also present challenges for those making contemporary policy in this area.

However, it would also be wrong to tell our 1940s visitor that no improvements have come about as a result of community care policy. Just because policy has been driven more by underlying economic pressures than need does not mean that the *idea* of care in one's own home is a bad one. Pilot schemes of community care in many different settings and with different client groups have demonstrated clear advantages of care at home over care in institutional surroundings. However, it will also be recalled that the advantages are not always clear cut, and that they depend on levels of funding and the ability to negotiate a complex system. Community care can be 'cheaper and better' than residential care, but only when the transition to 'the community' is well managed, or when staying in one's own home is sufficiently well resourced.

The advantages of the market system of social care introduced in the 1990s and continued by both New Labour and the Coalition Government into the twenty-first century over the previous system of domiciliary care are much less clear. This seems to be the case whether one is looking at the market from the point of view of those who operate the system, or of service users and carers.

Just as much depends on finance and resources as it did in the days before the introduction of a social care market. As pointed out in this chapter, this area remains – in relation to social security, health, education and many other areas of government spending – the 'Cinderella' service. More sustained resourcing is needed, as well as reform. However, reform without commitment of extra resources continues to be the chosen path of each successive government.

It will be interesting to see how far the ideas of personalization and user empowerment will make a difference to those who are in need of care. However, despite changes to the ways in which funding is provided and services are paid for, it is unlikely these changes will transform the landscape of social care. They could reflect government concern to respond to the increasingly combative and consumerist attitude among service users and carers rather than begin genuine reforms. On the other hand, while empowerment can be portrayed as empty rhetoric, it can nevertheless be exploited to criticize the limitations of official policy.

Changes may also yet take place following on from the Dilnot Commission. This remains to be seen, as New Labour when in power simply rejected a previous Commission's proposals for a simplified system of funding personal care. Thus, at the time of writing, the degree to which some of the Coalition Government's more recent policy changes will improve matters remains to be seen. What is more evident, as far as the present situation of social services is concerned, are widespread strains in the system. For instance there are widespread problems in the recruitment and retention of social workers and social care staff. An adequate supply of residential and nursing care places for the future is seriously threatened. And the ability of some cash-strapped local authorities to deliver services to people in their own homes, except for those in extreme need of care, means that the goal of a fair and equal standard of good quality social care across the UK is still a distant one.

Our visitor from the 1940s would probably be left with the impression that something had been lost from the ideals of the welfare state that had been newly built in their decade. From a time in which the emphasis was on collective responsibility, mutual support and access to 'free' health care, they would find our contemporary emphasis on the idea of social care as a 'package' of services in a market very strange.

On the other hand, the 1940s were a time in which no one had anticipated just how much chronic illness would replace acute illness as the main burden of the NHS, or how the needs for long-term care in the population would have grown. There would also be one element of continuity, despite changing needs and changing social policies. Our visitor would find, in the continued willingness of millions of relatives and others to provide care, a strand of altruism and responsibility that linked their decade with ours.

Summary of key points

- Current community and social care policy has followed the same general direction since the 1970s irrespective of the government in power. The state moved towards the provision of community care rather than institutional care and promoted the role of the market in service provision in this area. Recent Coalition Government policy is yet to be evaluated but outcomes will depend on the extent of funding provided.
- Social changes and demographic trends such as an ageing population with more complex health needs mean that more social care will be needed, and thus costs will continue to rise significantly.
- Longstanding problems in community care remain such as the divide between health and social care and the relative neglect of the social care sector.

Key terms and concepts

care management
carer
community care
consumers (of care services)
day centre
deinstitutionalization
domiciliary care (home care)
emotional labour
empowerment
mixed economy of care
needs-led assessment
purchaser–provider split
residential care
sheltered housing
social care market
welfare pluralism

Suggestions for further reading

Barnes, M. (2012) *Care in Everyday Life: An Ethic of Care in Practice.* Bristol: Policy Press.

In this book Barnes argues for care as an essential value in private lives and public policies. She examines the importance of care to well-being and social justice and applies insights from feminist care ethics to care work, and care within personal relationships. She discusses 'stranger relationships', how we relate to the places in which we live, and the way in which public deliberation about social policy takes place. This book is an excellent insight into social policy and practice.

Glasby, J. (ed.) (2012) *Commissioning for Health and Well-Being: An Introduction.* Bristol: Policy Press.

Commissioning is now a key task for health and social care, particularly after changes in the policy arena implemented by the Coalition Government. Commissioning was given higher policy importance under New Labour, but is now fundamental. Thus, this book explores what commissioning is, where it has come from and where it might be taking us. With edited chapters from key contributors within health care, social care and local government the book is a good introduction to the commissioning cycle.

Glasby, J. (2012) *Understanding Health and Social Care.* 2nd edition. Bristol: Policy Press.

This book highlights key developments under both the UK New Labour (1997–2010) and Coalition (2010–) governments, focusing on the key policy and practice dilemmas facing community health and social services. The book details the origins of community health and social care, partnership working, user involvement and support for carers.

Grey, A.M. and Birrell, D. (2013) *Transforming Adult Social Care: Contemporary Policy and Practice.* Bristol: Policy Press.

The focus of this book is on the contemporary major themes in policy and provision such as personalization, integration, user participation, the cost of long-term care, risk and safeguarding, care quality and workforce issues. This is an up-to-date book that is critically written and accessible.

Means, R. and Smith, R. (1998) *From Poor Law to Community Care: The Development of Welfare Services for Elderly People 1939–1971.* Bristol: Policy Press.

This book examines the historical growth of welfare services from the outbreak of the Second World War through to the establishment of social services departments in 1971. The authors discuss changing perceptions of the needs of elderly people, the extent to which they have been a priority for resources and the possibilities for a policy which combines respect for elderly people with an avoidance of the exploitation of relatives. A good introduction to historical policy that underpins contemporary approaches.

It is also worth reading the weekly publication *Community Care*, which provides a lively journalistic overview of topical issues in the field of social care and social services.

13 Devolution and social policy

Key learning outcomes

By the end of this chapter you should:

- be able to understand what devolution is as well as the types of devolution that the UK has
- be able to identify the impact of devolution in a variety of policy sectors such as education and health
- be able to assess the significance of European Union Social policy for devolution in the constituent countries of the UK

Overview of the chapter

This chapter focuses on the creation of devolved governments of various types across the UK in Scotland, Wales and Northern Ireland (the last only briefly). Since 1999, devolution represents a historic change to the government and character of the UK. Its impact has been felt in many ways, and especially in the area of social policy and welfare, as this chapter illustrates. Nor has the impact of devolution been restricted to the countries with devolved administrations. Policy *divergence* from a standard 'UK model' in Northern Ireland, Scotland and Wales has increasingly had implications for social policy in England. As devolution takes effect, people in England have begun to realize that, in some cases, what they have been told is not desirable or cannot be implemented in their own country *is* being adopted or implemented in one or more of the other countries in the UK. The same, of course, is true for inhabitants of the devolved nations in relation to what is happening in England. Thus one way that social policy in England has gradually become distinctive is by default, as the other countries have tried out new arrangements, but England has also innovated in ways in which the other countries have not.

In education policy, for instance, the increase in tuition fees for higher education (see Chapter 8) applies to England but not Scotland, where Scottish students can complete an undergraduate degree without the need to pay fees. Thus other countries choose to continue with existing policies towards education or other services and, by remaining the same as they were, accentuate their differences from England.

In this chapter, further examples of the growing differences in health, education and social services between England, Northern Ireland, Scotland and Wales will be examined. The chapter will also illustrate the links between globalization and devolution. However, in the limited space available here, a comprehensive guide to all the distinctive policies and services in each country will not be provided. The chief aim of the chapter is to discuss the broad implications of devolution and its impact on social policy in the UK. Key examples illustrate the effects devolution seems to be having in different areas of welfare (such as education, health and social services) in the different countries of the UK. As devolution is a fast-changing area of government and politics, any detailed description of policies and services in the different countries dates very quickly – new policies are coming on stream at a rapid rate. To obtain updates on new policy developments, or to find details about particular policies or services, it is a good idea to consult official, annual publications by the devolved administrations or to consult their websites and other Internet sources.

What is devolution?

The term 'devolution' refers to a transfer of government powers to make laws and policy. In the case of the UK, this means a transfer and loss of certain powers and functions from the Westminster Parliament and the government in London, which are at the centre of the UK's administration.

Devolution can be thought of as a process of transferring power and responsibility *upwards* as well as *downwards*. Table 13.1 outlines the different transfer of power related to devolution.

Table 13.1 Transfer of power within devolution

Upwards transfer of power	Downwards transfer of power
• Upwards devolution involves giving up some of the independence of the nation-state. • The right to take certain important decisions is passed to a supranational or international organization such as the EU. By becoming a member of the EU in 1973, the UK Parliament agreed to regulation by EU laws and policies in key areas of economic and social life. Latterly, this has included wider areas of social policy.	• Devolution downwards has been achieved in recent years by other Acts of Parliament that have transferred a limited range of powers and responsibilities from Westminster to elected assemblies or parliaments in each of the constituent countries of the UK. • These legislatures are the Northern Ireland Assembly in Belfast, the Scottish Parliament in Edinburgh and the Welsh Assembly Government in Cardiff. • Devolution in Northern Ireland is more complex because it is related to the peace process. Thus, some policy areas are now devolved while others remain in the control of Westminster.

A case for elected regional assemblies in England has been made in the past, but despite support from New Labour for an elected assembly in the north-east of England, it was rejected in a referendum in 2004, effectively killing the issue at the time. The Coalition Government has also made changes in relation to regional administrations; for example, since 2012 many regional institutions will no longer exist, and their related funding streams were also closed down.

Though devolution has advanced significantly in the UK in recent years, a degree of self-rule in certain parts is not a new phenomenon. For instance, the Isle of Man and the Channel Islands (Jersey, Guernsey and other smaller islands) are not part of the UK. They are Crown Dependencies and, though the UK Parliament retains the right to legislate for them, they have their own legislatures and historic rights to follow independent policies in many important areas. These include not only separate taxation and economic policies but also distinctive social policies. For instance, in Guernsey and Jersey there are quite different arrangements for running health services from those which pertain to the NHS in England and other parts of the UK.

Scotland, in terms of its size and political distinctiveness, is perhaps an even more significant example of historic 'devolution'. Strictly speaking, however, the Act of Union 1707 that joined together the two royal families, parliaments and administrations of England and Scotland was supposed to be an equal partnership rather than devolution of power from Westminster to Edinburgh. In practice, as England became the leading industrial economy and London the centre of political power in the UK, the principle of equal partnership of two nations was smothered by English dominance. However, the terms of the Act of Union meant that Scotland was able to retain its own distinctive laws and legal system, and a distinctive (and some would say superior) education system. Further changes are also being considered.

Northern Ireland also represents an example of a historic devolution of power from Westminster to a locally elected government in the province. However, as mentioned in Table 13.1, Northern Ireland is a special case because of its troubled history. However, despite periods of direct rule from Westminster, it has long been recognized by the British government – since the splitting away of southern Ireland as the Irish Free State in 1922 – that because of its distinctive history, geography and social make-up Northern Ireland needs its own administration and electoral system.

What type of devolution does the UK have?

As Northern Ireland, Scotland and Wales developed substantially different historic relationships with England, and with the UK as a whole, the more recent devolution reforms have been grafted onto these different historical relationships and political differences. Consequently, the type of devolution that the UK has chosen is called **asymmetric devolution**. Complete the first activity of this chapter to explore the differences that devolution means across Northern Ireland, Scotland and Wales.

Activity 13.1 Asymmetric devolution across the UK

Use the Internet to access the BBC News website and the report 'Devolution: A beginner's guide' at http://news.bbc.co.uk/1/hi/uk_politics/election_2010/first_time_voter/8589835.stm.

1. Read the article and compare the devolved powers across the UK.
2. Scotland will have a referendum on independence in 2014 – take time to learn more about this by accessing 'Scottish independence: the essential guide' a report in the *Guardian* newspaper, available at www.guardian.co.uk/politics/scottish-independence-essential-guide. (By the time you are reading this book it may already be decided!)
3. Visit the Welsh National Assembly at www.assemblywales.org/index.htm and find the history of Welsh devolution.
4. What is your view on devolution – do you think that it is a positive or negative development? Make a list of the advantages and disadvantages of devolved administrations using the Internet to help you to explore this issue further.

Completing the learning activity will have helped you to understand asymmetric devolution in the UK. However, remember that **symmetric devolution** exists in some other countries. Symmetric devolution is a type of government in which the constitution grants the same powers to each of the devolved states or administrations. In such cases more or less the same rules govern each devolved administration in its relationship with central government – as in the USA, for instance, where a written constitution prescribes the distinctive responsibilities and powers of all the US states and the federal government.

Why did the UK decide to take the road of asymmetric devolution, rather than scrap the existing constitution and start again with a more symmetric approach? This is perhaps a question of more interest to historians and political scientists than to social policy analysts. However, it can be said with certainty that a change to 'symmetric' devolution would have been very far-reaching. It would almost certainly have led to the federal government of the United Kingdom. A federal state is one in which there is a separate federal government, and in which there is a state or provincial government for *every* region or major province. Thus, federal UK government would have automatically led to the setting up of a (state) government of England – or, more likely, the splitting up of England into state governments of different English regions. In addition, federal government would mean state governments in Wales, Scotland and Northern Ireland and a separate federal administration to govern the UK as a whole.

As far as the future development of social policy is concerned, the main implications of the asymmetric pattern of devolution chosen by the UK are illustrated in Box 13.1.

Box 13.1 The implications of asymmetric devolution within the UK

- The powers of the devolved administrations to make their own social policies vary, with the Scottish Parliament having the most independence and the Welsh Assembly Government the least.
- Even though some government responsibilities have been devolved, the British government and the Westminster Parliament have retained control of some of the most important functions of central government – notably taxation, National Insurance and defence. In these matters – the so-called 'reserved powers' – the government in London continues to exercise its control in the whole of the UK, though at the time of writing proposals were being considered to give the Welsh Assembly Government more powers to make its own laws.
- The election of members or representatives to each of the devolved assemblies or parliaments is based on systems of proportional representation. This has resulted in a more even distribution of seats in each of the devolved assemblies, according to the various political parties, than is the case at Westminster – where the traditional 'first past the post' method of election can lead to a large majority of seats for the winning party. Therefore, power sharing between parties and coalition politics are the hallmarks of government in Northern Ireland, Scotland and Wales. Power sharing is now occurring in England too under the Coalition Government and this has implications in any context in relation to decisions about key policy implementation. For example, in Scotland and Wales, coalition government by Labour and Liberal Democrat members has forced each administration to consider policies that were not the agreed policy of the previous Labour government in London (for example, a reversal of policies on higher education students' tuition fees in Scotland).

- In large measure, devolved politics is social politics or policy. Most of the policy-making activity of the devolved governments is concerned with health, education and other social policy areas. Important policy areas – foreign and defence policy and economic policy, for example – are wholly or mainly reserved to Westminster. (Note that social security policy has also not been devolved and remains a Westminster responsibility.) So in discussing the social policies of the devolved governments, we are in fact describing their main activities (Chaney and Drakeford 2004: 121).
- Social policy was to some extent devolved already, before the creation of the devolved assemblies. This is most obvious in the case of Northern Ireland, which existed as a devolved 'state within a state' with its own representative assembly – Stormont – from 1921 to 1972 and pursued a partially distinctive social policy path (incidentally illustrating the dangers of devolution, because to some extent social policy, for example, in relation to housing, was used as a tool to reinforce sectarian divisions and to disadvantage the Catholic and nationalist minority).

Devolution has many implications, as Box 13.1 clearly illustrates, and is related to historical policy development too. For example, the historical distinctiveness of Scottish education has already been noted. The Scottish Office was created in 1885 and the Welsh Office in 1964 as departments of Whitehall/Westminster government headed by secretaries of state; these agencies represented administrative rather than political devolution, but to some extent policies, for example in relation to health, were allowed to differ from the English model. It is sometimes hard, in reading some of the accounts of post-devolution social policy, to determine whether what is being described is some genuinely new departure or the continuation of trends and tendencies from the pre-devolution situation.

One further important point about the nature of devolution in the UK is that per capita public spending in Northern Ireland, Scotland and Wales has been significantly higher than in England. These imbalances in spending have a long history, beginning with the introduction of formula funding of Scottish expenditure in the 1890s, and have been permitted to grow incrementally thereafter from an initial baseline of equal spending. Formula funding for Northern Ireland and Wales was established in the 1930s and 1960s respectively, and became subject to similar processes of incremental upwards drift. The reasons for higher spending levels in the devolved nations are complex, having more to do with political expediency than with any principled approach to the sharing of resources. Past secretaries of state for Scotland have, for example, used the spectre of resurgent nationalism, secession and defence of the Union to wring more resources out of Whitehall and Westminster (McLean 2001: 431). In recent decades spending has been regulated by a central (UK) government funding formula introduced in 1978 by the Labour politician Joel Barnett, Chief Secretary to the Treasury 1974–9 – the 'Barnett formula' – which grants Scotland, Wales and Northern Ireland additional amounts of the UK's public money every year (Glennerster 2003: 190). In fact the purpose of the Barnett formula was not to redistribute resources from England to Scotland and the other nations but to equalize spending between England and the other nations, a purpose in which it has failed. The main social services affected by the Barnett formula are health and education. Social security, as a national service, is outside this framework. These spending inequalities have survived devolution and the creation of national assemblies and have come to look increasingly anomalous, particularly so in the case of Scotland, which was given a measure of tax-raising powers. The Barnett formula has been subjected to powerful criticism on various grounds, including inefficiency, inequity and perverse incentives, and critics have argued that it is unsustainable in the long run (McLean 2005: 356–7). The Blair government reiterated its commitment to the Barnett formula in 1997 while attempting to narrow the public spending gap between England and the other countries. Their attempts failed (see Hetherington 2001a: 1). More recently Conservative politicians called for a review of the formula, and its replacement with a system that is based upon need and thus is fairer (Kirkup 2012).

A sense of unfairness in England about the privileged status of Scotland, Wales and Northern Ireland as the 'big spenders' of the UK is not restricted to border regions. English discontent has spread more widely, taking two different forms. First, there have been calls for renewed efforts to narrow the spending gap between England and the remainder of the UK, and perhaps to abolish the Barnett formula. Second, a strong case has been made by those representing English regions to give them devolution and additional spending too. As it stands, current arrangements seem to discriminate against the more disadvantaged parts of England with declining industry and agriculture. Also, special financial incentives can be used in Wales, Scotland and Northern Ireland to attract new businesses, whereas such incentives are not available in regions such as the south-west or north-east of England.

Whether devolution in England and matched funding to new English regional governments will occur in the future is, however, very doubtful. As Bogdanor (2001) suggests, the kind of regional identity that would guarantee the development of regional assemblies and governments in England is not present in sufficient strength. Also, regional devolution in England would necessitate further local government reforms that have already been achieved in Scotland and Wales. However, as he concludes, these factors do not rule out the piecemeal development of devolution in England in the future – whereby one or several regions gain a measure of self-government, rather than the whole of England being subdivided into devolved regional governments.

There is also another point to bear in mind, when comparing public spending and social services in England with those in the other UK countries. Although the Barnett formula grants a higher amount of public money to Scotland, Wales and Northern Ireland overall, this does not mean that spending on a particular *service* or category of 'service user' is always higher in all the 'Celtic' countries.

Devolution and education policy

The education systems of Scotland and Northern Ireland have long followed their own paths. Devolution of education policy in these two examples has therefore built upon foundations that were already very different from those in English education. In Scotland particularly, much of the driving force behind support for the whole project of devolution was a determination to preserve Scottish distinctiveness in education.

In Wales, on the other hand, schools have traditionally been run on English lines, in terms of the structure of the school system, the curriculum and the system of administration. However, Welsh distinctiveness has long been apparent in the ethos and culture of the education system in Wales. This is particularly apparent in the teaching of the

Welsh language and literature, which used to occur in some, and now in all, primary and secondary schools (with some schools teaching entirely in the medium of Welsh). But Welsh distinctiveness is also demonstrated by the development of a nationwide, 'federal' university – the University of Wales – and in other significant ways such as a widespread commitment to the value of education, as manifested in traditions of adult education and a desire for learning.

However, of the three countries, Scotland had the most distinctive education system before devolution was agreed in 1998, as illustrated in Box 13.2.

Box 13.2 The distinctive education system in Scotland

- no statutory or centrally imposed national curriculum, along the lines introduced by the Education Act 1988 in England and Wales (see Chapter 8)
- its own examinations and qualifications system, leading to a broad curriculum of subjects or Scottish Highers (presently under review) – rather than to A-Level examinations, as in England and Wales
- an earlier school leaving age (17) for those completing the high school or secondary stage of education, and a tradition of four-year rather than three-year degree courses
- a significantly lower proportion of children being educated in private (fee-paying) schools, compared to England (though this is not distinctive in comparison with Northern Ireland and Wales, where the percentages of the privately educated is also low)
- a low level of church involvement in state schools compared with the rest of the UK

Starting from a base that was distinctively different from the rest of the UK, the Scottish Parliament has already introduced several reforms in education that have had significant repercussions beyond Scotland as well as within the country.

The first was to reverse the policy to introduce up-front tuition fees for higher education that had been brought in by New Labour in London. Increased fees have since been introduced following Coalition Government policy changes (see Chapter 8) and again Scotland has continued with its own approach, rather than following Westminster. The main argument for this continuation was that tuition fees are particularly discouraging to potential students from disadvantaged backgrounds, or families with no tradition of attending university. At the time of writing, students from Northern Ireland, England and Wales are paying around £9000 per year towards their tuition costs (though Welsh students may receive considerable subsidies or grants to reduce costs, depending on personal circumstance). Scottish students do not have to pay tuition fees before university courses are taken. Instead, graduates will have to contribute to a 'graduate endowment' scheme after they have graduated, but only if they earn over a certain amount. Some Scottish students will get all their tuition fees paid from public funds, following a means test.

Scotland also took a distinctive path in funding higher education students by introducing bursaries (grants). The bursaries payable to Scottish students replace part of the student loan and do not have to be repaid after graduation. In 2012, the maximum bursary was £2640 a year. It falls to £2163 a year for a household income of £22,000 and then down to zero for a household income over £34,195 a year. By reintroducing student grants for higher education students from less well-off backgrounds, Scotland was the first of the 'Celtic' countries to challenge UK government policy in this area, and thus provided a concrete example of what could be achieved through devolution. Welsh students too, as noted above, also have a different support package for those in higher education, with a tuition fee grant available from the devolved government irrespective of the location in which students choose to complete their studies. The Welsh government has also frozen tuition fees to a maximum of £9000 until 2015. Thus, higher education policy is arguably the area of greatest divergence (McLean 2005: 353).

English higher education policy diverged further from Welsh and Scottish policy with the introduction of so-called 'top-up' fees in England in 2006, and then subsequent increases in tuition fees introduced after the Browne review (2010). Although this is an England-only policy, there are implications for higher education in the devolved nations. No account was taken by English policy-makers of the possible consequences for Scotland and Wales – for example, under the Scottish government system, Scottish students and those from EU member states outside the UK have their fees paid, thus there have been increased numbers of students choosing to attend Scottish universities. There are also other significant, unforeseen, resource consequences. All this amounted to, in the words of one observer, 'quite a failure of government – of all four governments involved' (McLean 2005: 354).

A second major innovation in education policy in Scotland has been in relation to teachers' pay and work contracts. In 2001, the Scottish Executive (government) approved a pay increase for Scottish teachers of 23 per cent over three years, combined with a reduction in their working week to 35 hours. There is also a guarantee that primary school teachers will not have to spend more than 22.5 hours a week in front of their classes. These conditions remain the same at the time of writing.

Thus the changes in higher education fees policy and teachers' pay and working conditions illustrate the way that Scotland has struck out in its own direction. But Scottish distinctiveness in education is also being maintained by important decisions *not* to change in line with the direction English education is taking. Not only has the National Curriculum remained non-statutory, as mentioned above, but also the Scots decided not to follow the English system of SATs at ages 7, 11 and 14. As Slater (2001: 20) puts it, 'Despite the mania for testing south of the border, Scottish pupils still do not sit national tests until 14 or 15'. Similarly, the policy of the literacy hour centrally enforced on English schools has been ruled out in Scotland as being too much of an intrusion on professional freedom and the ability of Scottish teachers to decide for themselves how best to teach. And though there is a small number of specialist high schools and colleges in Scotland, the Scottish Executive has no plans to increase the number of this type of school.

Therefore, in significant ways Scottish education has been protected from the impact of the type of reform introduced by Mrs Thatcher's government in the 1980s and continued vigorously by both New Labour and the current Coalition Government more recently. As discussed in Chapter 8, recent education policy in England is characterized by the continued break-up of the comprehensive school system through expansion of the numbers of specialist and 'faith' schools, academies and constant scrutiny of schools' and teachers' performance. As Scotland has been able to turn its back on these changes, Scottish education policies offer a comparative test of the value of the English reforms. If the performance of the Scottish education system is at least as good as that in England, what does this tell us about the wisdom of the government's approach to education in England?

Before the impact of devolution can be assessed, however, education policy in Wales and Northern Ireland also needs to be put into the picture. The Welsh example is interesting because, despite the more limited powers of the National Assembly compared with the Scottish Parliament, considerable divergence from English education policy has already occurred since devolution became a reality in 1999. As in Scotland, much of this divergence is coming about because of Welsh decisions not to follow the English educational road. Though the Education Act 1988 led to the introduction of opted-out, grant-maintained schools (see Chapter 8) in Wales, there is no Welsh plan to continue to diversify the secondary school system, as in England. Wales will continue with the established system of comprehensive schools and there will be no encouragement to develop specialist schools and colleges. Similarly, and as in Scotland and Northern Ireland, the National Assembly for Wales has ruled out the idea of involving the private sector in running state education.

These are two major planks of English education policy. But education in Wales now differs from English practice in other ways too – for instance, in the decisions to suspend SATs, to abolish published league tables of school performance, and to abandon the system of literacy and numeracy training used in England (see summary in Table 13.2).

Table 13.2 Education in the UK: how countries compare

	England	Scotland	Wales	Northern Ireland
Private companies allowed to set up state schools	Yes	No	No	No
Specialist schools	Yes	No	No	No
Limit on teachers' working week	No	Yes	No	Yes
Performance-related pay for classroom teachers	Yes	No	Yes	No
Secondary league tables	Yes	Yes	No	No
Statutory curriculum	Yes	No	Yes	Yes
Primary school literacy and numeracy strategies	Yes	No	No	Yes
National tests for 11-year-olds	Yes	No	No	Yes
Selective education	Yes*	No	No	Yes
Class size limits for 7- to 11-year-olds	No	No	Yes	Yes

Note: *In some areas
Source: Slater (2001: 21). The information in Table 13.2 has been reproduced with kind permission of the *Times Educational Supplement.*

Complete Activity 13.2 to explore the implications of devolution within education policy across the UK.

Activity 13.2 The impact of differential educational approaches achieved via devolution

Use the Internet to access the following websites:

1. www.bbc.co.uk/news/education-17238298: a news report about the implications of proposed changes to the GCSE examination across the UK
2. http://news.bbc.co.uk/1/hi/education/2602201.stm: a news report about the Welsh approach to school education
3. www.bbc.co.uk/news/uk-scotland-15912106: a news report about Scottish educational standards
4. www.bbc.co.uk/news/uk-northern-ireland-21502780: a news report about education in Northern Ireland and issues with both standards and segregation

Now that you have read all of the news reports, consider the impact of devolved education policy – has it been positive in all respects for students in the countries with devolved governments? Does education in Scotland, Wales and Northern Ireland face generally the same problems and issues as in England?

Finally, in Northern Ireland there is also a mood of significant educational change and a widespread desire to set education policy in new, distinctive directions. However, unlike the changes envisaged in Wales and Scotland, the plans for education in Northern Ireland are deeply affected by the legacy of selective education in the province. In Northern Ireland, not only are most schools identified with having either a largely or wholly Catholic or Protestant intake of children, but also they are divided by a selective system of grammar and secondary schools. While the rest of the UK gradually introduced comprehensive education in the 1960s and 1970s, Northern Ireland did not. It has retained its long-standing system of selection, which includes a 'transfer test' at the age of 11 (the eleven-plus).

The Northern Irish system produces better GCSE and A-Level results than the education systems of England and Wales (Woodward 2001c). Despite this, however, leading opinion in Northern Ireland is now promoting the need to change to a non-selective – or at least a less selective – system. As Woodward points out, research commissioned for the Northern Ireland Assembly underlined the drawbacks of the old selective system. These include narrowing of the primary school curriculum (in order to focus on the selective examination at age 11), the biases in the test itself and underachievement among the 'failed' students in secondary schools.

The Northern Irish system differs from that of England in many other ways. As in the other 'Celtic' countries, there is currently no teacher shortage in Northern Ireland, for instance (Woodward 2001c: 7). Nor are the province's teachers affected by the interventions of Ofsted, the standards watchdog, which does not exist in any of the three 'Celtic' countries. Also, as in Wales and Scotland, Northern Ireland has very few independent or private schools – it has an almost entirely state-run education system. All these characteristics will have an impact on the progress of Northern Ireland's education reform programme.

However, setting aside these factors, the educational debates in the rest of the UK can seem irrelevant in Northern Ireland. The success or otherwise of the proposed educational reforms there still depends a great deal on changes to historical segregation and the ability of the Northern Ireland Assembly to work out a widely accepted set of policies.

Devolution: health and social care

There is a long-running public debate in the UK about the problems of the NHS and the funding of social care. The Coalition Government has intensified this debate following recent policy changes in this area (see Chapter 10). Problems such as waiting lists for treatment, adequate care for older patients and the doctor shortages are increasingly seen not only as a comment on the NHS and social care system, but also as a test of the government's general credibility.

The health systems of the four devolved nations have always been slightly different in terms of policy emphasis, although sharing the same basic features. The NHS was fundamentally the same in all countries, although, as noted above, the English system is less generously financed than the rest (Ham 2004: 102). Particular areas of policy, such as public health and community care have been allowed to vary, and administrative structures relating to, for example, social care, have differed from the English model. It is noteworthy, however, that the Thatcher–Major reforms of the NHS implemented in 1991 were imposed on the whole of the UK.

In February 2002 the BBC conducted an opinion survey to find out the public's views on priorities in health and social care. Interestingly, the goal of providing 'free' care to older people – whether in a hospital, nursing home or residential home – topped the poll by a wide margin. This was significant for two reasons. First, it showed that, though the government has put a higher priority on health service spending than on social services (see Chapter 12), public attitudes in England as well as the rest of the UK reflect continued concern about both halves of the health and social care equation. There is a surprisingly large amount of public support for attending to the 'social' as well as the 'health' care needs of an ageing population. Second, public endorsement of 'free' care showed widespread support for a policy that is now developed in both Scotland and Wales.

As in education policy, Scotland's recent policies on social care show how devolution is leading, in some ways, to a return to a traditional, universalistic welfare state philosophy. In Scotland it has been agreed that all older people will be entitled to free personal care if they are in need of it in their own homes, or in residential or nursing home facilities. Personal care costs will include such items as cooking and laundry costs, or 'hotel' costs in residential homes. In addition, both the Scottish and Welsh NHS offer free prescriptions, and in Wales there is free hospital car parking. Both countries have largely rejected the market and the private sector (Brimelow 2011).

Historically, the New Labour government in London rejected a Royal Commission's key recommendation (see Chapter 12; see also Sutherland 1999) that personal care should be provided 'free' to all older people in the UK. It was agreed by the government in London that *nursing* care will be provided free of charge – though, as noted in Chapter 12, this has led to continuing wrangles over what counts as 'nursing' and as 'social' care in different areas.

In terms of public image and approval, then, the Scottish policy to provide free personal (that is, social and nursing) care to everyone who needs it seems to win hands down when compared with the niggardly and variable means-tested approach in England. From July 2002 there were no charges for personal care in Scottish older people's own homes, and free nursing care is provided whether the patient is at home or in a care home. However, there have been questions recently raised about whether this is a sustainable approach (BBC News Scotland 2012).

And though this policy met with a very positive response from the public, it is worth noting that it is an example of 'middle-class welfare state' provision. The main beneficiaries are relatively well-off older people who own substantial property or have above-average savings and retirement incomes. 'Free' personal care helps this group of older people to avoid using their own money or assets to pay for their care. Older people living on low incomes and with fewer assets would not have had to pay means-tested care costs under the former system in Scotland. Therefore a policy that has given considerable political and electoral rewards to the politicians who have introduced it, and a policy that *appears* to promote equality and fairness, in fact subsidizes the care costs of affluent older people.

The Scottish policy on long-term care has been favourably reviewed (Scottish Assembly Health Committee 2006). Policy in England on long-term care of older people has more recently been in the melting pot (see Chapter 12). Recent analysis and recommendations on social care (which of course may not be adopted by the government), differ from the Scottish policy, although they are interpretable as a movement in a Scottish direction. It is, however, not clear that the government's decision to launch a policy review owes anything to the Scottish experience.

In Wales there has also been considerable support in the National Assembly for policies on health and social care that are distinctively different from those in England, and which will seek to address the hardship faced by some older people when faced with care costs. The National Assembly does not have, however, either the degree of financial independence or the level of resources that are at the disposal of the Scottish Parliament. The way that nursing care costs are met is already different in Wales. A standard amount is payable to older people in care to help meet these costs. In England, a more complicated – and, some suggest, a less fair – system operates. Those qualifying for means-tested help to pay for nursing care are paid according to their level of need. As a result, residents of a single residential or nursing home in England can find that relatively small and sometimes arbitrary differences in their nursing care needs have led to marked differences in the amounts of money they receive (or rather that the home receives on their behalf). Managers of residential and nursing homes find the system difficult to cope with (again see Chapter 12). The example of the Welsh solution to this problem – a flat-rate sum to help people with nursing-care costs – shows how devolution is beginning to develop opportunities to experiment with different ways of *implementing* or *administering* policies, as well as opportunities to make different policies in the first place.

An interesting Welsh attempt to diverge from English policy by eliminating all home care charges for disabled people – a commitment contained in the 2003 Welsh Labour manifesto – was abandoned in 2006 amid considerable recrimination. A less generous package of support, which nevertheless diverges from English policy, was provided (Constitution Unit 2006: 17–18). Interestingly, Welsh politicians also clashed with David Cameron, the Prime Minister, during the development of the Health and Social Care Bill, which is now being implemented (Williamson 2012).

However, the more significant changes resulting from devolution will come from divergence in *policy* rather than as a result of different ways of interpreting or implementing common UK policies. In this respect the devolution of health and social care policy, like education, is building on rather different foundations in each of the 'Celtic' countries.

One recent observer of health politics in the UK has suggested that the style of politics has started to vary among the four countries, and, among the three devolved nations, to revert to pre-Thatcher styles of policy-making, which can be characterized as *professionalism* in Scotland, *markets* in England, *localism* in Wales and *permissive managerialism* in Northern Ireland (Greer 2004: 78, 156, 193; McLean 2005: 354–5).

So a *status quo* established under the Thatcher and Major governments regarding the organization of the NHS has dissolved; all four systems have been in movement, the English one taking a more radical direction, the others in various ways trying to put the clock back.

In Scotland, however, it is perhaps more significant that the NHS is beginning to seem to be distinctively different from the NHS in England and Wales because the Scottish system is not being reorganized at the same pace or on the same scale as it is in England and Wales. The Scottish Executive has decided to use the independence that it has to avoid many of the upheavals and changes being planned south of the border.

Recent NHS reforms in England following on from the Health and Social Care Act (2011) does not apply to the devolved nations. However, the changes that result from the implementation of this policy will affect some areas of the devolved nations because some services cross borders, such as the blood transfusion service, which crosses into north Wales. Furthermore, some services such as organ donation cover the entirety of UK, thus a more fragmented English NHS will impact in some senses across all devolved countries (Unison 2012).

Historically in Scotland and the other devolved nations the NHS has not been pushed so vigorously towards the kind of changes that are currently taking place in the UK. However, the future may not be as different as it currently seems within the devolved nations because in the past there have been some attempts to import English market models to the devolved nations. These include the implementation of Independent Sector Treatment Centres in Scotland and payment by results in Northern Ireland (Unison 2012). For the moment, however, the structure and organization of health care under the badge of the NHS remains different in each devolved country. Table 13.3 outlines these differences.

Table 13.3 The differences in the four UK NHS systems

Country	NHS structure and organization
Scotland	• Current provision of health care is the responsibility of 14 geographically based local NHS Boards and a number of National Special Health Boards. • There are proposals further the integration of health and social care for services to adults and children but these have yet to be realized. • NHS Scotland has a unique system of employee relations that is more positive than the existing English approach.
Wales	• The NHS in Wales is made up of seven Local Health Boards who plan, secure and deliver healthcare services across their own designated areas. • A National Advisory Board holds the responsibility for providing independent advice to the Minister for Health and Social Services. • In 2011, a five-year vision for the NHS in Wales was published (Welsh Government 2011). Currently service provision is under review with a future called for in which there will be greater emphasis on community provision of health services, as well as redesign of current hospital provision.
Northern Ireland	• The system in Northern Ireland differs from the rest of the UK in that it covers both health and social care. • The Northern Ireland Executive's Health Department is organized under a Permanent Secretary into several groups and one agency. • In the wake of recent budget cuts, service provision has been revisited and now there is a stronger emphasis on privatization.

Table 13.3 illustrates some differences in the structural organization of the NHS across the devolved nations. Currently there is significant restructuring happening in the English NHS which is not applicable to the devolved nations. However, this does not mean that there is no change in the devolved nations' healthcare systems. One of the main effects of devolution appears to be the instigation of a wider range of local initiatives and health service developments than might have otherwise occurred. In both Scotland and Northern Ireland (where health and social services were grouped together long ago), there have been innovations in the care of people with mental health problems, for instance. There have also been targeted preventive strategies to improve the poor health record in both countries in terms of heart disease and cancer, with additional money for these programmes from the devolved administrations.

In Wales, however, progress in developing such initiatives has been somewhat hampered by the task of reorganizing the structure of the NHS. Because of its more limited independence than that of the Scottish Parliament, the National Assembly in Wales has historically had to provide a Welsh equivalent to the main NHS reforms being carried out in England. Unlike England, however, the NHS in Wales was structured around local health boards rather than primary care groups, which are now in the process of being restructured.

However, there are signs that devolution has encouraged innovations and distinctive changes in Wales despite problems with reorganization. For instance, Wales is distinctive in instituting a Children's Commissioner – a role similar to that of an 'ombudsman' who can monitor the quality and effectiveness of educational, health and social services for children, respond to individual cases of abuse, mistreatment or injustice, and protect children's interests generally. Also, Wales has taken innovative steps in several other ways – for instance, in developing unified budgets for the provision of social, educational and health services for children, and more generally in terms of building statutory (that is, legally required) partnerships between the National Assembly, the voluntary sector and business organizations. These partnerships are intended to build a foundation for further developments in urban renewal and employment in poorer communities, as well as health improvement and social or community development.

Another interesting health policy divergence between Wales and England was the Welsh Assembly Government's decision in 2005 to detach itself from NICE requirements. NICE is the body established in 1999 to assess new medical technology and make recommendations about its use. The reasons for this withdrawal are not clear, but the Assembly Government did state that it will take account of NICE recommendations, but does not wish to be bound by them. Some concern has been expressed by Assembly members that the decision may result in the return of so-called 'postcode rationing', to the detriment of Welsh patients (Constitution Unit 2005c: 24).

Some recent commentaries on devolved health policy suggest that a degree of scepticism about the benefits of devolution hitherto may be in order. Bevan et al. (2010) illustrate that, historically, Scotland, Wales and Northern Ireland have had higher levels of funding per capita for NHS care than England. However, this has not led to improved outcomes within the devolved nations. Bevan et al.'s (2010) analysis suggests that the NHS in England spends less on health care and has fewer doctors, nurses and managers per head of population than the health services in the devolved countries, but that it is making better use of the resources it has in terms of delivering higher levels of activity, crude productivity of its staff, and lower waiting times.

The end of British social policy? The impact of devolution and of the EU

As this brief survey of examples of recent social policy in Northern Ireland, Scotland and Wales has shown, there are now clearly detectable trends in the development of devolution in the UK. Some of the changes are relatively small scale and subtle. They have involved behind-the-scenes changes in management or funding arrangements rather than obvious or far-reaching changes in the way welfare or health services are provided or experienced by service users. But all these relatively minor changes are mounting up, and are leading to a gradual divergence of the social policies of England and the three 'Celtic' countries. In time, important social institutions – the NHS, social services, the education system – that used to share at least parts of a common 'national' (British) identity may lose much of that common identity. The NHS and the social services, for instance, may begin to look different in the different parts of the UK, and they will have increasingly different patterns of provision, goals and ways of working.

In summing up the impact of devolution, however, some caution is needed before reaching the conclusion that a very diverse patchwork of social policies and social services will develop across the English regions, and between Wales, Northern Ireland and Scotland. Box 13.3 summarizes the reasons for this.

Box 13.3 The impact of devolution debated

- Some distinctively different policies have been launched, especially in Scotland, in such areas as higher education and funding of care for older people. But in other ways devolution seems to be having a significant braking effect on changes that would have come about if the 'Celtic' countries had had to follow the English lead. Examples of this are rejecting the involvement of the private sector in some sectors despite this occurring within England, or rejecting school league tables.
- Second, devolution in the UK is asymmetrical. Only Scotland has enough independence to become a semi-autonomous country within the UK, and currently only Scotland wishes to become independent. The National Assembly for Wales can pass only **secondary legislation** (though at the time of writing some new powers to introduce **primary legislation** had been granted) and has none of the tax-varying powers of the Scottish Parliament. The Northern Ireland Assembly has the potential to develop a considerable degree of autonomy for the province but the troubled political history of Northern Ireland casts doubt on how quickly any radically new policies could be agreed by the different sides of the community. It would be wrong to be too optimistic about the Northern Ireland Assembly given the difficulties in forming a government with a working majority.
- One of the main ways in which devolution has an impact is by *example*. As discussed in this chapter, for instance, the examples of the reintroduction of student maintenance grants in Scotland, or of free personal care for older people in Scotland, seem to show in both a concrete and obvious way that 'devolution works'. One argument is that people in one country will draw unfavourable conclusions about their own social policies from the social progress and improvements in welfare being made in neighbouring countries. However, there are some flaws in this argument. They boil down to a question of whether people in one country will notice what is happening in the other countries. In population terms, England is the giant of the group. Not surprisingly, English politicians and policy-makers tend to be

preoccupied with the much larger population on their own doorstep, or in their own regions, than they are with developments in what can be seen, ethnocentrically, as the 'Celtic margins'. Historically, the English have dominated the Union, and to this day there is still some cultural distance – increased by national differences in newspapers, radio and television output – between English people on the one hand, and Scottish, Welsh and Northern Irish people on the other. Therefore even if the growing distinctiveness of the 'Celtic' countries in politics and social affairs is going to be noticed, it is not yet clear what the impact of this will be. One possibility is that, rather than demand that similar welfare policies to those in Scotland, Wales or Northern Ireland are developed in England, the English will demand the scrapping of the Barnett formula.

- It is commonly assumed that devolution will bring increasing, never-ending divergence in social policy, not only between England and the rest of the UK but also between the three main 'Celtic' countries. Taken to its logical limits, this argument would suggest that future differences between England, Scotland, Wales and Northern Ireland will be as marked as between, say, the social welfare systems of Sweden, Norway, Denmark and Finland today. Increasing divergence is not inevitable, however, for a number of reasons. First, the 'Celtic' countries might converge on approximately similar solutions and policies for common issues and problems – there is already a considerable amount of 'policy learning' and sharing of experience among the three devolved administrations. Second, the impact of devolution might be one of allowing one of the countries in the UK to experiment with certain limited areas of social policy but with the end result that the others also adopt the same kind of innovation. For instance, England and Wales could 'converge' on some of the developments pioneered in Scotland, rather than forging ahead with increasingly different social policies.

None of the reasons outlined in Box 13.3 means that it is certain that devolution will have a limited impact on social policy in the UK. They are simply reasons for exercising caution about any claims that devolution will inevitably and completely transform the map of British social policy.

The significance of the EU

As mentioned at the start of this chapter, devolution can be seen as the passing of state power and responsibility 'upwards' as well as 'downwards' to devolved administrations, as in Scotland, Wales and Northern Ireland. Some have argued that the ceding of authority by the UK government and Parliament to the EU is at least as significant as the recent devolution of power to the 'Celtic' countries of the UK. Is the Westminster Parliament, and British governments led by prime ministers in London, going to be increasingly powerless and irrelevant in the future, when it comes to deciding important social issues? Whether or not the UK should stay in the European Union is a hotly debated political topic, with frequent calls from some quarters for a referendum on the question. The Coalition Government has yet to make a clear decision about this, though at the time of writing the Prime Minister, David Cameron, has promised that a referendum will be held after the next general election, should the Conservatives win a majority in the House of Commons. Complete Activity 13.3 to explore the issues related to European Union membership.

Activity 13.3 The European Union and devolution of power

1. Use the Internet to learn about the UK Independence Party – a political party that calls for the UK to leave the EU. See www.ukip.org.
2. Visit BBC news to search for latest reports about the Coalition Government and their approach to the EU.
3. What are your views about EU membership? Think about the positives and the negatives of devolution 'upwards' and your own political and ideological standpoint.

In thinking about Britain's membership of the EU, you will have realized that this is a complex issue. As with 'downwards' devolution, however, it is quite difficult to judge whether the impact of EU policy will lead to the end of the British welfare system as we know it. In one way Europe is becoming pervasive. The number of social policy areas and the depth of involvement in policy areas have all increased in recent years. This is especially the case since 1997, when the previous Labour government signed the 'Social Chapter' (section) of the Single European Act 1986. The Single European Act was a key piece of legislation and has been 'acclaimed as the most important and successful step in the process of European integration since the Treaty of Rome' (McCormick 1999: 77). Blair's signing up meant that legislation agreed under the Social Chapter since the 1991 Intergovernmental Conference (Maastricht Treaty) applies to the UK.

The EU has become less of a foreign policy issue and is now more a part of domestic politics and social administration than formerly. However, despite the increasing impact of the EU on social policy and politics in the UK, it would be wrong to portray the EU as an all-powerful juggernaut that flattens all domestic or national policies in its path. There are strong limitations to the impact of the EU. These limitations are both practical (limits to the effective capacity of EU institutions and organizations to enforce legislation) and constitutional (all member states – not just the UK – retain significant controls).

The balance between the EU's and nation-states' powers is not settled and there is still a major question as to whether the UK will fully participate in the process of further European integration and will be prepared to secede more national policy-making powers to the EU. An alternative to a single, unified and increasingly powerful 'superstate' is a two-speed Europe, or a two-*tier* Europe, or some variation of the two things. This is possible, given the recent enlargement of the EU to include 27 member states. These possibilities allow for an inner core of countries to press ahead with integration, whether in terms of defence, economics, or social policy and domestic issues such as immigration control and policies on refugees and asylum.

Thus, any estimation of the impact of the EU on the UK, and on British social policy, needs to include discussion of what role the UK itself wants to play in the Europe of the future. Will the UK be committed to being a member of any inner core of member states – alongside France and Germany, for instance – or will it wish to continue to deal with the EU at arm's length? Given the political debates about this issue that are still going on, the future of the UK within the EU is seemingly undecided.

The EU and social policy

There has been a lot of interest across Europe in the effect that the growing powers of the EU will have on social policy and on existing welfare states. As far as the UK is concerned, the impact of EU social policy on British social policy can be described as limited, but significant in particular areas such as employment conditions and equality at work. As Timonen (1999: 253) points out, the direct effects of EU policy are limited because 'EU social policy does not for the most part fall within the traditional definition of social policy (a structure of transfers and services aimed at redistribution among the entire population)'.

The EU's impact is more in terms of establishing a common framework of standards and goals in social welfare rather than imposing a blueprint of how each country should run its system of social security, education, health care, housing and so on. EU legislation is governed by a principle of subsidiarity, which means that member states build European law into their own legislation and policies. Key areas of EU legislative action are summarized in Table 13.4.

Table 13.4 Key areas of EU legislative action

Area of legislative action	What this means
Free movement of workers	• All nationals of EU member states have the right to live and work in any member state. If they do, they have the same rights to social security, working conditions and access to jobs as nationals in the country they have moved to (with certain exceptions, such as access to employment in defence, law and police forces).
Equal pay and equal treatment	• An Equal Pay Directive (1975) requires member states to abolish all overt discrimination between men and women in pay. After 1975 they also had to introduce legislation to recognize equal pay for work of equal *value* – a point that had a particular impact in the UK, which had to replace previous equal pay legislation with a new law that fell in line with the Directive. • An Equal Treatment Directive established the principle of equal treatment between men and women in access to employment and training. It also governs working conditions.
Social security	• Article 119, a Social Security Directive, covers not only wages but also overtime, sick pay, bonuses and occupational pensions. The main aim of this Directive is to eliminate sex discrimination in the calculation of benefits for men and women. In 1986 this legislation was extended to cover private pension and insurance schemes. As a result of one successful challenge to the UK under this legislation, the UK government was ordered to treat single and married carers equally in payment of benefits.
Parental leave	• EU Directives in this area are part of a wider programme of EU initiatives to help both men and women balance the demands of work and home. For instance there has been a Directive (1992) on the protection of pregnant women at work and on employment protection for such women. There has been a noticeable impact in the UK in relation to this. Several leading court cases involving wrongful dismissal of pregnant women from the armed forces were referred to the European Court of Justice and have resulted in the payment of large compensation sums to the women involved.
Part-time work	• With the acceptance of the Social Chapter, Directives on part-time work since 1991 have become binding on British employers. They mean that part-time workers must be given the same rights to pensions, employment benefits and health and safety protection as full-time workers.
Working hours and welfare at work	• There have been a number of Directives from the EU on the subject of working time (the maximum number of hours per week permitted in most occupations, with some agreed exceptions) and on employee participation in decision-making at work.

Table 13.4 illustrates the areas of policy in which EU directives have had a significant impact on the UK. When we look at other areas of social policy – that is, outside the areas of social security, welfare in employment, or equality laws and sex discrimination – the impact of the EU is much less noticeable.

Some of these other areas of policy have benefitted the UK. The European Social Fund was set up in 1960 to assist member states with the provision of retraining schemes, job creation and migration assistance – all designed to meet the social and human costs of industrial restructuring and the consequences of unemployment. Two main groups have been helped over the years: the long-term unemployed and unemployed young people. The Social Fund takes less than 10 per cent of the total EU budget (far less than the 50 per cent or so going to support agriculture) and it has been criticized for being cumbersome and inefficient. On the other hand, it has had considerable impact on the development of innovative schemes to address youth unemployment.

The EU has also funded a wide range of other initiatives – for example, to support disabled people in employment and to remove the obstacles that prevent disabled people from obtaining work. Similarly, the EU funds schemes to tackle economic disadvantage and to revitalize inner-city and other economically depressed areas. These initiatives often have a 'social' element and include such things as community development schemes, community transport projects and funds to develop childcare services or facilities, and several initiatives have been supported in the UK.

Globalization and devolution

While the future role and membership of the EU is a highly important issue for the UK, however, we should not forget that globalization represents a whole set of other international influences on the British economy, on British politics and therefore, in turn, on social policy in the UK. In some senses the EU represents a bulwark or protection against globalization, but it is unlikely to be able to mitigate all its influences very much.

As earlier chapters have highlighted, globalization is an important aspect of the contemporary policy-making process (see Chapter 4). The trend towards devolution as discussed throughout this chapter is not unique to the UK, as many countries are following a similar pattern. Complete Activity 13.4 to explore a range of contexts in which devolution is taking place.

Activity 13.4 Global trends in devolution

Using the Internet, access YouTube:

1. Watch 'Tibet in the Aftermath of Devolution of Political Authority' available at www.youtube.com/watch?v=q5rygSelMds. This is a lengthy clip so you do not need to view it all; watch it until you have a sense of the impact of devolution in this context.
2. Watch 'The devolution deal' discussing Kenya, available at www.youtube.com/watch?v=lpZQWuV84So.

Now take time to consider the following questions:

- What does devolution mean in the context of global policy-making? If there are significant global policy issues how might these be addressed via local policy implementation in devolved systems?
- Is devolution positive in the sense that it allows more power within specific locales and policy arenas, or is it more complex and a mechanism for national governments to shift responsibility?
- Consider your own standpoint – what is your opinion about devolution? What context and history has helped to shape your views?

Activity 13.4 will have illustrated that many governments devolve a variety of powers to a more local level. However, there are some areas in which policy is also made at a global level in terms of devolution upwards. Thus, some of the policies illustrated in Chapter 4, such as the Kyoto Protocol, and the Framework Convention on Tobacco Control are indicative of devolution upwards in terms of the decision-making process. Given some of the global challenges that current policy-makers are facing, this is an area of social policy development that will be worth watching in the future.

Conclusions

Devolution – both 'upwards' to the EU and 'downwards' to the elected legislatures in Scotland, Wales and Northern Ireland – poses some important questions about the future of the British welfare state. As stated at the outset, devolution to the 'Celtic' countries is beginning to lead to some exciting changes in the way social policies are formulated and how services are going to be delivered in the different parts of the UK. There are already signs of considerable divergence in education, health and social care policies, though for a variety of reasons we must be cautious about how much difference devolution is going to make.

A key question raised by devolution within the UK is how far the independence of the devolved administrations in Wales, Scotland and Northern Ireland will be used not only to develop their own distinctive approaches in social policy, but also to *protect* the 'traditional' welfare state. There are certainly signs in the 'Celtic' countries of a greater commitment than in the Westminster government to supporting older, or existing forms of social provision – rather than following a Coalition Government drive towards ever more re-organization and involvement of the private sector in welfare management and provision.

For instance, as will be recalled, the Scottish Executive's approach to the NHS and the Welsh approach to favouring the retention of standard comprehensive schools are illustrations of this more traditional welfare strategy. Also, the use of public money to fund improvements in personal care and student maintenance show a similar commitment to more traditional pro-welfare values and a commitment to investment in the social infrastructure. How strongly devolution will protect or revive the 'old' social democratic approach to building a welfare state, and how far the devolved administrations will be able to resist the centralizing pressures of the UK government, remains to be seen.

As far as the effect of devolution upwards to the EU is concerned, there has been little or no discussion of the EU weakening or watering down Britain's welfare services or social security provisions. This is because Britain's welfare system underwent a considerable squeeze and restructuring by Mrs Thatcher's government in the 1980s, and UK social expenditure is only average for comparable developed countries. The Coalition Government approach is also one of squeezing social spending and restructuring welfare. As mentioned above, the Conservatives are promising a referendum on the future of the UK within the EU, if they are re-elected at the next general election. Should this happen, the referendum will take place at some point in 2015. The referendum will not be a simple opt-out option; rather, it will be about the UK renegotiating its relationship with the EU.

Not surprisingly, in countries that joined the EU more recently and that have more developed welfare systems than in the UK – notably Finland and Sweden – the debate has been quite different. Here, concerns have focused on the worry that the EU's impact would lead directly to considerable erosion of their advanced welfare systems (Gould 1999; Timonen 1999).

Thus we may sum up the impact of upwards and downwards devolution as follows. First, for the minority of the UK's population living in the 'Celtic' countries there will be perceptible changes in the health and social care system, and in education, compared to England. Most of these changes will have a practical impact and a mostly beneficial effect on certain groups in the Scottish, Welsh and Northern Irish populations.

For the majority of UK citizens – the English – neither devolution nor the growing influence of the EU look like making as much difference. The global policy-making context may also become more relevant to the UK in the future. However, at the moment it seems that the EU is likely to have a greater impact, if only in specific areas such as parental leave or new regulations governing working time. Otherwise, it is hard to see how devolution within the UK will much affect English social policy, except by example and unless there is some regional devolution in England. However, the ability to draw comparative examples, and to see how things can be done differently, will perhaps turn out to be one of the most underrated effects of devolution. For everyone in the UK, the examples of EU social policy and the policies being worked out in the devolved administrations offer alternatives to the social policies emanating from central government in London.

Summary of key points

- Devolution in the UK has broadly taken two forms. First, power has been devolved downwards in which separate administrations for Scotland, Wales and Northern Ireland have a varying level of control over specific policy areas. Second, devolution upwards can be seen with the UK being a member of the European Union, whose directives have led to changed policies within the UK in a number of areas.
- Devolution has resulted in some divergent policies across the UK, and thus unsurprisingly there are already divergent outcomes. Education and health were the main areas used as examples in this chapter because it is in these areas that devolved administrations have been able to bring about most change.
- The future of devolved policy is one in which the UK is part of a global community, and one in which its membership of the EU is currently being debated.

Key terms and concepts

asymmetric devolution and symmetric devolution
devolution
divergence
legislation
primary legislation and secondary legislation
subsidiarity

Suggestions for further reading

Birrell, D. (2009) *The Impact of Devolution on Social Policy.* Bristol: Policy Press.

With new devolved administrations in Scotland, Wales and Northern Ireland, this book assesses the impact of devolution on social policy via a comparison of the devolved nations. The book looks at the nature and scope of social policies, ranging from major innovations and policy distinctiveness, to differences in implementation, policy convergence and areas of overlap. It also examines the outcomes of the different policies across the devolved nations.

Bogdanor, V. (2001) *Devolution in the United Kingdom.* Oxford: Oxford University Press.

This book looks at the historical context, from Gladstone's espousal of Home Rule in 1886 right up to the 1998 legislation governing the Scottish Parliament and the Welsh Assembly. The book examines historical lessons related to contemporary devolution as well as the implications of devolution in Scotland and Northern Ireland and analyses the 1998 Good Friday Agreement, as well as considering the impact and implications of the new arrangements for the government of London under the Mayoral system implemented in May 2000.

Greer, S.L. (ed.) (2009) *Devolution and Social Citizenship in the UK.* Bristol: Policy Press.

This timely study explores how changing territorial politics are having an impact on social citizenship rights across the UK. The book adopts the standpoint that devolved politics are increasingly producing different social citizenship rights in different parts of the UK. This book offers insight into the connections between the politics of devolution and the meaning of social citizenship in the UK. It also examines numerous issues related to devolution including policy divergence, public opinion, finance and the European Union.

Habermas, J. (2012) *The Crisis of the European Union: A Response.* Cambridge: Polity Press.

In the midst of the current crisis that is threatening to derail the historical project of European unification, Habermas explains why the current proposals to transform the system of European governance into one of executive federalism are a mistake. His central argument is that the European project must realize its democratic potential by evolving from an international into a cosmopolitan community. This is an interesting analysis of the European Union at a time when it has been critically questioned, and its future is open to debate.

You may also wish to access an archive project held online at UCL (University College London): www.ucl.ac.uk/constitution-unit/research/research-archive/archive-projects/devolution-monitoring99-05, where there is a large amount of devolution-related material.

14 Conclusion: the future of social policy

Key learning outcomes

By the end of this chapter you should:

- be able to understand the rapid changing context of social policy within the UK and indeed further afield
- be able to evaluate the impact of the UK New Labour government, 1997–2010
- be able to describe the trend towards postmodern government and understand what this means for the UK Coalition Government

Overview of the chapter

This book has aimed to introduce you both to the academic subject of social policy and to 'real' social policies evident in the world around us. It has included discussion of recent developments in social security, criminal justice, education, employment policy, health services, housing and social care. It has also included discussion of key themes in the subject of social policy and some of the academic debates that have developed in the discipline, as well as the increasing importance of the broader context in which policy is made with influences from the European Union (see Chapter 13), and the wider global policy-making agencies (see Chapter 4) now important within the field. This chapter summarizes the context of the book and evaluates policy changes made within the UK in recent years, including the New Labour and Coalition governments. Finally, the chapter ends with a consideration of the challenges that the future holds for those who are making policy.

Social policy and rapid social change

Years ago, in the era of welfare consensus (a term still of use in understanding mid-twentieth-century social policy: see Deakin 1994), studying social policy meant learning about the workings of the welfare state: a growing giant of welfare service provision in the postwar years. In more recent years, fundamental changes have begun to undermine old assumptions about both the subject of social policy and the welfare state itself. As suggested at the beginning (see Chapter 1), it is probably better to think of welfare today as a *system* of more or less connected agencies in different sectors (the public, private, voluntary and informal) than as a 'welfare state' that is almost entirely a government-run operation.

As the old welfare state fragments and changes, it will be increasingly important to rethink the subject of social policy. If social policy continues to define itself as a subject that concerns itself only with traditional areas of study, focusing on need, inequality and social services in well-demarcated areas such as education and health, important aspects of social change and reform will be missed. The old association between the subject of social policy and the welfare state needs to be questioned seriously. 'Social policy' will become much more concerned than it is now with such themes as the role of NGOs in providing welfare, with the changing nature of work, or with other aspects of human welfare, including leisure, transport and patterns of consumption (see Cahill 1994).

The changing and broadening nature of the subject matter of social policy is indicated by the inclusion of a chapter on the global policy environment (Chapter 4) in this edition. Having said that, you will have noticed that this book has concentrated for the most part on the traditional fields of social policy, from education and health to housing and community care. This is because there are continuities in social policy and, though the pace of change has been very rapid in the context of welfare (the economic and political scene), it makes sense to look forward from a well-understood base to developments on the horizon. It is also dangerous to make too many guesses, even about the near future, when a week is as long in the politics of social policy as it is in anything else.

This concluding chapter therefore aims to encourage you to look over your shoulder at recent policy in such areas as education, the health service and social care, as discussed earlier in this book. It also encourages you to think about the future in terms of some of the policy challenges that are likely to affect us and the wider world in the future. However, it is important to try to reflect on these recent changes in a way that helps us to think about the general direction of social policy – and to see the 'bigger picture' as it unfolds. Before moving on to reflect upon the UK context, complete the first activity of this chapter to think about one of the key global challenges that is frequently brought to our attention by the media, by academics and by some politicians.

Activity 14.1 The challenge of persistent inequalities

There is a large evidence base that illustrates the existence of inequalities within countries including the UK and the USA, as well as between countries, such as those with a higher income and those that have a lower income.

Use the Internet to read Zygmunt Bauman's analysis of contemporary inequalities – 'Does The Richness Of The Few Benefit Us All? By Zygmunt Bauman' available at www.social-europe.eu/2013/01/does-the-richness-of-the-few-benefit-us-all.

For many who write about inequalities, social policy is one mechanism by which inequalities can be changed and there are many state approaches to poverty reduction and other facets of inequalities. This is a key challenge for policy-makers across the world, as Chapter 4 indicated.

1. Think about all of the policy sectors that can have an impact upon inequalities.
2. Think about how specific policies may impact upon inequalities. For example, think about education policy and the changes to fee prices in Higher Education. You may also consider employment policy and welfare provision.

3. Think about how politicians understand inequalities – do they understand inequalities? See the *Metro* report 'Shift to the White' for an analysis of the social characteristics of the current UK cabinet - http://metro.co.uk/2012/09/04/cabinet-reshuffle-summary-critics-say-david-cameron-has-gone-too-white-too-male-and-too-rich-565566.What do you think that this means in relation to understandings of inequalities?
4. What do you think is the future for policy in relation to inequalities within the UK, given the cuts in public spending described throughout this book?

As the activity reminded you, persistent social inequality remains a challenge for policy-makers and a key aspect of the social context in which policy is made. At this point it may help to review the context in which British social policy finds itself following the long period of Labour rule, 1997–2010 and subsequently a Coalition Government. What are the implications of this political context for social policy?

Second, and tied to the thesis that the old welfare state is crumbling away, is a set of debates about the emergence of a *postmodern social order*. Depending on one's viewpoint, the notion of postmodernism is either a very useful way of summarizing trends that have great significance for social policy, or a set of ideas that cloud the picture and obscure such realities as growing inequality and exclusion from welfare.

'Not so New' Labour and social policy: the evaluation of a policy legacy

The election of a Labour government in May 1997 seemed to herald the dawn of a new political era. This was especially the case because Labour's victory over the Conservatives was so decisive and because it followed nearly 20 years of uninterrupted Conservative government.

As mentioned in Chapter 8, the British electoral system allows governments with large majorities to do what they want to a degree that other constitutions with more checks and balances do not. Thus the Labour government seemed to set out in 1997 with a free hand to change policy. Tony Blair's newly elected government promised bold changes in a number of areas.

First, it gave the impression that one change of policy would be to break with the 'Old Labour' approach of 'tax and spend' in dealing with the economy and public services. Labour's 1997 election manifesto stated that a Labour government would not raise basic and higher income tax rates to fund an expanded welfare budget (Labour Party 1997: 11–13), a commitment reiterated in the 2005 manifesto (Labour Party 2005: 16–17). At the time, an anti-taxation stance seemed vital to Labour's campaign to win the general election. The political mood in 1997 was anti-Conservative but not, apparently, supportive of any kind of radical programme for social reform. The tax commitment was in fact quite ambiguous and perfectly compatible with a policy of increasing the tax burden - precisely what has happened. The manifesto also stated a commitment to increased spending on health and education.

Second, the Labour Party under Blair had built its ideas for change around a rejection of the Conservative approach to economic management and welfare reform. Blair insisted that New Labour did not want to follow the neo-liberal, free-market principles that had become a marked feature of Conservative thinking and strategy in the governments led by Margaret Thatcher and John Major. Instead, New Labour would follow a

'Third Way' (see Powell 1999) – a new, distinctive approach to both economic and social policy that would be neither a version of 'Old Labour' socialism nor another kind of free enterprise, laissez-faire version of Conservatism.

However, the Third Way as a policy approach soon disappeared into the policy archives and instead New Labour discussed 'pragmatic' policies, and justified its actions on the principle that 'whatever works' was the best policy choice. For instance, New Labour justified the policy of involving private sector companies in takeovers of 'failing' schools or local education authorities in this way.

Some observers argue that this suggests that New Labour did not so much lose direction after 1997 but never had a clear direction to follow in the first place. Powell (1999: 298) and others have suggested that New Labour's supposedly big idea was never built around 'a coherent concept that can be applied more or less uniformly to different policy sectors. Instead, it appears to be . . . a poorly specified, pick and mix strategy, largely defined by what it is not'. Complete Activity 14.2 to explore different views on the impact that New Labour had in the UK.

Activity 14.2 Thinking about the impact of New Labour

1. Use the Internet to access You Tube and to listen to the short speech by a politician from a different party, The UK Independence Party, 'New Labour's record': www.youtube.com/watch?v=UUGZBHVQweM.
2. Again use the Internet to access a transcript of a speech from a New Labour politician, John Hutton, also evaluating their term in office: www.britishpoliticssociety.no/Speech_Hutton.PDF.
3. Compare and contrast these different views about the impact that New Labour had while in office, taking time to consider the ideological standpoint of each view and any bias.
4. What are your thoughts about the impact that New Labour had while in office – were there any notable successes from your point of view? Were there any policy changes that you felt were negative or that affected you and your family in a detrimental manner?

The New Labour government, and indeed any government in office, is subject to criticism from numerous directions, as Activity 14.2 should have helped you to understand. The reluctance of the government led by Blair to commit itself to a particular direction had two main effects in the political context. First, the strategy seemed to work, in some ways, in helping to secure the second and third terms in government for New Labour. The government's 2001 and 2005 election strategies, as in 1997, were to make some modest commitments but not to promise the earth. This at least succeeded in not scaring away voters by raising concerns about higher taxes or (in 2001) about the UK adopting the common European currency.

Second, however, this strategy seemed to foster voter apathy. Labour voters grudgingly gave the government another chance to continue in office in 2005, but more out of a sense that there was no credible alternative to Labour than as a result of strong support for the Labour programme. Blair's promise to quit some time after the general election also helped to shore up support for Labour among many voters, as by 2005 Tony Blair had become less popular than the party he led. However, the New Labour Government approach did not succeed in a successful fourth term in government.

The lack of a clear programme suggests that New Labour's achievements were few and far between, but this was not the case. The government did succeed in passing a great deal of legislation and introducing many policy reforms, including reforms in the area of social welfare. The point is rather that the social policy achievements of New Labour turned out to be both modest and working in different directions. For example, the Labour government's strategy after 1997 included some remarkably right-wing policies. Abolishing the lone-parent premium in income support for new claimants, the introduction of student loans and tuition fees, and adoption and expansion of the Conservatives' Private Finance Initiative to fund hospital building and other public infrastructure are all examples of policy in which New Labour 'out-Conservatived' the Conservatives.

On the other hand, some left-of-centre policies aiming to redress decades of increases in social inequality and poverty were introduced. The minimum wage, an extension of disabled people's rights, commitments to reduce child poverty and to improve access to child care facilities, and tax credits to working families on low incomes are all examples of this kind of policy.

Therefore New Labour's period in government so far has been like a river marked by swirling currents and eddies rather than a river flowing strongly and consistently in one direction. Table 14.1 provides an evaluation of New Labour's years in office.

Table 14.1 shows the contradictions evident within New Labour's policy approach. It is fair to say that no government's policies are ever entirely consistent, and every government has policy failures as well as successes. For example, as mentioned in Chapter 3 (see concluding section), even Mrs Thatcher's single-minded approach did not mean that all

Table 14.1 New Labour: successes and failures

Policy successes	Policy failures
New Labour did succeed in introducing a lot of specially targeted measures to improve the earnings and employment prospects of people on low incomes. Some of these measures did make a substantial difference.	Any improvements in health and social services took place against a backdrop of sharp and persistent social and economic inequalities. The gap between rich and poor in the UK is one of the highest in the world. The needs and social problems that are increased by poverty – for instance, poor health, illiteracy, crime and social exclusion – simply continued to put pressure on stretched public services during New Labour's term of office.
New Labour increased spending on public services during the time in office, which for many was seen as a positive policy move.	However, this increased spending was against the backdrop of two or three decades of relative underfunding and therefore it can be argued that the public services – notably, education, health and social services – did not recover despite the increased spending. Indeed, many public services still have critical shortages of professional practitioners – doctors, nurses, teachers, social workers and other staff.
In terms of employment policies, New Deal and anti-poverty policies aimed to improve the social inclusion of disadvantaged and socially excluded groups – for instance, by improving their chances of a good education, and of access to worthwhile employment and training opportunities.	However, overall education policy aimed to increase 'diversity' in the secondary school system, and to foster selection by 'aptitude' if not 'ability'. These policies seemed to be about pleasing New Labour's middle-class constituency. It is hardly a recipe for social inclusion to continue to break up the comprehensive school system (in England) and to widen the social divisions that already exist between the intakes of schools in better-off and poorer neighbourhoods.

her government's policies were working in the same direction. Given Labour's record in involving the private sector in funding and managing health, education and social services, and its determination to continue and extend the Conservatives' strategy of building a market in welfare provision, all investments in the welfare system were made with strings attached. In this respect there is at least one consistent thread in government policy – a steady increase in central government control of the various services. This, combined with the use of the private sector to fund and run services, has resulted in the continued break-up of the old structures of local authorities, professions and managers that used to run the welfare system.

The UK Coalition Government: an interim evaluation

The UK Coalition Government came into office in May 2010, and extended some of the policy approaches that had been started by the New Labour administration. As the chapters throughout this book have shown, there has been a clear continuation of policy in certain areas, particularly the increased use of market principles in service provision:

- Employment policy – increased involvement of private sector companies in assessing individual's ability to work, and the subcontracting out of employment support to private companies who are paid on the basis of the results that they achieve.
- Criminal justice – payment by results as part of rehabilitation.
- Education – reform of higher education following the Browne review, which resulted in increased tuition fees for those wishing to access higher education.
- Health – significant restructuring and reorganization of the NHS in England with the development of local clinical commissioning groups who will buy required services. This will advance the principle that increased competition and market forces will deliver a more efficient NHS.

These are just some of the examples of continuation of policy despite change of government. There are, however, some areas of policy divergence since New Labour. The biggest changes have been brought about by the Coalition Government's austerity measures and budget cuts. Some analysts have argued that these will have the most negative impact on those who need the services most, and that rather than being in this together as the Prime Minister, David Cameron has claimed, it is those who are the poorest and most in need that are affected more significantly than others. Complete Activity 14.3 to examine this suggestion.

Activity 14.3 The impact of the cuts

Use the Internet to visit the following websites

1. Joseph Rowntree Foundation: Austerity in the UK – available at www.jrf.org.uk/topic/austerity?gclid=CMCg5eOFjbUCFW_KtAodKGEA2Q. Here you can download summaries of investigations related to the impact of the austerity measures.
2. The Centre for Welfare Reform: the home page is located at www.centreforwelfarereform.org, and there is a variety of analysis about the impact of the welfare cuts available on this website.

Having read around these two websites, what can you conclude about the impact of the austerity measures and spending cuts?

Are there any positive aspects to these measures? What are the negative consequences?

Finally, what do you think are the implications for the future of welfare provision?

Having completed Activity 14.3, you will now have some understanding of the impacts that recent policy changes are having. Further cuts and policy changes will continue to impact beyond the time of writing, given the fast-paced change taking place in this sector.

The changing context of social policy: a 'postmodern' era?

The 'modern' world has proved to be bewildering and confusing, if we take the twentieth century to be representative. In that century there were two world wars, numerous acts of barbarism and mass murder, and stupendous rises not only in agricultural and industrial production but also in human population. There were mighty clashes of political ideology accompanying the rise of mass democracy in many states and – in the industrialized world – the rise of 'welfare states'.

The twenty-first century is possibly even more bewildering, anxious and insecure. It is therefore not surprising that, at the end of the twentieth century, commentators referred to the 'end' of almost everything: the end of socialism, for instance, or the end of the industrial age (**postindustrialism**).

However, before we leap to the conclusion that social policy, along with everything else, really is being swept into a new world order, it is worth contemplating what theories of postmodernism have suggested and whether they ring true in helping to explain both recent policy and emerging trends. Postmodernism as an intellectual and cultural phenomenon and its relation to other 'post' entities is hard to summarize and embraces a number of different ideas. In the 1990s there was a brief surge of interest in academic journals in postmodernism and its possible applicability to the understanding of social policy, an interest which seems now to have subsided. Social policy experts differed about the value of the idea of postmodernism. For example, Mishra (1993) found the concept useful, while Taylor-Gooby (1994) was strongly critical.

First, it may be helpful to make a distinction between postmodernism, a general term implying the end of the 'modern' era as we have known it in the twentieth century, and postindustrialism. The latter term refers more specifically to certain trends in the economy and the world of work (Penna and O'Brien 1996). The theory of postindustrialism can be summarized as in Box 14.1.

Box 14.1 The theory of postindustrialism

- The collapse of manufacturing as a major source of jobs and the rise of service-sector jobs.
- Associated with this, a fundamental set of changes in the ways both organizations and work itself are structured. The earlier industrial world provided work based on principles of mass manufacturing (Fordism). That is, people tended to work in organizations or factories run as hierarchies. Each worker had an allotted role and a predictable work pattern. But in the postFordist world, the old hierarchies based on traditional skills or on bureaucratic organizations are disappearing. Organizations are said to have become 'flatter' (less like pyramidal power structures) and decentralized, while part-time work has expanded at the expense of full-time; people will increasingly move from one workplace to another and develop more flexible portfolios of skills.

- As a result of the two trends identified above, old class and gender divisions based on industrial society are breaking down. However, new divisions are arising: there is likely to be a well-rewarded section of the workforce who are the more skilled in postindustrial, knowledge-based employment, while a poorer section will be relegated to casual, temporary and part-time work.
- The postindustrial world, it is suggested, will also be increasingly affected by globalization (see Chapter 4). This means that revolutions in production and information transfer permit production of goods and services on a worldwide basis. In the new world order, the nation-state will become increasingly unable to manage or control the economy within its own borders. The pressures to compete in a global market will force the more 'expensive' countries to reduce their welfare and labour costs. As a result, according to this view, not only will nation-states find it increasingly difficult to independently run their own economies, they will also find that their social policies (which are largely determined by economic success and failure) slip out of their grasp too.

All the points in Box 14.1 represent a *theory* about what is happening in the world today, not a set of firm conclusions. How much can be explained convincingly by this theory, and what use is the idea of postindustrialism in understanding social policy trends?

For those such as Penna and O'Brien (1996) and Fitzpatrick (1996), who believe that the concept does have some value, postindustrialism helped to explain a number of recent trends in the way the welfare system is developing. For instance, the *casualization* of employment in welfare services, as a result of the imposition of short-term and part-time work contracts, reflects wider changes in the workforce. The development of internal markets in most areas of welfare provision is resulting in the break-up of the old welfare bureaucracies. These changes also reflect the broader postindustrial trend towards working in fragmented, decentralized organizations. More generally, the emergence of a postindustrial type of economy is eroding the old norms of secure, permanent employment for men and leading to a situation in which the former 'Beveridgian' welfare state (see Chapter 3) is increasingly outmoded and unsuited to people's needs.

For such authors as Hillyard and Watson (1996) it is vitally important to include what are termed *poststructural* accounts and ideas in the study of social policy. Poststructural accounts of contemporary social life and society have appeared to call into question such universalistic creeds and norms as socialism, social justice and equality. These were the master narratives or so-called 'grand narratives' of 'modernist' societies, associated with the 'Fordist' economic production and the classic welfare states that arguably dominated much of the twentieth century. (The historical dimension to the popularity of post-structuralist/postmodernist theorizing may be significant; it emerged in the 1970s and 1980s, when 'the system' appeared to be in crisis, and also under challenge from various quarters.) Poststructuralism allegedly challenges the universalistic ways of thinking that underpinned the old 'Beveridgian' welfare state: for instance, the assumption that all people who fit a certain category (for example, older people, or women) have similar needs, and that a universalistic welfare state should provide for everyone's needs in a similar way.

For some commentators on social policy these ideas, although bold and interesting, obscure more than they reveal. For instance, Carter and Rayner (1996) take as an example a particular area of social policy (education) to see whether concepts of **postFordism** and postindustrialism help to interpret recent changes in the education system. They conclude that these theories downplay important elements of continuity in British policy-making. According to them, there is little evidence of the scale of change anticipated in theories of a postmodern society, either in the way the education system is being run or in the content of the system. Postmodernism may therefore exaggerate the idea of a complete change from one era to another, with associated social policy changes.

Taylor-Gooby (1994) also argues this point, suggesting that postmodernism is a set of ideas that is likely to deflect attention from such continuities as poverty and inequality. Far from ushering in a new postmodern era, Taylor-Gooby argues, the market economy and its accompanying values that now so dominate the world have led to a re-emergence of social conditions and relationships that are reminiscent of the period before the welfare state. The 're-emerging past' includes such things as a deregulated and exploitative labour market and a retreat from the idea of using universal, society-wide policies to reduce poverty. Complete the final learning activity of this chapter to explore the concept of postmodernism.

Activity 14.4 Exploring postmodernism

1. Use the Internet to access YouTube, and to listen to the brief talk 'Postmodernism – Postmodern Worldview', available at www.youtube.com/watch?v=ynMS0g6zu5E.
2. Here you will be able to listen to an introduction to postmodernism as a concept and what this means in economics, for the state and science.
3. Do you agree that the concept of postmodernity is useful in understanding society today, and that it throws light on welfare and social policy?
4. Are any of your views postmodern?

The above learning activity will have helped you to develop some understanding of postmodernism as a view of the world. Postmodernist styles of thinking have influenced social policy analysis in a number of indirect ways: for example, the highlighting of 'social construction' and 'social constructionist' methodological and theoretical approaches found in some texts (Saraga 1998). In so far as social constructionism as an approach to social analysis amounts to anything significant, it is probably in its emphasis on pluralism and diversity of viewpoints and its highlighting of social differentiation and division. In social policy this is associated with the discovery of 'identity' politics, the highlighting of new rather than old social divisions and inequalities, and the questioning of the traditional redistributionist agenda in terms of socio-economic or class inequalities. The embrace of 'diversity' and multiculturalism, the recognition of disability, age and sexuality as well as gender as social divisions might be taken as evidence of 'postmodernist' influence. In this sense postmodernist or poststructualist social policy thinking represents the impact of the 'new social movements'. Of course, it might seem inconsistent and incoherent for poststructuralist-influenced writers to appear to offer a critique of 'modernist' values such as equality on the one hand, while highlighting and apparently deploring a variety of 'new' social divisions on the other.

Endnote: a postmodern government and postmodern social policies?

In the persistence of poverty there is certainly a lot of evidence to support Taylor-Gooby's scepticism about postmodernity and its value as a concept in understanding the present-day world. As discussed in Chapter 6 there is still a lot of 'old-fashioned' poverty about in the UK today – the poverty of older people trying to live on inadequate pensions, for instance, or the poverty of people who are working on low incomes.

However, it would be wrong to write off postmodernism and associated ideas about the social changes resulting from the drawing to a close of the industrial era. As pointed out in Chapter 6, 'new' poverty and increasingly different experiences of poverty mean that it is no longer the 'mass experience' of, say, the 1930s. 'The poor', never a homogeneous social group, are becoming an increasingly fragmented and differentiated mixture of categories or groups in society. For instance, with regard to one major social category – older people – divisions in this group are becoming more significant than they were. Some older people – an increasing number in today's society – are relatively well off. Among those who are not so well off, there are rising numbers of older people who are 'asset rich but income poor' – those who own their own homes but are on low pension incomes. And there are yet other subgroups, such as older people on varying levels of pension income but with few savings and no substantial property.

Not surprisingly, therefore, there is a sound argument to suggest that the old universalistic policies of the welfare state will look increasingly anachronistic in a postmodern world in which new social distinctions and a greater diversity of values and social groups are emerging. But it might be helpful to picture this as a change in which the old, or traditional, elements of the welfare state continue to shape the postmodern welfare system. The development of the NHS (see Chapter 10) in the twenty-first century – a much-adapted 1940s-style health system that still retains its basic design – is a case in point. However, recent changes to the NHS in England suggest we need to continue to question that the traditional NHS will always be with us.

Similarly, it would be misleading to conclude with the view that the Coalition Government is a pure and simple example of a postmodern approach to politics and social policy. There are certainly some strong signs of postmodernity in the way that the Coalition Government works, as summarized in the examples within Box 14.2.

However, despite these elements of postmodernity that are visible in some aspects of the Coalition Government's work none of these postmodern characteristics neatly sums

Box 14.2 A postmodern coalition?

- The Coalition Government has developed its appeal to the public and has been able to gain much support for austerity measures despite their impact. Many support the 'need' for such an approach as well as welfare retrenchment.
- The 'postmodernity' of the Coalition Government's approach to making policy can also be seen in the rapidity with which the government can implement that policy. Sometimes this has been done without heeding opinion, without genuine consultation and with no piloting or careful consideration of policy options. An example of this can be seen in health policy, where abrupt changes of direction took place in 2011 regarding the restructuring of the NHS, the role of the private sector and the increased role of market mechanisms.
- Further signs of the government's postmodern approach to politics can be seen in its preoccupation with style, appearance and mass media reactions to its policies. Media reports about student demonstrations in relation to tuition fee hikes constructed students as violent and allowed space for the policy changes to be made, which arguably suited the Coalition Government's agenda.

up the nature of the current government and its policies. As always the policy picture is indeed filled with complexity and contradictions. In social policy, the Coalition Government's approach has also been affected by old-fashioned assumptions and thus there are many traditional elements to its policy approaches. The Coalition Government in some senses tells people what is best for them: work, traditional family values and the importance of community. This kind of paternalism is far from postmodern because it has echoes of 1940s Britain. Devolution and the growing significance of EU social policy have weakened this trend in some areas but only to a limited degree, or in relatively minor ways to date (see Chapter 13). The Coalition Government has been less traditional than might have been expected, mainly as a result of the influence of Liberal Democratic members. The public recognition of inequalities is something that is new from the Conservative party, as is the focus on tackling these via clinical commissioning within the health policy arena. However, despite this positive move other policy contradictions mean that inequalities may increase because of the state of the economy, spending cuts and welfare retrenchment. The future of the UK as an equal society is a utopian vision, despite some limited progress in this area under the previous New Labour government.

Serious social divisions still remain. As students of social policy, even of a postmodern generation, we may feel that these dimensions of inequality are relatively unimportant, perhaps just cosmetic or surface changes, and that the underlying material reality of poverty and socioeconomic inequality are more important. As we saw in Chapter 6, New Labour attempted to effect change in this area but despite their policies there was little improvement in overall income inequality, some improvement in indices of child poverty, and no improvement in non-family rates of poverty (Stewart 2005). Much remains to do but, given the overall policy approaches adopted by the Coalition Government, and the focus upon economics and the need for growth, inequality has seemingly slipped off the policy agenda within the UK for the moment. This is perhaps true across the globe, as many national governments focus upon the need to improve economies and the focus upon neo-liberal approaches to economic growth remain dominant.

In the final analysis, therefore, it is difficult to sum up recent government policy and it needs more than just the tag of postmodern government. The Coalition Government and the social policies it has developed and implemented are a combination of many things, as this book has illustrated: ideology, policy continuation and budgetary constraints to name just a few. Waiting to find out what the actual combination is, how the character of the government will change, and how this will affect the policies and the people of the future is what makes the study of social policy so exciting.

Summary of key points

- Social policy is a rapidly changing field; it moves at a fast pace and there are many influences within the policy process.
- The context in which social policy is made has also changed significantly over recent years, and for many theorists social policy is made within a postindustrialist and postmodern era. Some aspects of postmodernity can be seen in some areas of Coalition Government policy-making.
- The future of social policy is one that remains exciting because of the constant change which is taking place within the field, and because of the challenges that face policy-makers nationally and globally.

Key terms and concepts

casualization
globalization
paternalism
postfeminism
postFordism
postindustrialism
postmodernism
poststructuralism

Suggestions for further reading

Bale, T. (2011) *The Conservative Party: From Thatcher to Cameron.* Cambridge: Polity Press.

This book looks at how the Conservatives re-gained power in 2010 and addresses key questions, such as: Has Britain's prime minister really changed his party as much as he claims? Is the party really committed to the Big Society or just the 'same old Tories', keen on cuts and obsessively Eurosceptic? The book is based upon in-depth research and interviews with the key players, and therefore makes very interesting reading.

Bochel, H. (2011) *The Conservative Party and Social Policy.* Bristol: Policy Press.

With the Conservative Party breaking new ground in forming a coalition government with the Liberal Democrats, this book examines the development and content of the Conservatives' approaches to social policy and how they inform the Coalition Government's policies. Chapters cover a variety of policy areas such as family policy, criminal justice and welfare.

Jordan, B. (2010) *Why the Third Way Failed.* Bristol: Policy Press.

This book explains why the Third Way's combination of market-friendly and abstract, value-led principles has failed, and shows what is needed for an adequate replacement as a political and moral project. It criticizes the economic analysis on which the Third Way approach to policy was founded and suggests an alternative to its legalistic and managerial basis for the regulation of social relations.

Kilkey, M., Ramia, G. and Farnsworth, K. (eds) (2012) *Social Policy Review 24: Analysis and Debate in Social Policy, 2012.* Bristol: Policy Press.

Part One of this edition examines current developments under the UK's Coalition Government across a range of key policy areas. Part Two includes an examination of social policy in 'developing' countries, including in Africa and the Arab nations. Part Three turns to the fate of social welfare in countries among the worst hit by the 'economic crisis', including Ireland, Greece, Spain, Portugal and Iceland.

Powell, M. (2002) *Evaluating New Labour's Welfare Reforms.* Bristol: Policy Press.

The New Labour Government placed significant emphasis upon service delivery within its programme of welfare reform. This book addressed the question of whether New Labour actually delivered on this reform. The book explores the first term of office of New Labour by comparing achievements with stated aims and examining success in the wider context.

On a final and more general note, you will find that the *Journal of Social Policy* is well worth consulting for any research or coursework that you may have to do, or just to keep up to date with current policy issues and debates. Each issue contains a section titled 'Digest', which helpfully summarizes key changes in various policy areas such as the health services, education, housing, gender issues and so on.

Glossary

The key terms and concepts in this glossary are highlighted in bold throughout this book. Therefore, by reading the text of the relevant chapter(s) you will be able to find examples of the ways in which they can be applied. Relevant chapter(s) are indicated after each definition with an abbreviation (for example, 'Ch. 1' for Chapter 1).

The definitions that follow are summaries of the way concepts are used in *social policy*. You may find different interpretations of terms in a dictionary or a reference book.

Where terms are closely related (for instance, 'maximalist' and 'minimalist' types of equal opportunity policy), they have been placed together for convenience. Otherwise, the terms are arranged alphabetically.

Active labour market policy: a term that sums up a variety of government policies to maximize the number of people in employment. These policies include initiatives to improve people's employability through additional training and to give personal advice to individuals on the types of work they could do. They may also include (for example, in Sweden) incentives to take paid employment such as providing grants for travelling to work or moving house, or childcare facilities. This type of policy includes groups who have previously experienced difficulties in finding work – for instance, disabled people, lone parents, older workers and the long-term unemployed. Active labour market policies represent a state interventionist philosophy that assumes that the job market alone cannot be relied on to maximize the number of people in work. They connect economic and social policy, and operate on the principle that welfare and social security are enhanced through being employed rather than being unemployed and dependent on 'passive' welfare benefits. (Ch. 9)

Acute illnesses: serious life-threatening illnesses that are resolved in a relatively short period of time (usually a matter of days or weeks), either by death or by the patient regaining health. Medical intervention may help either to restore health or to manage acute illness, which may then become a chronic condition (see **chronic illnesses**). Acute infectious illnesses were common in Britain up to the early part of the twentieth century. (Chs 3, 10)

Asymmetric devolution and symmetric devolution: devolution is a process in which certain central government powers and functions are granted to regions or countries within the larger nation-state. If devolution is *asymmetric*, central government grants more powers of self-rule to some regions or countries than to others. If it is *symmetric*, each part of the country and each devolved administration has the same powers and functions. (Ch. 13)

Autonomy: when applied to individuals, this term refers to the ability of a person to decide their own fate; the autonomous individual has the freedom and the ability to make decisions independently or to exercise choices for themselves. 'Autonomy' can also be used to refer to government institutions and organizations (see **quangos**) or to devolved administrations (see **asymmetric devolution**). See **oppression** and **social control**. (Chs 2, 5, 7)

Basic needs: these are universal human needs that are considered to be fundamental, not simply to enable human beings to survive, but as basic requirements for the development of independent individuals. Autonomy has been seen as a basic need, as well as adequate nutrition and housing, for instance. (Ch. 2)

Business cycle: this refers to the tendency for economic activity (including production, rates of employment and unemployment, profit rates) to rise and fall over time. Both economic and social policies are concerned to smooth out the 'bumps' and crises in the business cycle. For instance, policies may aim to stimulate employment in times of high unemployment and sluggish economic growth (see **active labour market policy**). Or government policies might try to reduce the problems of 'overheating' of the economy in times of rapid growth by raising taxation (thus reducing consumer demand) or by trying to solve shortages of skilled labour. (Ch. 9)

Care management: a term associated mainly with the provision and organization of services in the community, or with managing services for people who are moving in or out of hospital or institutional settings. Care management is an approach which stresses the importance of co-ordinating health and social services in ways which not only best serve the interests of service users but also maximize the efficiency of service delivery. Care managers are often social workers, but can be appointed from other fields, such as occupational therapy, and their job is to take the lead responsibility for co-ordinating the various services needed. (Ch. 12)

Carer: this is a formal way of defining the role of someone who either willingly and voluntarily cares for someone, usually on a continual and permanent basis, or feels obliged to provide care or is paid to do so. The invention of the term 'carer' has had some unfortunate consequences, in that it tends to suggest that all the 'care' goes in one direction (from carer to 'cared for'), and it can overemphasize the helplessness and passivity of people who need help with managing their daily activities. (Chs 6, 12)

Casualization (of employment): a process of change in working conditions and work contracts. It refers to the way in which permanent work contracts and full-time jobs are replaced by short-term and part-time work. When work is casualized, employees tend to lose important rights and the protection of laws that should safeguard their welfare: for instance, laws against instant or unfair dismissal, laws to ensure safety at work and contributions by employers to social security, insurance and pension schemes. See **deregulation**. (Ch. 9)

Chavs: this is a negative term used to label and stereotype working-class individuals within the UK. The origins of the term are debated but the word has become popular and frequently features in British media reports, particularly newspapers. (Chs 1, 7)

Chronic illnesses: these are illnesses that are, in most cases, incurable. However, they may or may not be disabling and often they can be successfully managed by medical intervention. Chronic illnesses are thus long-term problems, in that they are not immediately life-threatening (for instance, Parkinson's disease), and they have replaced **acute illnesses** as the main causes of illness in modern society. (Chs 3, 10)

Civil rights: the rights of individuals to liberty and security under the law: for instance, the right to move freely from one place to another, freedom from arbitrary arrest or detention without legal cause, and the right to own property. Sociologist T.H. Marshall (1950) saw civil rights as a first step to the development of other rights (**political rights** and **social rights**). (Ch. 2)

Climate change: this refers to the changing patterns of weather distribution across the world, and therefore changes to the global climate. The evidence that climate change is happening is documented in a variety of ways, although there are some who dispute that climate change is occurring and instead suggest that it is the result of natural changes within weather patterns. Climate change is a term usually used to illustrate the human impact upon the environment. (Chs 2, 4)

Coalition Government: the UK since 2010 has been governed by a coalition; this is a government made up of members of more than one party – in this case, the Conservative Party and the Liberal Democrats. (Chs 5, 6, 8, 9, 10, 11, 12, 13, 14)

Coercion: this term can be used to define a wide variety of methods with which those in power constrain or force people without power to do something or to act in a particular way. Coercion may be subtle and may be exercised as a result of the way a particular organization or institution is run (for instance, a residential home for disabled people), or it may be direct and consciously applied by those with power. (Chs 2, 7)

Community care: this refers to caring activities or services that exist outside large-scale institutions such as hospitals. The 'community' may be defined as a wide range of non-institutional settings (for instance, **day centres**, 'halfway houses' or **sheltered housing** schemes, foster homes), but in most cases 'community care' is another way of describing the care of people living alone or in families. See **domiciliary care** and **residential care**. (Chs 6,12)

Comparative analysis: the study of the institutions or policies of more than one country, usually identifying and exploring similarities and differences, for the purpose of policy learning or to throw light on the causes of institutional or policy change. (Chs 3, 5)

Comparative need: a way of defining need in a group in relation to what other comparable groups have, or do not have. An observer may find that one group of disabled people, for instance, receive very little help in the form of social services even though it is clear that they need such services. Finding a second comparable group that does receive services may help to establish a case for providing services to the first group as well. (Ch. 2)

Consumers (of services): the idea of portraying users of public services as 'consumers' gained importance as a result of the introduction of market-style reforms of the **welfare system** in the 1980s. Its significance lay in the goal of giving individual service users greater choice of services or a greater say over how services should be delivered to them. Thus people who used public services such as NHS hospitals, schools or social services were to be seen *as if* they were purchasing goods or services in the private market, even though (in the case of 'free' services) they were not paying for them at the point of use. (Ch. 12)

Consumerism: this refers to the idea that individuals are encouraged by social forces within their environment to buy goods and services in large and ever-increasing amounts. This pattern of purchasing can now be seen on a global scale and has been encouraged by economic policies that aim to support consumerism, particularly in western societies. (Ch. 4)

Contract state: a role for government which seeks to ensure that certain services are provided (such as education), but not by the government itself. Instead of public provision, the contract state draws up contracts with private and voluntary organizations to provide services. These organizations are then paid for services by government, which restricts its role to regulating providers and to making sure that value for money is obtained. (Ch. 3)

Contributory benefits and non-contributory benefits: payment of social security benefits to people is based on two different principles. *Contributory* benefits work on the principle that people qualify for them because they have paid (contributed) National Insurance payments to the government's social security scheme. The state retirement pension is an example of a contributory benefit. To qualify for benefit, the recipient must also belong to a certain social category or group (for example, be over retirement age). *Non-contributory* benefits work on a different principle. They are payable to anyone who qualifies on grounds of **need** and do not depend on having paid contributions to the National Insurance scheme. Income support is an example of a non-contributory benefit. (Ch. 6)

Convergence and divergence: as countries develop, they become more alike, or perhaps *converge* on a uniform model of social organization, institutions and policies. This might be because of either certain imperatives in the process of development (for example, arising from technology or market forces, or perhaps because of 'social' or 'policy learning' – exchange of policy ideas between societies). The question might be asked of international institutions like the EU, whether it is promoting convergence of member countries because of such policies as the single market, imposed on all member countries. In comparative studies *divergence* refers to a process of change in which the social policies of the countries or other units being compared become increasingly different from one another. However, it is a process and does not mean that the policies of the different countries become completely different from one another – they are just less alike than they were. Equally, convergence does not mean that policies in different countries or regions become the same or similar. Convergence is also a process in which policies become more alike than they were, but still might retain a lot of difference and distinctiveness. (Chs 3, 5)

Corporatist welfare states: a model or type of welfare state that is based on the principle of legal or informal agreements between the major 'corporate groups' of society: for instance, organized labour (trade unions), employer organizations, voluntary organizations (such as leading churches or religious organizations) and government. Germany is an example of a corporatist welfare state. Some welfare and service provision is in the hands of Church organizations, while employers' and workers' organizations come to agreements with government over **social security** benefits and other aspects of welfare. (Ch. 3)

Council housing: rented accommodation provided and owned by elected local government councils. See **social housing**. (Ch. 11)

Critique: a critical discussion of someone's idea, position, theory or set of findings. A critique appraises others' ideas and suggests new insights. (Ch. 1)

Curative medicine: an approach in medicine that emphasizes the treatment of disease to effect cures and restore health. The 'curative model' or approach implies a policy that puts more resources into treating sick people (with doctors, other medical practitioners, hospitals and drug therapy) than into preventing the onset of disease. (Chs 3, 10)

Day centre: a social services term to describe a facility which provides services during the day (for instance, meals, recreation, therapy) for people who continue to reside in their own homes. See **community care**. (Ch. 12)

Deinstitutionalization: a policy or process of change through which institutions such as mental hospitals and residential homes are closed down. It can also refer to a process of personal change in which former residents or patients lose their 'institutionalized' identities and behaviour patterns. (Chs 7, 12)

Democratic pluralist model of power: this is one of several perspectives on the way power is distributed and exercised in society (see also **elite control** and **political economy** models of power). The democratic pluralist view suggests that power is distributed widely among a large number (plurality) of different groups in society (for example, business interests, political parties, campaign groups). No one group monopolizes power or decision-making. Democratic elections make governments accountable to ordinary citizens. (Ch. 8)

Deregulation (of employment): this refers to the abolition or suspension of rules and regulations governing work contracts. Those in favour of deregulation suggest that it is a necessary process to eliminate restrictive 'red tape' that often prevents employers from hiring more workers or expanding their businesses. Those who are critical of deregulation see it as an attack on the legislation that protects workers' welfare – for instance, health and safety legislation, or rules about working time or unfair dismissal. See **casualization**. (Chs 6, 9, 12)

Deserving poor and undeserving poor: terms from the nineteenth century that imply a distinction between those who are destitute and have a moral right to state welfare or charitable support (for instance, orphaned children or disabled people unable to work), and those who could support themselves but do not do so, preferring to make undeserved claims on the state or on charities. See **dole**. (Ch. 3)

Deterrence: approach to crime control and criminal justice which states that the aim of punishment is to deter the offender (from offending again), or to deter other would-be offenders. (Ch. 5)

Development: this term has a number of meanings but is used in this book to describe the international economic development paradigm. It is used within global policy-making as an approach to improve the conditions in which people live. It is also related to economic growth, in the sense that such growth is seen as part of the conditions necessary to improve the lives of people. (Ch. 4)

Devolution: see **asymmetric devolution** and **symmetric devolution**.

Disciplines: used in this book to discuss the status and identity of different academic subjects or fields of study, such as social policy. A discipline is a recognized university subject that has generated its own body of research and has developed a distinctive set of theories. (Ch. 1)

Disposable income: the money that people have and are able to spend or invest (including the cash benefits they receive), minus any direct taxes they have to pay (see Figure 6.1). (Ch. 6)

Divergence: see **convergence**.

Dole: one of the earliest terms related to welfare. 'The dole' was the daily or weekly payment (in bread or money) to the poor of the parish. The dole was given to those who were regarded as the **deserving poor** and who could receive 'outdoor relief' (assistance from the parish or Poor Law authorities while continuing to live at home, rather than in an institution such as the workhouse). (Ch. 3)

Domiciliary care: home care, that is, social services delivered by a local authority, voluntary or private sector agency to the home (domicile). See **community care** and **residential care**. (Ch. 12)

Dual labour market: in some countries or economies – particularly in developing countries – the labour market is segmented. In the formal sector of employment, workers normally receive wages on a regular basis and work according to formal contracts; they are also protected by legislation governing their terms of employment and retirement. In the informal sector, there are no permanent jobs with regularly paid wages. Workers in the informal sector either are self-employed, or work for employers who are not bound by formal contracts governing wages, job security, health and safety, working hours, leave and so on. (Ch. 9)

Due process: term more often used in the United States than the UK, meaning approximately the same as Rule of Law. (Ch. 5)

Ecological sustainability: this means the capacity of the environment to maintain biological diversity and a range of eco-systems. Ecological sustainability is important for the planet as well as for humans and other living organisms in general in order for survival. (Ch. 4)

Economic activity and the economically active: these terms refer to employment. The total of 'economically active' in the population is a combination of everyone in paid employment *and* the unemployed. When counting unemployment, the International Labour Organization recommends that everyone aged over 16 and below retirement age is included, as long as they are seeking a job and are available to start work within two weeks' time. This is a more comprehensive measure of unemployment than counting only those who have registered as unemployed to claim state benefits. The economically active, then, normally means everyone in work plus everyone who is employable and is seeking paid work. (Ch. 9)

Economic growth: the size of an economy can be measured by statistical estimates of the total value of all the goods and services produced every year. Economic growth occurs when one year's total production exceeds a previous year's. However, economic growth measures can be criticized because they are usually based on what is known as the 'formal economy' and production or work that has been statistically measured by economists. Official economic estimates often neglect the millions of hours and the resources devoted to family care and domestic work – an 'informal economy' of welfare. (Ch. 6)

Economics: this is an academic discipline that analyses the production, distribution and consumption of goods. Political economy is also a term used with the same meaning. (Ch. 4)

Egalitarianism: a broad term, which encompasses a variety of socialist points of view. However, all egalitarians believe in the importance of absolute equality and of creating a society which minimizes distinctions of rank or status, and of income and wealth. (Ch. 2)

Eligibility: see **less eligibility**.

Elite control model of power: an analysis or view of power in society which suggests that power is concentrated in the hands of an elite, or several connected elites. Elites may be defined as extremely small groups of people who occupy the leading positions in business, government and political parties, cultural institutions and the military. (Ch. 8)

Emotional labour: this is a commonly used term used to describe aspects of jobs that involve caring. It is describing emotional regulation and control within specific occupations such as nursing and caring. (Ch. 12)

Empirical research: research (on the natural or social world) that is based on observation, experience and testing of hypotheses against factual evidence. Empirical research is used to test theories, but is not itself highly theoretical. (Ch. 1)

Empowerment: a process of change in which oppressed groups discover their ability to challenge those who oppress them. Empowerment can be brought about by change in the power structures that govern communities and social service organizations. For instance, women living in a housing estate who were previously isolated and powerless might bring themselves together to form their own campaigning group to challenge street crime, domestic violence, a lack of community services and inadequate housing maintenance. See **oppression**. (Chs 2, 11, 12)

Equality: when applied to human societies, equality describes a state in which people are closely similar in social status, income, wealth, opportunities and living conditions. See **egalitarianism**. (Ch. 2)

Equality of opportunity: exists if everyone has the same or near-similar chances to achieve their ends or goals (for instance, through educational success or seeking employment). Therefore, equality of opportunity says nothing about final outcomes, which may be highly unequal in terms of success, educational qualifications or income. Equality of opportunity is often a measure of how fair or equal conditions are at the 'starting gate' before the race, though it can also be applied to promotion, career development and further opportunities after people have entered the job market. (Ch. 2)

Equity: this term refers to justice and fairness in the distribution of something (for instance, social benefits, jobs, income and wealth). It may be just and fair for one individual or group to receive more than another because needs differ. (Ch. 2)

Expressed needs: needs which are publicly known and which have been identified as important by an individual or a group. Not all expressed needs are met, but the expression of need is an important first step in placing a demand on government or some other body. (Ch. 2)

External benefits: a term often used by economists to refer to additional benefits that could be gained from a particular policy or course of action. Rather than being a narrowly defined or individual benefit, an external benefit is likely to be something that brings a gain or payoff to the community as a whole. For instance, education brings individual benefits or payoffs (because it allows people with qualifications to obtain higher pay) but it also brings external benefits such as a general increase in productivity and efficiency. (Chs 6, 8)

Felt need: this is need which not only objectively exists (i.e. there would be agreement among observers that a particular individual or group needs something) but which also the people or groups in question realize that they have, and consciously express their feelings about. See **wants**. (Ch. 2)

Flat-rate (contributions and benefits): a rather old-fashioned term which refers to everyone paying in the same amount to a social security scheme and, if benefits are also flat-rate, all beneficiaries receiving the same amount. (Chs 3, 6)

Freedom: this may be defined 'negatively' as the absence of restraint or **oppression** (for instance, freedom from crime, freedom from arbitrary arrest), or 'positively' as freedom to do certain things, such as the freedom to follow educational courses to one's full potential. Positive freedoms have greater resource implications than negative freedoms because they often involve increases in welfare and educational spending. See **social rights**. (Chs 2, 7)

Full employment: this term describes a state of the economy and the job market in which there is plentiful employment and in which almost everyone who is economically active (except for a very small percentage who are changing jobs) is in paid work. Not only is there negligible unemployment, but also there may even be labour shortages in some areas and a slight surplus of jobs compared to the numbers of people available for work. (Chs 3, 9)

Global capitalism: this refers to the dominant economic pattern of the world within contemporary society. Most societies are capitalist in their economic approach, in that they use economic systems based upon the private ownership of capital goods and most natural resources, with the goal of making a profit. (Ch. 4)

Globalization: a world trend in which national barriers to international trade and production are being eroded away. At the same time as an international or global market in goods, services and capital is being developed, it is also argued that globalization will lead to an erosion of national differences in ideology, culture and politics. According to this argument, distinct differences in social policy between countries will gradually disappear. There could be an overall reduction in welfare provision, among industrialized countries, towards the lowest common denominator. (Chs 2, 4, 9, 14)

Global policy-making: policy is increasing influenced by global organizations and actors whose approaches transcend the boundaries of national governments. Thus, policy is made at a higher level than that of national governments. (Ch. 4)

Global priorities: this is a term used to describe the issues that are identified as priorities within policy-making at the global level. Global priorities are often debated because not everyone agrees with those that are identified as the most significant, and there are concerns about the unequal power held across the nations that influence the global priorities. (Ch. 4)

Gross domestic product (GDP): a measure of the total value, in money terms, of all the goods and services produced in a country, excluding exports and 'invisible' earnings (for example, from insurance services provided to other countries). (Chs 4, 6)

Home care: see **domiciliary care**.

Homelessness: lack of a home, which may exist even if people have a place to stay or 'a roof over their head'. People who inhabit overcrowded or hazardous dwellings, or who are unable to enjoy freedom of movement, may be described as homeless.(Ch. 11)

Human rights: fundamental moral claims – for example, the rights to life, right to a fair trial, freedom of speech, freedom of worship, right to vote, and in some cases rights to welfare – for example, health care or education – often or usually presented in constitutional documents or international declarations such as the UN Declaration of 1948 or the European Charter of 1961 and in the UK in the 1998 Human Rights Act. (Chs 3, 5)

Hypothecated taxation: a way of linking or pledging the revenue gained from taxation to public spending on clearly specified services or developments. For instance, the Liberal Democrat Party proposed an increase in income tax that could be hypothecated to increased spending on education. In this example all the extra revenue gained from the tax increase would be spent on education services and none of it could be spent on anything else. There has been a public debate about whether most taxes should be hypothecated or linked to particular services or items of public spending, or whether this would introduce too much inflexibility into the government's management of the economy. The main attraction of hypothecated taxation is an apparent greater certainty for the taxpayer about 'where all the money goes' after it has been collected in taxes. (Ch. 10)

Hypothesis: an assumption or guess that is used to explain something. Hypotheses are 'working assumptions' that need to be tested against evidence. They are developed as ways of finding out whether broader theories are correct. (Ch. 1)

Iatrogenic disease: disease that is caused or aggravated by medical treatment. (Ch. 10)

Ideology: this refers to a set of philosophical ideas or views about the social world. Ideology as a term is commonly used to discuss politics and associated policy approaches, with a range of differing views being evident in contemporary political systems. (Chs 1, 7)

Implementation (of policy): the process of carrying out a policy and turning it from a written policy statement, law or guideline into action 'on the ground'. Note, however, that even when implemented, some policies do not bring about much change. (Chs 1, 3, 8)

Income (original, gross and final income): the distinctions between original, final and gross income help to illustrate the effect of welfare provision upon people's incomes. *Original* income represents the sum that a household receives (including cash benefits). *Gross* income is the sum before taxes and other deductions are taken away. *Final* income is what is left after **taxation**, plus an estimate of the value of social/welfare services and **social security benefits** that the household receives. A year's primary schooling, for instance, might be valued at £5000 and added to the household's final income (see Figure 6.1). (Chs 3, 6)

Industrial paternalism: this term refers to the examples of employers in the nineteenth and twentieth centuries who sought to improve the living and working conditions of their employees and their families. Such concerns have been termed 'paternalist' because employers tended to assume that they knew what was best for their workers. Further, in accepting improved conditions, workers were expected to show deference and loyalty to employers. Modern industrial paternalism can be seen in the management styles of Japanese companies. See **paternalism**. (Ch. 11)

Industrial relations: a useful but now rather outdated term to describe employer–employee relations. It does not have to be restricted to 'industrial' companies or organizations, and can be used to describe the state of relations between management and trade unions in service industries – for instance, the health service. Industrial relations cover such things as wage bargaining and negotiations over work contracts. (Ch. 9)

Institutional care: see **residential care**.

Internal market: this term is used to define the way in which competition and market-*like* ways of operating have been introduced into state-run organizations and services. Thus an internal market can be developed without any privatization. Public services (for example, local authority social services) are divided into 'purchasing' and 'providing' divisions. The 'purchasing' side of the organization is then free to 'shop around' to find the service provider that will provide the best value in terms of costs and quality of services provided. See **purchaser–provider split**. (Chs 8, 10, 12)

International Monetary Fund: this is an organization of 188 countries, who work together in relation to global monetary co-operation, with the aim of securing financial stability, facilitating international trade, promoting high employment and sustainable economic growth, and reducing poverty around the world. (Ch. 4)

Justice: in social policy, justice is discussed with reference to the fairness or rightness of policies. A socially just policy, for instance, will result in the fairest possible distribution of welfare, services or resources. See **equity**. (Chs 2, 5)

Keynesian strategy/policy: named after the famous economist John Maynard Keynes on whose theories it is based, this is a policy to use government borrowing and public money to manage the economy. In times of economic slow-down or recession, for instance, Keynes advocated the careful use of public spending to generate employment and stimulate production. When unemployment is reduced, more people are able to pay tax, thus replenishing government income and enabling the government to repay its debts. This strategy was used to good effect in various countries both before and after the Second World War. More recently, there have been attempts to apply Keynesian principles in new ways (neo-Keynesianism), but the advent of a global economy (see **globalization**) has made it difficult for national governments to follow Keynesian strategies as they did in the past. (Ch. 9)

Less eligibility: a term used in the framing of the 'New' Poor Law of 1834. Eligibility in this old-fashioned usage can be taken to mean 'satisfactory'. The argument put forward by those who wanted to reform the old (pre-1834) Poor Laws was that the income and living conditions of those in receipt of public assistance (poor relief) should always be 'less eligible' (satisfactory) than the lowest-paid labourer's. (Ch. 3)

Liberal welfare states: one of several major categories or types of welfare system. A country with a 'liberal' welfare system typically has minimal welfare provision. Where public services and welfare benefits are provided, they tend to be strictly means tested (see **means tests**) and restricted to the poorest sections of society. The dominant philosophy is one of laissez-faire, and the majority make their own arrangements (through private insurance and private facilities, or reliance on family support) to safeguard their welfare. Esping-Andersen's *The Three Worlds of Welfare Capitalism* (1990) refers to this type of welfare system. (Ch. 3)

Marginalization: a social and political process in which weaker or poorer groups and individuals are excluded from, or pushed to the margins of, mainstream society. Marginalization means that the views and the needs of excluded groups tend not to be taken into account in policy-making. See **social exclusion**. (Chs 6, 7)

Maximalist policies: see **minimalist policies** and **maximalist policies**.

Means tests: rules which are used to target benefits or services upon people whose incomes (means) fall below a certain level, so that only poorer groups are eligible. Means-tested benefits may be contrasted with universal benefits, which are available to all. See **selective benefits** and **social security benefits**. (Chs 3, 6)

Medicalization: a process of social change in which perceptions of human and social problems shift towards the view that problems can best be explained as 'illnesses' which must be dealt with by medical treatment. For instance, much deviant behaviour that might once have been described as 'evil' or 'mad' is now portrayed as illness that must be treated. Natural phenomena such as childbirth have also been extensively medicalized. (Ch. 10)

Millennium Development Goals (MDGs): following the Millennium Summit of the United Nations in 2000, eight goals were defined to support international development. All of the UN member states (193 in total) have agreed to work towards these goals by the deadline of 2015, in an attempt to tackle world poverty. (Ch. 4)

Minimalist policies and maximalist policies (of equal opportunity): the terms 'minimalist' and 'maximalist' could be applied to any kind of policy, in that the former suggests the idea of doing the minimum and the latter suggests maximum government intervention and effort. In relation to equal opportunities, a minimalist policy is one that seeks to ensure that competition for jobs or education is fair and not openly discriminatory in any way. Maximalist policies are those that seek more ambitiously to change outcomes by equalizing numbers of men and women, ethnic and 'racial' groups and other under- and overrepresented groups in the workforce. See **positive action**. (Chs 2, 9)

Mixed economy of care: a phrase that summarizes the complex modern system of social and health services, which are provided and funded by a variety of different types of organization in the local authority or central government, voluntary and private sectors. The idea of a 'mixed economy' was developed originally to describe countries that combined capitalism with nationalized (state) industries. See **social care market**. (Ch. 12)

Models (of welfare or social policy): in academic discussion the term 'model' is used to describe a set of ideas that summarizes the essence or essential characteristics of something. A model is not expected to be an accurate or detailed description: it is a way of picturing or generalizing basic types. In welfare, we may therefore develop ideas or models of different types of welfare system, such as the 'Scandinavian model' of social policy. (Chs 1, 2, 3)

Need: in social policy, the term 'need' is usually reserved for objective definitions of resources, skills or other things that are required and which an individual or a group lacks: for example, psychological needs for security or personal development, or physical needs for adequate nutrition. See **comparative need**, **expressed needs**, **felt need** and **normative needs**. (Ch. 2)

Needs-led assessment: a principle of basing assessment of people's eligibility for services or welfare upon an objective definition of their needs – as opposed to 'resource-led assessment', which works on the principle of assessing need on the basis of what limited services or resources are available. (Ch. 12)

Neo-liberalism: this is a clear political approach which supports the liberalization of the economy, as well as free trade and the opening up of markets to competition. Neo-liberal ideology holds that privatization, deregulation and a smaller public sector will support the development of a larger private sector that will in turn benefit the economy, for example, in terms of growth. (Chs 2, 4)

Non-contributory benefits: see **contributory benefits**.

Normative needs: needs defined by professionals' standards and their judgement of what is lacking and what ought to be provided. (Ch. 2)

Normative policies: policies that express social norms and strong public views of what ought to happen in society. (Ch. 2)

Objectivity: this is a key term in any discussion of social science. It is particularly important in social policy because the assessment of policies is often influenced by values and political opinion rather than by objective assessment. Although complete objectivity may be impossible, this does not mean that all statements have equal validity or that one person's observations are always as valid or reliable as another's. An objective appraisal or piece of research is one that is as free of prejudice as possible. Objectivity is attained when evidence and reasoned argument show that a particular phenomenon – a government policy, for instance – has certain characteristics that exist independently of the perceiver's mind or personal opinions. (Ch. 1)

Oppression: this term is now widely used in sociology and politics, and in social work training, where 'anti-oppressive practice' is a key training goal. Oppression refers to a wide variety of behaviours and practices that unfairly deprive others (the oppressed) of their rights to **autonomy** and self-expression. In traditional and wider usage, oppression suggests tyranny and extremes of cruelty. However, in social science and social work, oppression is used to imply a broad range of discriminatory behaviour and prejudiced beliefs that exclude and demean powerless groups and individuals. See **empowerment** and **social control**. (Ch. 1)

Outcomes: the results or achievements of policies: for instance, health policy outcomes can be measured in terms of rates of various illnesses, or education policy outcomes can be measured by rates of literacy or by percentages of the population attaining various skills. (Ch. 10)

Parliamentary democracy: a form of democratic government in which almost all elected representatives are members of political parties which compete for power (although independent representatives or MPs who do not represent any political party are sometimes elected). The party that has the largest group of elected members after an election then forms the government, though it may have to rely on the support of another party if it does not have an overall majority in Parliament. In a parliamentary democracy, elected members are bound by the policies and discipline of their parties rather than by the wishes of their constituents. If there were a democracy in which those elected to power *directly* represented the wishes of the voters (for instance, to restore capital punishment), representatives would become 'delegates'. (Ch. 8)

Paternalism: a general term meaning any kind of policy or politics that is based on the view that a leader, government or influential group knows best what is in the public interest, or in the interests of less well-informed classes or social groups. Paternalistic policies tend to impose the views and policy solutions of an elite or dominant group on the rest of society, and such policies are usually shaped without much public consultation or participation. See **industrial paternalism** and **welfarism.** (Chs 2, 7, 14)

Pauperism: a state or condition of absolute poverty and of dependence on public welfare. The Victorians drew a distinction between general poverty, which many experience, and pauperism. (Ch. 3)

Payment by results (in education): a phrase associated with education policy in the last quarter of the nineteenth century. Public funding of schools was based on a system of assessing school attainment (the numbers of pupils passing tests in the 'three Rs' - mainly tests of numeracy, literacy and rote learning of basic facts) and school attendance. The more pupils a school could 'process' successfully through the tests of rote learning, the more money was received from government. (Chs 3, 8)

Penal-welfare state: term employed by sociologists influenced by Foucault to describe modern societies that combine high levels of welfare with surveillance and regulation or social control of the population through criminal justice policy. Welfare and crime control go together; crime control is the dark side of the welfare state. (Ch. 5)

Philanthropy: charity and the practice of 'good works' in the community, either by donations or benevolent action. (Ch. 11)

Policy agenda: the main public issues or topics that are seen as a priority by government and/or the general public and the mass media. There is no completely objective way of defining which issues are on the policy agenda at any particular time, because there is a constantly changing list of concerns that drift in and out of the limelight. The absence of public issues from the policy agenda may have nothing to do with their importance. Many important issues or examples of need are ignored and never reach the policy agenda. (Chs 2, 8)

Policy learning: a concept of policy development, often used in comparative analysis, implying transfer or exchange of policy ideas between one country and another. Implies that the policies of other countries provide lessons or examples on how to do things that a policy-maker can use. (Chs 5, 13)

Political economy model of power (see also the democratic pluralist and elite control models of power): this view suggests that vested political and economic interests tend to be the dominant influences on decision-making and policy. For instance, the deep-seated interests of capitalist business exert a strong influence on government decisions about public spending and social welfare. However, these influences may be subtle and hard to detect. For various reasons, including a political ideology that supports the prevailing economic system, those who are relatively powerless might nevertheless support dominant interests (for instance, by voting for political parties that are pro-business and which reduce state-provided welfare). The political economy model is primarily a Marxist view of power. (Ch. 8)

Political rights: these are rights to political expression and freedom: for instance, the right to organize and to hold political meetings, to demonstrate publicly in groups, to organize political parties, to publish political views, to hold elections and to vote without being intimidated. See **civil rights** and **social rights**. (Ch. 2)

Positive action: a term used to define a particular approach to equal opportunities policy. Positive action includes measures which go further than minimalist policies. Positive action encourages people from underrepresented groups to apply for jobs or for educational places (whereas a minimalist policy would simply try to ensure fairness or similarity of treatment of applicants). However, positive action does not go as far as positive discrimination or 'reverse discrimination', which is a policy to ensure that formerly underrepresented groups are equally represented in the workforce or in educational institutions. (Chs 2, 9)

Postfeminism: feminist perspectives show how inequalities between men and women are constructed and maintained. Postfeminist perspectives do not deny that major inequalities remain as a result of traditional patterns of male dominance. However, postfeminist perspectives point to the growing instability of men's and women's identities in the '**postmodern**' world (the identity and economic status of many men have been profoundly affected by changes in the nature of manual work, for instance). Rather than taking for granted the idea that existing gender divisions will continue, postfeminism suggests that a greater variety of male and female roles and identities will develop. (Ch. 14)

PostFordism: 'Fordism' refers to the dominant pattern of work organization in modern society. Whether one works in a factory or not, Fordist organizations tend to be large-scale, hierarchical and bureaucratic, and to divide work into specialized units. However, as a result of profound changes in the economy and in technology, the nature of work is changing. To manage these changes, organizations – whether private firms or public organizations such as NHS hospitals or social services departments – are also changing. A postFordist economy or society is one in which the majority of organizations are becoming less centralized than before, and in which employees are expected to work flexibly with a range of skills rather than as specialized workers with narrowly defined skills. (Chs 9, 14)

Postindustrialism: a term that sums up key changes in the world of work and work organization. It is held that, as the industrial society of the twentieth century gives way to a postindustrial society, work and production will no longer take place in centralized plants and offices. Increasingly, work will be performed in decentralized units and in less hierarchical or bureaucratic working environments. Knowledge-based work and the ability to use and control information will become increasingly important, while 'traditional' patterns of work in manufacturing industry will decline in significance. (Chs 9, 14)

Postmodernism: a term that refers to a wide variety of ideas about the ways in which society is changing from a 'modern' period to an emergent, postmodern period. Postmodern society is characterized by the break-up or fragmentation of all the major social institutions and social groups. For instance, working patterns, social class groups and even categories such as 'older people' are undergoing major transformations. Lifestyles, expectations and social groups are becoming increasingly diverse. This will have major implications for social policy. The 'modern' notion of centralized government and universal or 'one size fits all' policies may have to give way to more diverse patterns of government intervention (for instance, partnerships between business and government) and flexible policies. (Chs 2, 14)

Poststructuralism: a way of thinking that challenges the idea of universal truths. Poststructural ideas question the assumption that there is an underlying rationality in the social structures that we live with (such as government and state policies). A poststructural approach suggests that different ideas and views of a subject (such as poverty) all have a certain validity (even if they are not all equally valid). There may be no single or most authoritative view of a problem such as poverty and what to do about it. Therefore poststructural thinking, like **postmodernism** in general, poses questions about the basic idea of having a commonly defined policy that is based on a single, 'rational' set of goals. (Ch. 14)

Poverty (absolute and relative definitions): *absolute* definitions of poverty are ways of measuring poverty that are based on the idea that it is possible and valid to identify an objective, fixed 'poverty line'. People or groups above the line are judged not to be in poverty; those below it are. The poverty line is therefore a supposedly objective standard of living, and it may be expressed in terms of income or money, percentage of household income that has to be spent on 'basics' such as food, heating or rent, or measurements of food consumption and diet. Absolute definitions can be regularly updated to keep up with changing standards. *Relative* poverty, on the other hand, is a concept that tries to move beyond the idea of a fixed standard at a particular point in time, or poverty line. Relative definitions stress that poverty can be understood only in relation to the standard of living of the majority in society, and what society as a whole sees as necessary items or patterns of consumption to fully participate in social life. For instance, not having a television set could be seen as a valid indicator of poverty even if a family has enough food to eat and adequate housing. See **pauperism**. (Chs 1, 6)

Power: this term has a number of definitions depending upon the context in which it is used. Power is used to describe the control that some individuals/groups have over others. Political power is central to discussions of social policy and economic power; that is, the power to purchase goods and services is also relevant within policy discourse. (Chs 1, 2)

Preventive health policies/services: an approach to designing, planning and delivering policies which aims above all to prevent people from becoming ill. 'Secondary' prevention refers to the concept of preventing further illness among people who have already contracted a disease. (Ch. 10)

Primary legislation and secondary legislation: these terms have become important in debates about devolution in the UK. When laws can be made independently by a parliament or legislature in matters over which it has authority, this is *primary* legislation. For instance, the Scottish Parliament has the authority to pass primary legislation in certain policy areas (for example, education) but not others (for example, defence, foreign relations). When laws have to be made with reference to primary legislation in another legislature or parliament, as occurs in the National Assembly for Wales with reference to the UK Parliament at Westminster, then this is *secondary* legislation. (Ch. 13)

Principles: as used in this book, the term 'principles' refers to the rules or guiding ideas that govern or inform social policies. (Chs 1, 2)

Public administration: the subject or field of study that is concerned with the ways in which government policies are administered: that is, how government is organized and run, how decisions are made and how services are delivered. See **social administration**. (Ch. 1 and throughout)

Public health: this term refers to governmental and medical concern with maintaining a healthy environment and with preventing outbreaks of disease in the community. (Chs 1, 3, 10)

Purchaser–provider split: the formal separation of the two separate functions of purchasing (paying for) services and providing and delivering them. This term gained currency as the internal market was developed in health and social services during the 1980s. Formerly integrated departments (for instance, social services departments in local authorities) were divided into separate units, some of which played the 'purchaser' role, while others provided services (such as home care teams). (Ch. 12)

Quangos (quasi-autonomous non-governmental organizations): these are public bodies or organizations that have been created by government but which are not actually part of central government. Therefore, the appointees who run quangos are not civil servants. Some are experts and professionals, but many are drawn from the business world. Quango managers usually work part-time for a quango while continuing to work for other employers or as managing directors of business firms. The phrase 'quasi-autonomous' means that these organizations are partially free of government control. Quangos function at arm's length from government to oversee and manage a wide range of services. (Chs 1, 8)

Real increases/decreases (for example, in spending, wages or benefits): a technical term to indicate that, when amounts of money are compared from year to year, inflation and other distortions have been removed from the calculations. For instance, when government expenditure in 1950 and the year 2000 is compared 'in real terms', it means that like is being compared with like, in terms of the currency values that are being referred to. (Ch. 6)

Recession: a term used to identify when a country's economy has produced less in one year than the previous year. A recession is when an economy slows down so much that it actually 'shrinks', in GDP terms (see **gross domestic product**). Unemployment and other social problems associated with economic slow-down tend to get worse in times of recession. (Chs 6, 9 and throughout)

Redistribution: simply, a distribution or sharing out that is different from before. It is important to remember that redistribution of resources does not necessarily mean a shift from the rich to the poor; wealth and resources can be redistributed in favour of better-off groups. (Chs 2, 6)

Rehabilitation: a model or theory of criminal punishment, implying reform of the offender, through, for example, education, training for employment, counselling, psychiatric or social work-type interventions, to restore them to being a 'useful' member of society. Distinguished as a justifying aim of punishment from the deterrence and the 'retributivist', 'just desserts' models of punishment. (Ch. 5)

Residential care: a broad term to describe a variety of living arrangements and social care for people who cannot, or do not wish to, live in their own family homes. The term 'residential care' tends to be reserved for descriptions of social service establishments (including the private and voluntary sectors), whereas 'institutional care' is an even broader term that can include not only social services but also healthcare establishments such as hospitals and nursing homes. See **community care** and **domiciliary care**. (Chs 2, 12)

Residual (approach to state services): a residual approach or policy is one that assumes that most people will purchase welfare services, care or social security from the private sector (the market), or will look after themselves, or obtain help and care from their families. However, those who cannot fend for themselves or who cannot afford to do so form a residual (remaining) group, and a residual safety net of public services is provided for them. (Ch. 3)

Residualization: a process of change in which public services or facilities are increasingly restricted to the poor, who cannot afford better-quality private services or other forms of welfare. (Chs 11, 12, 13)

Resource-led assessment: see **needs-led assessment**.

Reverse discrimination: see **positive action**.

Risk society: term coined by the German sociologist Ulrich Beck to describe modern or perhaps **postmodern** societies in which concern about risks grows and intensifies. Old risks may be less salient, but are replaced by newer risks: for example, the environment, terrorism, crime and health risks. May have a link with the concept of 'moral panic'. (Ch. 5)

Rule of law: basic principle of a liberal society and politics, where decisions are made according to law, a system of public rules, rather than being the product of unlimited discretion by powerful individuals, groups or a political elite. For example, individuals can only be prosecuted for known offences. (Ch. 5)

Secondary legislation: see **primary legislation** and **secondary legislation**.

Selective benefits: these are means-tested social security benefits. They are 'selective' in that they target or select for assistance only those people who cannot afford to pay fees or charges, or who cannot provide for themselves. See **means tests, targeting** and **universal benefits**. (Ch. 6)

Sheltered housing: a form of accommodation for people who are relatively independent and can manage most of the tasks of daily living by themselves, but who may be frail or vulnerable in some way. Sheltered housing is usually adapted in various ways to meet the needs of those who have physical or mental impairments, or who may benefit from having access to a supervising warden. See **community care**. (Chs 7, 11, 12)

Social administration: the subject or field of study which focuses on the structure and organization of social welfare services (in particular, health, education, the personal social services, housing and community care services). While social administration has a theoretical element (administrative theory), it has traditionally been seen as less theoretical than the discipline of social policy, and more concerned with the study of the 'nuts and bolts' of service provision – the content of social services and how they are administered. See **public administration**. (Ch. 1 and throughout)

Social care market: the concept of a 'social care market' suggests competition among a number of care providers. Consumers of care, or service users, may therefore choose between providers (assuming that they have the means and resources to do so). See **mixed economy of care**. (Ch. 12)

Social consensus: general agreement. When applied to welfare policy, the idea of social consensus suggests that there is no support for any reversal or significant change to the direction of policy. (Ch. 7)

Social contract: an agreement between major social groups which may be binding (and expressed in legal terms) or may exist more loosely as a set of 'understandings' and political compromises. For instance, a social contract may develop in which trade unions expect government to follow certain economic and welfare policies in order to protect their members' livelihoods; in return, government may expect trade unions to moderate their wage demands. However, this is only one example; a 'social contract' can develop between government and any major sectional interests, or between government and the community as a whole. (Ch. 7)

Social control: any kind of relationship or social setting in which an individual's or a group's behaviour is brought into line with social norms and general expectations. Social control may be highly visible, direct and coercive (for instance, if police tactics get out of hand and become brutal and confrontational), or it may be more subtle and generally acceptable (as in preventive or community policing). See **autonomy** and **oppression**. (Chs 1, 7)

Social democratic welfare states: 'social democracy' is difficult to define in precise terms, but all social democratic states and political parties stress the importance of equality, openness and participation, and of the role of a centrally managed welfare state. Social welfare in social democratic states therefore tends to be inclusive and available to all on an equal basis. The best-known examples of the social democratic model (such as Sweden) are renowned for the comprehensiveness and generosity of their social services and social security benefits. (Chs 2, 3)

Social engineering: a philosophy or approach to government which suggests that it is possible to plan solutions to social problems and to create a new social order. (Ch. 11)

Social exclusion: a process that results in certain social groups and individuals being marginalized (see **marginalization**) and separated from 'mainstream' society. When disadvantaged and powerless groups are socially excluded, this can be observed in high rates of unemployment and the geographical concentration of excluded groups in certain types of housing or urban areas. See **underclass**. (Chs 6, 7, 11)

Social housing: housing provided for people in need who, for one reason or another, cannot purchase accommodation on the open market. Social housing may be built by and/or rented from the private sector, but usually the term 'social housing' refers to accommodation provided by, or rented from, housing associations and the voluntary sector of housing. Social housing can mean voluntary and public sector housing – in which case it is a wider category than **council housing**. (Chs 1, 11)

Social rights: these rights are associated with the development of the welfare state. In welfare states, full citizenship is expressed in rights to certain services (such as 'free' education) and social security. See **civil rights** and **political rights**. (Ch. 2)

Social security benefits (contributory, non-contributory, income-related and non-income-related): entitlement to and size of *contributory* benefits is worked out on the basis of need and also on how much an individual has previously contributed to the scheme through taxes and National Insurance contributions. *Non-contributory* benefits are provided on the basis of need only; neither the amount of benefit nor a person's right to it are affected by the contribution record. *Income-related* benefits are adjusted in amount according to the recipient's means (a means test is applied so that poorer benefit claimants receive more and the better-off receive less). *Non-income-related* benefits are standard and are calculated irrespective of income. (Chs 1, 6)

Speenhamland system: an informal system, widespread in Britain before the introduction of the 'New' Poor Law in 1834, to supplement the income of poorer agricultural and rural workers. Public money, gathered in the form of local rates or taxation, was used to subsidize poorer workers' pay on a 'sliding scale' (the lower the wage, the higher the subsidy). (Ch. 3)

Stigmatization: social stigmata are public and obvious signs of 'spoiled identity' and shame. Stigmatization refers to a process of applying such signs of deviant status and shame either to groups and individuals or to particular kinds of public services. In residual welfare systems, for instance, both those who rely on public welfare and the services themselves are likely to be stigmatized. (Chs 3, 7, 11)

Subsidiarity: the concept of allowing policies to be applied or implemented in ways that are decided at a lower (subsidiary) level of decision-making. The EU, for instance, has developed a range of social policies and (depending on their status) some of these must be adopted by member states. However, the principle of subsidiarity allows each country to develop the policy in its own way, as long as the main aims and objectives of the policy are achieved. 'Subsidiarity' also refers to the idea (underlying many social policies in European countries) of expecting the family and local community to meet welfare needs wherever possible. (Chs 4, 13)

Symmetric devolution: see **asymmetric devolution.**

Targeting: developing policies and services (in particular social security benefits) that are aimed to meet the needs of particular groups only. See **selective benefits.** (Chs 5, 6)

Taxation (direct, indirect, progressive and regressive): income taxes are examples of *direct* taxation, while *indirect* taxes are levied on goods and services. *Progressive* taxes are those that become progressively higher as income and wealth rise, so that better-off groups pay high taxes and the low-paid relatively little. *Regressive* taxes, on the other hand, take similar amounts from everyone, so that the less well-off end up losing a higher proportion of their income in tax than the better-off. (Chs 2, 6)

Tenure: a legal expression of the claim or right that someone has to live in a property, for instance by ownership, or by renting or leasing. (Chs 6, 11)

Theory: an idea to explain phenomena or facts that have been observed. (Ch. 1)

Theories of crime: a range of different ideas that are used to explain the causes of crime, as well as its existence (Ch.5)

Third age: intended to promote a positive view of later life, this concept suggests that the life course can be divided into different phases – a first age of learning, growing up and socialization, a second age of work, production and acquiring responsibility, and a third age of creative development and further learning, leisure and fulfilling activity. One drawback of the 'third age' concept is that it prompts thoughts of a 'fourth age' of decline and dependency – and has been criticized because it promotes a view of ageing that relies too much on sharply divided stages of life. (Ch. 9)

Underclass: a sociological term to describe a category or group that is excluded from the labour force. This term is highly contentious because there is disagreement about whether an underclass exists as a single group. The socially excluded comprise many different groups, such as older people, the long-term unemployed, some minority ethnic communities and lone parents. Also, there has been much disagreement about what the causes of **social exclusion** and a possible underclass might be. For instance, some suggest that members of the underclass exclude themselves from the rest of society by adopting a deviant and/or criminal lifestyle. But others suggest that, if an underclass exists, it is composed mainly of people who wish to work and to join the mainstream but are prevented from doing so for various reasons – for instance, by discrimination. (Chs 2, 7)

Undeserving poor: see **deserving poor**.

Universal benefits: universality implies that a service or benefit is available to everyone irrespective of their income or social position, so universal benefits are available to all without **means tests.** See **selective benefits**. (Ch. 6)

Utilitarianism: a school of thought which developed in the early nineteenth century, largely through the efforts of Jeremy Bentham. Utilitarianism aims to assess the value of all human action (including government policy) in terms of its 'utility' or use.

Briefly, utility or usefulness is itself assessed by the ability of an action or a policy to bring 'the greatest happiness to the greatest number'. (Ch. 2)

Values: ideas and standards which are highly important in a social group or culture. Certain values may be evident in social policies: for instance, US policies on poverty express core American values concerning self-reliance and individualism. (Ch. 1)

Wants: wants are (in social policy terms) expressions of a subjective desire for something (resources, care, a service) irrespective of need. For instance, a person might want to have a particular surgical operation but not need it. **Felt need** occurs when the person subjectively feels an actual need for something. (Ch. 2)

Welfare: an extremely difficult term to define briefly. Almost every commentator has a different definition of the main ingredients or components of human welfare. However, a comprehensive definition would include not only measures of well-being in the present, such as health and material well-being, but also opportunity and autonomy. (Chs 1, 2)

Welfare capitalism: a 'late' stage in the development of capitalist society in which the provision of welfare becomes an integral and essential part of that society and its market economy. (Ch. 7)

Welfare dependency: a term which suggests not only financial dependence on welfare benefits and services but also a state of mind – a psychological state on which those dependent on welfare lose motivation, skills, independence and self-reliance. (Chs 2, 4, 7)

Welfare pluralism: this is a useful term that sums up the way in which many observers see the future of welfare. 'Welfare pluralism' suggests that welfare provision will increasingly become the responsibility of a number – a plurality – of providers (state, voluntary, private and informal) rather than being mainly the responsibility of the state. (Ch. 12)

Welfare system: a phrase which can be used to suggest that a structure of welfare services and social security exists, but that this is not provided by, or organized solely, by, government. Where welfare *is* still mainly a government-run concern, we may continue to use the term 'welfare state'; otherwise, 'welfare system' may be more appropriate. (Ch. 1)

Welfarism: a set of political and social values that strongly support the existence and continuation of a comprehensive welfare state. Sometimes welfarism may underpin paternalistic, condescending attitudes towards certain social groups – for instance, disabled people. Welfarism might lead to the assumption that everyone in a particular group such as disabled people needs support and is bound to be dependent on welfare services. See **paternalism**. (Chs 1, 2, 7)

'Whole system' comparisons: as an alternative to comparing individual social policies in one country with those of another (for instance, policies in the Netherlands and Britain towards the idea of decriminalizing certain drugs), it is possible to compare the 'whole systems' of each country (or groups of countries). This means comparing their economic systems, political systems, belief or value systems and so on. This will help to put their respective social policies in context (see Jones 1985). (Ch. 3)

Workfare: policies which seek to make eligibility for benefits and welfare conditional upon willingness to work – in other words, claimants receive benefits only if they have completed a specified total of hours of work per week. (Chs 3, 6, 7)

Workhouse: a centuries-old social institution which provided shelter and subsistence to the poor. If people were able-bodied they were usually expected to work in the institution at menial and/or backbreaking tasks, but workhouses were also a form of residential care for the non-able-bodied. (Chs 2, 3)

World Bank: this is an international financial institution, the remit of which includes the provision of loans to lower-income countries. It is different from a traditional bank in the sense that its goal is the reduction of poverty. The bank is also committed to promoting foreign investment, international trade, and the facilitation of capital investment. (Ch. 4)

World Health Organization: this is a United Nations (UN) agency with a remit to deal with international public health. It was established in 1948, and its most notable success is the successful eradication of smallpox. Priorities have varied over the years, but currently include tackling communicable diseases such as HIV/AIDS, malaria and tuberculosis; encouraging development; and working towards food security. The organization reports upon a variety of international health issues and produces various publication such as the *World Health Report* on an annual basis. (Ch. 4)

Bibliography

Abbott, P. and Sapsford, R. (1990) Health Visiting: Policing in the Family?, in P. Abbott and C. Wallace (eds) *The Sociology of the Caring Professions*, pp. 120–52. Basingstoke: Falmer Press.

Abel-Smith, B. and Titmuss, K. (eds) (1987) *The Philosophy of Welfare: Selected Writings of Richard M. Titmuss*. London: Allen & Unwin.

Acheson, D. (1998) *Independent Inquiry into Inequalities in Health Report*. London: Stationery Office.

Addison, P. (1994) *The Road to 1945: British Politics and the Second World War*. London: Pimlico.

Alcock, P. (1996) *Social Policy in Britain: Themes and Issues*. Basingstoke: Macmillan.

Alcock, P. (1997) *Understanding Poverty*, 2nd edn. Basingstoke: Macmillan.

Aldridge, H., Parekh, A., MacInne, T. and Kenway, P. (2011) *Monitoring Poverty and Social Exclusion 2011*. York: Joseph Rowntree Foundation.

Annesley, C. (2003) Americanised and Europeanised: UK Social Policy since 1997, *British Journal of Politics and International Relation* 5(2): 143–65.

Arber, S. and Gilbert, N. (1988) Men: The Forgotten Carers, *Sociology* 23(1): 111–18.

Atkinson, R. (2003) Urban Policy, in N. Ellison and C. Pierson (eds) *Developments in British Social Policy 2*. Basingstoke: Palgrave.

AUT (Association of University Teachers) (2001) Swansea AUT News, unpublished Newsletter, 7 June.

Audit Commission (1986) *Making a Reality of Community Care*. London: HMSO.

Baggott, R. (1994) *Health and Health Care in Britain*. London: Macmillan.

Balchin, P. (1995) *Housing Policy: An Introduction*, 3rd edn. London: Routledge.

Barnett, C. (1986) *The Audit of War*. London: Macmillan.

Barr, A., Stenhouse, C. and Henderson, P. (2001) *Caring Communities: A Challenge for Social Inclusion*. York: York Publishing Services.

Barr, N. (1998) *The Economics of the Welfare State*. Oxford: Oxford University Press.

Barrow, B. (2012) The North–South Mortgage Divide: Negative Equity Map of UK Shows Clear Disparity, *Daily Mail*, www.dailymail.co.uk/news/article-2128825/The-North-South-mortgage-divide-Negative-equity-map-UK-shows-clear-schism.html (accessed 2 January 2013).

BBC News (2010a) Pay Gap Between Men and Women Narrows, Says ONS, *BBC*, www.bbc.co.uk/news/business-11947127 (accessed 6 December 2012).

BBC News (2010b) Tuition Fees Protest Violence 'Unacceptable', Says PM, *BBC*, www.bbc.co.uk/news/uk-politics-11732264 (accessed 24 July 2012).

BBC News (2011a) Cameron Criticises 'Coasting' State Schools, *BBC*, www.bbc.co.uk/news/education-14860352 (accessed 27 November 2012).

BBC News (2011b) Thousands March in Student Protest over University Fees, *BBC*, www.bbc.co.uk/news/education-15646709 (accessed 24 July 2012).

BBC News (2011c) 'Sarah's Law' Scheme Covers all England and Wales, *BBC*, www.bbc.co.uk/news/uk-12952334 (accessed 27 July 2012).

BBC News (2012a) Abuse Secretly Filmed in 'Excellent' London Care Home, *BBC*, www.bbc.co.uk/news/uk-17810136 (accessed 26 September 2012).

BBC News (2012b) Bickleigh Down 'Eco Village' Plans Approved for Plymouth, *BBC*, www.bbc.co.uk/news/uk-england-devon-20266407 (accessed 3 January 2012).

BBC News (2012c) CBI Complains of 'Exam Factory' Schools, *BBC*, www.bbc.co.uk/news/education-20355664 (accessed 27 November 2012).

BBC News (2012d) Compulsory Retirement Age at 65 Fully Abolished, *BBC*, www.bbc.co.uk/news/business-15127835 (accessed 18 September 2012).

BBC News (2012e) Governments Turn to Indirect Taxes to Boost Revenue, *BBC*, www.bbc.co.uk/news/business-17673436 (accessed 17 September 2012).

BBC News (2012f) Athens Clashes as Greek Police Fire Tear Gas, *BBC*, www.bbc.co.uk/news/world-europe-19724284 (accessed 26 July 2012).

BBC News (2012g) Spain Police Fire Rubber Bullets at Madrid Protest, *BBC*, www.bbc.co.uk/news/world-europe-19712203 (accessed 26 July 2012).

BBC News (2012h) Whipps Cross Hospital: Three Charged over Abuse Claims, *BBC*, www.bbc.co.uk/news/uk-england-19371636 (accessed 26 September 2012).

BBC News Scotland (2012) Robert Black: Free Public Services Need 'Revisiting', *BBC*, www.bbc.co.uk/news/uk-scotland-19839096 (accessed 21 January 2013).

Beck, U. (1999). *World Risk Society.* Cambridge: Polity Press.

Bellamy, K., Bennett, F. and Millar, J. (2006) *Who Benefits? A Gender Analysis of the UK Benefits and Tax Credits System.* London: Fawcett Society.

Beland, D. and Waddan, A. (2012) The Obama Presidency and Health Insurance Reform: Assessing Continuity and Change, *Social Policy and Society* 11(3): 319–30.

Benjamin, A. and Carvel, J. (2006) The Cost of Cutting Edge, *Guardian*, 5 April.

Bennett, F. (1998) Social Policy Digest, *Journal of Social Policy* 27(3): 397–420.

Bennett, F. (2000) Social Policy Digest, *Journal of Social Policy* 29(4): 669–96.

Bennett, O. (1996) It's Really Nice Once You Get Inside, *Independent on Sunday* (Real Lives section), 8 September: 3.

Bentham, J. (1982) *An Introduction to the Principles of Morals and Legislation*, edited by J.H. Burns and H.L.A. Hart. London: Methuen.

Bentley, D. and Churcher, J. (2010) Cameron Defends Wellbeing Measure, *Independent*, www.independent.co.uk/news/uk/politics/cameron-defends-wellbeing-measure-2143595.html (accessed 26 September 2012).

Berkel, R.V. and Borghi, V. (2008) Introduction: The Governance of Activation, *Social Policy and Society* 7(3): 331–40.

Best, G. (1979) *Mid-Victorian Britain 1851–75.* London: Fontana.

Bevan, S. (2000) *Family-Friendly Employment: The Business Case.* Research Report No. 136. London: DfEE.

Bevan, G., Mays, N. and Connelly, S. (2010) *Funding and Performance of Health Care Systems in the Four Countries of the UK Before and After Devolution.* London: Nuffield Trust.

Beveridge, Sir W. (1942) *Social Insurance and Allied Services* (Beveridge Report). Cmnd 6404. London: HMSO.

Bexell, M., Tallberg, J. and Uhlin, A. (2010) Democracy in Global Governance: The Promises and Pitfalls of Transnational Actors, *Global Governance* 16: 81–101.

Bhagwati, J. (2004) *In Defense of Globalization.* Oxford: Oxford University Press.

Bingham, J. (2011) Kenneth Clarke Questions whether Date Rape is Really 'Rape', *Telegraph*, www.telegraph.co.uk/news/politics/8520940/Kenneth-Clarke-questions-whether-date-rape-is-really-rape.html (accessed 26 July 2012).

BIS (2011) *Higher Education: Students at the Heart of the System.* CM8122. London, Stationery Office.

Black, C. (2008) *Working for a Healthier Tomorrow.* London: The Stationery Office.

Blair, T. (1993) Why Crime is a Socialist Issue, *New Statesman*, 29 January: 27–8.

Blakemore, K. and Drake, R.F. (1995) *Understanding Equal Opportunity Policies.* Hemel Hempstead: Prentice Hall.

Blank, R.H. and Burau, V. (2004) *Comparative Health Policy.* Basingstoke: Palgrave.

Bogdanor, V. (1999) *Devolution in the United Kingdom.* Oxford: Oxford University Press.

Bogdanor, V. (2001) England May Get Its Turn, *Guardian*, 23 April: 17.

Bolton, P. (2010) *Changes to Higher Education Funding and Student Support in England from 2012/13.* House of Commons Library SN/SG/5753.

Bornat, J., Johnson, J., Pereira, C., Pilgrim, D. and Williams, F. (eds) (1997) *Community Care: A Reader.* 2nd edn. Basingstoke: Macmillan.

Boseley, S. (2000a) Cancer Diagnosis Errors no worse than Average, *Guardian*, 15 June: 6.

Boseley, S. (2000b) Doctor's Errors Led to Agony and Death, *Guardian*, 21 October: 6.

Bowcott, O. (2012) Prisoners Must Be Given Right to Vote, European Court Rules, *Guardian*, www.guardian.co.uk/politics/2012/may/22/prisoners-right-to-vote-echr (accessed 26 July 2012).

Box, S. (1987) *Recession, Crime and Punishment.* London: Macmillan.

Bradbury, J. and Mawson, J. (1996) *British Regionalism and Devolution: The Challenges of State Reform and European Integration.* London: Jessica Kingsley.

Bradshaw, J. (1972) The Concept of Social Need, *New Society* 30: 640–3.

Brautigam, D. (2000) *Aid Dependence and Governance.* Expert Group on Development Issues, Sweden.

Brewster, C. and Teague, P. (1989) *European Community Social Policy and its Impact on the UK.* London: Institute of Personnel Management.

Brimelow, A. (2011) Devolution Points Way to Different Types of NHS, *BBC,* www.bbc.co.uk/news/health-13122448 (accessed 21 January 2013).

Brindle, D. (1995) Government Backs Bill to Recognise Carers, *Guardian,* 3 March: 7.

Brindle, D. (1998) Civil Liberty Row on Mental Health Law, *Guardian,* 9 December: 14.

Brown, G. (2003) State and Market: Towards a Public Interest Test, *Political Quarterly* 74(3): 266–84.

Brown, P. (2012) A Nudge in the Right Direction? Towards a Sociological Engagement with Libertarian Paternalism, *Social Policy and Society* 11(3): 305–17.

Brown, P., Green, A. and Lauder, H. (2001) *High Skills: Globalization, Competitiveness and Skill Formation.* Oxford: Oxford University Press.

Browne, A. (2000) Ageist NHS Lets Elderly Suffer, *Observer,* 13 August: 3.

Browne, J. (2010) *Securing a Sustainable Future for Higher Education: An Independent Review of Higher Education and Student Finance,* www.gov.uk/government/uploads/system/uploads/attachment_data/file/31999/10-1208-securing-sustainable-higher-education-browne-report.pdf (accessed 5 June 2013).

Bryson, B. (1996) *Notes from a Small Island.* London: Black Swan.

Budge, I., Crewe, I., McKay, D. and Newton, K. (1998) *The New British Politics.* Harlow: Addison Wesley Longman.

Bullard, R.D. (1990) *Dumping in Dixie: Race, Class and Environmental Quality.* Boulder, CO: Westview.

Bulmer, M. and Rees, A.M. (eds) (1996) *Citizenship Today: The Contemporary Relevance of T.H. Marshall.* London: UCL Press.

Burchardt, T. (2000) *Enduring Economic Exclusion: Disabled People, Income and Work.* Joseph Rowntree Foundation Report. York: York Publishing Services.

Burden, T. (2000) Poverty, in J. Percy-Smith (ed.) *Policy Responses to Social Exclusion: Towards Inclusion?* Buckingham: Open University Press.

Busfield, J. (2010) A Pill for Every Ill: Explaining the Expansion in Medicine Use, *Social Science & Medicine* 70(6): 934–41.

Butler. P. and Ferguson, B. (2012) Homeless Families to Be Expelled from London by Councils, *Guardian,* www.guardian.co.uk/society/2012/nov/04/london-boroughs-housing-families-outside-capital (accessed 3 January 2013).

Bytheway, B. and Johnson, J. (1997) The Social Construction of Carers, in A. Symonds and A. Kelly (eds) *The Social Construction of Community Care.* London: Macmillan.

Cahill, M. (1994) *The New Social Policy.* Oxford: Blackwell.

Callender, C. (2012) The 2012/13 Reforms of Higher Education in England: Changing Student Finances and Funding, in M. Kilkey, G. Ramia and K. Farnsworth (eds) *Social Policy Review 24: Analysis and Debate in Social Policy 2012.* Bristol: Policy Press.

Cameron. D. (2010) Return to Responsibility: With Less Bureaucracy and Greater Personal Responsibility, People are More Likely to Make Ethical Decisions, *Guardian,* www.guardian.co.uk/commentisfree/2010/feb/27/david-cameron-personal-responsibility (accessed 21 June 2012).

Cammack, P. (1999) The Mother of all Governments: The World Bank's Matrix for Global Governance, in R. Wilkinson and S. Hughes (eds) *Global Governance: Critical Perspectives.* London: Routledge.

Campbell, D. (2012a) Patients with Rare Conditions Face Postcode Lottery, *Guardian,* www.guardian.co.uk/society/2012/oct/20/patients-rare-conditions-postcode-lottery (accessed 14 December 2012).

Campbell, D. (2012b) Survey Reveals NHS Staff Fears over Reforms, *Guardian,* www.guardian.co.uk/society/2012/sep/11/survey-reveals-nhs-staff-fears-reforms (accessed 27 November 2012).

Carter, H. (2012) Six Arrested over Alleged Mistreatment of Elderly Care Home Residents, *Guardian*, www.guardian.co.uk/society/2012/oct/10/six-arrested-alleged-mistreatment-elderly (accessed 9 January 2013).

Carter, J. and Rayner, M. (1996) The Curious Case of Post-Fordism and Welfare, *Journal of Social Policy* 25(3): 347–67.

Carvel, J. (2001) Tories Dispute Waiting List Fall, *Guardian*, 12 May: 4.

Carvel, J. (2005) 'Age Shall Not Weary Him . . .', *Guardian*, 2 February.

Carvel, J. and MacLeod, D. (1995) Learning Swerve, *Guardian*, 14 June: 15.

Casserley, C. (2000) The Disability Discrimination Act: An Overview, in J. Cooper (ed.) *Law, Rights and Disability*. London: Jessica Kingsley.

Cassidy, S. (2012) Nearly 10,000 Homes Repossessed in First Three Months of 2012, *Independent*, www.independent.co.uk/news/uk/home-news/nearly-10000-homes-repossessed-in-first-three-months-of-2012-7734533.html (accessed 2 January 2013).

Cavadino, M. and Dignan, J. (2000) Penal Systems: A Comparative Approach, in W.E. C.A. Valkenburg, M. Cavadino and J. Dignan (eds) *Comparative Criminal Law*. Tilburg: Katholieke Universiteit Brabant.

Cavadino, M. and Dignan, J. (2006) *Penal Systems: A Comparative Approach*. London: Sage.

Challis, D., Darton, R., Johnson, L., Stone, M. and Traske, K. (1995) *Care Management and Health Care of Older People: The Darlington Community Care Project*. Aldershot: Arena.

Chaney, P. and Drakeford, M. (2004) The Primacy of Ideology: Social Policy and the First Term of the National Assembly for Wales, *Social Policy Review* 16.

Chaney, P., Hall, T. and Pithouse, A. (eds) (2001) *New Governance: New Democracy?* Cardiff: University of Wales Press.

Chaplin. R., Flatley, J. and Smith. J. (2011) *Crime in England and Wales 2010/11*. London: Home Office.

Citizens' Advice Bureau (1998) *Flexibility Abused*. London: National Association of Citizens' Advice Bureaux.

Clark, I. (2001) Globalization and the Post-Cold War Order, in J. Baylis and S. Smith (eds) *The Globalization of World Politics: An Introduction to International Relations*, 2nd edn. New York: Oxford University Press.

Coalition Government, The (2010) *The Coalition: Our Programme for Government*. London: HM Government.

Cohen, S. (1987) *Folk Devils and Moral Panics*. London: MacGibbon and Kee.

Cole, C. and Furbey, R. (1994) *The Eclipse of Council Housing*. London: Routledge.

Collini, S. (2011) From Robbins to Mckinsey, *London Review of Books*, www.lrb.co.uk/v33/n16/stefan-collini/from-robbins-to-mckinsey (accessed 28 November 2012).

Commission on Global Governance (1995) *Our Global Neighbourhood: The Report of the Commission on Global Governance*. Oxford: Oxford University Press.

Commission on the Social Determinants of Health (2008) *Closing the Gap in a Generation: Health Equity through Action on the Social Determinants of Health*, www.who.int/social_determinants/thecommission/finalreport/en/index.html (accessed 23 October 2012).

Constitution Unit (2005a) Devolution Monitoring Programme, *Northern Ireland Report*, 23 July.

Constitution Unit (2005b) Nations and Regions: The Dynamics of Devolution, *Quarterly Monitoring Programme, Scotland: Quarterly Report*, April.

Constitution Unit (2005c) Nations and Regions: The Dynamics of Devolution, *Quarterly Monitoring Programme, Wales: Quarterly Report*, April.

Constitution Unit (2006) *Wales Devolution Monitoring Report*, May.

Cooper, J. (ed.) (2000) *Law, Rights and Disability*. London: Jessica Kingsley.

Council of Europe, The (2010) *Criminalisation of Migration in Europe: Human Rights Implications*. Issue Paper commissioned and published by Thomas Hammarberg, Council of Europe Commissioner for Human Rights, https://wcd.coe.int/ViewDoc.jsp?id=1579605 (accessed 25 July 2012).

Crinson, I. (2009) *Health Policy: A Critical Perspective*. London: Sage.

Crowther, A. (1988) *Social Policy in Britain 1914–1939*. Basingstoke: Macmillan.

Crowther, A. (2008) When Good Times Turn Bad. *Health Service Journal*, 4 December 2008: 20–2.

CSO (Central Statistical Office) (1996) *Social Trends 26*. London: HMSO.

Curtis, B. (2005) Government to Revamp Academy Schools Plan, *Guardian*, 23 July: 8.
Dahl, R.A. (1961) *Who Governs? Democracy and Power in an American City*. New Haven, CT: Yale University Press.
Dahlburg, J.-T. (1995) Sweatshop Case Dismays Few in Thailand', *Los Angeles Times*, 27 August.
Dale, J. and Foster, P. (1986) *Feminists and State Welfare*. London: Routledge.
Davies, R. (1999) *Devolution: A Process, not an Event*. Cardiff: Institute of Welsh Affairs.
Davies, S.E. (2010) *Global Politics of Health*. Cambridge and Malden, MA: Polity Press.
de Grazia, V. (2005). *Irresistible Empire: America's Advance through 20th Century Europe*. Cambridge, MA: Harvard University Press.
de Swaan, A. (1989) The Reluctant Imperialism of the Medical Profession, *Social Science and Medicine*, 28(11): 1165–70.
Deakin, N. (1994) *The Politics of Welfare*, 2nd edn. Hemel Hempstead: Harvester Wheatsheaf.
Dean, H. (1991) *Social Security and Social Control*. London: Routledge.
Dean, H. (2012) *The (Non-)Boundaries of Social Policy*, www.politybooks.com/blog/post.aspx?id=124 (accessed 25 May 2012).
Dean, H. and Hartley, G. (1995) Listen to Learn, *Community Care*, 30 March: 22–3.
Dearing, Sir R. (1994) *National Curriculum and Assessment: Final Report*. London: School Curriculum and Assessment Authority.
Denny, C. (2000) Tories' Legacy of Poverty, *Guardian*, 12 January: 2.
DETR/DSS (Department of Environment, Transport and the Regions / Department of Social Security) (2000) *Quality and Choice: A Decent Home for All*. London: DETR/DSS.
DHSS (Department of Health and Social Security) (1977) *The Way Forward*. London: HMSO.
DHSS (Department of Health and Social Security) (1983) *NHS Management Inquiry* (the Griffiths Report). London: DHSS.
Dilnot, A. (2001) Our Unequal Society, *Guardian*, 2 June: 20.
Directgov (2012a) *Crime and Justice: Alcohol and Crime*, www.direct.gov.uk/en/CrimeJusticeAndTheLaw/CrimePrevention/DG_181558 (accessed 27 July 2012).
Directgov (2012b) State Pension and Pension Credit Rate: What You'll Get, www.direct.gov.uk/en/Pensionsandretirementplanning/StatePension/DG_188551 (accessed 18 September 2012).
Dixon, A., Le Grand, J., Murray, R. and Poteliakhoff, E. (2003) *Is the NHS Equitable? A Review of the Evidence*. Health and Social Care Discussion Paper 11. London: LSE.
DoH (Department of Health) (1989) *Caring for People: Community Care in the Next Decade and Beyond*. London: HMSO.
DoH (Department of Health) (1996) *The National Health Service: A Service with Ambitions*. Cm 3425. London: The Stationery Office.
DoH (Department of Health) (1997) *The New NHS: Modern, Dependable*. London: DoH.
DoH (Department of Health) (1998a) *Modernising Social Services*. London: The Stationery Office.
DoH (Department of Health) (1998b) *Our Healthier Nation: A Contract for Health*. London: The Stationery Office.
DoH (Department of Health) (2001) *Shifting the Balance of Power within the NHS: Securing Delivery*. London: DoH.
DoH (Department of Health) (2005) *Independence, Well-being and Choice*. Cm 6499. London: The Stationery Office.
DoH (Department of Health) (2006) *Our Health, Our Care, Our Say: A New Direction for Community Services*. Cm 6737. London: The Stationery Office.
DoH (Department of Health) (2009) *Shaping the Future of Care Together*. London: The Stationery Office.
DoH (Department of Health) (2010a) *Equity and Excellence: Liberating the NHS*. London: The Stationery Office.
DoH (Department of Health) (2010b) *Healthy Lives, Healthy People: Our Strategy for Public Health in England*. London: The Stationery Office.
DoH (Department of Health) (2011a) *Government Launches NHS Listening Exercise*, http://healthandcare.dh.gov.uk/nhs-engagement-exercise (accessed 5 June 2013).
DoH (Department of Health) (2011b) *Government Changes in Response to the NHS Future Forum*. London: DoH.
Donnison, J. (1988) *Midwives and Medical Men*. 2nd edn. London: Heinemann.

Donoghue, J. (2008) Antisocial Behaviour Orders (ASBOs) in Britain: Contextualizing Risk and Reflexive Modernization, *Sociology* 42(2): 337–55.

Donzelot, J. (1980) *The Policing of Families: Welfare Versus the State*. London: Hutchinson.

Doogan, K. (2009) *New Capitalism: The Transformation of Work*. Cambridge: Polity Press.

Dorling, D. (2010) *Injustice: Why Social Inequality Persists*. Bristol: Policy Press.

Dorling, D. and Thomas, B. (2011) *Bankrupt Britain: An Atlas of Social Change*. Bristol: Policy Press.

Downes, D. (1988) *Contrasts in Tolerance: Post-War Penal Policy in the Netherlands and England and Wales*. Oxford: Oxford University Press.

Downes, D. and Morgan, R. (2002) The Skeletons in the Cupboard: The Politics of Law and Order at the Turn of the Millennium, in M. Maguire, R. Morgan and R. Reiner (eds) *Oxford Handbook of Criminology*. Oxford: Oxford University Press.

Doyal, L. and Gough, I. (1991) *A Theory of Human Needs*. Basingstoke: Macmillan Education.

Drabble, M. (1988) *Case for Equality*. Fabian Tract 527. London: The Fabian Society.

Drake, R.F. (1999) *Understanding Disability Policies*. Basingstoke: Macmillan.

Drake, R.F. (2001) *The Principles of Social Policy*. New York: Palgrave.

DSS (Department of Social Security) (1994) *Households Below Average Income: A Statistical Analysis 1979–1991–92*. London: HMSO.

DSS (Department of Social Security) (2000) *Opportunity for All*. Cm 4865. London: DSS.

DWP (Department for Work and Pensions) (2004) *Work and Pension Statistics*. London: DWP.

DWP (Department for Work and Pensions) (2010a) *A New Approach to Child Poverty: Tackling the Cause of Disadvantage and Transforming Families' Lives*. London: DWP.

DWP (Department for Work and Pensions) (2010b) *21st Century Welfare*. London: DWP.

DWP (Department for Work and Pensions) (2010c) *The Work Programme Framework*, www.dwp.gov.uk/docs/work-programme-prospectus.pdf (accessed 11 July 2011).

DWP (Department for Work and Pensions) (2010d) *Universal Credit: Welfare that Works*. London: DWP.

DWP (Department for Work and Pensions) (2012a) *Social Security Benefits and Expenditure*, www.parliament.uk/briefing-papers/SN02656.pdf (accessed 18 September 2012).

DWP (Department for Work and Pensions) (2012b) *Policy*, www.dwp.gov.uk/policy/welfare-reform/universal-credit (accessed 18 September 2012).

DWP (Department for Work and Pensions) (2012c) *Welfare Reform*, www.dwp.gov.uk/policy/welfare-reform (accessed 17 September 2012).

DWP (Department for Work and Pensions) (2013) *Policy: Simplifying the Welfare System and Making Sure Work Pays*, www.gov.uk/government/policies/simplifying-the-welfare-system-and-making-sure-work-pays (accessed 22 May 2013).

DWP and DfE (Department for Work and Pensions and Department for Education) (2011) *A New Approach to Child Poverty: Tackling the Causes of Disadvantage and Transforming Families' Lives*. London: The Stationery Office, www.gov.uk/government/uploads/system/uploads/attachment_data/file/177031/CM-8061.pdf (accessed 22 May 2013).

Easton, M. (2012) Housing Crisis Deepens, *BBC*, www.bbc.co.uk/news/uk-18416365 (accessed 2 January 2013).

Elliott, L. (2000) It's Working, *Guardian*, 17 October: 19.

Esping-Andersen, G. (1990) *The Three Worlds of Welfare Capitalism*. Cambridge: Polity Press.

Eurostat (2012a) *Eurostat News Release, Euro Indicators: Euro Area Unemployment Rate at 11.6%* (September), http://epp.eurostat.ec.europa.eu/cache/ITY_PUBLIC/3-31102012-BP/EN/3-31102012-BP-EN.PDF.

Eurostat (2012b) *Labour Market Participation by Sex and Age*, http://epp.eurostat.ec.europa.eu/statistics_explained/index.php/Labour_market_participation_by_sex_and_age (accessed 6 December 2012).

Exworthy, M., Blane, D. and Marmot, M. (2003), Tackling Health Inequalities in the United Kingdom: The Progress and Pitfalls of Policy, *Health Services Research* 38: 1905–22. doi: 10.1111/j.1475-6773.2003.00208.x.

FAO (Food and Agriculture Organization of the United Nations) (2010) *The State of Food Insecurity in the World 2010: Addressing Food Insecurity in Protracted Crises*. Rome: FAO.

Faulkner, D. (2001) *Crime, State and Citizen*. Winchester: Waterside Press.

Feacham, R.G.A. (2001) Globalisation is Good for Your Health, Mostly, *British Medical Journal* 323: 504–6.

Field, F. (1995) The Poison in the Welfare State, *Independent on Sunday*, 14 May: 27.

Fink, J. (ed.) (2004) *Care: Personal Lives and Social Policy*. Bristol: Policy Press.

Finn, D. (2003) Employment Policy, in N. Ellison and C. Pierson (eds) *Developments in British Social Policy 2*. Basingstoke: Palgrave Macmillan.

Firth, J. (1987) *Public Support for Residential Care: Report of a Joint Central and Local Government Working Party*. London: DHSS.

Fitzpatrick, T. (1996) Postmodernism, Welfare and Radical Politics, *Journal of Social Policy* 25(3): 303–20.

Ford, J. (2003) Housing Policy, in N. Ellison and C. Pierson (eds) *Developments in British Social Policy 2*. Basingstoke: Palgrave Macmillan.

Forrest, R. and Murie, A. (1988) *Selling the Welfare State*. London: Routledge.

Foucault, M. (1977) *Discipline and Punish: The Birth of the Prison*. Harmondsworth: Penguin.

Fowler, A.F. (1998) Authentic NGDO Partnerships in the New Policy Agenda for International Aid: Dead End or Light Ahead? *Development and Change* 29: 137–59.

Fraser, D. (1984) *The Evolution of the British Welfare State*. Basingstoke: Macmillan.

Fraser, D. (2003) *The Evolution of the British Welfare State*. 3rd edn. Basingstoke: Macmillan.

Friedman, M. (1962) *Capitalism and Freedom*. Chicago: University of Chicago Press.

Gabbatt, A. (2011) 'Occupy' Anti-Capitalism Protests Spread Around the World, *Guardian*, www.guardian.co.uk/world/2011/oct/16/occupy-protests-europe-london-assange (accessed 19 December 2011).

Gant, W. (2012) Worst Outlook for 18yrs Faces School Leavers, *Metro*, 15 August 2012.

Garland, D. (1985) *Punishment and Welfare*. Aldershot: Gower.

Garland, D. (2001) *The Culture of Control: Crime and Social Order in Contemporary Society*. Oxford: Clarendon Press.

Gatrell, V.A.C. (1990) Crime, Authority and the Policeman State, in F.M.L. Thompson (ed.) *The Cambridge Social History of Britain 1750–1950*. Cambridge: Cambridge University Press.

George, V. and Wilding, P. (2009) Globalization and Human Welfare: Why Is there a Need for a Global Social Policy? in J. Douglas, S. Earle, S. Handsley, L. Jones, C.E. Lloyd and S. Spurr (eds) *A Reader in Promoting Public Health*. London: Sage: 27–34.

GHS (General Household Survey) (1983) *General Household Survey 1983*. London: OPCS.

Gibbs, G. (2000) Doctor Blundered in More than 200 cases, *Guardian*, 14 May: 4.

Giddens, A. (1994) *Beyond Left and Right: The Future of Radical Politics*. Cambridge: Polity Press.

Giddens, A. (2009) *Sociology*. 6th edn. Cambridge: Polity Press.

Gillard, D. (2010) Chapter 12: 2010 What Future for Education in England?, in *Education in England: A Brief History*, www.educationengland.org.uk/history (accessed 27 November 2012).

Gilmour, Sir Ian (1992) *Dancing with Dogma*. London: Simon & Schuster.

Girling, R. (2005) *Rubbish! Dirt on Our Hands and Crisis Ahead*. London: Transworld Publishers.

Glendinning, C. and Millar, J. (eds) (1992) *Women and Poverty in Britain*. Hemel Hempstead: Harvester Wheatsheaf.

Glennerster, H. (1995) *British Social Policy Since 1995*. Oxford: Blackwell.

Glennerster, H. (2003) *Understanding the Finance of Welfare: What Welfare Costs and How to Pay for It*. Bristol: Policy Press.

Glennerster, H. (2005) The Health and Welfare Legacy, in A. Seldon and D. Kavanagh (eds) *The Blair Effect 2001–5*. Cambridge: Cambridge University Press.

Glennerster, H., Hills, J., Piachaud, D. and Webb, J. (eds) (2004) *One Hundred Years of Poverty and Policy*. York: Joseph Rowntree Foundation.

Glover, S. (2012) Cuts? WHAT cuts? Ignore the BBC and the Left, Public Spending is HIGHER than under Labour, *Daily Mail*, www.dailymail.co.uk/news/article-2146571/Cuts-What-cuts-Ignore-BBC-Left-public-spending-HIGHER-Labour.html (accessed 18 September 2012)

Goffman, E. (1991) *Asylums: Essays on the Social Situation of Mental Patients and Other Inmates*. Harmondsworth: Penguin.

Goodwin, M. (2011) English Education Policy after New Labour: Big Society or Back to basics?, *The Political Quarterly* 82(3): 407–24.

Gordon, D. and Pantazis, C. (1997) *Breadline Britain in the 1990s*. Aldershot: Ashgate.
Gordon, D., Adelman, L., Ashworth, K., et al. (eds) (2000) *Poverty and Social Exclusion in Britain*. York: Joseph Rowntree Foundation.
Gough, I. (1979) *The Political Economy of the Welfare State*. London: Macmillan.
Gould, A. (1999) The Erosion of the Welfare State: Swedish Social Policy and European Union, *Journal of European Social Policy* 9(2): 165–74.
Gould, L. (2008) Scandal of Recycled Rubbish Ending up in India, *Mirror*, www.mirror.co.uk/news/top-stories/2008/09/07/scandal-of-recycled-rubbish-ending-up-in-india-115875-20727734 (accessed 19 December 2011).
Gov.UK (2012) *National Minimum Wage Rates*, www.gov.uk/national-minimum-wage-rates (accessed 8 December 2012).
Graham, H. (2000) *Understanding Health Inequalities*. 2nd edn. Buckingham: Open University Press.
Grant, C. (ed.) (1992) *Built to Last? Reflections on British Housing Policy*. London: ROOF Magazine/Shelter.
Gray, J. (1986) *Liberalism*. Milton Keynes: Open University Press.
Gray, J. (1995) Beggaring our Own Neighbours, *Guardian*, 17 February: 12.
Greer, S. (2004) *Territorial Politics and Health Policy*. Manchester: Manchester University Press.
Gregory, A. and Myall, S. (2012) Scandal of Dirty Hospitals: 43,000 Patients Struck down by Deadly Superbugs on NHS Wards Last Year, *Mirror*, www.mirror.co.uk/news/uk-news/nhs-superbugs-43000-patients-struck-1412556 (accessed 14 December 2012).
Griffiths, R. (1988) *Community Care: Agenda for Action*. London: HMSO.
Groves, J. (2010) Coalition's Internet 'Consultation' Sham as Ministers Reject every Single Suggestion, *Daily Mail*, www.dailymail.co.uk/news/article-1300049/Coalitions-internet-consultation-sham-ministers-reject-suggestion.html (accessed 27 November 2012).
Guardian, The (2001) Better Late than Never, *Guardian*, 3 January: 19.
Guardian, The (2011) Carol Vorderman Wants to Split Maths in Two: A Good Formula?, *Guardian*, www.guardian.co.uk/commentisfree/2011/aug/08/school-subjects-carol-vorderman-maths (accessed 27 November 2012).
Hallett, C. (1995) *Women and Social Policy: An Introduction*. Hemel Hempstead: Prentice Hall.
Ham, C. (2004) *Health Policy in Britain*. Basingstoke: Palgrave.
Ham, C. and Hill, M. (1993) *The Policy Process in the Modern Capitalist State*. London: Harvester Wheatsheaf.
Ham, C., Dixon, A. and Brooke, B. (2012) *Transforming the Delivery of Health and Social Care: The Case for Fundamental Change*. London: The King's Fund.
Hancock, C. (1995) Who'll Take Care of the Caring? *Guardian*, 8 March: 2–3.
Hanley, L. (2007) *Estates: An Intimate History*. London: Granta.
Hantrais, L. (2000) *Social Policy in the European Union*, 2nd edn. Basingstoke: Macmillan.
Harman, C. (2009) *Zombie Capitalism: Global Crisis and The Relevance of Marx*. N.p.: Bookmark Publications.
Harris, J. (1977) *William Beveridge: A Biography*. Oxford: Oxford University Press.
Harrison, S. and Macdonald, R. (2008) *The Politics of Healthcare in Britain*: London: Sage Publications.
Hasluck, C. (2000) Early Lessons from the Evaluation of New Deal Programmes, *Labour Market Trends* 108(8): 353–80.
Hayek, F.A. (1944) *The Road to Serfdom*. London: George Routledge & Sons.
Heidensohn, F. (2002) Gender and Crime, in M. Maguire, R. Morgan and R. Reiner (eds) *Oxford Handbook of Criminology*. Oxford: Oxford University Press.
Hennessy, P. (1992) *Never Again: Britain 1945–51*. London: Jonathan Cape.
Henry, J.S. (2003) *The Blood Bankers: Tales from the Global Underground Economy*. New York and London: Four Walls Eight Windows.
Henwood, M. (1995a) Measure for Measure, *Community Care*, 6–12 July: 18–19.
Henwood, M. (1995b) *Making a Difference? Implementation of the Community Care Reforms Two Years On*. London: Nuffield Institute for Health / The King's Fund.
Herbert, N. (2010) *Criminal Justice Reform*, speech to Policy Exchange, 23 June.
Hetherington, P. (1998) Council Houses Unloved, Unlettable, *Guardian*, 10 November: 9.

Hetherington, P. (2001a) Scots and Welsh Face Subsidy Axe, *Guardian*, 24 April: 1.
Hetherington, P. (2001b) English Learn the Scottish Way, *Guardian*, 24 April: 3.
Higginson, J. (2012) 45p-a-Unit Booze Price to 'Save Lives and Cut Crime', *Metro*, 29 November 2012.
Hill, M. (1990) *Social Security Policy in Britain*. Aldershot: Edward Elgar.
Hill, M. (1997) *The Policy Process in the Modern Society*. 3rd edn. London: Prentice Hall.
Hills, J. (1997) *The Future of Welfare: A Guide to the Debate*. 2nd edn. York: Joseph Rowntree Foundation.
Hills. J. (2001) Poverty and Social Security. What Rights? What Responsibilities?', in A. Park, J. Curtice, K. Thomson et al. (eds) *British Social Attitudes: The 18th Report*. London: Sage Publications.
Hills, J. (2002) Floowing or Leading Public Opinion? Social Security Policy and Public Attitudes since 1997, *Fiscal Studies* 23(4): 539–58.
Hills, J. (2004) *Inequality and the State*. Oxford: Oxford University Press.
Hills, J. and Stewart, K. (eds) (2005) *A More Equal Society? New Labour, Poverty, Inequality and Exclusion*. Bristol: Policy Press.
Hills, J., Brewer, M., Jenkins, S. et al. (2010) *An Anatomy of Economic Inequality in the UK: Report of the National Equality Panel*. London: Centre for the Analysis of Social Exclusion.
Hillyard, P. and Percy-Smith, J. (1988) *The Coercive State: The Decline of Democracy in Britain*. London: Fontana.
Hillyard, P. and Watson, S. (1996) Postmodern Social Policy: A Contradiction in Terms?, *Journal of Social Policy* 25(3): 321–46.
HMG (HM Government) (2011) *Laying the Foundations: A Housing Strategy for England*. London: DCLG.
HM Revenue and Customs (2012) *Tax Credits: Effect of Budget Changes from 6 April 2012*, http://webarchive.nationalarchives.gov.uk/+/www.direct.gov.uk/en/MoneyTaxAndBenefits/TaxCredits/DG_194914 (accessed 5 June 2013).
HM Treasury (2004) *2004 Spending Review*. Cm 6237. London: The Stationery Office.
HM Treasury (2005) *Public Expenditure Statistical Analyses*. Cm 6521. London: The Stationery Office.
HM Treasury (2009) *Trends in Public Sector Expenditure Statistical Analysis 2009*, www.hm-treasury.gov.uk/d/pesa09_chapter4.pdf (accessed 18 September 2012).
HM Treasury (2010) *Spending Review 2010*, London: The Stationery Office.
Hodgson, A. and Spours, K. (2005) Divided We Fail, *Guardian*, 1 March: 4.
Home Office (2000) *The Criminal Justice System of England and Wales*. London: Home Office.
Horowitz, R. (1995) *Teen Mothers: Citizens or Dependents?* Chicago: University of Chicago Press.
House of Commons Health Committee (2005) *NHS Continuing Care Sixth Report 2004–05 Vol. 1 HC 399-1*. London: The Stationery Office.
Hudson, B. (2002) Punishment and Control, in M. Maguire, R. Morgan and R. Reiner (eds) *Oxford Handbook of Criminology*. Oxford: Oxford University Press.
Humphrys, J. (2011) JOHN HUMPHRYS: How our welfare system has created an age of entitlement, *Daily Mail*, www.dailymail.co.uk/news/article-2052749/Our-Shameless-society-How-welfare state-created-age-entitlement.html (accessed 21 June 2012).
Hunter, D. (1992) Lost tribes of the NHS, *Health Service Journal*, 20 August: 19.
Hurst, G. (2012) Students Must Get More for Their Money, Says Watchdog, *The Times*, 20 April.
Hutton, W. (1995) *The State We're In: Why Britain is in Crisis and How to Overcome It*. London: Jonathan Cape.
IDeA (2010) *Big Society Policy*, www.idea.gov.uk/idk/core/page.do?pageId=23536490 (accessed 13 December 2010).
Ignatieff, M. (ed.) (2005) *American Exceptionalism and Human Rights*. Princeton, NJ: Princeton University Press.
Illich, I. (1990) *Limits to Medicine – Medical Nemesis: The Expropriation of Health*. London: Marion Boyars.
Insley, J. (2012) Budget 2012: Flat-Rate State Pension Confirmed, *Guardian*, www.guardian.co.uk/money/2012/mar/21/budget-2012-flat-rate-pension-scheme (accessed 19 September 2012).

IRHEFSF (Independent Review of Higher Education Funding and Student Finance) (2010) *Securing a Sustainable Future for Higher Education: An Independent Review of Higher Education Funding and Finance*, www.bis.gov.uk/assets/biscore/corporate/docs/s/10-1208-securing-sustainable-higher-education-browne-report (accessed 30 November 2012).

Islam, F. and Mathiason, N. (2001) Labour Spending Less than Thatcher, *Observer*, 27 May: 1.

Jack, A. (2006) Decision on Herceptin to Come 'Within Six Months', *Financial Times*, 16 February.

Jack, A. and N. Timmins (2006) Alzheimer's Decision a Test for Ministers, *Financial Times*, 24 January.

Jack, R. (1992) Case Management and Social Services: Welfare or Trade Fare?, *Generations Review* 2(1): 4–6.

James, O. (1998) *Britain on the Couch*. London: Arrow Books.

James, O. (2007) Infected by Affluenza: Blair's Encouragement of Free Market Capitalism Has Boosted Spiralling Levels of British Mental Illness, *Guardian*, www.guardian.co.uk/commentisfree/2007/jan/24/comment.politics (accessed 30 May 2012).

Joffe, M. and Mindell, J. (2004) A Tentative Step Towards Healthy Public Policy, *Journal of Epidemiology and Public Health* 58: 966–8.

Johnson, J. (1997) Care as Policy, in A. Brechin, J. Katz, S. Peace and J. Walmsley (eds) *Care Matters*. London: Sage.

Johnson, J. and Slater, R. (eds) (1993) *Ageing and Later Life*. London: Sage.

Johnson, N. (1999) The Personal Social Services and Community Care, in M. Powell (ed.) *New Labour, New Welfare State?* Bristol: Policy Press.

Johnson, P., Tanner, S. and Thomas, R. (2000) Money Matters: Measuring Poverty, Wealth and Unemployment, in S. Kerrison and A. Macfarlane (eds) *Official Health Statistics: An Unofficial Guide*. London: Arnold.

Jones, C. (1985) *Patterns of Social Policy: An Introduction to Comparative Analysis*. London: Tavistock.

Jones, K. (1994) *The Making of Social Policy in Britain 1830–1990*. 2nd edn. London: The Athlone Press.

Jones, O. (2011) *Chavs: The Demonization of the Working Class*. London: Verso.

Joseph, K. and Sumption, J. (1979) *Equality*. London: John Murray.

Kangaspunta, K., Joutsen, M. and Ollus, N. (eds) (1998) *Crime and Criminal Justice in Europe and North America 1990–1994*. Helsinki: European Institute for Crime Prevention and Control (HEUNI).

Kemp, P. (1999) Housing Policy under New Labour, in M. Powell (ed.) *New Labour, New Welfare State?* Bristol: Policy Press.

Kennedy, I. (1980) The Reith Lectures: Unmasking Medicine, *The Listener*, 13 November: 641–4.

Kennedy, I. (1983) *The Unmasking of Medicine*. 2nd edn. St Albans: Granada Publishing.

Kennedy, I. (2001) *The Report of the Public Inquiry into Children's Heart Surgery at the Bristol Royal Infirmary 1984–1995*. Cm 5207. London: The Stationery Office.

Kennett, P. (2001) *Comparative Social Policy*. Buckingham: Open University Press.

Kesey, K. (1962) *One Flew Over the Cuckoo's Nest*. London: Methuen.

Kincaid, J. (1984) Richard Titmuss 1907–73, in P. Barker (ed.) *Founders of the Welfare State*. London: Heinemann Educational.

King's Fund, The (2011) *Briefing: The Dilnot Commission Report on Social Care*, 13 July. London: The King's Fund.

Kirkup, J. (2012) Scrap Formula Giving Scots Extra Cash, Say Tory MPs, *Telegraph*, www.telegraph.co.uk/news/uknews/scotland/9008823/Scrap-formula-giving-Scots-extra-cash-say-Tory-MPs.html (accessed 16 January 2012).

Kisby, B. (2010) The Big Society: Power to the People?, *The Political Quarterly* 81(4): 484–91.

Kitwood, T. (1997) *Dementia Reconsidered*. Buckingham: Open University Press.

Klein, R. (1984) Edwin Chadwick, in P. Barker (ed.) *Founders of the Welfare State*. London: Heinemann Educational.

Klein, R. (1993) The Goals of Health Policy: Church or Garage? in A. Harrison (ed.) *Health Care UK 1992/93*. London: King's Fund Institute.

Klein, R. (1995) *The New Politics of the NHS*. 3rd edn. London: Longman.

Klein, R. (ed.) (1998) *Implementing the White Paper: Pitfalls and Opportunities*. London: The King's Fund.

Klein, R. (2006) *The New Politics of the NHS*. 5th edn. Abingdon: Radcliffe Publishing.

Klein, R. (2010) *The New Politics of the NHS: From Creation to Reinvention.* 6th edn. Abingdon: Radcliffe Publishing.

Knapp, M., Cambridge, P., Thomason, C. et al. (1992) *Care in the Community: Challenge and Demonstration.* Aldershot: Arena.

Labbock, M. and Nazro, J. (1995) Breastfeeding: Protecting a Natural Resource. Washington, DC: Institute for Reproductive Studies, Georgetown University cited in T. Macdonald (2005) *Third World Hostage to First World Health.* Abingdon: Radcliffe Publishing.

Labonte, R. (2010) Health Promotion, Globalisation and Health, in J. Douglas, S. Earle, S. Handsley (eds) *A Reader in Promoting Public Health.* London: Sage: 235–45.

Labour Party (1997) *New Labour: Because Britain Deserves Better.* London: Labour Party.

Labour Party (2005) *Britain Forward not Back.* London: Labour Party.

Lansley, S. (2011) *The Cost of Inequality: Three Decades of the Super-Rich and the Economy.* London: Gibson Square.

Lawlor, E. and Nicholls, J. (2008) *The Gap Years: Enterprise and Inequality in England 2002–2006.* London: New Economics Foundation.

Lawson, R. (1995) The Challenge of 'New Poverty': Lessons from Europe and North America, in K. Funken and P. Cooper (eds) *Old and New Poverty.* London: Rivers Oram Press.

Le Grand, J. (1982) *The Strategy of Equality.* London: Allen & Unwin.

Le Grand, J., May, N. and Mulligan, J.A. (eds) (1998) *Learning from the NHS Internal Market: A Review of the Evidence.* London: The King's Fund.

Le Grand, J. (2007) *The Other Invisible Hand: Delivering Public Services Through Choice and Competition.* Princeton, NJ: Princeton University Press.

Lea, J. (2003) Institutional Racism in Policing: The Macpherson Report and its Consequences, in R. Matthews and J. Young, *The New Politics of Crime and Punishment.* Cullompton: Willan.

Leathard, A. (2000) *Health Care Provision.* 2nd edn. Cheltenham: Stanley Thornes.

Lechner, F.J. and Boli, J. (2012) *The Globalization Reader Fourth Edition* (eds). Chichester: Wiley-Blackwell.

Letwin, O. (1988) *Privatising the World: A Study of International Privatisation in Theory and Practice.* London: Caswell Educational Ltd.

Lewis, J. (1980) *The Politics of Motherhood: Child and Maternal Welfare in England, 1900–1939.* London: Croom Helm.

Lewis, J. (1983) *Women's Welfare, Women's Rights.* London: Croom Helm.

Lewis, P. (2011) Upskilling the Workers Will Not Upskill the Work: Why the Dominant Economic Framework Limits Child Poverty Reduction in the UK, *Journal of Social Policy* 40(3): 535–56.

Lianos, M. (2003) Social Control after Foucault, *Surveillance & Society* 1(3): 412–30.

Lindsay, C. (2010) Reconnecting with 'What Employment Means: Employability, the Experience of Unemployment and Priorities for Policy in an Era of Crisis, in I. Greener, C. Holden and M. Kilkey (eds) *Social Policy Review 22: Analysis and Debate in Social Policy, 2010.* Bristol: Policy Press.

Lister, R. (1998) *Citizenship: Feminist Perspectives.* Basingstoke: Macmillan.

Lloyd, T.O. (1993) *Empire, Welfare State, Europe: English History 1902–1992,* 4th edn. Oxford: Oxford University Press.

Loader, I. and Sparks, R. (2002) Contemporary Landscapes of Crime, Order and Control: Governance, Risk, and Globalisation, in M. Maguire, R. Morgan and R. Reiner (eds) *Oxford Handbook of Criminology.* Oxford: Oxford University Press.

Lowe, R. (1993) *The Welfare State in Britain since 1945.* Basingstoke: Macmillan.

Lowi, T.J. (1966) Distribution, Regulation, Redistribution: The Functions of Government, in R.B. Ripley (ed.) *Public Policies and their Politics: Techniques of Government Control.* New York: W.W. Norton.

Lukes, S. (1974) *Power: A Radical View.* Basingstoke: Palgrave.

Lukes, S. (2005) *Power: A Radical View.* 2nd edn. Basingstoke: Palgrave.

Mabbett, D. and Bolderson, H. (1999) Theories and Methods in Comparative Social Policy, in J. Clasen (ed.) *Comparative Social Policy: Concepts, Theories and Methods.* Oxford: Blackwell.

Macdonald, T. (2006) *Health, Trade and Human Rights.* Abingdon: Radcliffe Publishing.

Macdonald, T. (2007) *The Global Human Right to Health: Dream or Possibility?* Abingdon: Radcliffe Publishing.

Mack, J. and Lansley, S. (1985) *Poor Britain.* London: Allen & Unwin.

Maguire, M., Morgan, R. and Reiner, R. (eds) (2002) *Oxford Handbook of Criminology*. Oxford: Oxford University Press.

Malpass, P. (1984) Octavia Hill, 1838–1912, in P. Barker (ed.) *Founders of the Welfare State*. London: Heinemann Educational.

Malpass, P. (2005) *Housing and the Welfare State*. Basingstoke: Palgrave.

Malpass, P. and Murie, A. (1994) *Housing Policy and Practice*. 4th edn. London: Macmillan.

Manji, F. (2000) Collaboration with the South: Agents of Aid or Solidarity?, in D. Eade (ed.) *Development, NGOs and Civil Society*. Oxford: Oxfam GB: 75–9.

Marchant, C. (1995) Care Managers Speak Out, *Community Care*, 30 March: 16–17.

Marcuse, P. (1993) What's So New about Divided Cities? *International Journal of Urban and Regional Research* 17(3): 355–65.

Marmot, M. (2010) *Fair Society, Healthy Lives: The Marmot Review. Strategic review of health inequalities post 2010*. London: The Marmot Review.

Marshall, T.H. (1950) *Citizenship and Social Class, and Other Essays*. Cambridge: Cambridge University Press.

Marshall, T.H. (1963) *Sociology at the Crossroads*. London: Heinemann.

Marshall, T.H. (1964) *Class, Citizenship and Social Development*. Chicago: University of Chicago Press.

Marshall, T.H. (1970) *Social Policy*. London: Hutchinson.

Martell, L. (2010) *The Sociology of Globalization*. Cambridge: Polity Press.

Mays, N., Goodwin, N., Killoran, A. and Malbon, G. (1998) *Total Purchasing: A Step Towards Primary Care Groups: National Evaluation of Total Purchasing Pilot Projects*. London: The King's Fund.

McCartney. M. (2011) Well Enough to Work? *British Medical Journal* 342: 308–9.

McCormick, J. (1999) *Understanding the European Union*. Basingstoke: Macmillan.

McKeown, T. (1979) *The Role of Medicine: Dream, Mirage or Nemesis?* 2nd edn. Oxford: Blackwell.

McLean, I. (2001) The National Question, in A. Seldon (ed.) *The Blair Effect*. London: Little, Brown.

McLean, I. (2005). The National Question, in A. Seldon and D. Kavanagh (eds) *The Blair Effect 2001–5*. Cambridge: Cambridge University Press.

Mcquaid, R.W. and Lindsay, C. (2002) The 'Employability Gap': Long-Term Unemployment and Barriers to Work in Buoyant Labour Markets, *Environment and Planning C: Government and Policy* 20(4): 613–29.

Meikle, J. (1994) Puppets on a String? *Guardian*, 8 November: 2.

Metro (2012) Postcode Lottery Denies 2m Children a Decent Schooling, *Metro*, 28 November.

Midwinter, E. (1994) *The Development of Social Welfare in Britain*. Buckingham: Open University Press.

Mills, H., Silvestri, A. and Grimshaw, R. (2010) *Police Expenditure, 1999–2009*. London: Centre for Crime and Justice Studies.

Ministry of Health (1963) *Health and Welfare: The Development of Community Care*. Cmnd 1973. London: HMSO.

Ministry of Justice (2010) *Breaking the Cycle: Effective Punishment, Rehabilitation and Sentencing of Offenders*. London: Ministry of Justice.

Ministry of Security and Justice (2012) *Youth Policy*, www.government.nl/issues/youth-policy/documents-and-publications/press-releases/2011/06/25/more-severe-punishments-for-at-risk-youths.html (accessed 24 July 2012).

Mishra, R. (1990) *The Welfare State in Capitalist Society*. Hemel Hempstead: Harvester Wheatsheaf.

Mishra, R. (1993) Social Policy in a Postmodern World, in C. Jones (ed.) *New Perspectives on the Welfare State in Europe*. London: Routledge.

Morgan, J. (2012) Figures Reveal Huge Drop in Students Starting University, *Times*, www.timeshighereducation.co.uk/story.asp?storycode=421152 (accessed 27 November 2012).

Morris, J. (2003) Community Care or Independent Living? in N. Ellison and C. Pierson (eds) *Developments in British Social Policy 2*. Basingstoke: Palgrave.

Morris, T. (1983) Crime and the Welfare State, in P. Bean and S. MacPherson (eds) *Approaches to Welfare*. London: Routledge.

Morris, T. (1989) *Crime and Criminal Justice Since 1945*. Oxford: Basil Blackwell.

Morris, T. (2001) Crime and Penal Policy, in A. Seldon (ed.) *The Blair Effect*. London: Little, Brown.

Moyo, D. (2009) *Dead Aid: Why Aid Makes Things Worse and How There is Another Way for Africa*. London: Penguin Books.

Mullholland, H. (2011) David Cameron Defends Sentencing U-Turn, *Guardian*, www.guardian.co.uk/politics/2011/jun/21/david-cameron-prison-u-turn-sentences (accessed 27 July 2012).

Mullholland, H., Walker, P. and Curtis, P. (2012) *London Tory Councils Consider Moving Claimants to Midlands*, www.guardian.co.uk/society/2012/apr/24/tory-westminster-council-tenants-derby (accessed 3 January 2013).

Murie, A. (2012) Housing, the Welfare State and the Coalition Government, in M. Kilkey, G. Ramiak and K. Farnsworth (eds) *Social Policy Review 24: Analysis and Debate in Social Policy*. Bristol: Policy Press.

Murphy, J. (2011) Ed Miliband and Unions Clash Over Reforms, *London Evening Standard*, www.standard.co.uk/news/politics/ed-miliband-and-unions-clash-over-reforms-6429163.html (accessed 6 December 2012).

Murray, C. (1994) *Underclass: The Crisis Deepens*. London: Institute of Economic Affairs.

Naik, A. (2008) Did Jamie Oliver Really Put School Dinners on the Agenda? An Examination of the Role of the Media in Policy Making, *The Political Quarterly* 79(3): 426–33.

NAO (National Audit Office) (2012) *Welfare and Benefits: Department for Work and Pensions 2010–11 Accounts*, www.nao.org.uk/report/department-for-work-and-pensions-2010-11-accounts (accessed 22 May 2013).

NEF (New Economics Foundation) (2010) *Cutting it: The 'Big Society' and the New Austerity*. London: NEF.

Nelken, D. (2002) Comparing Criminal Justice, in M. Maguire, R. Morgan and R. Reiner (eds) *Oxford Handbook of Criminology*. Oxford: Oxford University Press.

Newman, I. (2011) 'Work as a Route out of Poverty: A Critical Evaluation of the UK Welfare to Work Policy' *Policy Studies* 32(2): 91–108.

Newton Dunn, T. (2012) You're Fired! Ministers Make it Far Easier for Bosses to Sack Bad Workers in Labour Law Reforms, *Sun*, www.thesun.co.uk/sol/homepage/news/politics/4531682/Ministers-make-it-far-easier-for-bosses-to-sack-bad-workers-in-labour-law-reforms.html (accessed 8 December 2012).

Novak, T. (1988) *Poverty and the State: An Historical Sociology*. Milton Keynes: Open University Press.

Nozick, R. (1974) *Anarchy, State and Utopia*. Oxford: Blackwell.

Oliver, M. (1990) *Politics of Disablement*. London: Macmillan.

Ollilia, E. (2005) Global Health Priorities: Priorities of the Wealthy? *Globalisation and Health* 1(6): 1–6.

ONS (Office for National Statistics) (2001) *Social Trends* No. 31. London: The Stationery Office.

ONS (Office for National Statistics) (2005) *Social Trends* No. 35. Basingstoke: Palgrave.

ONS (Office for National Statistics) (2009) *Pension Trends*. London: The Stationery Office.

ONS (Office for National Statistics) (2011a) *The Effects of Taxes and Benefits on Household Income, 2009/10*, Statistical Bulletin. Newport: Office for National Statistics.

ONS (Office for National Statistics) (2011b) *Labour Force Survey Employment Status by Occupation, April–June 2011*. London: The Stationery Office.

ONS (Office for National Statistics) (2012a) *Labour Market Statistics, February 2012*, Statistical Bulletin. Newport: Office for National Statistics.

ONS (Office for National Statistics) (2012b) *The Effects of Taxes and Benefits on Household Income, 2010/11*. Statistical Bulletin. Newport: Office for National Statistics.

ONS (Office for National Statistics) (2012c) *Pension Trends*. London: The Stationery Office.

ONS (Office for National Statistics) (2012d) *Public Expenditure Statistical Analyses 2012*. London: Stationery Office.

ONS (Office for National Statistics) (2012e) *Annual Crime Survey for England and Wales*, www.ons.gov.uk/ons/guide-method/surveys/list-of-surveys/survey.html?survey=Crime+Survey+for+England+and+Wales (accessed 23 December 2012).

Orton, M. (2008) State Approaches to Wealth, in T. Ridge and S. Wright (eds) *Understanding Inequality, Poverty and Wealth*. Bristol: Policy Press.

Oxfam (2010) *21st Century Aid: Recognising Success and Tackling Failure*. Oxfam Briefing Paper. Oxford: Oxfam International.

Page, D. (2000) *Communities in the Balance: The Reality of Social Exclusion on Housing Estates*. York: York Publishing Services.

Palmer, I. (2012). David Cameron: Jimmy Carr's Tax Avoidance is 'Morally Wrong', *International Business Times*, www.ibtimes.co.uk/articles/354476/20120620/david-cameron-morally-wrong-jimmy-carr-tax.htm (accessed 26 July 2012).

Pantazis, C., Gordon, D. and Levitas, R. (eds) (2006) *Poverty and Social Exclusion in Britain: The Millennium Survey*. Bristol: Policy Press.

Parker, R. (1990) Elderly People and Community Care: The Policy Background, in I. Sinclair, R. Parker, D. Leat and J. Williams (eds) *The Kaleidoscope of Care: A Review of Research on Welfare Provision for Elderly People*. London: HMSO.

Parkinson, J. (2012) Lib Dem Conference: Clegg Pledges £100m for Childcare, *BBC*, www.bbc.co.uk/news/uk-politics-19704174 (accessed 9 December 2012).

Pascall, G. (1986) *Social Policy: A Feminist Analysis*. London: Tavistock.

Pascall, G. (2008) Gender and New Labour: After the Male Breadwinner Model?' in T. Maltby, P. Kennett and K. Rummery (eds) *Social Policy Review 20*. Bristol: Policy Press.

Paton, G. (2010) Spending Review: What it Means for the Department of Education, *Telegraph*, www.telegraph.co.uk/news/newstopics/spending-review/8035164/Spending-Review-what-it-means-for-the-Department-of-Education.html (accessed 27 November 2012).

Paton Walsh, N. (2001) UK Matches Africa in Crime Surge, *Observer*, 3 June: 11.

Peach, C. and Byron, M. (1994) Council House Sales, Residualisation and Afro-Caribbean Tenants, *Journal of Social Policy* 23(3): 363–83.

Pease, K. (2002) Crime Reduction, in M. Maguire, R. Morgan and R. Reiner (eds) *Oxford Handbook of Criminology*. Oxford: Oxford University Press.

Peel, Q. (2005) America's Exceptionally Poor Choice of Friends, *Financial Times*, 11 August.

Penna, S. and O'Brien, M. (1996) Postmodernism and Social Policy: A Small Step Forwards? *Journal of Social Policy* 25(1): 39–61.

Phillipson, C. (1982) *Capitalism and the Construction of Old Age*. London: Macmillan.

Philpott, J. (ed.) (1997) *Working for Full Employment*. London: Routledge.

Piachaud, D. (1981) Peter Townsend and the Holy Grail, *New Society*, 10 September: 419–21.

Pickvance, C.G. (1986) Comparative Urban Analysis and Assumptions about Causality, *International Journal of Urban and Regional Research* 10(2): 162–84.

Pierson, C. (1991) *Beyond the Welfare State?* Oxford: Blackwell.

Piven, F. and Cloward, R. (1971) *Regulating the Poor: The Functions of Public Welfare*. New York: Pantheon Books.

Powell, M. (1995) The Strategy of Equality Revisited, *Journal of Social Policy* 24(2): 163–85.

Powell, M. (ed.) (1999) *New Labour, New Welfare State?* Bristol: Policy Press.

Powell, M. (ed.) (2002) *Evaluating New Labour's Welfare Reforms*. Bristol: Policy Press.

Prime Minister's Strategy Unit (2005) *Improving the Life Chances of Disabled People*. London: PMSU.

Qureshi, H. and Walker, A. (1989) *The Caring Relationship: Elderly People and Their Families*. Basingstoke: Macmillan.

Ranson, S. and Travers, T. (1994) Education, in P. Jackson and M. Lavender (eds) *Public Services Yearbook*. London: Chapman & Hall.

Rawls, J. (1972) *A Theory of Justice*. Oxford: Oxford University Press.

Rawnsley, A. (2000) *Servants of the People: The Inside Story of New Labour*. London: Hamish Hamilton.

Rawnsley, A. (2001) A Conspiracy that Threatens Democracy, *The Observer*, 13 May: 29.

Revell, K. and Leather, P. (2000) *The State of UK Housing*. 2nd edn. York: Joseph Rowntree Foundation/Policy Press.

Riddell, M. (2001) The *New Statesman* interview – Peter Morris, *New Statesman*, 10 December: 20–1.

Ritzer, G. (2008) *The McDonaldization of Society*. Los Angeles, CA: Pine Forge Press.

Rix, J. (2011) Price of Suing the NHS too High, *Guardian*, www.guardian.co.uk/society/2011/mar/29/cost-suing-nhs-too-high (accessed 13 December 2012).

Robertson Elliot, F. (1996) *Gender, Family and Society*. Basingstoke: Macmillan.

Robinson, R. and Le Grand, J. (1994) *Evaluating the NHS Reforms*. London: King's Fund Institute.

Rogers, S. (2012) Homeless England: The Statistics for Your Area, *Guardian*, www.guardian.co.uk/news/datablog/2012/mar/08/homelessness-statistics-data (accessed 2 January 2013).

Rose, N. (1985) *The Psychological Complex: Psychology, Politics and Society in England, 1869–1939*. London: Routledge.

Rosenau, J.N. (1997) *Along the Domestic–Foreign Frontier: Exploring Governance in a Turbulent World.* Cambridge: Cambridge University Press.
Ross, T. (2012) Budget 2012: Four More Years of Cuts to the Welfare Bill, *Telegraph*, www.telegraph.co.uk/finance/budget/9159397/Budget-2012-Four-more-years-of-cuts-to-the-welfare-bill.html (accessed 18 September 2012).
Rostow, W.W. (1978) *The World Economy: History and Prospect.* London: Macmillan.
Rowntree, B.S. (1937) *The Human Needs of Labour*. London: Longman.
Royle, E. (1987) *Modern Britain: A Social History*. London: Edward Arnold.
Rust, V. and Blakemore, K. (1990) Education Reform in Norway and in England and Wales: A Corporatist Interpretation, *Comparative Education Review* 34(4): 500–22.
Sage, D. (2012) Fair Conditions and Fair Consequences? Exploring New Labour, Welfare Contractualism and Social Attitudes, *Social Policy and Society* 11(3): 359–73.
Saraga, E. (ed.) (1998) *Embodying the Social: Constructions of Difference*. London: Routledge.
Scholte, J.A. (2000) *Globalization: A Critical Introduction.* Basingstoke: Macmillan.
Scottish Assembly Health Committee (2006) *Tenth Report: Care Inquiry*. Edinburgh: Scottish Assembly.
Scourfield, J. and Welsh, I. (2003) Risk, Reflexivity and Social Control in Child Protection: New Times or Same Old Story?, *Critical Social Policy* 23(3): 398–420.
Scruton, R. (1984) *The Meaning of Conservatism*. 2nd edn. London: Macmillan.
Scull, A.T. (1984) *Decarceration: Community Treatment of the Deviant – A Radical View*. 2nd edn. Cambridge: Polity Press.
Seckinelgin, H. (2009) Global Social Policy and International Organizations: Linking Social Exclusion to Durable Inequality, *Global Social Policy* 9: 205–27.
Seldon, A. and Kavanagh, D. (2005) *The Blair Effect 2001–5*. Cambridge: Cambridge University Press.
Sen, A. (1980) Equality of What? in S.M. McMurrin (ed.) *Liberty, Equality and Law*. Salt Lake City, UT: University of Utah Press.
Sen, A. (1985) *Commodities and Capabilities*. Oxford: Oxford University Press.
Sen, A. (1987) *The Standard of Living*. Cambridge: Cambridge University Press.
Sen, A. (1999) *Development as Freedom*. Oxford: Oxford University Press.
Sernau, S. (2011) *Social Inequality in a Global Age*. 3rd edn. Los Angeles, CA: Sage.
Sharpe, R. (2010) *An Inconvenient Sandwich: The Throwaway Economics of Takeaway Food*. London: New Economics Fund.
Shaxon, N. (2011) *Treasure Islands: Tax Havens and the Men who Stole the World*. London: The Bodley Head.
Shepherd, J. (2011) English Universities still Failing Poor Students, Says Government Watchdog, *Guardian*, www.guardian.co.uk/education/2011/sep/29/british-universities-fail-poor-students (accessed 27 November 2012).
Sherman, J. (2001) Internet and TV Blamed for NHS Claims Bill, *The Times*, 3 May: 4.
Simon, B. (1990) *Education and the Social Order, 1940–1990*. London: Lawrence & Wishart.
Simon, J. (1997) Governing Through Crime, in L. Friedman and G. Fisher (eds) *The Crime Conundrum: Issues in Criminal Justice*. Boulder, CO: Westview Press.
Sklair, L. (2002) *Globalisation: Capitalism and Its Alternatives*. 3rd edn. Oxford: Oxford University Press.
Slater, J. (2001) Thriving out of the Slipstream, *Times Educational Supplement*, 5 October: 20–1.
Sly, F. and Stillwell, D. (1997) Temporary Workers in Great Britain, *Labour Market Trends*, September. London: The Stationery Office.
Smith, H. (2012) Fee Degrees: The £53,000 Cost of Going to University, *Metro*, 16 August 2012.
Smith, R. (2012) NHS Waiting Times Rise for First Time in a Year: Official Figures, *Telegraph*, www.telegraph.co.uk/health/healthnews/9479664/NHS-waiting-times-rise-for-first-time-in-a-year-official-figures.html (accessed 14 December 2012).
Smithers, R. (2005) Researchers Raise more Doubts on City Academies, *Guardian*, 30 June: 7.
Smithers, R., White, M. and Ward, L. (2004) Blair Insists A-Levels Will Stay in Shakeup, *Guardian*, 19 October: 1.
Social Exclusion Unit (1998) *Bringing Britain Together: A National Strategy for Neighbourhood Renewal*. Cm 4045. London: HMSO.

Spicker, P. (1993) *Poverty and Social Security*. London: Routledge.
Squires, P. (2006) New Labour and the Politics of Antisocial Behaviour', *Critical Social Policy* 26(1): 144–68.
Stainton, T. (1994) *Autonomy and Social Policy*. Aldershot: Avebury.
Steintrager, J. (1977) *Bentham*. London: George Allen & Unwin.
Stevenson, J. (1984) *British Society 1914–45*. Harmondsworth: Penguin.
Stewart, J. (2004) *Taking Stock: Scottish Social Welfare after Devolution*. Bristol: Policy Press.
Stewart, K. (2005) Equality and Social Justice, in A. Seldon and D. Kavanagh (eds) *The Blair Effect 2001–5*. Cambridge: Cambridge University Press.
Stigliz, J. (2006) *Making Globalization Work: The Next Steps to Global Justice*. London: Allen Lane.
Stratton, A. and Kowelle, J. (2012) Welfare Bill Soars as Coalition Counts Cost of Austerity Drive, *Guardian*, www.guardian.co.uk/politics/2011/jan/02/welfare-bill-soars-coalition-austerity (accessed 17 September 2012).
Summerskill, B. and Hinsliff, G. (2001) An Impossible Dream? *The Observer*, 24 June: 13.
Sutherland, S. (1999) *With Respect to Old Age: Long-Term Care – Rights and Responsibilities*. Cmnd 4192. London: The Stationery Office.
Tait, N. (2006) Cancer Sufferer Loses Drug Fight, *Financial Times*, 16 February.
Tak, P.J.P. (2008) *The Dutch Criminal Justice System*. Nijmegan: Wolf Legal Publishers.
Tawney, R.H. (1964) *Equality*. 4th edn, with an introduction by R.M. Titmuss. London: George Allen & Unwin.
Taylor, M. (2005) New Blow to City Academies, *Guardian*, 3 December: 3.
Taylor, M. (2006) Academies Fail to Improve Results, *Guardian*, 22 May: 4.
Taylor, M. (2010) Student Fees Protest: Lawyers Launch Legal Challenge to Kettling, *Guardian*, www.guardian.co.uk/education/2010/dec/14/student-fees-protest-kettling-human-rights (accessed 24 July 2012).
Taylor, S. and Field, D. (1997) *Sociology of Health and Health Care: An Introduction for Nurses*. 2nd edn. Oxford: Blackwell Scientific Publications.
Taylor-Gooby, P. (1994) Postmodernism and Social Policy: A Great Leap Backwards? *Journal of Social Policy* 23(3): 385–404.
Teodorazuk, A., Welfare, M., Corbett, S. and Mukaetova-Ladinska, E. (2009) Education, Hospital Staff and the Confused Older Patient, *Age and Ageing* 38: 252–53.
Thaler, R.H. and Sunstein, C.R. (2009) *Nudge: Improving Decisions about Health, Wealth and Happiness*. London: Penguin.
Thane, P. (1996) *The Foundations of the Welfare State*. 2nd edn. London: Longman.
Thomas, B., Dorling, D. and Davey Smith, G. (2010) Inequalities in Premature Mortality in Britain: Observational Study from 1921 to 2007. *British Medical Journal* 341: 3639.
Thompson, A. and Dobson, R. (1995) Death of an Ideal, *Community Care*, 6–12 July: 20–1.
Thompson, N. (1998) *Promoting Equality*. London: Macmillan.
Timmins, N. (1995) *The Five Giants: A Biography of the Welfare State*. London: HarperCollins.
Timmins, N. (2006a) Review of Social Care Funding Launched, *Financial Times*, 27 March.
Timmins, N. (2006b) Scrap Means-Testing on Care of Old, Says Study, *Financial Times*, 25 March.
Timonen, V. (1999) A Threat to Social Security? The Impact of EU Membership on the Finnish Welfare State, *Journal of European Social Policy* 9(3): 253–61.
Tinker, A. (1981) *The Elderly in Modern Society*. London: Longman.
Tinker, A. (1997) *Older People in Modern Society*. 4th edn. New York: Addison Wesley.
Titmuss, R.M. (1950) *Problems of Social Policy*. London: HMSO.
Titmuss, R.M. (1958) *Essays on the Welfare State*. London: Allen & Unwin.
Titmuss, R.M. (1968) *Commitment to Welfare*. London: Allen & Unwin.
Titmuss, R.M. (1970) *The Gift Relationship*. London: Allen & Unwin.
Tomlinson, S. (2001) *Education in a Post-Welfare Society*. Buckingham: Open University Press.
Tomlinson, M. (2004) *14–19 Curriculum and Qualifications Reform (Final Report)*. Annesley: DfES Publications.
Townsend, M. (2010) Black People are 26 Times more Likely than Whites to Face Stop and Search, *Guardian*, www.guardian.co.uk/uk/2010/oct/17/stop-and-search-race-figures (accessed 26 July 2012).
Townsend, P. (1979) *Poverty in the United Kingdom*. London: Allen Lane/ Penguin Books.

Townsend, P. and Davidson, N. (1982) *Inequalities in Health: The Black Report.* London: Penguin.

Toynbee, P. (2000) Targets for Pensions, *Guardian*, 22 September: 19.

Toynbee, P. and Walker, D. (2001) *Did Things Get Better? An Audit of Labour's Successes and Failures.* London: Penguin.

Toynbee, P. and Walker, D. (2005) *Better or Worse? Has Labour Delivered?* London: Bloomsbury.

Travis, A. (2010) Crime in England and Wales at its Lowest since 1981, Says Survey, *Guardian*, www.guardian.co.uk/uk/2010/jul/15/crime-figures-fall-bcs-survey (accessed 25 July 2012).

Travis, A. and Stratton, A. (2011) David Cameron's Solution for Broken Britain: Tough Love and Tougher Policing, www.guardian.co.uk/uk/2011/aug/15/david-cameron-broken-britain-policing (accessed 23 July 2012).

UK Parliament (2011) *Regeneration. Regen 54*, www.publications.parliament.uk/pa/cm201011/cmselect/cmcomloc/writev/regeneration/m54.htm (accessed 3 April 2013).

UNEP (United Nations Environment Programme) (2012) *21 Issues for the 21st Century: Results of the UNEP Foresight Process on Emerging Environmental Issues.* Nairobi: United Nations Environment Programme (UNEP).

Ungerson, C. (1987) *Policy is Personal: Sex, Gender and Informal Care.* London: Tavistock Publications.

Unison (2012) *Health & Social Care Act 2012: Making Sense of the New NHS*, www.unison.org.uk/file/Understanding%20Health%20Act%20-%20MV%20-%20June%202012.pdf (accessed 21 January 2013).

United Nations (2011) *Discriminatory Laws and Practices and Acts of Violence Against Individuals Based on their Sexual Orientation and Gender Identity.* Report of the United Nations High Commissioner for Human Rights. Vienna: United Nations.

United Nations (2012) www.un.org (accessed 20 July 2012).

UNDP (United Nations Development Programme) (2010) *The Millennium Development Goals.* New York: United Nations Development Programme.

UNODC (United Nations Office on Drugs and Crime) (n.d.) *United Nations Survey on Crime Trends and the Operations of Criminal Justice Systems*, www.unodc.org/unodc/en/data-and-analysis/United-Nations-Surveys-on-Crime-Trends-and-the-Operations-of-Criminal-Justice-Systems.html (accessed 3 June 2013).

Valentine, S. (2011) Coalition: What Does it Mean for Schools, *Nutrition Bulletin* 36: 117–19.

Vandenbroucke, F. (1998). *Globalisation, Inequality and Social Democracy.* London: Institute for Public Policy Research.

Vaughan, A. (2009) Elimination of Food Waste Could Lift 1bn out of Hunger, Say Campaigners, *Guardian*, www.guardian.co.uk/environment/2009/sep/08/food-waste (accessed 19 December 2011).

Vickerstaff, S. (2003) Work and Welfare, in J. Baldock, N. Manning, S. Millar and S. Vickerstaff (eds) *Social Policy*. 2nd edn. Oxford: Oxford University Press.

Vidal, J. (1994) Health Over Wealth, *Guardian*: 4–5.

Vivian, J. (1994). NGOs and Sustainable Development in Zimbabwe: No Magic Bullets, *Development and Change* 25: 181–209.

Wacquant, L. (2009) *Punishing the Poor: The Neoliberal Government of Social Inequality.* Durham, NC: Duke University Press.

Wadham, J. and Mountfield, H. (1999) *Blackstone's Guide to the Human Rights Act 1998*. London: Blackstone Press.

Wainwright, M. (2001) Bradford Warned on Segregation Trend, *Guardian*, 20 June: 6.

Walker, A. (1990) The Benefits of Old Age? Age Discrimination and Social Security, in E. McEwen (ed.) *Age: The Unrecognised Discrimination*. London: Age Concern England.

Walker, P. (1994) What Happens when You Scrap the Welfare State? *Independent on Sunday*, 13 March: 17.

Walton, J. (2010) Election 2010: Turnout Mapped, *BBC*, http://news.bbc.co.uk/1/hi/uk_politics/election_2010/8672976.stm (accessed 16 November 2012).

Wanless, D. (2006) *Securing Good Care for Older People: Taking a Long-Term View*. London: The King's Fund.

Wardrop, M. (2012) NHS facing £15.7bn for Rising Number of Clinical Negligence Claims, *Telegraph*, www.telegraph.co.uk/news/politics/9065534/NHS-facing-15.7bn-for-rising-number-of-clinical-negligence-claims.html (accessed 13 December 2012).

Warner, N. (1995) *Community Care: Just a Fairy Tale?* London: Carers' National Association (unpublished report).

Waterhouse, R. (2000) *Lost in Care: Report of the Tribunal of Inquiry into the Abuse of Children in Care in the Former County Council Area of Gwynedd and Clwyd since 1974.* London: DoH.

Warnock, M. (ed.) (1966) *Utilitarianism*. London: Collins/Fontana.

Welsh Government (2011) *Together for Health: A Five Year Vision for the NHS in Wales*, http://wales.gov.uk/docs/dhss/publications/111101togetheren.pdf (accessed 4 June 2013).

White, A. (2011) *The State of Men's Health in Europe*. n.p.: European Union, Directorate-General for Health and Consumers.

White, M. and Taylor, M. (2005) Blair Sweeps aside Critics of School Reform, *Guardian*, 25 October: 1.

WHO (World Health Organisation) (2007) *World Health Statistics, 2007.* Geneva: WHO.

WHO (World Health Organisation) (2008) *Closing the Gap in a Generation: Health Equity through Action on the Social Determinants of Health.* Geneva: Commission for the Social Determinants of Health.

Wilkinson. P. (2005) Global Environmental Change and Health, in A. Scriven and S. Garman (eds) *Promoting Health: Global Perspectives.* Basingstoke: Palgrave Macmillan: 129–38.

Wilkinson, R. (2011) How Economic Inequality Harms Societies, *Ted Talks*, www.ted.com/talks/richard_wilkinson.html (accessed 17 May 2013).

Wilkinson, R.A. and Homenidou, K. (2012) *Working Futures 2010–2020: Evidence Report 41*, www.ukces.org.uk/assets/ukces/docs/publications/evidence-report-41-working-futures-2010-2020.pdf (accessed 6 December 2012).

Wilkinson, R.G. and Pickett, K. (2009) *The Spirit Level: Why Equality is Better for Everyone.* London: Allen Lane.

Williamson, D. (2012) Updated: David Cameron attacks Welsh Government's Health Policy – But Is Accused of Getting his Facts Wrong, *Wales Online*, www.walesonline.co.uk/news/health/updated-david-cameron-attacks-welsh-2035555 (accessed 29 May 2013).

Wilson, G. (2011) 'Feral Underclass' to Blame for Riots, *Sun*, www.thesun.co.uk/sol/homepage/news/3797021/Feral-underclass-to-blame-for-riots.html (accessed 26 September 2012).

Wilson, R. (2012) Tuition Fees: Nick Clegg Should Come Clean about what Really Happened, *Guardian*, www.guardian.co.uk/commentisfree/2012/sep/21/nick-clegg-tuition-fees (accessed 28 November 2012).

Winnett, R. (2011) Feckless Parents Would only Spend Extra Benefits on Themselves, Says Iain Duncan Smith, *Telegraph*, www.telegraph.co.uk/news/politics/8929809/Feckless-parents-would-only-spend-extra-benefits-on-themselves-says-Iain-Duncan-Smith.html (accessed 22 June 2012).

Wistow, G., Knapp, M., Hardy, B. and Allen, C. (1994) *Social Care in a Mixed Economy*. Buckingham: Open University Press.

Woodcock, A. (2012) Thousands Escape Child Benefit Axe, *Independent*, www.independent.co.uk/news/uk/politics/thousands-escape-child-benefit-axe-7580493.html (accessed 17 September 2012).

Woodward, W. (2001a) UK Spending on Education Lags Behind Rivals, *Guardian*, 14 June: 8.

Woodward, W. (2001b) Schools 'Resemble Third World', *Guardian*, 1 June: 8.

Woodward, W. (2001c) Test Paper, *Guardian*, 23 October: 6–7.

Woodward, W. (2006) View from on High, *The Guardian*, 14 February, 1–2.

World Bank (2004) *Governance Matters IV: Governance Indicators for 1996–2004*, http://econ.worldbank.org/WBSITE/EXTERNAL/EXTDEC/EXTRESEARCH/0, contentMDK:20696276~pagePK:64214825~piPK:64214943~theSitePK:469382,00.html (accessed 22 May 2013).

World Bank and International Bank for Reconstruction (2007) *A Decade of Measuring the Quality of Governance. Governance Matters 2007. World Wide Governance Indicators 1996–2006 Governance Indicators: 1996–2004.* Washington, DC: World Bank and International Bank for Reconstruction.

World Resources Institute (2000) *Repairing the Fraying Web: A Call to Action by UNDP, UNEP, World Bank, and WRI*, www.wri.org/publication/content/8148 (accessed 20 July 2012).

Worrall, L. and Cooper, C. (1998) *The Quality of Life: 1997 Survey of Managers' Changing Experiences.* London: Institute of Management.

Worsthorne, P. (1971) *The Socialist Myth*. London: Cassell.

Wragg, T. (ed.) (2005a) *Letters to the Prime Minister: The Future of Education*. n.p.: The New Vision Group.

Wragg, T. (2005b) Opinion, *Guardian*, 1 March: 7.

Wyn, H. (1991) Women, the State, and the Concept of Financial Dependence, in J. Hutton, S. Hutton, T. Pinch and A. Shiell (eds) *Dependency to Enterprise*. London: Routledge.

Yamey, G. (2002) Why Does the World still Need WHO? *British Medical Journal* 325, 1294–8.

Yapp, R. (2012) Working Women 'Still Do Housework', *Daily Mail*, www.dailymail.co.uk/news/article-206381/Working-women-housework.html (accessed 6 December 2012).

Yeates, N. (2008) *Understanding Global Social Policy. Understanding Welfare: Social Issues, Policy and Practice.* Bristol: Policy Press.

Yeates, N. and Holden, C. (eds) (2009) *The Global Social Policy Reader*. Bristol: Policy Press.

Young, J. (2002) Crime and Social Exclusion, in M. Maguire, R. Morgan and R. Reiner (eds) *Oxford Handbook of Criminology*. Oxford: Oxford University Press.

Young, J. and Matthews, R. (2003) New Labour, Crime Control and Social Exclusion, in R. Matthews and J. Young (eds) *The New Politics of Crime and Punishment*. Cullompton: Willan.

Yuill, C., Crinson, I. and Duncan, E. (2010) *Key Concepts in Health Studies*. London: Sage.

Index

Locators shown in *italics* refer to tables, boxes and figures.